The Books of Ezra and Nehemiah

an Exegetical and Doctrinal Commentary

Lange's Commentary on the Holy Scripture

BY

FR. W. SCHULTZ,

PROFESSOR IN ORDINARY OF THEOLOGY IN THE UNIVERSITY OF BRESLAU, PRUSSIA.

TRANSLATED, ENLARGED, AND EDITED

BY

REV. CHARLES A. BRIGGS, D.D.,

PROFESSOR OF OLD TESTAMENT EXEGESIS IN THE UNION THEOLOGICAL SEMINARY, NEW YORK.

Wipf & Stock
PUBLISHERS
Eugene, Oregon

Wipf and Stock Publishers
199 W 8th Ave, Suite 3
Eugene, OR 97401

The Books of Ezra and Nehemiah
an Exegetical and Doctrinal Commentary
By Schultz, Frederick William
ISBN 13: 978-1-55635-405-2
ISBN 10: 1-55635-405-3
Publication date 4/4/2007
Previously published by Charles Scribner, 1877

THE

BOOKS OF EZRA AND NEHEMIAH.

INTRODUCTION.

§ 1. THEIR SIGNIFICANCE, CHARACTER AND CONTENTS.

1. *Their Significance.*—It might readily seem as if the development of Israel subsequent to the exile had been backwards, and it had had but a negative significance with reference to the history of redemption; that is, as if it was merely through the deficiencies of the present, that the desire for a better future had been awakened and pointed forward to it. If, however, it was the final destiny of Israel to overcome the empires of the world, and set up the kingdom of God, not through political, but religious forces; not as a nation in battle with the nations of the world, but as leaven cast in among them; not from without, but from within, and without political independence or power—in other words: if the kingdom of God, the preparation for which is here considered, was to be a higher spiritual kingdom, then even the circumstances of the exile, still more those subsequent to the exile, were peculiarly appropriate to prepare Israel for its work in a positive way, likewise; yea, they constrained this people at once from the very beginning to become a community which was not so much political as religious, which, in distinction from the previous royal kingdom, we may call a priestly kingdom. (Comp. J. P. LANGE, *Introd. to the Scriptures* in the vol. of the *Comm. on Matt.*, p. 4.) In all their public undertakings, even after the close of the exile, although so dependent upon their heathen rulers and overseers that they could not even build their temple, not to speak of the walls of Jerusalem, without permission, they yet had the important task of showing that in spite of the loss of their national independence, they were in a position to maintain victoriously their internal religious peculiarities, and that they had in them a treasure through which, if they faithfully cherished the inheritance entrusted to them from above, they might be enabled to rise above all external oppressions —yea, through which they might arise in the most powerful and glorious manner even from their apparent defeats. It is true that they still for a long time could not entirely dispense with externalities. It was necessary that their God should ever have a temple, in which to dwell among His people, though apart from them; their hearts were not yet sufficiently won and purified to become His dwelling and temple. And so Israel itself still needed a city in which they might be near the temple, in which more than any where else they might live as a religious community, and they must still secure it with walls and gates. But in view of their higher and proper aims, they were no longer called to reconquer their political independence and re-establish a worldly kingdom. The efforts of the Maccabees, so far as they tended to this result, and their consequences, were in a false and round-about way.

The development of the people of God, as such, at that time necessarily required that the external vessel, which indeed was entirely appropriate to its times and even indispensable, should gradually more and more completely fall away and disappear, as the chrysalis, out of which the butterfly, attired in the most beautiful colors, soared upward to the bright sky; so that that which was spiritual and belonged to eternity might attain its pure representation as spiritual and eternal, and that the words whose depth and fullness we still to-day so insufficiently appreciate: "My kingdom is not of this world," might be more and more understood.

Now the more Israel was referred to their religion and religious customs, the more weight would they be likely to give to those things which still seemed to give their religion its greatest stability; the more decidedly they found their calling in being a holy people, the more might it seem that they were commanded to clothe with religious consecration those things which were externally as well as those which were ethically holy, *e. g.* the sanctuary, especially the temple and the institutions of worship, the ancient writings also which guided to the religion, the people which had its existence through the religion and the law over against the heathen world; yea, the city itself, in which alone they were able to preserve all these holy things. Yes, they were in great danger of regarding reverence and care for these sacred things as the highest and most important of all things, and thus of externalizing religion in a worse way than before the exile, when it was through the undue estimation of other things. In short both tendencies were possible. The times following the exile might just as well prepare the way for the new, real and internal organization of the kingdom of God, commencing with Christ and the apostles, as be the beginning of that entirely opposite extreme of Pharisaism through the cultivation of externals and of antichristian Judaism. And both possibilities have been realized. It is the great significance of the books of Ezra and Nehemiah that they historically describe that effort, yea, likewise power and might of Israel in rising up again and maintaining the field, even without political independence, as a purely religious community, thus of struggling for the New Testament and spiritual mode of existence, so likewise it at least lets us, through the entire character of the persons with whom they have to do, yea even through the condition of the entire congregation, forebode the danger pointed out of a new external religion putting itself in place of the old. The book of Esther also shares in this characteristic, as on the one side it brings into view the faithfulness of Israel to the law of their fathers in the midst of the severest temptations and trials; whilst on the other it does not extol this faithfulness as being as pure and exalted as we could wish. Thus these three books were given for instruction, edification, consolation and warning, especially for those times when the congregation is again in the condition of doing away with their previous unreliable and frail props, of becoming poorer in apparent blessings and of being obliged to return to the real and substantial blessings. They bear witness to the congregation in the plainest and most unmistakable manner that it can show itself as internally, really rich even in external poverty, and can rise above all difficulties, trials and oppressions in spite of external weakness, yea, they prophesy to it, that whilst not of this world, it will abide ever anew as indestructible and eternal. But they likewise warn, in such times of mortification and trouble, not to be careless of self, or to find true piety, which can only consist in sincere devotion to God, in the estimation and cultivation of those things which are really the products of piety itself.

2. *Their Character.*—It might be questionable whether the period subsequent to the exile afforded the appropriate material for a sacred history. Sacred history had previously had especially to do with the government of God as it was more or less revealed in Israel. If now there were no longer any such manifestations of God as had previously been described, no more such preservation, deliverance, revival and advancement of the people; if the people continued to exist merely as a religious community, and accordingly lead merely a quiet, so to say a hidden life, without rejoicing in new revelations—then at least it is not quite clear why the history should still maintain a sacred character. But on the other hand the history might, yea, must exhibit, on the one side, the new beginning at all events, so far as the people had such a beginning in Jerusalem as a religious community, and thus the return of a portion of the exiles and the restoration as well of the temple as of the city with its walls, as a secure place of the community; but especially likewise the re-establishment of the community itself as a people separating themselves decidedly from the heathen, and living in accordance with the divine law in communion with God.

This beginning had been expressly set in prospect by the prophets as God's own act, and so could not come to pass without the especial co-operation of God, that is, unless He had made the heathen world-powers subservient to His purpose, and inclined a portion of the exiles to return to their devastated land. Moreover, on the other side, the preservation of the portion remaining in the lands of the exile might at all events take such a form that it would not be an entirely inappropriate theme of sacred history. That is, if a danger should arise for this Judaism in the Diaspora too great to be overcome through human power and sagacity without a higher divine providence; if it should especially threaten Judaism as such, that is, on account of the law and their lawful reverence of God so that it became doubtful whether obedience to the divine law could be maintained in spite of the human claims to obedience—then there could, yea, must be such a preservation. That portion of Judaism remaining in heathen lands had by no means been dismissed as such from communion with Jehovah; it had a not unimportant part to play for the kingdom of God, as is manifest in the apostolic times, where it constituted with its synagogues the best starting-point for the preaching of the gospel; and their remaining behind in exile was in some measure approved by the word of God itself, inasmuch as the prophets had placed the proper return in connection with the appearance of the Messiah.

The new beginning we find described in the books of Ezra and Nehemiah, and a preservation of the character above pointed out in the book of Esther. The books of Ezra and Nehemiah by no means intend to narrate the history of the entire period which they embrace from Zerubbabel to Nehemiah; but they would in reality merely treat of that which was essential to the new beginning. This is clear not only from what they narrate, but also from that which they omit. And with respect to the book of Esther, the principal thing is not so much the person of Esther or Mordecai and their exaltation, as the deliverance of Israel, for which all else is as the means to the end. As it was to be expected, however, the history of this new period has a new method and a different tone. Whilst the representation of the times before the exile regarded the external affairs, that is, the people and their possession of the land, as the bearers of the internal; and the lower, that is, the political fortune as the outflow of the highest; and thus had ever occupied itself with the proper soul of that which occurred, with the thoughts and plans of God, especially with the holy and glorious acts of God: the historian of the times subsequent to the exile naturally took the external itself at once as an internal thing, so that he stopped with the lower, earthly and human. Whilst the history of the times previous to the exile, as a faithful copy of the great conflict, which the Lord had then conducted for the existence of His truth, against all heathenish influences within and without Israel, had on its part most earnestly taken part in the struggle, and become especially great and strong through its simple, constantly-repeated, but at the bottom the only valid criticism of the heathenish influence, the apostacy from Jehovah, the carnal impulses and errors—the history of the times subsequent to the exile contented itself with a simple account of that which transpired, and purposed merely to excite a grateful remembrance of that which God had done, or of the services of the prominent men and families. Whilst the history of the pre-exile times had a genuine prophetic character, in that it had immediately taken part in real life, as it then was also conducted by prophets; that of the post-exile times assumed a priestly Levitical character without doubt likewise proceeding from priests and Levites. This new method of conception and treatment had likewise its propriety. The view which supported this method was that ultimately all depends upon the divine service, and that which is connected therewith, that hence the temple and the capital deserve the most attention as the places of the divine service. This was sufficiently sustained by that advance in development, which marked the post-exile time and the new arrangement of affairs, and is entirely correct. And if now the singers and musicians appeared alongside of the priests, this is all the more established, as alongside of and after the offerings the worship must more and more gain through the word a higher and more spiritual value. We must find sufficiently good reasons for this, and recognize it with thankfulness that a historian subsequent to the exile in the books of Chronicles treated the entire history previous to the exile from the same point of view and according to the same principles.

But we must also bring into consideration a difference in the method of using the sources, which, if it is more of a formal character is yet not unimportant. Whilst in the pre-exile history the use of the sources was the subordinate and secondary thing, and the independent representation in accordance with practical aims was the principal thing; in the post-exile history, as it appears in the books of Ezra and Nehemiah, the chief thing appears to be the use of the sources. The author lets his own representation remain in the back-ground, at least so far as that he merely gives a sufficient introduction to the sources or original documents respecting the subject in hand, so far as he can use them, and seeks to put them in proper connection with one another, and even in the Chronicles he does not revise, but compiles. Hence he heaps up the original documents, especially in the book of Ezra, official letters, which naturally seem too detailed, and in addition registers of names, which strike us as too long-winded. But when we ask what induced him to make these so prominent, we might bring into consideration in general and above all that which was involved in the entire development of the times, the above-mentioned estimate of ancient pieces of composition as holy treasures; but the chief reason for the adoption of such epistolary documents, as we find especially in the book of Ezra, was certainly in the circumstance that the whole existence of the community subsequent to the exile, politically so dependent, was based upon them, so that they really had an inestimable worth; with respect to the register of names, we are likewise to consider, that in a time when the existence of the community gathered about the temple was no longer given by the simple mention of their membership in the tribe or people, but was dependent on the free resolution of the individuals who would return from Babylon, and as a matter of fact limited itself to individual households of the ancient families and tribes, that it was no longer sufficient to speak in general of Judah or Benjamin, but was natural to mention the individual families and households, yea, here and there likewise of individual persons, and to hold them as worthy of a thankful remembrance. These registers of names cannot but remind us from this point of view of the fact that the farther the congregation developed itself in accordance with this idea, the more the personality of the individual gained in importance and came into estimation.

3. *Their Contents.*—The chief topics of consideration after the exile were, on the one side, the temple as the dwelling-place of God; on the other side the city with its walls as the place of the congregation, and besides the congregation itself. Thus in the book of Ezra the temple stands decidedly in the foreground, in the book of Nehemiah the city with its walls, whilst both books, in their second parts, take up the congregation itself, that is the organization of their life in accordance with the law. The book of Nehemiah, moreover, embraces the city walls and the life of the congregation in accordance with the law once more in a brief closing section. More closely considered there are only a few principal topics treated of with reference to these subjects. The book of Ezra begins with the year in which Cyrus gave the Jews permission to return (536), and extends at least to the seventh year of Artaxerxes (458), embracing accordingly a space of about eighty years. The book of Nehemiah alludes to the twentieth year of Artaxerxes, and touches besides upon what happened after his thirty-second year, thus after 433. Limiting itself, however, to the beginnings, the book of Ezra occupies itself merely with the fundamental permission of Cyrus, the building of the temple under Zerubbabel and Jeshua, and finally merely with the negative consolidation of the life of the congregation under the law, which still so readily mixed itself with heathenism, namely, with the exclusion of heathen women by Ezra; it thus, after narrating the building of the temple, leaps over the entire period between the seventh year of Darius Hystaspis and the seventh year of Artaxerxes, a period of fifty-six years. The book of Nehemiah discourses merely respecting the restoration of the city-walls and the positive strengthening of the life under the law through the renewal of the covenant between God and the new congregation, with an emphasis of the conditions then particularly important. How much the author is inclined to make use of the documents and sources respecting the re-establishment of the congregation, or rather give them after a short introduction, is manifest enough from the beginning. After referring to Jeremiah's words with reference to the end of the exile and re-establishment of Jerusalem, by which the subsequent history is put in the light of an act

of God in fulfilment thereof, the edict of Cyrus follows, that called upon the Jews to return to Jerusalem and build the temple, and moreover called upon those who remained to assist the departing. The restoration of the vessels of the temple, once carried away from Jerusalem by Nebuchadnezzar to Sheshbazzar, the prince of Judah, is likewise mentioned (chap. i.). This is, however, in a certain sense, merely the introduction to chap. ii. Without going further into a description of the return, yea, without even simply mentioning it in so many words, the author at once gives the register of those who returned with Zerubbabel and Jeshua, whilst he adds at the close their number and the number of their servants, maid-servants, horses, *etc.*, at the same time, moreover, the sum which the heads of fathers among them offered for the building of the temple (chap. ii.). In chap. iii. he again continues his narrative. The returned people again assembled from the different cities in which they had settled, towards the seventh month, and in order to be able to celebrate the feast of tabernacles, restored at first merely the ancient altar, then, moreover, directly prepared also for the building of the temple. Already in the second year and indeed in the second month occurred the laying of the foundation of the temple, when shouts of joy and cries of lamentation touchingly mingled. But sad to say (chap. iv.) the adversaries of Judah and Benjamin, the Samaritans, interfered, who would have gladly assisted, but were necessarily excluded from the work, and in consequence of this had the permission to build revoked at the Persian royal court, who still even in the time of Ahasuerus and Artaxerxes raised obstacles by their calumniations. The author narrates this to us in order now directly to insert in Chaldee the letter of complaint of the Samaritans which they addressed to Artaxerxes, and the answer of the king to it, documents without doubt preserved in Jerusalem. In chaps. v. and vi. he continues the history of the building of the temple in the time of Darius Hystaspis, but so that first of all he gives the report that the Persian officers sent to their king and his answer thereto. He concludes this section in ch. vi. 19–22 with a short account of the celebration of the first passover after the completion of the temple and the re-establishment of the worship.

A new section begins with chap. vii. as it passes over from the seventh year of Darius Hystaspis, from Zerubbabel and Jeshua to Ezra. It narrates chap. vii. 1–10 summarily, that the priest Ezra, whose high-priestly origin is shown, in the seventh year of Artaxerxes had departed from Babylon for Jerusalem, and had arrived in the fifth month, in order to set up and teach the law of the Lord in Israel. But this is again only for an introduction to documents, which he has to communicate and directly subjoins. First a letter in the Chaldee language follows, which Artaxerxes gave Ezra to take along with him, in order to secure him the support of the officers for the complete establishment of the worship in Jerusalem, in order also to give him ample authority for the improvement of the administration of judgment, for the appointment of judges and officers of justice (chap. vii. 25); then comes the conclusion in the Hebrew language added by Ezra himself, in which he praises God for this decree of the king (chap. vii. 11–28). Next we have a list prepared by Ezra of the families who went up with him to Jerusalem (chap viii. 1–14); furthermore a somewhat more extended narrative of Ezra's, respecting the equipment of his company, respecting his journey to Jerusalem, and respecting the delivery of the treasures and vessels that he brought with him for the temple (chap. viii. 15–36); finally in chap. ix. respecting his action against the intermarriage with heathen women or men, especially respecting his prayer that he made with reference to this matter. Chap. ix. introduces Ezra's activity in Jerusalem. It is true it seems to treat only of a particular part of his activity; but this is yet in truth the foundation of all the rest, yea, it already involves the rest to a certain extent: it is the strengthening of the life of the congregation in the law; only it is merely the negative side, which alone could be undertaken at once, namely, the separation of the congregation from heathenism and from the life of the heathen. The author himself, as it seems, again takes the word in chap. x. in order to append what success Ezra had at first with the heads, but then also, when they had called all the Jews together to Jerusalem, with the great congregation, how he obtained the solemn promise of all, to dismiss the heathen women and its fulfilment. But even here there follows again a list, which he doubtless had come upon in some way, namely, an enumeration of all those who had married heathen women, and now dismissed them. The whole is divided into two parts, the first part again into three sections, and the second part into two sections; each of these sections, however, amounts to a principal document.

Part I. *The Temple as the place of the Lord* (times before Ezra). Chaps. i.–vi.

SECTION 1. The most important foundations. Chaps. i. and ii.
Chap. i. The permission to build, and those who returned for this purpose.
Chap. ii. The document respecting the names of the returning.
SECTION 2. The first effort. Chaps. iii. and iv.
Chap. iii. Re-establishment of the altar and the preparation for building the temple.
Chap. iv. The interruption and a document respecting the machinations of the enemies.
SECTION 3. The renewal and completion of the work. Chaps. v. and vi.
Chap. v. The renewal of the work and the report of the officers to Darius.
Chap. vi. Darius' answer, with the completion of the temple. The Passover feast.

Part II. *The congregation as the people of the Lord. Negative strengthening of their life in the law* (Ezra's activity). Chaps. vii.–x.

SECTION 1. Ezra's emigration to Jerusalem. Chaps. vii.–viii.
Chap. vii. Ezra's journey and purpose, and Artaxerxes' letter of authority.
Chap. viii. Ezra's own documentary report (his companions, their completion and journey).
SECTION 2. The chief fault of that time, and its removal. Chap. ix.–x.
Chap. ix. Chief fault of that period, and Ezra's penitential prayer on that account.
Chap. x. The removal of that fault, and documentary list of those who purified themselves from it.

In the book of Nehemiah the entire first part, chaps. i. to vii., is devoted to the rebuilding of the walls of the city by Nehemiah, in spite of many hinderances and disappointments, but throughout taken from a documentary written source, namely, from Nehemiah's own memorial. The second part then occupies itself with the congregation, in order now to give an account of the further activity of Ezra with reference to it, or rather its results, the positive strengthening of the congregation in the life in the law, which led to the renewal of the covenant relation between the people and God; since, however, he adduces the names of the families belonging to it, he runs out into traditional lists. The third part describes the dedication of the city walls and the removal of various evils in that period; the latter is again accompanied with the documentary words of Nehemiah himself. The three chief parts may be again divided each into two sections, so that the following summary results:

Part I. *The city as the place of the congregation. Re-establishment of the city walls and list of the first emigrants.* Chaps. i.–vii.

SECTION 1. How the re-establishment of the city walls came about. Chaps. i.-iii.

Chap. i. Nehemiah hears of the sad condition of Judah and Jerusalem, and prays to the Lord for help.

Chap. ii. He asks permission of Artaxerxes, and journeys with authority from him to Jerusalem. There he brings about the resolution to re-establish the walls, in spite of the adversaries of the Jews.

Chap. iii. Each family of the congregation undertakes a certain portion of the work.

SECTION 2. How Nehemiah overcame all difficulties. Chaps. iv.–vii.

Chap. iv. The difficulties from without: Sanballat, Tobia, *etc.*, threaten to fall upon the Jews with force of arms; Nehemiah organizes against them a troop of warriors, and also arms the laborers themselves.

Chap. v. The difficulties from within; the poor complain of oppression on the part of the rich; Nehemiah does away with usury, and works through the example of his own unselfishness.

Chap. vi. The difficulties that arise from the co-operation of external and internal factors. Sanballat frightens the Jews, as if Nehemiah stood in the odor of a rebel. The prophet Shemaiah attempted in the pay of Sanballat to deprive Nehemiah himself of courage, as if a real danger threatened him; the companions of Tobia carry on tale-bearing. But all these efforts fail on account of Nehemiah's foresight.

Chap. vii. Nehemiah completes the building of the walls, and gives a review of the first emigrants after the exile.

Part II. *The congregation as inhabitants of the city of God. Positive strengthening of their life in the law by the renewal of the covenant between them and God, and list of the members of the congregation.* Chaps. viii.–xii. 26.

SECT. 1. The history of the renewal of the covenant. Chaps. viii.-x.

Chap. viii. The reading of the law under the leadership of Ezra and Nehemiah leads at first to a feast of tabernacles according to the law, and then

Chap. ix., to a prayer for grace and redemption from the afflictions that were still present; finally,

Chap. x., to a renewal of the covenant under conditions then particularly important, and indeed for many heads of families, who are especially adduced.

SECT. 2. The constituent parts of the entire congregation at that time. Chaps. xi.–xii. 26.

Chap. xi. The inhabitants of Jerusalem, and at the same time of the other cities of Judah.

Chap. xii. The priests and Levites, at first the earlier families who had already come up with Zerubbabel and Jeshua, vers. 1-11, and then also the later ones, vers. 12-26.

Part III. *The city and the congregation. Dedication of the city walls. Removal of various evils in the life of the congregation.* Chaps. xii. 27–xiii. 31.

SECT. 1. Dedication of the city walls. Chap. xii. 27-43.

SECT. 2. Removal of various evils in the life of the congregation. Chaps. xii. 44–xiii. 31.

§ 2. SOURCES, COMPOSITION AND AUTHENTICITY.

1. *Sources.*—There can be no doubt but that the author really had original documents and sources before him, and introduced them unchanged in his narrative, to a great extent. That the list of names in Ezra ii. is such an original document is the less to be disputed that already Nehemiah came upon it as an ancient piece of writing and used it in chap. vii. 6-73. It must have been composed already in the earliest times of the re-establishment of the congregation. The same is true with reference to the letters that are given in chaps. iv.-vi., and that constitute the principal contents of the statements there made. Many interpreters even regard it as very probable that the few verses of a historical character that introduce the letters in chaps. iv.-vi., or unite them with one another, were taken from other sources, namely, a Chaldee history of the building of the temple. Yet the reasons given therefor are not very tenable, whilst those that are adduced against this view, are well worthy of attention. They appeal to the Chaldee language of these verses, which our author would have had no occasion to use himself. But perhaps he found some of these verses as an introductory superscription already on the letters themselves; the others, however, which he himself added and inserted between Chaldee passages, would have made the narrative too much mixed, if he had wished to write in Hebrew. They also appeal to the fact that the first person is used in chap. v. 4, "then we spake to them" (the Persian officers), whereby the writing shows itself to be a work composed long before, by a man who participated in the building of the temple in the time of Darius Hystaspis, whilst the work as a whole could have originated only at a far later period. But the correctness of this first person is very doubtful, as we will see in the exegesis of chap. v. 4. Still further they appeal to the fact that there occur here statements respecting names, close accounts of transactions and individuals, which, as Bertheau says, must have been derived altogether from written documents. Nevertheless there is nothing further in this respect than what is suggested by the letters. On the other hand, already in chap. vi. 14,

Artaxerxes is mentioned alongside of Cyrus and Darius, as one of the Persian kings, through whose favor the Jews had re-established the temple, which shows at least that this piece cannot have been written already in the time of Darius, but at the earliest in the time of Artaxerxes. This name must then have been added at the later revision, at which time also Artaxerxes seemed well worthy of mention. In vers. 16-18 furthermore, in the closing verse of the Chaldee section, the dedication of the temple, especially in ver. 17, the offering of sacrifices, in ver. 18, the arrangement of the priests and Levites, are spoken of in such a manner, and besides the arrangement of the priests and Levites, in accordance with the law, is so expressly emphasized, as is peculiar only to our author himself (comp. the parallel passages brought forward upon the verses in question). Finally, the 24th ver. of chap. iv., which refers back to ver. 5, has manifestly been added by the same person who in vers. 6-23 has given the letter of Artaxerxes before. That this, however, was done by our author himself, there can be no doubt, since it only commended itself thus to his purposes and arrangement.—Again, on the other hand, that the lists of names, as they are given further in the book of Ezra (chaps. viii. and x.) especially, however, in the book of Nehemiah, were already met with as ancient pieces of writing, is not only said by the author himself quite plainly, since he speaks of different registrations of the Levites at different times (Neh. xii. 23), but is likewise in itself probable, and is all the more sure, that a part of the register given in Neh. xi. 3-36, occurs also in 1 Chron. ix. 3-33, and indeed with many deviations, which is best explained from the supposition that the author found the same writing in different places and in different forms.

It is only questionable, whether in Ezra vii. 27 sq. likewise, we may speak of an original document, or whether the author of that which could be regarded as such, that is, Ezra, speaking of himself in the first person, must be regarded as the author of the rest of the second part, and accordingly also, as the Rabbinical tradition will have it, the author of the entire book. This leads us to our second point.

2. *Composition.*—That Ezra wrote a narrative of his journey to Jerusalem, and what he accomplished there, is clear from the passages in which the first person is used, without doubt. Yet it cannot be denied that, against the view still advocated by KEIL [PUSEY, RAWLINSON, WORDSWORTH], that Ezra is the proper author of the book named after him, many very weighty arguments are opposed, which make it more probable that a later author compiled our book, as we now have it, with the use of Ezra's writing. In general against Ezra as the author, is the incompleteness, we might say the fragmentary character of the second part; Ezra himself would, we should suppose, have communicated something more, and something more systematic respecting his work in Jerusalem We learn from our book only the one thing, that he opposed the intermarriage with the heathen, whilst yet he was empowered to undertake a far more comprehensive work. More in detail comes into consideration, especially the circumstance, that in the genealogy of Ezra (vii. 1-5) his immediate ancestors are passed over, that at once the high-priest Seraiah, who lived at the beginning of the exile, is mentioned, since the design without doubt was to make him known above all as a descendant of the high-priestly family. Ezra himself would rather have been led by filial reverence to mention his own father before all. Furthermore we are struck by the honorable mention of Ezra in chap. vii. 6, that he was a סֹפֵר מָהִיר, a skilful scribe,* then also the circumstance, that chap. vii. anticipates chap. viii., so that there is a repetition, which is only natural, if the author in chap. viii. yet again cites from an original document the same thing that he had already previously briefly mentioned in chap. vii.; furthermore the fact, that in chap. vii. 1 sq. the third person is used,† first in chap. vii. 27 sq. the first person,—finally and especially

* [Pusey, p. 339: "It is added merely that he was a *ready*, fluent expositor of it. He mentions of himself, what others have observed of him in the books of Chronicles, that the law of his God was the great study of his life, and that he made progress in it. Perhaps he meant, as one of the Psalmists, whose expression he used, said before him, that he was a "ready writer" of what he was taught by God, ascribing to himself only that he was, what he was, the instrument of God."—TR.]

† [Rawlinson *in loco:* "But exactly parallel changes of person occur in the Book of Daniel (*e. g.*, the third person from i. to vii. 2, the first from vii. 2–ix. 27; the third in x. 1, and the first from x. 2 to the end), which there is good reason to regard as the work of Daniel himself, and not of a compiler; changes too, not very dissimilar occur in the nearly contemporary Greek writer Thucydides. Thucydides begins his history in the third person

this fact, that the book of Ezra has so many things in common with the Chronicles in the manner of expression, and at the same time in many matters of fact, as the preference for the different Levitical officials in the sanctuary, especially for musicians and door-keepers, besides the interest in genealogies and registers of names. This is shown in the Com. of ZOECKLER upon the Chronicles, Introduction, § 2. The view in recent times wide-spread and discussed in the Introduction to the Chronicles, §§ 2 and 3, by ZOECKLER that the author of Chronicles at the same time brought Ezra, yea also Nehemiah into the present form in which we have them, has decidedly the most reasons in its favor. If it were really a fact, that the observed resemblances in Ezra and Nehemiah throughout occurred even in the original documents and written sources with entire indifference, then they would not have to be regarded as individual peculiarities of a common author, but be ascribed in general to the later period, to which the books in question belong, especially if they likewise occurred in other writings of essentially the same period. But this is true of only a proportionally few of them, as for example with the expressions brought forward by KEIL, בִּזָּה, קַבֵּל and כְּיַד אֱלֹהַי עָלַי (the last is not found indeed in other books, but in the written sources, Ezra vii. 28; viii. 18, 22, 31, as well as in vii. 6–9, and besides Neh. ii. 8). By far the most of them occur, as we must at once remark, if we review the passages cited by ZOECKLER in the Introduct. to Chronicles, § 2, not to speak of Chronicles, on the one side, in Ezra i. and iii., as well also in the other passages not presenting themselves as original documents or sources, and on the other side in Neh. viii.–x. Here belong most decidedly these very phenomena of the language, which may be regarded most properly as idiomatic expressions of the books of Chronicles, Ezra, and Nehemiah; thus the expression, עַל־עָמְדָם, 2 Chron. xxx. 16; xxxv. 10; Neh. viii. 7; ix. 3; xiii. 11,—הֶדְוָה, 1 Chron. xvi. 27; Ezra vi. 16; Neh. viii. 10,—כְּפוֹר = goblet, 1 Chron. xxviii. 17; Ezra i. 10; viii. 27; עַד־לְמֵרָחוֹק, 2 Chron. xxvi. 15; Ezra iii. 13; פְּלֻגָּה, of divisions of the Levites, 2 Chron. xxxv. 5; Ezra vi. 18; so also *termini*, which emphasize the being in accordance with the law, which in the later period seem so particularly important, especially כַּמִּשְׁפָּט, 1 Chron. xxiii. 31; 2 Chron. xxxv. 13; xxx. 16; Ezra iii. 4; Neh. viii. 18, for which in the older writings כַּכָּתוּב בַּתּוֹרָה occurs frequently, furthermore liturgical formula, as הוֹדוּ וְהַלְלוּ לַיהוָה, 1 Chron. xvi. 4; xxiii. 30; xxv. 3, *etc.*; Ezra iii. 11, לְהוֹדוֹת וּלְהַלֵּל, and "that Jehovah is good, and his mercy endureth forever," 1 Chron. xvi. 34, 41; 2 Chron. v. 13; Ezra iii. 11,—the standing expressions in connection with descriptions of festivals and the like: בְּשִׂמְחָה, 1 Chron. xii. 40, *etc.*; Ezra iii. 12; and עַל־יְדֵי דָוִיד, 1 Chron. xxv. 2, 6; Ezra iii. 10,—finally, the official names of the musicians and servants in the temple that only occur in our books, מְצִלְתַּיִם מְשֹׁרְרִים and נְתִינִים. But even those phenomena, which seem in general to belong to the later language on the whole, because they are found here and there in other books likewise, are found besides in the Chronicles, at least pre-eminently in those very parts of our books under consideration. To these belong 1), the brief method of subordination of the relative clauses, together with their collocation after a *stat. constr.*, 1 Chron. xxix. 3; 2 Chron. xxxi. 19; Ezra i. 5; Neh. viii. 10; 2) the case of the infin. with לְ, in order to express a potential mood, 1 Chron. v. 1; ix. 25; xiii. 4, *et al.*; Ezra iv. 3; x. 12; Neh. viii. 13; 3) the extraordinarily frequent use of the preposition לְ partly before the object as *nota accusativi*, partly after an accusative, to continue it, 1 Chron. xxviii. 1, *etc.*; Neh. ix. 32, as especially before כֹּל, when in enumerations everything is to be included, 1 Chron. xiii. 1; 2 Chron. v. 12; Ezra i. 5 (certainly moreover also vii. 28); Neh. xi. 2, after the preposition עַד, 1 Chron. xxviii. 7, 20, *etc.*; Ezra iii. 13; x. 14 (moreover also ix. 4, 6); 4) the redundant use of prepositions in general, *e. g.*, in expressions like בְּיוֹמָם, Neh. ix. 19; 5) the use of the article before a verb instead of the relative pronoun, 1 Chron. xxvi. 28; xxix. 8, 17, *etc.*: Ezra viii. 25; x. 14, 17; Neh. ix. 33.

(i. 1), and changes to the first after a few chapters (i. 20-22). Further on, in book iv., he resumes the third (104-106). In book v, 26 he begins in the third, but runs on into the first, which he again uses in book vii. 97."—TR.]

The manner in which the section Neh. viii. 1 sq. is connected with Chronicles and Ezra on the one side, and on the other is distinguished from the rest of the book of Nehemiah, is in a critical point of view very important. In order to carry out the latter point, how it separates itself from the rest of the book, we might already bring into consideration the subject-matter itself. This is not only suddenly entirely different from the previous context, since it no longer treats of the strengthening of the city wall and the like, but treats of religious acts, but it seems almost as if we might first have expected something else instead of it. Nehemiah in chap. vii. has given an account of the completion of the building of the walls; it is singular that there is no reference *here* to the dedication of the walls, but that this comes only afterwards in xii. 27 as supplementary. In chap. vii. 4 he has mentioned that the inhabitants of Jerusalem were too few; it is singular that their increase is first intimated in xi. 1, and indeed only incidentally. It is very true that the book, as it now is, has a tolerable continuity, since the author allows himself to make use of the remark respecting the inhabitants of Jerusalem in vii. 4, as an occasion for going over from the securing the safety of the capital, of which he had previously written, to the congregation and its organization, in order further on to mention the increase of the inhabitants and the dedication of the walls, merely as a supplement, and as it were incidentally. Nevertheless this kind of progress of thought compared with the first part, has something surprising in it. It seems as if here suddenly a point of view was taken, which for the previous part of the work had originally not been considered important. But besides this there are still many other circumstances which render the difference of subject here very significant. 1. Nehemiah very suddenly ceases to speak of himself in the first person. 2. He here in general retires to the background, whilst Ezra, who is mentioned in the book of Nehemiah elsewhere only at the dedication of the walls incidentally (xii. 23), is the chief person. Nehemiah occurs only as supplementary, and indeed only twice, viii. 9; x. 2. 3. He bears here both times the title of "the Tirshatha," whilst in v. 14, 15, 18, he is called "Pechah." 4. Whilst the chiefs are called ii. 16; iv. 8, 13; v. 7, 17; vi. 17; vii. 5; xii. 40; xiii. 11, הֹרִים and סְגָנִים, the term רָאשֵׁי הָאָבוֹת occurs in viii. 13. 5. The expressions peculiar and usual to Nehemiah are missing, as "according to God's hand over me," comp. ii. 8 and 18; furthermore, "God gave to me in my heart," comp. ii. 12 and vii. 5. Even KLEINERT (*Dorp. theol. Beitr.* I., S. 114 sqq.) and HÆVERNICK (*Einleit.* II. 1, S. 305 sqq.) find it probable that there was another author for vii. 73 *b*—x. 40; they suppose that this section was not composed by Nehemiah, but by Ezra as the leader of the religious transactions here described, and was only appropriated by Nehemiah.* But, 6. The author speaks also of the times of Ezra and Nehemiah as past, yea, considers likewise the times subsequent to Nehemiah, Neh. xii. 11, 22, and thereby makes himself known, as he does likewise in Chronicles as a later writer, as will be still more evident when we consider the time of its composition. The grounds adduced by KEIL for the traditional view that Neh. viii.–x. comes from the same hand as the rest of the book, namely, from Nehemiah himself, have little significance. That the previous threads of thought in Neh. viii. have been allowed so entirely to fall, yea, to be broken off, is to be explained, says he, simply and artlessly from the succession of the things narrated in time, as if the order in time could not yield at times to the logical order of facts, yea, in such cases as the present must not yield. What would have hindered the author in such a case, if, for the sake of chronological order, he would have come to the public reading of the law in viii. sq., from reserving the statement, that the inhabitants of Jerusalem were few, and therefore also the list of the exiles who first returned, for another place, where he then could have spoken at once of the increase of the inhabitants? That Nehemiah suddenly steps so decidedly into the back-ground with respect to Ezra, he says, has its ground in the fact that Nehemiah as civil governor was not authorized to lead the religious feast here narrated which alone belonged to the priest and scribe Ezra (—at first it speaks only of the public reading of the law, which Nehemiah might have very well occasioned,—), that he here rather could only co-operate subordinately

* [RAWLINSON *in loco* conjectures here that Zadok (or Zidkijah), Nehemiah's scribe, or secretary, was the author as an eye-witness of the proceedings.—TR.]

as *membrum præcipuum ecclesiæ Israeliticæ.* But if it were really so, the question would at once arise, how is it that Nehemiah narrates here something in which he had so little to do, since he elsewhere limits himself entirely to that which had been urged and brought about by himself. Moreover, under all circumstances, the failure of the first person, which is elsewhere so consistently retained in the writings of Nehemiah, is not explained. When KEIL refers to xii. 27 sq., where he says not "*we*," but "*they* sought the Levites," to prove that Nehemiah might very well put others in the foreground in connection with facts that did not originate primarily with himself, this very section suffices with reference to the principal point for a very decisive counter argument. For notwithstanding Nehemiah does not stand so much in the foreground as a matter of course as elsewhere, yet he uses the first person in vers. 31 and 38 even in this connection. What KEIL says respecting the *Tirshatha* and *Rashe haaboth* deserves no mention. With the different character of the section, Neh. viii.–x., if critical probability is worth anything, we are to suppose that here another author has supplemented Nehemiah's writing, whether from another document or from tradition. Who this was cannot remain in doubt in connection with the similarity of the style that is manifest here, in the book of Ezra and in the Chronicles.

The question whether this author is to be regarded moreover as the editor or the proper author of our two books, is answered from the foregoing of itself. It is possible, that already Ezra, when he described his journey to Jerusalem, and his principal work there, likewise collected the original documents respecting the previous times, and placed them, provided with historical introductions, before his book. Yet we have no right to derive from him in our present book, any more than chap. vii. 22, 28, and chap. viii.—ix. 15, that is, any more than the passages, which show clearly by the first person that they were written by him, which thereby distinguish themselves from all the other passages, especially from chap. vii. 1–10, and chap. x. Whatever is not as chap. ii. 4, 8–23, an original document, or as chap. v. 5, 6, 12, chaps. viii. and ix. sources, whatever serves as introduction to the original document or sources, as especially chaps. i. and iii. and v. 1–10, bears the stamp of the so-called chronicler, or at least of his time. When KEIL, in order to show that the whole, and therefore also the tenth chap. was composed by Ezra, raises the question, what could have determined the author to break off the further communication of the memoir of Ezra at the end of chap. ix. and narrate the end of the transaction in his own words,—criticism would not be required to answer this question, unless it knew something more of the memoir of Ezra than it can know at present. Now we may think of various reasons.—With more propriety the book of Nehemiah might be spoken of as merely edited. Since however the last author has inserted chaps. viii.—x., and indeed for the most part with the help of his own literary activity, he must be designated here at least as a supplementer. Although he already had before him the book of Ezra, and so also a book of Nehemiah, yet the form of these books, as it lies before us, originated first with him, and the design which he on his part pursued in his literary activity. Perhaps he had also transformed, to some extent, the text of the registers and original documents, which he reproduced in his work here and there in accordance with his method, as it may perhaps be seen, for example in Ezra ii. 68 sq., in comparison with Neh. vii. 71 sq., and so also Ezra vi. 16–18, if here an authority has been really used.

The question, when this last and real author actually lived, has already been answered by ZOECKLER (in his introduction to the books of Chronicles), who, it is true, with reference to Ezra and Nehemiah regards him only as an editor. In Neh. xii. 10, 11, 22 and 23, the line of high-priest is carried down to Jaddua, who, according to JOSEPHUS' statement, not to be doubted here (*Antiqu.* XI. 10) held his office in the time of Alexander the Great. KEIL'S supposition that the author had known Jaddua not yet as high-priest, but only as a child, and had mentioned him merely as grandson of the last high-priest of his own time, Joiada, is already in itself improbable, and besides has against it the fact that the same person is mentioned with the others as one in whose days the Levites were recorded. It seems that the meaning of ver. 22 is that under the four high-priests Eliashib, Joiada, Johanan and Jaddua, four registrations of Levites had been made. KEIL understands, it is true, that only one occurred, namely, under Eliashib and Joiada, and the others are mentioned merely because they then already lived. But this supposition is too clearly a mere evasion of the difficulty. If immediately afterwards only the one record of priests, which was made in the time of Darius, is mentioned, this is to be explained from the fact that this one chiefly, yea exclusively, comes into consideration for the author, since he according to the entire context, would mention only those belonging to the times of the beginning—at all events those living up to the time of Ezra and Nehemiah—as he then also in chap. xii. 1–11 expressly names only those of the time of Zerubbabel, and then in ver. 12 sq., only those of the times immediately following Joiakim, and in ver. 26, after mentioning the heads of the Levites, expressly adds that he thereby had given only those of the time of Joiakim and Nehemiah.—This mark of a late period of composition that has been adduced, stands, it is true, somewhat apart by itself, and would not signify much if anything else contradicted it; we might readily suppose that the names of the later high-priests (and so also those of the later posterity of Zerubbabel in 1 Chron. iii. 19–24) were subsequently added as a supplement by a late hand; but since there is nothing of the kind, since on the contrary the times of Ezra and Nehemiah are spoken of as of a previous period, and of themselves as of persons of the past in Neh. xii. 26, 27, so the probability is, so far as it can be established by criticism, that the author was one who at the earliest lived in the time of Jaddua,* at the end of the Persian or the beginning of the Greek supremacy. [RAWLINSON *in loco* thinks that Ezra, "who seems to have had only a temporary commission (vii. 14), returned to the Persian court when he had carried through the matter of the marriage, and either a little before or a little after his return wrote the Book which has come down to us." He thus accounts for the abrupt conclusion of the book, and gives the date as 457 or 6. With regard to Nehemiah he thinks that it is most probable that the various sections of the book of Nehemiah "were collected by Nehemiah himself, who had written, at any rate, two of them (i.–vii. 5 and xii. 27–xiii. 31). The date of the compilation would be about B. C. 430."—TR.]

3. *Authenticity.*—Already the style of composition, and also the kind of contents and the method of stating them, testifies that the author, even if he wrote a hundred or more years after Nehemiah, in general pursued a method that was entirely historical. We have seen that he supports almost every important event that he narrates, with original documents, or presents it in the language of the written authorities. There is not the least occasion for doubt with reference to the historical character of the original documents and written authorities. There is only one point that can be questioned, having no confirmatory document, unless we should recognize as such the report of the elders in Jerusalem given in the letter to Darius, chap. v. 16. This is where it is said that the returned exiles already in the first year of their emigration had re-established the altar, and already in the second year had laid the foundation of the temple (Ezra iii.). (Comp. SCHRADER *Theol. Stud. und Krit.*, 1867, S. 460 ff., and DE WETTE *Einl.*, 8 *Ausg.*, § 235). Since in later times SCHRADER supposes it has been presupposed that the returned exiles were pervaded with glowing love for the religion of their sires, were filled with the greatest joy over their finally successful redemption from Babylon, and of the most sincere thankfulness towards the God of their fathers, they have quite gradually it is true, and without having any historical foundation for it, been able to give way to the idea that the returned exiles, as soon as they arrived in the land of their fathers, had had nothing more speedily to be done than to think of the restoration of the temple. In reality, however, the congregation hardly went so far as to put their hands to this work until the time when they actually carried on the building to its completion, in the second to the sixth year of Darius. If they had really begun already in the time of Cyrus, we cannot think that they then would have let it remain idle for fourteen entire years: if they would not have ventured to undertake it again in the time of Cyrus, yet they might well do so under Cambyses or Smerdis. Yet these assertions gain some likelihood only from the fact that the prophets Haggai and Zechariah, in the time of Darius, speak not of a fresh undertaking of the building, but of the building simply, yea, that they speak still of a laying of the foundation of the temple, as if it really had now been proposed for the first time. In that Haggai

* [Pusey and Rawlinson agree in regarding this verse as an interpolation or marginal gloss of a later date, that has crept into the text.—TR.]

ii. 18. "Consider now from this day and upward, from the 24th day of the 9th month, as from the day when the foundation of the temple of the Lord was laid consider" assigns the laying of the foundation of the temple to the 24th day of the 9th month, that he adds the phrase לְמִן הַיּוֹם אֲשֶׁר יֻסַּד in apposition and accordingly as of like meaning with the phrase, "from the 24th day of the 9th month," is just as clear as the interpretation of KEIL, according to which לְמִן *etc.*, would be in apposition indeed, yet would reach back to the time of Cyrus, is artificial and untenable. And that Zech. viii. 9, "the prophets which were in the day when the foundation of the house of the Lord of hosts was laid, that the temple might be built," does not mean the prophets after the exile in general (KEIL) but those of the better times (KÖHLER), which were already bringing the fulfilment, as they, according to the immediately following verse, had not come previously, but for the first now after the failure of the harvest, that the laying of the temple's foundations accordingly also here is recognized as of the present, can as little be denied. But with all this the conclusions which SCHRADER derives from it are by far too hasty. As בָּנָה often means continue the building, or also, rebuild, comp. Ps. li. 20; lxix. 36, so יָסַד also may be used in different senses, since in a narrower sense it refers merely to the laying of the foundation stone, in a broader and fuller sense to the laying of the foundations in general. Only in the narrow sense had the laying of the foundation taken place in the time of Cyrus; for without doubt only a small portion of the congregation had as yet the leisure to occupy themselves therewith. Above all, moreover, the ruins had to be removed and the necessary new material be procured. In the fuller sense the laying of the foundations did not really take place until the time of Darius. Now for the first time was stone laid upon stone, as it was necessary, if the foundations as a whole were to be carried up. (Comp. Hag. ii. 15).*

That the returned, however, had constantly undertaken, already in the time of Cyrus, the re-establishment of the temple, yea, regarded it as most necessary and important, is entirely probable, and cannot be conceived of as otherwise. (Comp. EWALD, *Geschichte Israels* IV. S. 129 sq.). Not only because that the pre-exile prophets, as Jeremiah, by whose utterances the returning exiles allowed themselves to be chiefly led, that Ezekiel also had seen in the re-establishment and continuance of the temple worship and priestly office the best security for the continuance of the true religion itself, Jer. xxxiii. 17–26; Ezek. xx. 40; xxxiv. 26; xxxvii. 26 and 28, and especially in chaps. xl.–xlvii. (comp. EWALD IV. S. 43) and that in Jer. xliv. 28 the re-establishment of the temple under and by Cyrus was set down definitely as the will of God, comp. also Isa. lx. 7—against which it might perhaps be said that passages of contrary purport may be found in Jer. iii. 16 and Isa. lxvi. 1—but the edict of Cyrus itself, which constituted the foundation for the existence of the new congregation itself, had decidedly the same purport that the congregation should above all have the task of building the temple and restoring the temple worship, as is testified not only by Ezra i., but also by the original Chaldee document given in chap. vi. 3 sq. Over against this edict they would have lost the right of their existence in Jerusalem if they had set aside the building of the temple for the sake of any incident that changed the posture of affairs, or had postponed it for fully fourteen years. That they, however, did not touch the building for a long time after they had been interrupted, and did not even in the time of Cambyses attempt to take it up again, is easily explained from the many sad circumstances, especially also from the external dangers threatening them, under which they had to suffer, as is to be seen from the book of Ezra, and especially from the book of Nehemiah.

* According to Hag. i. 14, 15, it is true they had not for the first begun to work upon the house of the Lord on the 9th month and 24th day, when, according to chap. ii. 18, the foundation of the temple of the Lord was laid, but already in the 6th month. But that they then had merely performed the preparatory labor, removed the rubbish, and procured materials for building, that the proper work of building really began on the 24th day of the 9th month, is clear from the simple fact that the prophet makes this later day his great *terminus a quo*, with which the bad growth shall come to an end and a better and more fruitful time begin, and of a *quid pro quo* (Keil) there can be thought if we understand it thus.

§ 3. RELATION OF THE TWO BOOKS TO ONE ANOTHER, TO THE CHRONICLES, AND ESDRAS.

If the composition of the two books was in the manner above described, the question readily arises whether the last author from the first regarded the Chronicles, Ezra and Nehemiah as three particular books, or planned them as one work. That the unity, which has in recent times been asserted by ZUNZ (*Gottesdienstl. Vorträge der Juden*), EWALD, BERTH., *et al.*, really exists in a certain sense, cannot be ignored. The three books are so cut out that they unite to form a greater whole, not only in the looser way of the books of Samuel and Kings, but in a much more internal and firmer manner. Ezra begins with the same edict of Cyrus with reference to the return of the Jews, with which the Chronicles end. Ezra and Nehemiah, moreover, on their side are united together in the closest manner by Neh. viii.—xii. 26. Ezra's activity, the first part of which alone is narrated in the book of Ezra, is here described as to its continuance and results; the strengthening of the life of the congregation by this activity, the negative side of which is taken into consideration in the book of Ezra, is here carried on to its completion by the positive side. The book of Ezra is thus continued in the book of Nehemiah, and only finished therein. Neh. viii.—x. might have been added to the book of Ezra; it is annexed to the book of Nehemiah only because it describes a later period in which Nehemiah likewise came into consideration along-side of Ezra. Moreover, there is properly in all three books throughout one and the same subject treated; the history of the city of Jerusalem, the worship of God in it, and the most important persons who rendered services to it.

But it is just as easy to see likewise that the division into three particular books cannot have been made at a subsequent period, still less that it rests upon arbitrary grounds. The book of Nehemiah begins with a particular title, which designates it as the history of Nehemiah, and clearly enough separates it as a particular and independent writing from the book of Ezra. This title, moreover, cannot have been appended at a later period, but must have been placed there already by Nehemiah, otherwise the first person that constantly occurs, could not be explained. Moreover the supposition that the book, in spite of this title, should be regarded as merely a section of another larger book, would be against all Biblical analogies. And from this results also the independence of the book of Ezra. That which has been said in favor of the separation of Nehemiah, is also in favor of that of Ezra. To make Nehemiah independent, and append Ezra to the Chronicles (MOVERS) would be very inconsistent at any rate, and all the more so, indeed, that the book of Ezra treats of an entirely new period, which was separated by a great and gloomy chasm, from all that preceded it. Besides, if the author had written Chronicles and Ezra as a single book, he would have mentioned the edict of Cyrus but once, certainly, and he who separated Ezra would have caused the Chronicles to end before the introduction of this fact; in general, before the mention of Cyrus at all. That edict would have its proper place only at the beginning of the book of Ezra, where it formed the foundation for the subsequent history, and where it was therefore indispensable. To put it at the end of the Chronicles, moreover, would have been too refined for a mere arranger; this rather would come only into the mind of the author himself, who thereby would certainly merely satisfy the need of indicating by a brief word the restoration also after the exile and the destruction, which could not here be entirely absent.

In favor of the view that at least Ezra and Nehemiah originally constituted a single book, the circumstance is cited that both books from the most ancient times, namely, in the Talmud, yea, even in JOSEPH. and in the Alexandrine version, and accordingly also in MILETUS of Sardis and ORIGEN, in EUSEBIUS' *Church Hist.* II. 25, have been counted as one. But at the basis of this enumeration there is hardly more than the true recognition of the relationship that has been shown, and on the other side, the wish to have no more than just so many books in the Canon of the Old Test. as there are letters of the Alphabet. For the same reason the books of Judges and Ruth were connected together. For already JOSEPH. (*c. Ap.* I 8) enumerates, although he does not expressly give the reason, exactly twenty-two books, and JEROME says in the *prologus gal.*, expressly that the Hebrews had twenty-two canonical books, according to the number of the letters of their alphabet, which he, namely, mentions, and then adds that some, because the rabbins distinguish Sin and Shin, and for the sake of the sign of Jehovah, would set up a double yod in the alphabet, suppose that there are twenty-four, since they separate Ruth and Lamentations. That Ezra and Nehemiah are properly two books, can be the less denied, as they without doubt recognize two authors; for the book of Ezra, the priest of that name, of whom it is expressly said in the Talm. (*Bab. batr.* Fol. 14): "*Esra scripsit librum suum et genealogias librorum chron. usque ad sua tempora*," and for the book of Neh. with as much certainty the governor Nehemiah also makes himself known unmistakably as the author by the use of the first person. As for the Alex. version the connection of the two books is found indeed in *Cod. Alex.* and *Cod. Frid.-Aug.*, but not in the *Cod. Vatic.**

Now in the Alexandrine version there is found a translation at first of our book of Ezra, enlarged by additions, and only afterward a translation that conforms closely to our text, and the question arises what weight the former has with its deviations, as well critical as exegetical. The former is in the Alex. in the ancient Latin and in the Syriac versions (comp. *libri vet. test. apocryphi syriace e recogn. de Lagarde*) Ἔσδρας πρῶτος, the second Ἔσδρας δεύτερος, the book of Nehemiah Ἔσδρας τρίτος, or also (probably from the time of Jerome) Nehemias; in the Vulgate, on the other hand, the book of Ezra in its present unenlarged form, is called I. Esra, the book of Nehemiah, II. Esra, as then likewise already ORIGEN (in EUSEBIUS' *Church Hist.* IV. 25), then the council *Laodicæ can.* 80, and other lists, distinguish our books of Ezra and Nehemiah as Ἔσδρας πρῶτος and δεύτερος,—the enlarged translation however is called III. Ezra, and the apocalyptic, pseudepigraphic book of Ezra finally the IV. Ezra.—The enlargement of the translation was brought about on the one side by placing before the proper beginning the closing part of the Chronicles (chaps. xxxv. and xxxvi.), namely the description of the brilliant passover feast under Josiah, and at the same time the last history of Jerusalem before the exile, and by adding as a conclusion the beginning of the second part of Nehemiah, Neh. vii. 73—viii. 13, namely, the public reading of the law by Ezra before the door of the restored temple. We see that as in the original book, so also in this enlargement nothing is so much regarded as the history of the temple worship, and indeed especially its indestructibleness. The translator would first of all recall the evening sky in which he rejoiced shortly before the exile, for this reason, because it was to him to a certain extent a prophecy of the morning and the resurrection, which might be expected after the temporary ruin in exile, through the power and grace of God. He then lets the contents of our book of Ezra follow, and adds Neh. vii. 73—viii. 13, because here the fulfilment of that prophecy is narrated. For the public reading of the law before the door of the temple, Neh. vii. 73 sq., came into consideration for him without doubt as a kind of temple worship, yea, was regarded by him perhaps in accordance with the ideas subsequently formed, as the most suitable and important worship of God alongside of the sacrificial worship. He needed not to go further than Neh. viii. 13, however; it was already sufficiently established by the history preceding, up to this time, that the restoration had been completed, and especially in the last verse does it still stand forth, what seems to have come into consideration for the author therewith that the people by their worship of God had again been exalted to prosperity and joy.—On the other side, however, the author has taken into his book likewise a passage entirely foreign to the canonical Old Test., which gives an account of a banquet which the Persian king Darius prepared in the second year of his reign, where Zerubbabel found opportunity to gain the king's favor for himself and his people, so that he permitted the building of the temple, contributed to the restoration of the worship in Jerusalem and influenced many Jewish heads of

* [DAVIDSON's summary is as follows: "*Intro.* II., p. 148. The extended work of the Chronist embraced a post-exile as well as a pre-exile part; but the former was afterwards separated from the latter, and received a distinct name, the book of Ezra, including what is now Nehemiah. In this post-exile portion the Chronicle writer copied his sources more extensively than in the preceding part. In Ezra ii. 1-69 he gave an old list; in iv. 8—vi. 18 a fragment of an Aramean narrative which he had got. In vii. 12—ix. 15 he inserted a piece of Ezra's memoirs, and in x. 18-33, he put a list or register which had come into his hands. Thus more than two-thirds of the book of Ezra was transcribed from the sources at his disposal. With respect to the book of Nehemiah, which was merely intended as an appendix to the whole, he filled up gaps in Nehemiah's memoirs with vii. 73 *b*—ix.; xii. 1—xiii. 3, and with minor interpretations besides. We have then left for the authorship of Ezra vii. 12—ix. 15; for Nehemiah i. 1—vii. 73 *a*, x. at first; xi. *a*—xiii. 4-31."—TR.]

families to return. This is the section, chaps. iii.—v. 6, which may be compared with the "passages in Esther." It is quite probable that the author here had reproduced a popular tradition (FRITZSCHE, *Einl. zu.* III. Esra § 5); but without doubt, in the formation of the story the design had already co-operated of giving moral truth a historical dress (ZUNZ, *Gottesdienstl. Vort.*, S. 106 and 123). Zerubbabel and two other young men were at that banquet, body-guards of the king; they agreed, when the latter had gone to sleep, to lay down their opinions before him with reference to what was the mightiest on earth, and see to which he would give his recognition. The one wrote "wine," the second "the king," the third (Zerubbabel) wrote "women are mightiest;" the latter added, however, "but truth gains the victory over every thing," and this he explained afterwards so that every other thing, even the king, had fallen into unrighteousness, and hence likewise become perishable. Only truth lasts. The author might by this sentence of Zerubbabel, so to say, have indicated the spirit of his presentation of history; not the king, that is worldly power and glory, can do everything. Their victory over the Lord is only apparent. The worship of Jehovah and the existence of Jerusalem can only be interrupted by them for a time. The king is not the mightiest, because on the one side even wine, and on the other women, rule over him; in other words, because he belongs to the world and its lusts, that is, to vanities; but it is the truth, the divine truth, which guarantees the eternal duration of the worship of God, because it is one with it; it proceeds from the eternal, and must therefore endure forever.

Now with respect to the critical value of this enlargement, it is by no means in the condition to make probable to us the already rejected view of an original external unity of Chronicles, Ezra, and Nehemiah, notwithstanding the reasons for the opposite opinion; the internal connection is sufficient to explain why the author, if his object was the temple worship, went to work to collect material at the same time from the three fields. No more are we to suppose that he had found a basis in the original for the section, chaps. iii.—v. 6, that he inserted. "The language (of this passage) betrays itself throughout as originally Hellenistic (FRITZSCHE, *l. c.*). It seems to FRITZSCHE that only the conclusion, chap. v. 1–6, can be an exception. At any rate III. Ezra might come into consideration with reference to textual criticism. The translation is indeed frequently free, yet is as a whole in close conformity to the Hebrew text, in comparatively good Greek, and "is therefore an important evidence of the condition of our present Hebrew text at the time of this author" (BERTH., S. 15). However, the author could not have lived earlier than the first century before Christ, and the changes in the text that he recommends to us, are only to be admitted with great caution.

Exegetically and historically the III. Ezra might almost make it questionable for us whether we interpret the names of the Persian kings aright when we understand by the Darius mentioned after Cyrus, Darius Hystaspis, and by Artasasta, Artaxerxes. After having informed us of the edict of Cyrus in chap. ii. 1–14 and other matters contained in the canonical book of Ezra, III. Ezra lets the two original documents of Ezra iv. directly follow in vers. 15–25, the letter of the officer to Artaxerxes and its answer, and in addition the transition verse, by which it is carried back to Darius, "then the work on the house of the Lord was discontinued until the twentieth year of Darius." It also gains the appearance as if it had held the Artaxerxes, to whom the Samaritans turned themselves through the Persian offices, as one of the kings previous to Darius, perhaps Cambyses. Since then in chaps. iii.—v. 6, in his apocryphal addition, in that Zerubbabel still under Darius, and indeed still as a young man, stayed at the Persian court, he excites the appearance as if already before or even alongside of Cyrus, Darius had been favorable to the Jews, and had given them permission to return. The skein of difficulties, moreover, is entangled, as soon as it is supposed that the author in his statement, so to say, has made two beginnings, and indeed the second time in chap. v. 7, however little, there is here to be observed by the reader a larger pause. The announcement of the exiles who returned under Darius, which we read here in ver. 4 "these are the names of the men who went up," *etc.*, is only to be referred to the names that follow in vers. 5 and 6, that is to the priests, the sons of Phineas, to Jeshua the high-priest, and Joakim, the son of Zerubbabel, not at the same time to those following from ver. 7 onward. In ver. 7 a new announcement, corresponding to that of Ezra i. 2, introduces the names of those who returned already in the time of Cyrus, or as it is expressly said with Zerubbabel and Jeshua. The matter would be clearer if the fifth chapter did not begin until ver. 7. It seems as if the author, before he passed over to the statement of the history proper, as it lies before us in Ezra iii., would anticipate all that which subsequently would have too much interrupted the connection of the history of the temple at Jerusalem, and which was yet of importance with reference to the course that affairs took; at first the edict of Cyrus, which constituted the foundation for all that followed, but then also the letter of the adversaries to Artaxerxes, with reference to the building of the city and its walls, and his unfavorable answer to the Jews, which original documents at the very beginning would throw a strong light upon the adversaries who were active at the time of the building of the temple likewise, and which already, because they are brought out in so much detail in our canonical Ezra, must be mentioned somewhere—finally the apocryphal section respecting the events at the banquet of Darius, which explains the sentiments of this king as so favorable and so decided for the building of the temple. The letter to Artaxerxes and the reply, he probably placed before the apocryphal history from the time of Darius, because it would have interrupted the narrative if placed after it, that is, would have too much separated similar things,—the names of those who returned under Darius on the one side, and the list of those who returned under Cyrus on the other side. Perhaps it likewise comes into consideration, that the closing verse after the reply of Artaxerxes, "then the building of the sanctuary at Jerusalem ceased until the second day of the reign of Darius" (chap. ii. 25), which here really has no sense at all, provided that under Artasasta we are to understand Artaxerxes, and under Darius the Darius Hystaspis, who had already reigned previously,—was well calculated to form the transition to the section respecting Darius. If it should be thought that the author thought of Cambyses as Artasasta, and therefore had placed the letter in question before, objections are excited by the close of the 5th chap., where he says, changing our Ezra freely, "they, namely, the Samaritans, hindered, that the building was not completed the entire period of the life of king Cyrus, and they were restrained from building two years, to the reign of Darius," which sounds as if, according to his view, Darius had followed immediately after Cyrus, and indeed already two years after the interruption of the building of the temple.—That the author makes Zerubbabel still live in the time of Darius, and indeed still as a young man at the Persian court, although he yet, according to him, was already active in Jerusalem under Cyrus, rests perhaps on a corruption of the text; perhaps the young man who influenced Darius so favorably in chap. iii. was not Zerubbabel, as, it is true, it is expressly said in chap. iv. 13, but the son of Zerubbabel, Joiakim, who in chap. v. 5 is mentioned as one who returned under Darius, and at the same time, also, expressly as the one who spake wise words under Darius, the king of Persia. To be sure, however, the difficulty still remains that as the high-priest, not Jeshua's son, but Jeshua himself, stands alongside of him. It is possible that rather the name Joiakim in chap. v. 5, rests on an alteration, by which a copyist would assist the author, and the appearance of Zerubbabel as a young man at the court of Darius is to be explained from the fact that the author himself thought of Darius, who already so soon after the interruption of the building of the temple attained the sovereignty, as the immediate successor of Cyrus; at any rate it must properly be supposed that Zerubbabel, after the interruption of the temple building, returned again to Babylon.

§ 4. LITERATURE.

As in the books of Chronicles, so here we have to complain of the small amount of exegetical and critical literature. Of Jewish interpreters, besides the well-known R. S. JARCHI and ABEN EZRA, who wrote commentaries upon almost the entire Old Test., which are printed in the *Rabbin. Bible* of BUXTORF, we may mention R. SIMEON BEN JOIAKIM, whose Commentary on Ezra, Nehemiah and Chronicles, according to BARTOLOCCI, (*bibl. rabb.* IV., p. 412) appeared at Venice from Bomberg,—furthermore JOSEPH. BAR ABEN JECHIJJA, of whom a Commentary on the 5 *Megilloth* and the rest of the *Hagiographa* is mentioned, and ISAAK BEN R. SOLOMON JABEZ, whose *Thorath chesed* likewise embraces the *Megilloth* and the rest of the *Hagiographa*.

Of the Fathers of the Church only BEDA. VEN. comes into consideration, who composed two books of allegorical interpretation upon Ezra and Nehemiah (*op. t.* IV., p. 462 sq.); he would show by both books how those who have fallen into ruin by carelessness or error, must turn to repentance, how great God's grace is, *etc.* Of the Reformers, only JOHN BRENZ wrote a *Commentar. in Esdram*, and provided the first three chapters of Nehemiah with *annotationes*. VICT. STRIGEL'S *scholia in libr. Esræ* appeared at Leipsic, 1571; his *scholia in libr. Nehemiæ*, Leipsic, 1575; Erasmi Sarcerii *scholia in Nehemiam* and Cyriaci Spangenbergii *tabulæ* (Basel, 1563) are barely worthy of mention. The expository writings of the 16th and 17th Centuries are embraced, so far as they deserve mention, in the great collection "*Critici sacri*," London, 1660, 9 vol. fol., and in the selections therefrom of MATTH. POLUS, *Synopsis Criticorum s.*, London, 1669.

On the part of the Roman Catholics are to be mentioned: THOMAS DE VIO, Rome, 1553; DIONYS. CARTHUSIANUS, Cologne, 1534; CASPAR SANCTIUS, Lyons, 1627, and NICOLAUS LOMBARDUS (*Commentarius literalis, moralis, et allegoricus in Nehemiam et Esram.* Paris, 1643).

Of the Reformed Church are: LUDOV. LAVATERUS (38 Homilies upon Ezra, and 58 upon Nehemiah), Zurich, 1586; JOHANN WOLFF, *Nehemias de instaurata Hierosolyma seu commentarius in librum Nehemiæ*, Zurich, 1570; CHRISTIANUS SCHOTANUS, *bibliotheca hist. sacr.* V. T. T. II., p. 1154 sq.; GUILELM PEMBELIUS, *explicatio locorum obscurorum ex Esræ, etc., libro*, Lond., 1658; H. GROTIUS, *Annotatt. in Vet. Test.*, Paris, 1644, *ed. Vogel et Doederlein*, Halle, 1775–6.; FRANC. BURMANNUS, a Belgian Commentary upon the books of Kings, Chronicles, and Ezra, Amsterdam, 1694.

Of the 18th Century are only the works embracing the entire Old Test., or at least a greater part of it, by AUG. CALMET, *Commentaire literal*, Paris, 1707 sq.; by JO. CLERICUS, *Commentarius* (3 vols. *in Hagiographa*), Amsterdam, 1731; by JOH. HEINR. MICHAELIS, *adnotationes uberiores in hagiographos veteris testamenti libros*, Halle, 1720 (the book of Ezra, by J. H. MICHAELIS himself, the book of Nehemiah, by J. J. RAMBACH, both in the third vol.); by H. B. STARK *Notæ selectæ in Pent., etc.*, Leipsic, 1714,—by JOACH. LANGE, *Mosaisches, Prophetisches u. s. w. Licht und Recht*, Halle, 1729—38, by CHR. STARKE the Synopsis III.; by J. D. MICHAELIS, *Die Uebersetzung des Alten Testaments mit Anmerkungen für Ungelehrte. Theil* 12, 1785. Of the 19th Century we have, by J. B. D. MAURER, *Comment. gramm. crit. in V. T.*, vol. I., Leipsic, 1835; E. BERTHEAU, *Die Bücher Esra, Nehemia, and Esther* (17 *Lieferung des kurzgefassten exegetischen Handbuches zum A. Testament*), Leipsic, 1862; BUNSEN, *Bibelwerk* (Thl. I., *Abth.* 3, by AD. KAMPHAUSEN), Leipsic, 1865; C. F. KEIL, *Bibl. Kommentar über die nachexil. Geschichtsbücher*; *Chronik, Esra, Nehemia und Esther* (Thl. 5 *des bibl. Kommentars* of KEIL and DELITZSCH, Leipsic, 1870 —[Trans. in CLARK'S *For. Theol. Library*]; SCHIRMER, *observatt. exeget. crit. in* 1 *Esdræ*, Breslau, 1820. There are the following introductory critical treatises on the books of Ezra and Nehemiah; KLEINERT, *über die Entstehung, die Bestandtheile und das Alter der Bücher Ezra und Nehemia*, in the *Beitr. zu den theol. Wissenschaften* by the Professors of Theology at Dorpat, Hamburg, 1832, first volume; KEIL, *über die Integrität des Bücher Ezra* in his *Apol. Versuch über die Chronik*, S. 93 sq.; F. W. SCHULTZ, "*Cyrus der Grosse*" in the *Stud. u. Krit.*, 1853, S. 624 sqq.; BAIHINGER, "*zur Aufhellung der nachexil. Geschichte Israels*" *Stud. u. Krit.*, 1857, S. 87 sqq.; E. SCHRADER, "*die Dauer des zweiten Tempelbaus,*" *Stud. u. Krit.*, 1867, S. 460 sqq. E. SCHRADER'S book, "*die Keilinschriften und das Alte Testament,*" Giessen, 1872, contains contributions worthy of consideration with reference to the book of Ezra, fewer with reference to Nehemiah.

[To these we may add the few works upon Ezra and Nehemiah in English. The Holy Bible, with notes of the older MATTHEW HENRY and SCOTT, and the more recent Holy Bible, with Notes of WORDSWORTH, vol. II., new ed., London, 1873; the Bible or Speaker's Comm., vol. III., London, 1874, by RAWLINSON, to which frequent reference is made by the translator. See also DAVIDSON'S *Introduction to the Old Test.* II., 121–132, Edin., 1862; PUSEY on *Daniel*, p. 331 sq., 3d ed., London, 1869; also in KITTO'S *Cyclopædia*, 3d edit., 1865, and SMITH'S *Biblical Dictionary*—especially the American edition.—TR.]

THE BOOK OF EZRA.

PART FIRST.

The Temple as the Place of the Lord. (Period previous to Ezra.)

CHAPS. I.—VI.

FIRST SECTION.

The Most Important Fundamental Facts.

CHAPTERS I. II.

A.—THE DECREE OF CYRUS—THE DEPARTURE FROM BABYLON—THE RESTITUTION OF THE SACRED VESSELS.

CHAP. I. 1–11.

I. *The Decree of Cyrus.* Vers. 1–4.

1 Now in the first year of Cyrus king of Persia, that the word of the LORD by the
mouth of Jeremiah might be fulfilled, the LORD stirred up the spirit of Cyrus king
of Persia, that he made a proclamation throughout all his kingdom, and *put it* also
2 in writing, saying, Thus saith Cyrus king of Persia, The LORD God of heaven hath
given me all the kingdoms of the earth; and he hath charged me to build him a
3 house at Jerusalem, which *is* in Judah. Who *is there* among you of all his people?
his God be with him, and let him go up to Jerusalem, which *is* in Judah, and
build the house of the LORD God of Israel, (he *is* the God,) which *is* in Jerusalem.
4 And whosoever remaineth in any place where he sojourneth, let the men of his
place help him with silver, and with gold, and with goods, and with beasts, besides
the free-will offering for the house of God that *is* in Jerusalem.

II. *The Departure from Babylon.* Vers. 5, 6.

5 Then rose up the chief of the fathers of Judah and Benjamin, and the priests,
and the Levites, with all *them* whose spirit God had raised, to go up to build the
6 house of the LORD which *is* in Jerusalem. And all they that *were* about them
strengthened their hands with vessels of silver, with gold, with goods, and with
beasts, and with precious things, besides all *that* was willingly offered.

III. *The Restitution of the Vessels of the Temple.* Vers. 7–11.

7 Also Cyrus the king brought forth the vessels of the house of the LORD, which
Nebuchadnezzar had brought forth out of Jerusalem, and had put them in the
8 house of his gods; Even those did Cyrus king of Persia bring forth by the hand
of Mithredath the treasurer, and numbered them unto Sheshbazzar, the prince of
9 Judah. And this *is* the number of them: thirty chargers of gold, a thousand

10 chargers of silver, nine and twenty knives, Thirty basins of gold, silver basins of a
11 second *sort* four hundred and ten, *and* other vessels a thousand. All the vessels
of gold and of silver *were* five thousand and four hundred. All *these* did Sheshbazzar bring up with *them of* the captivity that were brought up from Babylon unto Jerusalem.

EXEGETICAL AND CRITICAL.

Vers. 1–4. The decree of Cyrus placed here at the beginning constituted the basis of all that followed, first of all, of the re-establishment of the temple and the renewal of the congregation. And although this decree was issued by a heathen prince, it yet involved a great act of fulfillment on the part of the Lord. It is manifest from the first verse that the Lord was there present and acting to fulfil His word.

Ver. 1. **And in the first year of Cyrus king of Persia.**—The וְ (and), which under other circumstances might be deemed unimportant, here, in view of 2 Chron. xxxvi. 22, connects the subsequent re-establishment with the previous destruction. The first year of Cyrus naturally refers to that first year, in which he began to come into consideration as ruler with reference to the Jews, that is, over Babylon, and indeed not mediately, as the sovereign of Darius the Mede, in view of Dan. vi. 1, but immediately. It was the year 536 B. C.—[Rawlinson contends that "by the first year of Cyrus is to be understood his first year at Babylon, which was the first year of his sovereignty over the Jews. This was B. C. 538."—Tr.]—כּוֹרֶשׁ corresponds with the old Persian *kurus*, the Greek *κῦρος*, and is perhaps connected with *kurus* the name of prince in ancient India [and the *kuru* race, according to Rawlinson, who also thinks that the Masoretic pointing is incorrect for כֻּורֻשׁ.—Tr.].—*Vid.* Delitzsch, Com., Isaiah xliv. 28. פָּרָס (in the best editions with pathah under resh, for which we have qametz in strong pause, as with silluq, ch. iv. 3) is in the cuneiform inscriptions *Paraça*, in the native dialect *Parça*, *vid.* Schrader, *Keilinschriften*, S. 244 [Rawlinson, Appendix to Com. on Persian words in Ezra.—Tr.].—**That the word of the Lord by the mouth of Jeremiah might be fulfilled.**—לִכְלוֹת would generally be rendered: in order that it might be completed. The subject would then be properly regarded as the period of seventy years which the divine word had determined (so Berth. and Keil); yet as this is not the subject, but rather the word of the Lord itself, we are compelled to render: in order that it might be fulfilled. כָּלָה means properly to be ready, and thence, on the one side, to be finished, *e. g.* Ex. xxxix. 32, especially of buildings, as of the temple, 1 Kings vi. 38, but likewise of predicted events, Dan. xii. 7; in the Piel, to finish, 1 Kings vii. 1 sq.; in Pual, to be completed, Gen. ii. 1; on the other side, to pass away. Taking it thus, לִכְלוֹת is essentially the same as לְמַלֹּאוֹת, which is used as its synonym, 2 Chron. xxxvi. 21 (Vulg. *ut compleretur*), although this term rests on a different idea. The word of God is not as with מְלֹאוֹת to be regarded as a measure to be filled full, but as the vital beginning of that which is to be carried out.—That our author, as well as the author of Dan. ix. 1, brings into consideration above all the prophecy of Jeremiah, xxv. 11 sq. and xxix. 10, not that of Is. xli. 2–4, 25; xliv. 24-28; xlv. 1–6, 13; xlvi. 11; xlviii. 13–15, is to be explained from the fact that he is concerned, as we see from 2 Chron. xxxvi. 21, not merely with the deliverance after the exile, but likewise with the time of that deliverance, that is, with its beginning, after the expiration of the seventy years of the exile, which is foretold in Jeremiah alone. Besides the prophecies of Jeremiah were the more popular as they were older and more fundamental.* The seventy years of the exile, to the first year of Cyrus, can only be made out by going back to the first beginning of all the Chaldean wars, conquests and captivities of Israel —that is, to the victory of Nebuchadnezzar over Pharaoh-Necho at Carchemish in the fourth year of Jehoiakim, 606 B. C. [Rawlinson and Smith both make the date 605 B. C. The former contends that seventy is a round number sufficiently fulfilled by sixty-eight years, which he makes between 605 and 538.—Tr.], when Jeremiah first uttered the prophecy under consideration (comp. ch. xxv. 1 sq. and xlvi. 1). We are fully justified in doing this, as is now again generally recognized. That already in the fourth year of Jehoiakim there was really a conquest of Jerusalem and a carrying into captivity of Jews of the principal families, is shown not only by the fact that this year had to Jeremiah the significance of an important crisis, comp. ch. xxv., not only, moreover, from the statement, 2 Kings xxiv. 1, that Nebuchadnezzar made a first expedition against Jehoiakim, and then reduced him to submission for a long time, but likewise from the combination of very definite historical statements. Here belongs especially the remark of Jer. xlvi. 2, that Nebuchadnezzar defeated Pharaoh Necho in the fourth year of Jehoiakim at Carchemish, and in connection therewith the account of Berosus, that he pursued the Egyptians in conquest into their own land, and then when the account of the death of his father recalled him, had carried away captive the Jews among other nations. Besides, 2 Chron. xxxvi. 6 may be adduced as an evidence of this fact (with Bertheau), since the account there manifestly taken from ancient sources, that Nebuchadnezzar had ordered Jehoiakim to be bound with an iron chain, in order to bring him to Babylon, cannot be referred to the last campaign

* [The author adopts the view of Ewald, Hitzig, *et al.*, that the second part of Isaiah was written by "the great unknown in the latter part of the exile." This view is to be rejected, and the unity of Isaiah maintained with most evangelical critics. Hence the author's statement of the priority of Jeremiah falls.—Tr.]

against Jehoiakim, in which he perished in his native land, but only to a previous expedition. The fact that Jeremiah makes no mention of a capture of Jerusalem in the fourth year of Jehoiakim cannot count for the contrary opinion; for Jeremiah touches upon the history of Jerusalem only in so far as it determined his own history; and there is no more importance to be given to the fact that Jeremiah, ch. xxxvi. 9 sq., caused to be read in the fifth year of Jehoiakim and the ninth month a prophecy that Nebuchadnezzar would come and destroy the land. Jehoiakim was ever thinking of rebellion, and the people were of like spirit, and would not believe that ruin actually threatened them from the Chaldeans. They were therefore still in especial need of such a threatening, even if the misfortune had already begun. It might also under these very circumstances be as unwelcome to them as it appears from ch. xxxvi. 11 sq. In contrast with their hopes and efforts it was certainly the most undesirable (against Bähr on 2 Kings xxiv. 1). At that time they held a fast, and that they thereby would lament a misfortune already suffered, and not merely avert one that was to be feared, is in connection with the false security so natural to them, and their effort to suppress those gloomy thoughts that were anywhere about to have vent, is at least highly probable.—**The Lord stirred up the spirit of Cyrus.**—This does not mean that Cyrus was influenced in the same way as were the prophets, upon whom, with their greater susceptibility, the Spirit of the Lord came; but yet an influence in consequence of which Cyrus made the will of God his own will, and executed it in the things under consideration. God gave him the resolution and the desire to execute His intention, comp. 1 Chron. v. 26; 2 Chron. xxi. 16; Hag. i. 14 sq. That the Lord at this time chose a heathen, and indeed the ruler of a heathen empire, as His instrument, was in accordance with the new position that the empires of the world were henceforth to assume with reference to the kingdom of God.—**He made a proclamation throughout all his kingdom, and also** (made known) **by writing.**—Usually הֶעֱבִיר קוֹל means "to cause to be made known through heralds," comp. ch. x. 7; Neh. viii. 15; 2 Chron. xxx. 5; Ex. xxxvi. 6; that it is to be taken here in the same sense is clear from the use of גַּם before בְּמִכְתָּב, which is thus adjoined in zeugma, so that we must supply a new verb with a general meaning, such as "he made known."

Ver. 2. The decree of Cyrus immediately following was not merely designed for the Jews; accordingly was by no means merely to be communicated to them secretly; but, according to ver. 4, it was directed to all the subjects of the Persian empire. All the more striking therefore is the open confession of Jehovah, which Cyrus makes at the very beginning.—**All the kingdoms of the earth hath Jehovah the God of heaven given me, and He hath charged me to build Him a house.**—We are not therefore to suppose that the author simply imputed to Cyrus the acknowledgment of Jehovah or indeed that he altogether invented this entire edict. Chapter v. 17; vi. 3 suffice to disprove this supposition. It is not to be supposed, indeed, that Cyrus spake in his edict of Jehovah as the God of heaven who had given him the lands; for his subjects would have regarded it as an apostasy from the Persian religion, which might have been fatal to him; moreover such a thing would be without any analogy.* Against this view there cannot be cited the case of that king of Hamath who in the inscription of Sargon at Khorsebad and Nimrud is called *Jahubihd*, in another inscription however *Ilubihd*, who thus seems not only to have employed the name of El., but likewise of Jehovah. Comp. Schrader, *l. c.*, S. 3 sq. Without doubt the Persians had an entirely different self-consciousness from the Syrians, who as a matter of course were much more closely related to the Israelites. Notwithstanding this, however, it is clear from the fact of the edict itself and the dismission of the Jews, that Cyrus tolerated the religion of Jehovah, at least as much as so many others in his wide realm, yea we may certainly conclude therefrom that he favored it. He would not only have Jehovah recognised as a God alongside of other gods; for such a polytheistic syncretism would have accorded but little with the strong monotheistic bent of the Persian religion, and would still less accord with that recognition of Jehovah which is declared in the decree before us. Cyrus might very well have regarded the Jewish religion as a method of worshipping the highest God, which deserved a preference above many other sensuous conceptions of the Deity. He might have seen in Jehovah, so to speak, only another name for *Ahura mazda*, and might have been so much the more inclined to this conception, as the Persians had an idea of God which in itself was purer than that of other nations, which has been obscured for the first time by more sensuous religious elements, pressing in upon them from Media and the West. Comp. Döllinger, *Heidenthum und Judenthum*, S. 351 sq. [also Rawlinson's *Ancient Monarchies*, III., p. 97]. A good impression in this respect might have been made upon him by the fact that his conquest of Babylon had been very desirable to the Jews, yea that they had placed their hopes at once in him as their deliverer. It is then but probable that they made their disposition and expectations known to him, and if they laid before him, as Josephus (*Arch.* IX., i. 7) informs us, at once likewise the prophecies referring to him in Isa. xli. 2–4, 25 sq.; xliv. 24–28; xlv. 1 sq., this must have given him a very favorable disposition towards them. Moreover, as Cyrus recognised in the Jewish God, so might the Jews easily find in the Persian God one closely related to their own, yea identical with Him. Without regard to the fact that the divine name *Ahura* = *asura*, from *as* = *esse*, to a certain extent coincides with יְהוָֹה (compare Böttcher, *Rudimenta mythologiæ semiticæ*, spec. I.), the Zoroastrian religion was nearer to the religion of Jehovah than any other, and it is very remarkable that it is predicted in Isa. xli. 25; xlv. 3, not only

* [We have here not a citation of the very words of the decree, as is so often the case in Ezra and Nehemiah, but rather a free reproduction of it.—Tr.]

that Cyrus will call upon and proclaim the name of the Lord; that he will recognise Jehovah as the one who has chosen him, but likewise that he will be a mighty instrument in the hand of the Lord for overcoming the respect of the Chaldean gods. In fact, since Cyrus and the establishment of the Persian empire, the temptation to the rude worship of idols has declined as never before, not only in Israel, but likewise there gradually came over the other nations, even over the Greeks and Romans from that time forth more and more a spirit of enlightenment that certainly paved the way for the agency of the second great instrument of God, the servant of the Lord foretold in Isa. xlii.—The introduction given by Cyrus to his decree: "all the kingdoms of the earth hath Jehovah the God of heaven given me, and hath charged me with building him a house in Jerusalem," corresponds with the beginnings of the proclamations of the Persian kings, as they are preserved to us in the cuneiform inscriptions. These likewise frequently begin with the confession that they owe their dominion to the highest God, the creator of heaven and earth. (Comp. Lassen, *Die altpersischen Keilinschriften*, Bonn, 1836, S. 172; and more recently Joach. Menant, *Exposé des elements de la grammaire Assyrienne*, Par., 1868, p. 302 sq., according to whom the trilingual inscription of Elvend begins thus: *deus magnus Aüra-mazda, qui maximus deorum, qui hanc terram creavit, qui hoc cœlum creavit, qui homines creavit, qui potentiam (?) dedit hominibus, qui Xerxem regem fecit*, etc. [Also Rawlinson's *Monarchies*, III., 348, and his *Com. on Ezra*, where he gives the inscription of Darius: "The great God, Ormazd, who is the chief of the gods; he established Darius as king; he granted him the empire; by the grace of Ormazd is Darius king."—Tr.]). The words: "all the kingdoms of the earth" are explained from the wide extent of the Persian empire. When Cyrus conquered Babylon, he had already subjugated to himself almost the entire eastern Asia, even to the Indian Ocean (according to Berosus in Joseph. *c. Ap.*). Afterwards he pressed southward also, and entered even into Egypt and Ethiopia. The words of Cyrus: "He hath charged me to build Him a house," would be possible and justified even if he had merely felt himself charged by circumstances to build the temple at Jerusalem, but is still better explained if the Jews, as Josephus, *l. c.*, says, laid before him Isaiah xliv. 24 and 28, and xlv. 1 sq. [So also Rawlinson, who says: "It is a reasonable conjecture that, on the capture of Babylon, Cyrus was brought into personal contact with Daniel, and that his attention was drawn by that prophet to the prophecy of Isaiah.—Cyrus probably accepted this prophecy as a 'charge' to rebuild the temple." Keil also refers to Dan. vi., which states that Darius the Mede made Daniel one of the three presidents of the one hundred and twenty satraps of the empire, and valued him greatly at court.—Tr.]. J. H. Michaelis therefore explains the passage thus: *mandavit mihi, nimirum dudum ante per Jesaiam*, cap. xliv. 24-28; xlv. 1-13. The reference to these prophecies is all the more apparent since there, as well as here, the same fundamental fact is so strongly and repeatedly emphasized, namely, that the Lord gave to him the kingdoms of the earth, comp. especially Isa. xli. 2, 3, 25; xlv. 1 sq. Comp. A. F. Kleinert, *Ueber die Echtheit sämmtlicher in dem Buch Jesaia enthaltenem Weissagungen*, Berlin, 1829.

Ver. 3. Cyrus would first call upon the Jews, but yet turn to all his subjects with his address; because he had something to say to those also who were not Jews, but were dwelling with the Jews.—**Who among you, of all His people,** *etc.* With all the people of Jehovah he also properly includes the descendants of the ten tribes. Yet these seem not to have been thought of, nor does it seem that any important element of them made use of the permission of Cyrus. The blessing:—**His God be with him**—thus emphatic in position, shows that that which follows is not so much command as permission, as if he would say: His God be with him should he go up and build. Besides, this wish involves not only the permission to build the temple, but at the same time the consent to all that was necessarily connected therewith, especially the emigration to Palestine.* The additional clause, **He is the God who is at Jerusalem,** which would give the motive for building the temple of Jehovah, does not mean that Jehovah is present only in Jerusalem, and only has power in Canaan, for Cyrus has already ascribed to Him the power over the kingdoms of the earth—but it simply expresses the idea that He has chosen Jerusalem, above all other places, as the holy place which He would have distinguished for His worship. [Compare the confession of Darius, Dan. vi. 26, "He is the living God."—Tr.]

Ver. 4. **And as for every one of the survivors, let the people of his place assist him,** *etc.*—The heathen, on their part, are to assist. כָּל־הַנִּשְׁאָר, is accusative absolute, placed before for emphasis. The designation of the exiles as survivors, properly those left over, is connected with the thought of the great and severe judgments that had overtaken Israel, and is found therefore especially among the Israelites themselves, comp. Neh. i. 2 sq.; Hag. ii. 3 sq. This thought, however, was natural enough even for the heathen. The words: **From all the places where he sojourneth,** can only be connected with the subsequent clause. The Piel נִשֵּׂא here means to assist, as in 1 Kings ix. 11, *etc.*—**With silver and with gold, and with goods** (here perhaps clothing or tents) they are to enable the departing to emigrate.—**Besides the free-will offering.**—This was something additional (עִם comp. ver. 6) to the gifts, by which they were to contribute directly to the building of the house of God. Comp. chap. viii. 25; Ex. xxxv. 29; Lev. xxii. 25. [Rawlinson regards the free-will offering as that of Cyrus himself.—Tr.]

Ver. 5. The permission to march to Jerusalem was made use of by **the heads of the fathers of Judah and Benjamin and the priests and the Levites.**—We are to conclude as a

* I see no sufficient ground, with Ewald, *Lehrbuch*, 3 734, either to strike out entirely יְהִי or change it into יְהוָה, after 2 Chron. xxxvi. 23. In Esd. ii. 5, we have for it ἔστω.

matter of course that with the heads of the fathers* the fathers themselves set out, and with the fathers their families; that is, that the divisions of a higher and lower degree accompanied their heads. But it does not mean that all of the heads of the three tribes mentioned set out, but **all whose spirit God had raised.**—It certainly must have been the most of them, otherwise it would not have been said so distinctly the heads of the fathers. The simple לְכֹל (to be distinguished from וּלְכֹל, chap. vii. 28) does not serve, in enumerations, to add in a short and summary way all the others, which have not yet been mentioned, as if the meaning were that besides the heads there were others also who set out (Berth. [A. V.]), but it adds to that which has been already said a still closer definition, which is important to the context, (comp. Neh. xi. 2; 1 Chron. xiii. 1; 2 Chron. v. 12), so that it corresponds with our "namely," "that is" [Ew. § 310 *a*]. ל properly here, as elsewhere, indicates the belonging to a class or kind. The author has then, in a manner peculiar to himself, subordinated the following relative clause to the כָּל־ without אֲשֶׁר. God must awake the spirit of those who would ascend, that is, must make them willing (comp. ver. 1); for the return home was not a matter that required no consideration. Their native land lay either desolate or occupied with heathen and barbarous nations. Great dangers threatened the little nation, that would put itself in opposition with the inhabitants and indeed severe tasks awaited them. In Babylon, on the other hand, their circumstances had become such that they could very well endure them, yea, they were favorable, as we can see from Isa. lvi. 11—lviii., hence *πολλοὶ κατέμειναν ἐν τῇ Βαβυλῶνι τὰ κτήματα καταλιπεῖν οὐ θέλοντες.* (Many remained behind in Babylon, unwilling to relinquish their property (Joseph. *Arch.* XI. 1, 1).

Ver. 6. **All they that were about them.**—The call to assist the returning exiles was obeyed and their neighbors, who certainly included the Israelites, who remained behind, who if they had means, would especially contribute with liberality (comp. Zech. vi. 9) in order to a certain extent to make up for what they seemed to neglect by their remaining behind. But there were surely heathen, also, whom Cyrus had chiefly in view, under the supposition that the Israelites could not let his permission go by without using it. The example of the king and his exhortation must have already made them willing, but there were certainly here and there some who were influenced by their friendly relations to the departing. חִזְּקוּ בִידֵיהֶם means, like הֶחֱזִיק בְּיַד, first of all to take by the hand, in order to hold or support (Berth., Keil), then passes over as the German "*jemandem unter die Arme greifen,*" immediately to the meaning "assist" (although the construction with בְּ is against a full equivalence of the expression with the frequently-occurring חִזַּק יָד) as is clear from the context, which demands the meaning, assist, the בְּ before כְּלֵי־כֶסֶף the following noun זָהָב, and the נִשְּׂאוּ corresponding to it in ver. 4.—**Besides all that was willingly offered.**—לְבַד is here connected with עַל, (which properly would have sufficed by itself), for the usual מִן Gen. xxxii. 12. Comp. Ex. xii. 37; Num. xxix. 39. כָּל־ after עַל is certainly to be taken as neuter. הִתְנַדֵּב which is closely connected with the foregoing must have supplied not only אֲשֶׁר, but also the subject "what" he, namely, the giver, gave as an offering. הִתְנַדֵּב means properly "to act freely," is frequently used in this sense by our author, so likewise here "to give freely," comp. 1 Chron. xxix. 9; Ezra ii. 68; iii. 5, and indeed in the liturgical sense "give for the temple," to a certain extent as an offering, נְדָבָה. Comp. ver. 4.

Vers. 7–11. It was Cyrus himself who especially helped the returning exiles by bestowing upon them the vessels that had been plundered from the temple. These vessels might have been taken away by Nebuchadnezzar, at the very first capture of Jerusalem in the fourth year of Jehoiakim, comp. 2 Chron. xxxvi. 7; Dan. i. 2. That nothing of the kind is mentioned either in 2 Kings xxiv., or by Jeremiah, is explained naturally from the fact that in general so little is expressly said with reference to that first campaign of Nebuchadnezzar. When Jehoiachin (Jechoniah) was carried away captive, there was certainly a plundering of the temple, and that seemed more worthy of mention, 2 Kings xxiv. 13; Jer. xxvii. 16; xxviii. 1 sq.; whilst it is expressly said, 2 Kings xxiv. 13, that Nebuchadnezzar at this time brake off the gold of the vessels, which seems to indicate that there were no longer vessels of massive gold, but merely vessels overlaid with gold. When Zedekiah was set aside by the governor of Nebuchadnezzar, Nebuzaradan (2 Kings xxv. 13 sq.; Jer. lii. 18 sq.), the vessels remaining were mostly of brass.

Ver. 8. Cyrus delivered over the vessels by **the hand of the treasurer Mithredates.***—עַל־יַד, that is, so that he had at the same time to take them in his hands to inspect them, to recognize them as the vessels of the temple at Jerusalem, accordingly under his supervision. Comp. chap. viii. 33; Esth. vi. 9. גִּזְבָּר is the Zend *gaza-bara*, treasurer, whilst the other form, גְּדָבָר pl. גְּדָבְרִין Dan. iii. 2, 3, corresponds with the old Persian *gada-bara* (*gaint bara*, modern Per-

* [רָאשֵׁי הָאָבוֹת for the fuller form רָאשֵׁי בֵּית הָאָבוֹת, Ex. vi. 14, that is, heads or chiefs of the fathers' houses or families, which were subdivisions of the מִשְׁפָּחוֹת, as the latter were of the שְׁבָטִים or tribes. Thus the fathers' houses of the going up from Babylon are in striking contrast with the tribes of the going up from Egypt. —TR.]

* [*Mithredath.* Rawlinson: "The occurrence of this name, which means given by Mithra," Persian *Mithradata* = *Mithra*, "the Sun-God," and *data* past part. of *da* = "to give," or dedicated to Mithra, is an indication that the sun worship of the Persians was at least as old as the time of Cyrus. (Comp. Xen. *Cyrop.* ch. VIII. 3, § 24."—TR.]

sian *geng' war*) from *gada* or *ganda*. Comp. Keil, Dan. v. 36, *Anm.* 1.—**Sheshbazzar**, the prince of Judah, to whom Mithredates counted out the vessels, meets us again in the Chaldee passage, chap. v. 14, 16, and indeed as *pecha* or governor of the new community in Judea, who laid the foundation of the new temple, so that without question he is identical with Zerubbabel (chap. ii. 2; iii. 8; iv. 3) the son of Shealtiel (chap. iii. 2, 8; v. 2; Hag. i. 1, *etc.*, comp. also Matth. i. 12; Luke iii. 27), who, 1 Chron. iii. 19, is likewise a son of Pedaiah, a brother of Shealtiel, and belongs to the family of Daniel. Alongside of the more Chaldee name of Sheshbazzar, Zerubbabel was used as a more Hebrew name. The latter occurs even in the Chaldee part of the book, chap. v. 2. In the same way Daniel and his three companions had with their Chaldee names, which they received when they entered into the service of the king of Babylon, likewise Hebrew names, Dan. i. 7. The meaning of Sheshbazzar is still more uncertain than that of Zerubbabel. Not even the pronunciation of the word is certain. The Alex. version has, in most accordance with the Masoretic form Σασαβασάρ, but likewise Σαβαχασάρ, and Σαναβάσσαρος. The latter form is found in accordance with the best MSS. in Esdras, where the reading alongside of it is Σαμανασσάρ.

Ver. 9. In the *enumeration* of the vessels their names, as well as their numbers, afford difficulties. Instead of the usual names for temple vessels, others are chosen here, perhaps, because they were preferred as more comprehensive and popular terms. The detailed numbers do not correspond with the sum total in ver. 11. Thirty golden and one thousand silver אֲגַרְטְלִים were numbered first of all, according to the Alex. version ψυκτῆρες (wine coolers), Esdras ii. 11, σπονδεῖα, cups for drink-offerings, according to the interpretation of the Talmud in Aben Ezra from אָגַר to collect, and טָלֶה, lamb, vessels for collecting the blood of lambs, which is certainly untenable. Probably we have in the Arabic *kirtallat*, Syriac *kartolo*, Greek κάρταλλος, the same term, accordingly a basket coming to a point below (see Suidas). The twenty-nine מַחֲלָפִים which follow, are judged according to their small number merely a subordinate kind of the preceding, which differed from them in some special kind of decoration or arrangements, thus not *cultri*, sacrificial knives (Vulg.), according to rabbinical interpretation, from חָלַף to penetrate, to cut in two, but rather according to מַחְלְפוֹת = braids, Judges xvi. 13, 19, adorned with net work (Ew.) or provided with holes above, designed for incense (Berth.), or likewise from חלף in Piel and Hiph. to change, sacrificial dishes serving for the pouring out of the blood of the sacrifices.

Ver. 10. The thirty golden cups כְּפוֹרִים (properly covered vessels, 1 Chron. xxviii. 17) are followed by silver ones in parallelism with verse 9. מִשְׁנִים has been taken by the ancient and more recent interpreters as an adjective in the sense of *secundarii*, as if the silver cups were thereby compared with the golden as expressive of a less good, merely second sort and quality. Since this closer definition seems strange and at any rate superfluous, it is more appropriate to suppose that משׁנים (pointing it, as it were, as a Piel participle) designates a subordinate kind of *cups*, corresponding with the מַחֲלָפִים in the previous ver. and with essentially the same meaning, which likewise served for pouring out; or it has arisen from a numeral, perhaps אֲלָפִים (Esdras ii. 12), so that not 410 but 2410 silver cups were returned. If we find a subordinate sort indicated by משׁנים, then the number must be supplied to the previous principal sort. Of the subordinate sort there were 410, and of other vessels 1,000 more.

Ver. 11. The sum total, 5400, is more than double the detailed numbers given in our text of the 9th and 10th verses, 2499, and can only be made out by conjecturing the number of the silver cups as 1000 or 2000. If we supply 2000, the sum total of 4499 results, thus in round numbers 4500, and it is possible this may be the correct sum, arisen from 5400 by transposition of numbers. But at any rate the LXX. already favored the text, as we have it, and Esdras which has 1000 golden and 1000 silver σπονδεῖα; 29 silver θυίσκαι, 30 golden, and 2410 silver φιάλαι, and 1000 other vessels, in all 5469, has ventured to conjecture, in order to reach the sum total in some measure. [So Keil, but Ewald, *Gesch.* IV. p. 88, Bertheau *et al.* more properly find the key to the difficulty in Esdras.—Tr.]. It is however possible that the author, as J. H. Michaelis asserts against Clericus, passed over many subordinate vessels in the detail, but in the sum-total has taken them all into consideration. [Rawlinson thinks the sum-total in our passage a corruption.—Tr.].—**All these did Sheshbazzar bring up with** (or at) **the bringing up of the captives.**—(הֵעָלוֹת is the infin. Niph. with passive meaning as in Jer. xxxvii. 12). This statement passes over lightly the long and difficult journey from Babylon to Jerusalem. It is possible that the documents used by our author, contained something more on this subject. But the author himself has hardly given anything more that has been lost, but he hastens to his proper topic, to come to the building of the temple in Jerusalem. In Esdras v. 1–6 some verses are found respecting the journey of those who returned under Darius. Darius sent with them 1000 cavalry, in order to bring them in peace to Jerusalem, with musical instruments, with kettle-drums and flutes, and all their brethren played, *etc.* Fritzsch and Bertheau are of the opinion that these verses were taken from a Hebrew original and conjecture that they originally stood in our book of Ezra, and referred to the return under Cyrus. But their contents are so cheerful that we have no reason for finding any greater authority for them than that afforded by 1 Chron. xiii. 8, and similar passages.

THOUGHTS UPON THE HISTORY OF REDEMPTION.

Ver. 1. *That it might be fulfilled.*—This chapter contains nothing less than the beginning of the fulfilment of all the great and glorious prophecies with which the prophets before the exile brightened the gloomy night of the severe judgments of God—the dawning light of the grace of God in all its greatness, that would re-awaken the people of God from death and the grave, and enable them to live a new and glorious life—the glorious liberty of the children of God in the fullest and highest sense. What a great revolution of affairs was now to be expected! What a fulness of salvation after the night of misfortune—the entire extent of Messianic redemption! The beginnings were very small, very insignificant. There was no king to rule in strength out of Zion and conquer the world, to restore the ancient theocracy in the political sense, if it were only in the old proportions, not to speak of greater proportions and a more complete form. There were no people, great and strong, of their own increase in numbers, breaking through their boundaries and imparting themselves to the world (comp. Mic. ii. 12, 13). There was no territory, broad and free, yea, not even a little piece of land, that the people could really call their own, on which they could really feel that they were free. In other cases, when the Lord had redeemed His people from severe afflictions, or had intended to produce a new and better beginning of their development, He had awakened from their midst an instrument endued with an especial fulness of the Spirit and power. But now even this failed them. It was the heathen king whom He used as His instrument. Moreover not the people as such, but only a small portion of them, were permitted to re-people Jerusalem. The reorganization of a political commonwealth was not allowed, but only the reestablishment of the temple and its worship. Instead of a people, who might have organized and vindicated themselves as such, there could now only be a religious congregation in Jerusalem and Judah. Faith in God's faithfulness and truth, in Israel's lofty destiny and future glory, so far as it at all existed, or was about to awaken afresh, was now once more put to a severe test, even when its confirmation seemed to be in prospect. But if the Lord had so often and so long been obliged to wait until Israel turned in repentance to Him, how unreasonable and presumptuous would it have been, if now Israel had been unwilling likewise to wait and see whether the Lord would yet again turn in grace to them. The Lord was obliged to have such extraordinary patience with men, that men, if they knew themselves even to a very limited extent, could never find reason or justice in being impatient with the Lord. Besides it was very well calculated for those who were to be placed on a higher stand-point and have the eyes of their faith made more sensitive, and certainly for those who came after them, who might look over these small beginnings, in connection with their results, because of its very insignificance, to enable them to foresee, or at least forebode therein, the indications of the highest and brightest end, and to wonder all the more at the really divine operation of God; as indeed it was permitted to more than one pious singer, looking at the glorious end, to raise already his triumphal cry and ever re-echo it anew: the Lord is King, He clothes Himself with salvation. Comp. Ps. xciii. 1; xcvi. 10; xcvii. 1; xcix. 1 (on the basis of Isa. lii. 7).

The word of the Lord by the mouth of Jeremiah.—All the previous prophecies of the impending judgments of God, and the temporary ruin of Israel, had again combined in the words of Jeremiah, and developed into the greatest definiteness. As a great prophet, who on the ἀκμή of a critical period, yea, immediately on the brink of the abyss, had caused the call to repentance once more to sound forth with mighty power, and had brought the prophecy of the impending judgment to a conclusion; like Elijah he became typical of the angel which the Lord would send before Him, before the coming of the great and terrible day, Mal. iii. 1. As the Jews expected Elias, so did they Jeremiah, before the advent of the great Messianic events, Matth. xvi. 14; Luke ix. 19; Bertholdt's *Christol.* S. 58. Now it was just this preacher of repentance and chastisement who had become for the exile times and those immediately following, the most important preacher of salvation, as is clear likewise from Dan. ix. 2. The Lord could not limit through him the duration of the time of chastisement without therewith at the same time predetermining the time of the beginning of the period of redemption, so that, so long as the question of the time seriously occupied the soul, the references were made chiefly to Jeremiah. Thus in fact the divine word of chastisement ever goes hand in hand with His word of salvation, and His negative with His positive working. His chastening is in truth ever a helping; yea, His killing is a making alive. He puts to death only the dead.

The Lord stirred up the spirit of Cyrus, king of Persia.—The Lord had hitherto made use of the heathen nations and their kings, when He would chastise Israel. They had been His rods and had been obliged to act in a negative relation to Israel. Now, on the other hand, He makes the mightiest empire of the world, yea, its greatest king, to assist in the accomplishment of very positive ends, in the realization of His most important and greatest designs of redemption. Egypt had once been obliged to help Israel with her possessions (Ex. xi. 2), being a weak type, so now the heathen who had previously plundered Israel were obliged to restore a part of their possessions; and Cyrus, the king of the same empire that had robbed Israel of her most sacred possessions, was obliged to restore the holy vessels, in order to assist in rebuilding the temple of the Lord in Jerusalem. Comp. Esth. viii. 25 sq.; 2 Macc. iii. 35; xiii. 23. This was in fact much more and bore stronger witness to the truth of the Lord and His final victory over the heathen world and its idolatry than the awakening of a great king and prophet in Israel. It already involved something of what the great prophet had uttered in the severest times of affliction as the greatest consolation, that the same heathen who threatened to tread Israel as a worm under their feet, should bring the children of Israel near in their bosom; yea, in that the mightiest king of the earth, the great king of Persia, had assisted Israel even to the accomplishment of their highest and noblest task, the honoring of their God, the word that the kings should be the nursing fathers of Israel, and their queens their nursing mothers (Isa. xlix. 22, 23), already received the very best fulfilment. But it involved something still greater and more important. Since Israel remained in such a weak and dependent position, and was no longer able to give their spiritual blessings political security by a mighty commonwealth of their own; it must be shown, as never before, that the truth, whose bearers they were called to be, was able to stand by its own indestructible power, and was strong enough of its own fulness and glory to protect the congregation of its adherents and preserve them, notwithstanding their external dependence, in internal freedom and independence.

Ver. 2. With exalted self-consciousness Cyrus could say not only that all the kingdoms of the earth had been given to him, but also that God the Lord Himself had given them to him. Moreover he says this with humility, for it is with the feeling and recognition of the task thereby imposed upon him by God of building His temple. Naturally enough, he does not behold,—yea, he does not even surmise, what a high mission he has, that he is thereby bringing into existence the bud out of which the kingdom of God in its time is to break forth as the loveliest blossom and noblest fruit as well to the blessing of all nations, as for the complete glorification of the divine name; but however little he understood this, he yet nevertheless in praiseworthy respect before the holiest things of a nation reached forth his hand full of help, and fulfilled unconsciously the highest mission of a temporal prince. What he accomplished was indeed still something in embryo, but we can see in the covering still wrapped about it already the sprouting forth of the richest and most wonderful life. Hence it is that the sacred Scriptures have accorded him a significance that is given to no other foreign king. The Lord does not call him His servant as Nebuchadnezzar (Jer. xxv. 9; xxvii. 6; xliii. 10), but His shepherd, who will fulfil all His pleasure, yea, His *mashiah* (Is. xliv. 28; xlv. 1). It has been said that in Isa. xl.—xlviii. Cyrus comes into consideration even for Messianic prophecy; for the servant of the Lord is placed in prospect for the accomplishment of the higher Messianic hopes, Cyrus for the lower. This is correct, inasmuch as the external political work that is necessary for the accomplishment of salvation is assigned chiefly to him, since indeed the proper mediator of salvation is to execute a higher spiritual ministry. It may therefore be said with a certain propriety (Starke) that he is a type of Christ in His royal office. Placed at the beginning of a new period, when the congregation was to be constituted no longer as a political, but as a religious body, he is the first of those who put external political affairs in such a relation to that body, that whilst something different from, they are yet friendly, supporting and protecting; and he is well adapted to represent for all time this ministry of the *patron*. His name has been incorrectly explained as "sun." In modern Persian the sun is *char;* in Zend, *hvare;* sunshine is *charsid,* with a weak initial *ch,* which, according to Rawlinson, Spiegel, *et al.,* would lead us to expect in ancient Persian *uwara,* whilst Cyrus on the monuments is *kuru* or *khuru,* on a block of marble in the valley of Murghab, near the tomb of Cyrus; *k'ur'us,* so likewise *Beh.* I. 28, 39, *etc.* (comp. Schrader, *l. c.,* S. 244), with initial hard *k.* But the prophet did actually view him as possessed of a sunny nature and activity, since he represents the Lord as inquiring with reference to him; who raised up righteousness from the east; called him to his foot, *etc.* (Isa. xli. 2), and is constantly putting him in relation to the sunrise (xli. 25; xlvi. 11).

Ver. 3. *Let him go up and build.*—In former times Israel had needed external political independence and a government of their own, simply because they were still too weak to preserve the pound entrusted to them for the entire human race, without external props and means of protection; because the sweet and saving kernel which was to develope in Israel could only ripen as it were in a sufficiently firm shell. The danger of their giving themselves over internally to heathenism was for the most part overcome by their having been externally abandoned in exile among the heathen. The tendency to heathenism, that previous to the exile broke out again and again with ever-increasing strength, and which in the previous centuries could have been overcome with difficulty, owing to the fact that it had the appearance of being an advance in enlightenment beyond the ancient faith of their fathers, had been rendered disgusting to them by the cruelty and severity of the heathen themselves. Thus it was now possible that there should be a new form of life and activity entirely different from any thing previous. It was the most important change of affairs that could take place at any time before Christ (comp. Ewald, *Gesch. Israels* IV. S. 35). The task of establishing a grand independent form of government for the national life, and securing it by the development of power externally, could now be abandoned; the task of cultivating the worship of the true God could be made much more preponderating in its influence; Israel could become a religious congregation instead of a political commonwealth; they could—expressing the idea with the words of Cyrus—go up and build the temple of the Lord. That this great change was now actually accomplished, in that there was so little cohesion in Israel itself, and, for the most part, there was so little thought of again constituting a powerful body externally, whilst Cyrus, on his part, did not afford them political freedom, but only religious liberty; that was in truth no hindrance to the development of the kingdom of God, but an indication of what the Lord would accomplish with His people, a preparation of the kingdom of God as a kingdom which is not of this world, which in truth deserves to be called the kingdom of heaven. The blessing that was to come from Israel upon the families of the earth was thus too spiritual and internal to be brought about among the nations through a government with external means. Israel's proper and highest task could henceforth only be to let the external opposition to the nations of the world more and more pass away, to subordinate themselves more and more in external and temporal things; at the same time disappearing among them as an external body, in order to permeate them so much the more internally with the holy and divine things committed to their trust.

Ver. 5. "*And the heads of the fathers arose.*"—It was also already a step nearer to the end and a hint of what must transpire in greater and greater proportions, that Israel no longer as such, or according to an external necessity of nationality, but that only a part of Israel by virtue of free resolution marched to Jerusalem to constitute the new religious community at that place. Individual freedom, and accordingly the importance of the single person and the right of the personal subject, have their proper place in the kingdom of God. Only those marched up whom the Spirit of God awakened, that is, only the zealous and the awakened, whose spirits allowed themselves to be filled from God with courage and joy to overcome all the difficulties that opposed them, and with a longing for the land of their fathers that outweighed every other consideration. This limitation was, moreover, entirely in accordance with the divine purpose. They must bring with them a zeal for the service of the true God that could not be quenched, at least entirely by the difficult and gloomy circumstances in Judea, that might be enkindled and fed in some of them by these very circumstances. For although those remaining behind still retained an importance with reference to the kingdom of God, yet the most direct and greatest importance was henceforth to be given to the congregation in Judea; they were to constitute first and chiefly the ground in which the highest and noblest things might become possible.

Ver. 6. "*And all their neighbors helped them.*" The world generally will be pleased only with the worldly members of the congregation, the lukewarm and faint-hearted. The more decided and zealous provoke opposition, and are often enough met with hostility, oppression and affliction. Yet there are times when the world is obliged to make manifest the fact that they have more respect for the zealous than for the indifferent, when they cannot but show their good-will and friendship, yea, act favorably towards those very efforts that are directed towards divine things. Even the men of the world have, so long as they have not become entirely hardened, two kinds of hearts within them, and it is only necessary that a suitable impulse should be given them, that the better heart may assert itself within them. Even they have a certain feeling that their best and deepest needs can only be satisfied by God and His Spirit, as He comes near to them in the true congregation.

Vers. 7–11. *And Cyrus the king brought forth the vessels of the house of the Lord.*—Israel had not then been brought so far as to have been able to recognize with full clearness their pure spiritual calling, as to have been able to separate altogether with entire certainty the spiritual and the divine, in which their calling consisted, from the external, earthly and temporal. The time when God would have His place of worship neither in Jerusalem nor on Gerizim, could only come with a new and higher stage of the divine revelation of Himself, yea, only with the fulfillment of that revelation. Until that time the Lord had Himself ordered, in accordance with the lower and limited stand-point of His people, that one particular, chosen place, a special sanctuary, with its vessels, and a priesthood set apart from the people, should to a certain extent share in the sanctity which was properly appropriate only to the Holy One Himself. As the Lord brought about the restoration of the temple itself, so He did also the restitution of the sacred vessels; and the great numbers of them given back to the returning exiles, although in itself unimportant, yet was notwithstanding an evidence that He could re-establish His worship in a magnificence and dignity as great as possible in accordance with the ideas of the times.—In connection with the awakening of the enthusiasm for the ancient and honorable sanctuaries, it might easily happen that their sanctification might be overdone, yea, that they might take the place of the essence of religion itself, so that the externalizing of religion, although in a new form, might creep in anew, that a hierarchy might arise instead of the kingdom of God; but a congregation, in which the only truly holy one has once been recognized so decidedly as in Israel, carries the kernel of reformation ever in itself. And by the fact that the hierarchy also shows itself as something unsatisfying, empty and vain, the hunger after that of which it is the mere phantom must be awakened with all the more strength, at least in the souls of the more spiritual.

HOMILETICAL AND PRACTICAL.

The pledges of redemption possessed by the congregation of the Lord even in the severest afflictions: 1) God's unchangeable faithfulness, which fulfils the promises He has given at the right time; 2) God's infinite grace, which chastises indeed, but does not give over to death, but, on the contrary, breaks forth anew in its time in spite of the severest judgment; 3) God's unsearchable wisdom, which advances towards the end, even in the most improbable manner; 4.) God's all-conquering power, which even makes use of the powers of the world and their means. The redemption from Babylon a type of the redemption from the bonds of the devil and hell: 1) With reference to the Redeemer; He breaks into the kingdom of the enemy (Babylon) and conquers it; 2) With respect to the Redeemed; the susceptible arise in order to march home; 3) With respect to the *end of redemption;* the temple of the Lord, a tabernacle of God among men, is built. Or: 1) With reference to its occasion; the greatness of the misery excites God's compassion; 2) With reference to its source; it is the divine grace notwithstanding human sin; 3) With reference to its extent; the susceptible are awakened to accept redemption; 4) With reference to its end; it is the glorious freedom and blessedness in the internal communion with the Lord. BRENTIUS remarks respecting those remaining behind in Babylon: *adumbrant omnes illos, qui fiduciam suam in hunc mundum collocant, satius esse existimantes, felicitate hujus mundi frui, quam per infelicitatem ad perpetua gaudia ingredi.*—Divine grace after wrath: 1)

Its time; it waits until God's chastening judgment has been accomplished, but does not tarry, but rather corresponds with the divine veracity; 2) its method; it works often secretly, but shows itself to be all the more appropriate and glorious whether we regard the instruments that it uses or the persons in whose behalf it is employed, or the gracious acts that proceed from it; 3) its end; it is the highest and noblest that there is, the building of the temple, that is, the reconciliation of man with God for their salvation and His glory.—God's wonderful ways, that He chooses in leading His people: 1) Out of the depths up on high; 2) By changing enemies into friends; 3) From small beginnings to a glorious end.

Ver. 2. The universality of God's revelation of Himself: 1) To whom made; even the heathen, even a Cyrus; 2) What it reveals: *a*) that God is the author of all things, the source of all power and strength; *b*) That He is the end of all things, that every one is obligated to honor Him.—The prince endowed with God's grace: 1) He derives his power from God: 2) He puts himself at the service of the divine honor.—Man in his true subordination to God: 1) he ascribes his possessions to God; 2) he employs them in the divine honor.

Ver. 3. The work of the redeemed: 1) to be pilgrims, namely, on the march to the holy city; 2) To build the temple of God; 3) To honor God therein and be saved.

Starke: Ver. 1. No one will be ashamed who patiently waits for divine help (Ps. xxv. 3; Sir. ii. 7; xvi. 13). The king's heart is in the hand of the Lord as brooks of water, and He inclines it whither He will (Prov. xxi. 1; Job xii. 24). God often touches the hearts even of unbelieving princes, *etc.*; therefore let us ever pray for them (1 Tim. ii. 12).

Ver. 2. As Cyrus was of humble origin, lived in his childhood as an humble shepherd, and then God had been with him in a truly wonderful manner, used him, moreover, to deliver the people of God from captivity, so all this is to be found in Christ, although in a much more extraordinary manner. It is a very easy thing for God to make His enemies the benefactors of His Church (Prov. xvi. 7).

Ver. 6. We are bound, in whatever station in life we may be placed, to employ our means for the advancement of the true worship of God (1 Chron. xxx. 6; 2 Chron. xxiv. 4; xxxi. 10).

[Scott: When God has work to do, they whom He hath chosen to perform it find their minds enlarged to entertain noble designs.—That which is devoted to the service is entrusted to the protection of the Lord.—Henry: Those are much *honored* whose spirits are stirred up to begin with God and to serve him in their *first* years.—*Well-willers* to the temple should be *well-doers* for it.—Our spirits naturally incline to this earth and to the things of it; if they move upwards in any good affections, or good actions, 'tis God that raiseth them.—Wordsworth: Cyrus is contrasted with Pharaoh, who resisted God's Spirit.—Egypt gave up its gold and silver and jewels to Israel at their Exodus; Babylon gave back the vessels of gold and silver to God's house. The enemies of Christ will one day be made subjects tributary to Him (Acts ii. 35; 1 Cor. xv. 25).—Tr.]

B.—THE CATALOGUE OF THE RETURNING EXILES AND THEIR CONTRIBUTIONS FOR THE BUILDING OF THE TEMPLE.

Chapter II. 1–67. (Comp. Nehem. vii. 6–73.)

I. *The catalogue of the families and households of the people.* Vers. 1–35.

1 Now these *are* the children of the province that went up out of the captivity,
of those which had been carried away, whom Nebuchadnezzar the king of Babylon
had carried away unto Babylon, and came again unto Jerusalem and Judah, every
2 one unto his city; Which came with Zerubbabel: Jeshua, Nehemiah, Seraiah, Ree-
laiah, Mordecai, Bilshan, Mizpar, Bigvai, Rehum, Baanah. The number of the
3 men of the people of Israel: The children of Parosh, two thousand a hundred
4 seventy and two. The children of Shephatiah, three hundred seventy and two.
5, 6 The children of Arah, seven hundred seventy and five. The children of Pahath-
moab, of the children of Jeshua *and* Joab, two thousand eight hundred and twelve.
7, 8 The children of Elam, a thousand two hundred fifty and four. The children of
9 Zattu, nine hundred forty and five. The children of Zaccai, seven hundred and
10, 11 threescore. The children of Bani, six hundred forty and two. The children
12 of Bebai, six hundred twenty and three. The children of Azgad, a thousand two
13 hundred twenty and two. The children of Adonikam, six hundred sixty and six.

14, 15 The children of Bigvai, two thousand fifty and six. The children of Adin, four
16 hundred fifty and four. The children of Ater of Hezekiah, ninety and eight.
17, 18 The children of Bezai, three hundred twenty and three. The children of Jo-
19 rah, a hundred and twelve. The children of Hashum, two hundred twenty and
20, 21 three. The children of Gibbar, ninety and five. The children of Beth-lehem,
22, 23 a hundred twenty and three. The men of Netophah, fifty and six. The men
24 of Anathoth, a hundred twenty and eight. The children of Azmaveth, forty and
25 two. The children of Kirjath-arim, Chephirah, and Beeroth, seven hundred and
26 forty and three. The children of Ramah and Gaba, six hundred twenty and one.
27, 28 The men of Michmas, a hundred twenty and two. The men of Beth-el and
29, 30 Ai, two hundred twenty and three. The children of Nebo, fifty and two. The
31 children of Magbish, a hundred fifty and six. The children of the other Elam, a
32 thousand two hundred fifty and four. The children of Harim, three hundred and
33 twenty. The children of Lod, Hadid, and Ono, seven hundred twenty and five.
34, 35 The children of Jericho, three hundred forty and five. The children of Senaah,
three thousand and six hundred and thirty.

II. *The catalogue of the Priests, Levites, and Servants of the Temple.* Vers. 36–58.

36 The priests: the children of Jedaiah, of the house of Jeshua, nine hundred seventy
37, 38 and three. The children of Immer, a thousand fifty and two. The children
39 of Pashur, a thousand two hundred forty and seven. The children of Harim, a
40 thousand and seventeen. The Levites: the children of Jeshua and Kadmiel, of
41 the children of Hodaviah, seventy and four. The singers: the children of Asaph,
42 a hundred twenty and eight. The children of the porters: the children of Shallum,
the children of Ater, the children of Talmon, the children of Akkub, the children
43 of Hatita, the children of Shobai, *in* all a hundred thirty and nine. The Nethinim:
44 the children of Ziha, the children of Hasupha, the children of Tabbaoth, The children
45 of Keros, the children of Siaha, the children of Padon, The children of Lebanah,
46 the children of Hagabah, the children of Akkub, The children of Hagab, the
47 children of Shalmai, the children of Hanan, The children of Giddel, the children
48 of Gahar, the children of Reaiah, The children of Rezin, the children of Nekoda,
49 the children of Gazzam, The children of Uzza, the children of Paseah, the chil-
50 dren of Besai, The children of Asnah, the children of Mehunim, the children of
51 Nephusim, The children of Bakbuk, the children of Hakupha, the children of Har-
52 hur, The children of Bazluth, the children of Mehida, the children of Harsha,
53, 54 The children of Barkos, the children of Sisera, the children of Thamah, The
55 children of Neziah, the children of Hatipha. The children of Solomon's servants:
56 the children of Sotai, the children of Sophereth, the children of Peruda, The chil-
57 dren of Jaalah, the children of Darkon, the children of Giddel, The children of
Shephatiah, the children of Hattil, the children of Pochereth of Zebaim, the chil-
58 dren of Ami. All the Nethinim, and the children of Solomon's servants, *were* three
hundred ninety and two.

III. *The members of the People and the Priests without Genealogy.* Vers. 59–64.

59 And these *were* they which went up from Tel-melah, Tel-harsa, Cherub, Addan,
and Immer: but they could not shew their father's house, and their seed, whether
60 they *were* of Israel: The children of Delaiah, the children of Tobiah, the children
61 of Nekoda, six hundred fifty and two. And of the children of the priests: the chil-
dren of Habaiah, the children of Koz, the children of Barzillai; which took a wife
62 of the daughters of Barzillai the Gileadite, and was called after their name: These
sought their register *among* those that were reckoned by genealogy, but they were
63 not found: therefore were they, as polluted, put from the priesthood. And the Tir-
shatha said unto them, that they should not eat of the most holy things, till there
stood up a priest with Urim and with Thummim.

IV. *Sum total of those who returned, their Servants and Beasts of Burden.* Vers. 64–67.

64 The whole congregation together *was* forty and two thousand three hundred *and*
65 threescore, Besides their servants and their maids, of whom *there were* seven thou-

sand three hundred thirty and seven: and *there were* among them two hundred sing-
66 ing men and singing women. Their horses *were* seven hundred thirty and six;
67 their mules, two hundred forty and five; Their camels, four hundred thirty and
five; *their* asses, six thousand seven hundred and twenty.

V. *Contributions for the Building of the Temple, and Closing Remarks.* Vers. 68–70.

68 And *some* of the chief of the fathers, when they came to the house of the LORD
which *is* at Jerusalem, offered freely for the house of God to set it up in his place:
69 They gave after their ability unto the treasure of the work threescore and one thou-
sand drams of gold, and five thousand pounds of silver, and one hundred priests'
70 garments. So the priests, and the Levites, and *some* of the people, and the singers,
and the porters, and the Nethinim, dwelt in their cities, and all Israel in their cities.

EXEGETICAL AND CRITICAL.

The same catalogue as that here given is likewise found in Neh. vii. 6–73. The two texts differ, to some extent, in the names, and especially in numbers. This is not so remarkable, considering the long list; at the bottom these differences are insignificant enough. This is clear from the notes made in connection with the translation. We have passed over some very trifling deviations, which are manifestly to be regarded as due to oversight of the copyist. The peculiarities of Esdras are scarcely anywhere of such a character that we can find in them an evidence of the original reading. This catalogue of the constituents of the new community may be placed in parallelism with that of the constituents of the ancient community, Num. i. 5 sq.

Verses 1 and 2 give the individual members connected with the names of their heads.—**And these are the children of the province,** *etc.* מְדִינָה, from דִּין, properly, judicial or official district, is here the province given in charge to the judge or governor of Jerusalem (Neh. xi. 3), just as in chap. v. 8; Neh. i. 2. [“The children of the province are the Israelites who returned to Palestine, as distinct from those who remained in Babylon or Persia” (Rawlinson).—TR.] Instead of the usual form Nebuchadnezzar (with *a* in the last syllable), the Kethib has Nebuchadnezzor (with *o*), a form which, to a certain extent, is nearer to the Chaldee pronunciation of the name. Another approximation is the form Nebuchadrezzar (with *r* in the penult.) in Jer. xxi. 2, 7; xxxii. 1; xxxv. 11; xxxix. 11, *etc.*; Ezek. xxvi. 7; xxix. 18 sq.; xxx. 10,—and both approximations are combined in that of Nebuchadrezzor. The name in Chaldee, according to Ménant, *Grammaire Assyrienne*, 1868, p. 327, is *nabu kadurri usur*; according to Schrader, *die Keilinschriften, etc.*, S. 235, is *Nabiuvkudurrinsur* and means “*Nebo protect*, or protect the crown.” That in Hebrew a נ is usual in the penult. instead of ר is connected with the fact that the primitive form of *usur* is *nasar*.—**Every one unto his city.**—אִישׁ לְעִירוֹ is apparently used from the subsequent standpoint of the author of the document. It certainly does not mean, according to the city, which was already theirs from the time of the fathers—for only a small portion of the former southern kingdom was taken possession of by the new community. Thus many did not return to the cities where their ancestors had dwelt, but to the city which subsequently was their own when this catalogue was prepared (with Bertheau against Keil [Rawlinson]). Comp. v. 70.

Ver. 2. **Which came with Zerubbabel.**—Whilst וַיָּשׁוּבוּ in ver. 1 is conceived as merely a continuation of אֲשֶׁר הֶגְלָה, אֲשֶׁר בָּאוּ is in ver. 2, a parallel, co-ordinate clause. Hence it again has the preterite. Nehemiah in ver. 1 uses the participle בָּאִים corresponding with the הָעֹלִים in ver. 1.—Zerubbabel, now זְרֻבָּבֶל, and sometimes זְרֻבָּבֶל is formed not from זְרוּי (scattered), as would seem at first sight, but from זְרוּעַ (sowed) and בָּבֶל (that is born in Babylon). Comp. also chap. i. 11. **Jeshua**—יֵשׁוּעַ (later form of יְהוֹשׁוּעַ, comp. Neh. viii. 17) is here the first high-priest of the new community, the son of Jehozadak, the grandson of the high-priest Seraiah, 1 Chron. vi. 14, whom Nebuchadnezzar put to death at Riblah, in the land of Hamath, 2 Kings xxv. 18 sq. Comp. chap. iii. 2, and chap. v. 2. In Hag. i. 2 and 14, and Zech. iii. 1, we find the older form of his name Jehoshua. The other men here named who come into consideration as chiefs are unknown to us. For Nehemiah and Mordecai are not at all to be identified with the later persons who bore these names. Instead of Seraiah, Neh. vii. gives Azariah; but in Neh. x. 2 both names are found alongside of one another as names of families of priests in the time of Nehemiah, so that we may conjecture that both names were then favorites and in frequent use in the families of the priests, and therefore would be easily interchanged. If we count here the name of *Nahamani*, who is named in Neh. vii. 7, but is missing here, we have just twelve heads which, without doubt, refers to a new division of the community into twelve divisions. That the idea at the basis of this catalogue was that the new community represented entire Israel and its twelve tribes, is clear from the title that directly follows—**number of the men of the people of Israel**—especially however from the twelve sin-offerings in chap. vi. 1. Notwithstanding this fact it may be that the twelve were all from the three tribes to which almost all those that returned belonged, Judah, Benjamin, and Levi. The last words of the verse, “the number of the men of the people of Israel,” constitute the special title of the first section of the catalogue after the analogy of vers. 36, 40, 43 and 55.

Vers. 3–35. The families and households of the people. Many of the names mentioned in vers. 3–19 and ver. 32 meet us again in the register of the times of Ezra and Nehemiah, thus the children Parosh, Pahath-Moab, Adin, Elam, Shephatiah, Joab, Bebai, Azgad, Adonikam, Bigvai, and according to the original reading, the children of Zattu and Bani, in ch. viii., in the catalogue of those returning with Ezra; so likewise men of the sons of Parosh, Elam, Zattu, *etc.*, in ch. x., among these, who had strange wives, and also in Neh. x. 15 sq., "from which we see, *a*) that of many families only a part returned with Zerubbabel and Jeshua; another part followed under Ezra; *b*) that heads of the fathers' houses are not mentioned for the sake of their personal names, but for the names of the houses of which they were fathers originating without doubt from more ancient times" (Keil). Since in vers, 30–35 the inhabitants of the other cities are mentioned according to the names of their localities, so probably the most or all which bear the names of their fathers' houses are to be regarded as inhabitants of Jerusalem.

The names in vers. 3–19 are beyond question names of families or households, and those in vers. 20–29 and 33–35 are just as surely names of cities. This order seems, however, to be interrupted by vers. 30–32, in that perhaps Harim, according to ch. x. 21, the other Elam, after the analogy of ver. 7, and perhaps also Magbish, are names of persons, not of places. Yet Ezra x. 21 is not entirely decisive for Harim as the name of a person, since in Neh. x. 15 sq., likewise, names of places, as for example Anathoth, occur in ver. 19 in the middle among names of families. Besides it is possible that the text in vers. 30–32 may have been corrupted; it seems strange that with the other Elam here the same number, 1254, occurs as with the Elam of ver. 8, and that the name Magbish is not found either in Nehemiah or Esdras. In Esdras the other Elam is passed over, and instead of the children of Harim three hundred and twenty, there is (ch. v. 16) in the corresponding place, that is, among the names of families, ὑιόι Ἀρόμ, thirty-two. The cities mentioned in vers. 20–35 occur for the most part in other parts of the Old Testament: Gibeon, which, according to Neh. vii. 25, is to be read for Gibbah, already in Josh. ix. 3; Bethlehem in Ruth i. 2; Mic. v. 1; Netopha (apparently in the vicinity of Bethlehem) in 2 Sam. xxiii. 38 sq.; 2 Kings xxv. 23; 1 Chron. ii. 54; Anathoth in Josh. xxi. 18; Jer. i. 1; Kirjath arim, Chephira and Beeroth as cities of the Gibeonites, Josh. ix. 17; Rama and Geba already in Josh. ix. 25 sq., and then especially in the history of Samuel and Saul; Michmas in 1 Sam. xiii. 25; Isa. x. 28; Bethel and Ai in Josh. vii. 2 and Jericho in Josh. v. 13, *etc.;* all situated in the vicinity of Jerusalem, and first of all taken possession of by those who returned. On the other hand Azmaveth or Bethazmaveth, Neh. vii. 28, occurs besides only in Neh. xii. 29. Accordingly it was situated apparently in the neighborhood of Geba. It has not yet been discovered. Ritter's conjecture (*Erdk.* xvi. S. 519) that it is El-Hizme in the vicinity of Anata has nothing in its favor. Nebo, which has nothing to do with the mountain of this name, Num. xxxii. 32, has been identified with Nob, or Nobe, 1 Sam. xxi. 2, whose situation would certainly suit, especially as in Neh. xi. 31 sq., among many other places named here Nob, but not Nebo, is mentioned. Besides the sons of Nebo occur again in Ezra x. 43. Bertheau thinks of Nuba or Beit-Nuba (Robinson, *New Biblical Researches*, III. page 144). Lod is Lydda, where Peter healed the paralytic (Acts ix. 32 sq.), at present Ludd, comp. 1 Chron. viii. 12. Ono, which occurs again in Neh. xi. 35 and 1 Chron. viii. 12, must have been situated in the vicinity of Lydda. There also we must seek Hadid, now El Haditheh (Robinson, *B. R.*, p. 143), according to 1 Macc. xii. 38; xiii. 13. Senaah was regarded by the more ancient interpreters as Σεννὰ νῦν Μαγδαλσεννά, which, according to Jerome, was situated as *terminus Judæ in septimo lapide Jerichus contra septentrionalem plagam* (*Onom. ed. Lars. et Parth.*, p. 332), and which is hardly to be identified, as Robinson (*B. R.* III. p. 295), with Mejdel, which is too far distant, four German miles north of Jericho, situated on a lofty mountain-top. At the building of the walls of the city, Neh. iii., there are mentioned besides the men of Jericho, Senaah and Gibeon, inhabitants also of Tekoah, Zanoah, Bethhaccerem, Mizpah, Bethsur and Keilah, and a still greater number of cities occurs in Neh. xi. 25–35. From this it is clear that gradually the cities of Judah and Benjamin were taken possession of, and more and more of them inhabited.

Vers. 36–39. The priest-classes. Of the four names mentioned here three agree with the names of three classes of priests, which were among the twenty-four classes introduced by David, 1 Chron. xxiv. 7 sq.; Jedaiah was the second, Immer the sixteenth, Harim the third class. It is very probable, therefore, that the divisions here are connected with such classes. For additional remarks upon this subject, *vid.* notes upon Neh. xii. 1 sq. The house of Jeshua, however, may very properly refer to the house of the high-priest Jeshua, to which the children of Jedaiah belonged. This view is favored by the fact that among those who returned, in all probability, this family was more numerously represented perhaps by a class of priests belonging to it. It is true the high-priest Jeshua belonged to the line of Eleazar; the class of Jedaiah, on the other hand, it is supposed, we must seek as the second in the line of Ithamar, and yet the order of classes was determined by lot, 1 Chron. xxiv., and it is a very natural supposition, since there is some uncertainty in the passage as to the method of the lot, that the second class was of Eleazar's line. Else Jeshua might also be the name of an ancient head of the family; in 1 Chron. xxiv. 11 it is the name of the ninth class of priests.—The children of Pashur constitute a new class, which does not occur in 1 Chron. xxiv. as a class of priests, and this name does not occur among the nine classes subsequent to the exile, Neh. xii. They occur again, however, in Ezra x. 18–22 among the priests who had married strange wives, alongside of the sons of Jeshua, Immer and Harim.

The name Pashur is besides found even in more ancient times, 1 Chron. ix. 12; Nehem. xi. 12; Jer. xx., xxi.

Vers. 40–58. The Levites, servants of the temple (Nethinim), and servants of Solomon: The Levites fall into three divisions according to their different official duties; the first was the Levites in the narrower sense, the assistants of the priests in the divine worship, the second was the singers, the third the porters, 1 Chron. xxiv. 20–31; xxv. and xxvi. 1–19. The children of Jeshua and Kadmiel are mentioned in ver. 40 as Levites in the narrower sense. The additional clause: **of the children of Hodaviah**, belongs probably only to the last family, the children of Kadmiel, comp. notes on iii. 9; the name is not found in the lists of Levites in Chronicles.—Of the singers (ver. 41) only the members of the choir of Asaph returned with the first company. Yet in Neh. xi. 17 three classes are mentioned again as in times before the exile.—Of the six classes of porters (ver. 42) three, Shallum, Talmon and Akkub, are mentioned 1 Chron. ix. 17 as those who dwelt in Jerusalem already before the exile. Thirty-five families of the Nethinim are mentioned (vers. 43–54), of the servants of Solomon ten families (vers. 55–57). In Nehemiah the children of Akkub, Hagab and Asnah have fallen out, and some names are written differently, partly through oversight, partly on account of another method of writing them. The most of the families of the Nethinim may have descended from the Gibeonites, Josh. ix. 21–27. The children of Mehunim, however, in ver. 50, belonged, as the plural form of the name shows, to the tribe or people of the Mehunim, and were probably prisoners of war,—perhaps after the victory of the king Uzziah over that people (2 Chron. xxvi. 7) they had been given to the sanctuary as bondsmen. The children of Nephusim might have been prisoners of war from the Ishmaelite tribe of נָפִישׁ, Gen. xxv. 15. The children of the servants of Solomon, who are mentioned again in Neh. xi. 3, elsewhere connected with the Nethinim, with whom they are here arranged in the enumeration, were certainly not the descendants of those Amorites, Hethites, *etc.*, whom Solomon, 1 Kings ix. 20 sq.; 2 Chron. viii. 7 sq., had made tributary and bondsmen [Rawlinson], but apparently prisoners of war from tribes that were not Canaanites. The name פֹּכֶרֶת הַצְּבָיִים in ver. 57 probably denotes: catcher of gazelles.

Vers. 59, 60. Fellow-countrymen, who could not show their ancestry. They went up from Tel Melah (salt-hill), Tel Harsa (bush or wood-hill), Cherub, Addan and Immer. The last three words are probably not names of persons, they are first mentioned in ver. 60, but still as names of places. Like Tel Harsa, they might likewise be connected without מִן. Perhaps they may designate *one* district, that is, three places situated close to one another in the same district. We have then perhaps three districts for the three families named in ver. 60.—[Rawlinson regards these as villages of Babylonia, at which the Jews here spoken of had been settled. The first and third he regards as really identified with the Thelmé and Chiripha of Ptolemy.—Tr.]—**They could not show their fathers' house**, that is, could not prove to which of the fathers' houses of Israel their forefathers, after whom they were called, Delaiah, Tobiah and Nekoda, belonged.—**And their seed**, that is, their family-line, whether they were of Israelite origin or not. Clericus properly remarks: *Judaicam religionem dudum sequebantur, quamobrem se Judæos censebant: quamvis non possent genealogicus tabulas ostendere, ex quibus constaret, ex Hebræis oriundos esse.* It is possible that there was a doubt whether the children of Nekoda here mentioned did not belong to the Nethinim family of the same name in ver. 48, and with respect to the other two families, there were similar doubts (Bertheau). Since we do not find any of these names again in the enumeration of the heads of the people and fathers' houses in Neh. x. 15–28, or in the list of Ezra x. 25–43, it seems that although they were not expelled, yet the right of citizenship was withheld from them.

Vers. 61–63. Priests who could not show that they belonged to the priesthood, the children of Habaiah, Hakkoz and Barzillai. Whether these children of Hakkoz claimed to belong to the seventh class of priests of the same name, 1 Chron. xxiv. 10, is uncertain. The name occurs also elsewhere, comp. Neh. iii. 4.—The children of Barzillai were descended from a priest who properly bore another name, but who married a daughter of the Gileadite Barzillai, well-known in the history of David (2 Sam. xvii. 27; xix. 32–39; 1 Kings ii. 7). It is conjectured that she was an heiress (Num. xxxvi.), and to obtain possession of her inheritance, he assumed her name. Comp. Num. xxvii. 4. The name Barzillai and membership in a family of Gilead might have subsequently rendered the priestly origin of his posterity doubtful, although they would by no means have lost the right of the priesthood, if they could have proved in any way their priestly origin. The suffix with שְׁמָם must be referred back to בְּנוֹת. For the masc. form for the fem., comp. Gesen., § 121, *Anmerk.* 1. Their register in ver. 62 is their סֵפֶר הַיַּחַשׂ, Neh. vii. 5, their writing of genealogy, their register of their descent; this writing had the title of הַמִּתְיַחְשִׂים, those registered as to genealogy; for this word is in apposition with כְּתָבָם, and נִמְצָאוּ refers back to this plural, for which in Neh. vii. 64 the sing., נִמְצָא, referring back to כְּתָבָם, is found, as we say in Germany, not to be able to find their forefathers, instead of the register of their forefathers.—**They were as polluted put from the priesthood.**—וַיְגֹאֲלוּ is a pregnant term=they were declared polluted, so that they were excluded from the priesthood. The more definite decision respecting them was given according to ver. 63 by the *Tirshatha*, the civil governor of the community, according to Neh. vii. 65, comp. with ver. 70, Zerubbabel, who, Hag. i. 1, 14; ii. 2, 21, is called פַּחַת יְהוּדָה. In Neh. viii. 9 and x. 2 Nehemiah bears this title, who besides in Neh.

xii. 26 likewise has the title פֶּחָה, Tirshatha is without doubt the Persian designation of the governor. It is probably not connected with *taras*, fear = the one feared [Rawlinson, who regards it as the Persian *tarsata*, past part. of tars = to fear = the feared, a title which well might be given to one in authority. He compares the German *gestrenger Herr* and our title of "Reverend." — TR.], or with *tarash, acer, auster* = the severe lord, but is from the Zend *thuorestar* (nom. *thuoresta*) = *præfectus, penes quem est imperium*, Gesen., *Thes.*, p. 1521; Benfey, *die Monatsnamen*, S. 196. The reason why the name of Zerubbabel is not added, and why he is not mentioned in Neh. vii. 65–70 in connection with this title, is that there is no importance to be ascribed here to the person, but only to the position expressed by the title. It is not strange that the civil governor made this decision with reference to the priesthood, because of the close connection between the civil and religious affairs of the community at Jerusalem. Their prohibition from eating of the most holy things, that is, of those that were consecrated to the Lord, of which none but the priests could partake, and these only of certain prescribed parts in the holy place (comp. Lev. ii. 3), excluded them from participation in those revenues that were immediately connected with priestly occupations, and therefore without doubt likewise from the priestly occupations themselves. The children of Habaiah, *etc.*, were not to come near the most holy things, *e. g.* the altar of burnt-offerings (Ex. xxix. 37; xxx. 10), and especially were not to enter the most holy places (Num. xviii. 10). A portion of the general fees which were offered to the priests was not denied them, since their right to the priesthood was not expressly denied, but left *in suspenso*.—**Till there stood up a priest with Urim and Thummim.**—עָמַד is according to later usage for קוּם (comp. Dan. viii. 23; xi. 2, *etc.*). The question arises why the high-priest Jeshua could not have given the desired decision by means of Urim and Thummim, for the use of which we are to compare Ex. xxviii. 30. The reason could hardly have been of such a personal and external character as Ewald, *Gesch. Isr.* IV. 95 conjectures, as if Jeshua was perhaps not the eldest son of his father, and therefore not entirely suited to the high-priesthood. It is probable that in the times subsequent to the exile there was no longer as formerly any more decisions by means of Urim and Thummim. Little importance is to be given to the opinion of Josephus *Arch.* III. 8, 9, that its use had not ceased till two hundred years before his time, since he acts upon the opinion that it had been used for the purpose of predicting victory. The Rabbins reckon this method of divine revelation among the five things which from the beginning were lacking in the second temple. Comp. Buxtorf, *exercitt. ad historiam Urim et Thummim*, cap. V., and Vitringa *observatt.*, *s.* VI., cap. VI., p. 324 sq. We are rather to suppose that they believed that they must wait until such a time when the high-priest would again be able to fulfil his entire calling. The temple must first arise again, and the Lord must declare His presence again in some special practical and unmistakable manner, without which indeed a revelation through Urim and Thummim was inconceivable.

Vers. 64–67. The sum-total of those that returned, their servants and maid-servants and beasts of burden. The sum of 42,360 is given in our passage in Nehemiah and Esdras, for the whole congregation together (so manifestly here כְּאֶחָד, (it is otherwise in chap. iii. 9; vi. 20); a number which is not gained by adding the detailed numbers together, either here or in Neh. or Esdras, for the sum total is much too great for the detailed numbers, which amount to only 29,818 here, in Nehemiah 31,089, in Esdras 30,143. How then did this difference arise? Even Keil is convinced that it is due only to mistakes of copyists. "Any attempt to explain them (the differences) in any other way cannot be justified." But if this were really so, there would be greater differences between the detailed numbers as they are given here and in Nehemiah; and reckoned together they would, in accordance with one or the other texts, approximately make out the sum total of 42,360. If such essential mistakes as these occurred in copying, then the fact that the result of reckoning together the numbers agrees, at least in the main, and that each text is about the same number behind the sum total of 42,360, could not be possible unless the mistakes were above all in this sum total, which however is inconceivable in connection with the exact agreement which everywhere prevails. It is certainly clear that the sum total was not meant to embrace any others, such as those who returned of the ten tribes (*Seder Olam*, Raschi, Usserius, J. H. Mich., *et al.*) but only the constituent parts contained in the previous verses. But perhaps it was understood of itself according to the fundamental notions and ideas of the time that there were others still belonging to the 2172 sons of Parosh, *etc.*, who properly were not reckoned with them, but who yet united with them in constituting the "entire congregation," כָּל־הַקָּהָל, and were given with them in summing it up. It depends upon the idea of כָּל־הַקָּהָל. Possibly if the number of the children of Parosh, *etc.*, were to be given, only the independent people, especially the heads of families, came into consideration; whilst in the "entire congregation" there were, counted perhaps likewise the larger sons, who had reached the age of discretion, Neh. viii. 2, 3. If in Esdras v. 41 our ver. 64 reads "all of Israel from twelve years old and upwards, besides the servants and maid-servants, were 42,360," this addition, "from twelve years and upward," is indeed critically worthless, yet it might rest upon a correct knowledge of ancient customs, although perhaps the age of twelve years corresponds only with latter circumstances. If the servants and maid-servants were reckoned to the כָּל־הַקָּהָל, whose number is given in ver. 65, they might have been counted in the sum total, although they were not taken into consideration in the detailed numbers.

Ver. 65. **Besides their servants and**

maids.—אֵלֶּה, which is properly connected with the subsequent words by the accents, is explained as referring to the following sum, 7337 = besides their servants, *etc.*, who make out the following numbers. The additional clause: **And they had two hundred singing men and women**, can only mean: and they who returned—for the suffix לָהֶם, certainly refers to those to whom the suffix of עַבְדֵיהֶם, *etc.*, also refers,—had singing men and women, who because they were hired and paid, stood upon the same footing as the servants and maids, and since they were probably not of Israelite origin, did not belong to the congregation. They served, however, doubtless to increase the joy of the feasts, and for singing dirges in connection with sorrowful events, comp. Eccl. ii. 8; 2 Chron. xxxv. 25. At any rate these singing people are to be distinguished from the Levitical singers and musicians who took part in divine worship. J. D. Mich. would change these singing men and women into oxen and cows (as if מְשֹׁרְרִים were for שׁוֹרִים) since we would rather expect these here, after the domestics, and in connection with the horses, mules, camels, and asses. But it may be that the returning exiles only took with them beasts of burden, or at least chiefly of these, and obtained their cattle rather on their arrival in Canaan. If animals were intended here, we would not have לָהֶם, but the suffix as in the following verse.

Vers. 68–70. Contributions for the building of the temple and closing remarks.—Ver. 68. **And of the heads of the people** = some of them. Comp. וּמִן־הָעָם in ver. 70. Neh. uses instead וּמִקְצָת, a part, as Dan. i. 2, *etc.*. הִתְנַדְּבוּ they freely offered gifts, and indeed for the house of God. Comp. notes upon chap. i. 6. לְהַעֲמִידוֹ, = in order to erect it, rebuild it=לַהֲקִימוֹ, comp. ver. 63.

Ver. 69. **They gave to the treasure of the work,** that is, into the treasure that was collected for the work of the temple 61,000 darics of gold, (דַּרְכְּמוֹן here and Neh. vii. 70 sq., for which אֲדַרְכֹּן, with א, prosthetic. 1 Chron. xxix. 7, and Ezra viii. 27, the Greek δαρεικός, a Persian gold coin worth twenty-two German marks, [shillings, English] or seven and a half German thalers [five and a half American dollars], comp. 1 Chron. xxix. 7) = 457,500 German thalers, and 5,000 pounds of silver (above 200,000 German thalers) and 100 priests' garments. It seems that our author has here abbreviated the list that was before him, and given the figures in round numbers. We recognize here, as Bertheau properly points out, expressions peculiar to the author: "house of Jehovah, which is in Jerusalem," comp. chapter i. 4; iii. 8; הִתְנַדֵּב, comp. chapter i. 6; iii. 5; 1 Chr. xxix. 5, 6; לְהַעֲמִיד, comp. 1 Chron. xvi. 16; 2 Chron. ix. 8; Ezra ix. 9; כֹּחָם, comp. 1 Chr. xxix. 2; "they gave into the treasure," comp. 1 Chron. xxix. 8, *etc.* In Nehemiah the text of the document has been more faithfully retained.—In accordance with this some of the heads of fathers' houses contributed to the work, *viz.*, the Tirshatha (who comes into consideration as the first of these heads, and is mentioned by himself, with his contribution, which was probably especially large) gave to the treasure 1000 darics of gold, 50 sacrificial bowls, and 30 priests' garments, and 500, probably pounds, of silver). It cannot mean 530 priests' garments, for then the hundreds should stand first. Perhaps the things numbered have fallen away before the 500, in all, probably, וְכֶסֶף מָנִים. Some (*viz.*, others besides the Tirshatha) heads of fathers' houses gave 20,000 darics of gold, 2200 pounds of silver, and the rest of the people gave 20,000 darics of silver, 2000 pounds of silver, and 67 priests' garments. Accordingly the sum total amounted to 41,000 darics of gold, 4700 pounds of silver, 97 priests' garments, and 50 sacrificial bowls. An important difference between these statements and our text of the book of Ezra is found in 41,000 darics, for which Ezra has 61,000. Since this cannot be balanced by the 50 sacrificial bowls, which are passed over in our text, the 61,000 must be ascribed to a copyist's error.

Ver. 70. Here, in the closing remarks, the hand of our author may be recognized. The original text read somewhat thus: **And the priests and Levites and some of the people and entire Israel dwelt in their cities.**—But the author would in his own way specify the persons who took part in the divine worship, and adds therefore after those of the people, **the singers and door-keepers and temple servants**, and in connection therewith perhaps also that which directly followed the former, **in their cities**, which is missing in Nehemiah. In Nehemiah this statement is improved in this way, that he lets the Levitical singers and porters follow immediately after the Levites, and indeed the porters first, notwithstanding their office was less honorable than that of the singers, because he is not concerned with the dignity of their office, but with their membership among the Levites. It is true he had the disadvantage of being obliged to separate the Nethinim, whom he could not very well place "before those of the people," by וּמִן הָעָם from the porters and singers. וּמִן הָעָם at any rate does not mean "some," "many of the people;" the meaning cannot be that at first only some of them took possession of their cities, against which is the concluding statement "and all Israel were in their cities,"* but the others of the people, besides the priests and Levites. Respecting the **in their cities**, comp. remarks on ver. 1. Our author in a similar manner, as in the closing verse of the first chapter, passes over many things that would have seemed worthy of mention under other circumstances, as in what condition they found the cities, where they settled, whether they contended with the inhabitants of the land for them, how they accomplished their organization and the like. The reason is the same as that adduced in our notes upon chap. i. 11.

* ["All Israel" is interpreted by Rawlinson as referring to representatives of the ten tribes.—Tr.]

THOUGHTS UPON THE HISTORY OF REDEMPTION.

Ver. 2. Since the people formed the new congregation no longer as a nation, or according to their external membership in the nation,—since all depended upon the free choice of particular families,—there is no longer any mention of the ancient distinction of tribes which was based on merely natural laws. But the congregation, notwithstanding, again has its heads, and indeed again exactly twelve, as the people in the times before the exile had had twelve elders of tribes. Doubtless they needed them still just as much, if not even still more, since indeed the Persian king and his officers did not occupy themselves so immediately, and in so many ways, in their affairs as the previous royal government had done. The restoration of the temple and its worship was imposed directly and pre-eminently upon them, and they certainly had pre-eminently to take care that the law of God should prevail as thoroughly as possible in the life of the congregation. Hence there is sufficient reason that they should be placed foremost here just as the twelve elders of tribes had been in the time of Moses, Num. i. 15, 16. There must always be office-holders, ranks, and a corresponding subordination in the congregation of God, as surely as it ever needs guidance and training. And if the officials are no longer given by natural rank, or appointed by the state, if the relation to them is thus a more tender one, then they ought to meet them as those who have been freely chosen to positions of trust, with all the more respect, yea, reverence.

Vers. 36–39. The priests were disproportionately numerous in the new congregation. They made up about the seventh part of the whole. If in consequence of this they were obliged to be all the more discreet to maintain themselves, since the offerings falling to them hardly sufficed for their support,—if therefore it could not be permitted them to acquire land for themselves, work them, or to learn trades and practice them, then it was without doubt the very reverse of what they ought to have done, when they, in consequence of this, became conformed to the world and helped to favor the mingling with heathenism, as we observe to be the case even in the high priestly family itself. Comp. chap. x. 18. They ought, owing to their great numbers, to have offered to the congregation all the greater support against the worship of idols and apostasy from the law, and at any rate they should have been a living, practical reminder of their most appropriate and highest tasks. They should have more and more impressed upon the entire congregation a priestly, spiritual character. The universal priesthood, which the worldly Christians claim, in a false sense, should be imparted more and more decidedly to the true congregation in the true sense.

Vers. 64–67. The new congregation must have appeared to themselves extraordinarily small and weak, when they compared themselves with the first beginnings in the time of Moses, when the men of war were about 600,000. (Comp. Numb. i. 46 and xxvi. 51.) It was all the more incumbent upon them to maintain themselves as far as possible in unity with those who remained behind in exile, and cultivate the bond of communion with them, accordingly widen their views, and keep themselves from narrow-heartedness,—or, if their relation to them proved again to be only a loose one, to consider themselves as a mere remnant, that had been preserved from the divine judgment by grace, accordingly to let themselves be reminded by their weakness of the divine holiness as well as compassion. The weaker they were in themselves, the more were they prompted, at all events, to seek their strength in the Lord, and expect their help from Him. Moreover we may conclude from their small numbers that it is not the great multitude to which the development of the church leads; rather those by whom God's thoughts of redemption are to realize themselves chiefly and most immediately, constitute naturally only a small minority. Besides, we may conclude from vers. 65–67 that among those who returned there were likewise men who were quite wealthy, that therefore the idea is not at all correct that only those had sought out Jerusalem again who had nothing to lose in Chaldea (*Talm. bab. tract. Kidduschim*). Without doubt God was able already in the Old Testament times to awaken a living zeal for His cause, not only among the poorer, but also, at the least, of making here and there also the rich, with their possessions, serviceable to His cause.

Vers. 68–69. By offering gold and the other gifts which had reference to the restoration of worship, the new congregation showed their earnest desire to really become what was incumbent upon them to be. Christianity should never fall behind them; but although its task is mainly the internal and spiritual offerings, they should be ready to prove the truth of their spirituality, where it is necessary, by external offerings likewise.

HOMILETICAL AND PRACTICAL.

Vers. 1, 2. Take care that thou and thy house above all belong to those who constitute the congregation of the Lord. Only they are named and numbered in the book of life.

Vers. 68, 69. Let not thy house, but God's house, be thy chief care. With reference to the statements respecting the riches of the returned exiles in ver. 65 sq. BRENTIUS appropriately remarks: *Ejecti erant Judæi e Hierusalem propter scelera sua. Nihilominus fovit eos inter gentes et locupletavet eos. Unde Jeremiæ vigesimo nono dicitur: Ego scio cogitationes, quas cogito super vos, cogitationes pacis et non afflictionis, ut dem vobis finem.* With the same appropriateness STARKE: "The Lord killeth and maketh alive, leadeth into Sheol and again out of it, 1 Sam. ii. 6. Let no one, therefore, utterly lose courage in enduring crosses, suffering, poverty and misery, persecution and imprisonment. God extends His church amidst crosses and persecutions all the more, and causes it to bloom as a palm-tree, Psalm xcii. 13; Matth. xvi. 18; Acts xi. 19–21." Upon ver. 68: "Whatever we give to the glory of God, we should give willingly, for God loveth a cheerful giver." Upon ver. 70: "My God, if Thou wilt redeem me some day out of this body in the world, then remove me likewise to the eternal and true fatherland and Canaan, the right to which our first parents lost by their disobedience for themselves and all men, but which Christ has regained for us." [SCOTT: Our gracious Lord will carry us through those undertakings which are entered on according to His will with an aim to His glory, and in dependence on His assistance; and then we shall be made superior to all difficulties, hardships and dangers.—HENRY: 'Tis an honor to belong to God's house, though in the meanest office there.—Let none complain of the necessary expenses of their religion, but believe that when they come to balance the account, they will find it *quit cost.* —TR.]

SECOND SECTION.

The First Effort.

CHAPS. III. IV.

A.—THE RE-ESTABLISHMENT OF THE ALTAR AND THE PREPARATION FOR BUILDING THE TEMPLE.

CHAP. III. 1–13.

I. *Building of the Altar, Feast of Tabernacles, and anxiety for the Building of the Temple.* Vers. 1–7.

1 AND when the seventh month was come, and the children of Israel *were* in the
2 cities, the people gathered themselves together as one man to Jerusalem. Then
stood up Jeshua the son of Jozadak, and his brethren the priests, and Zerubbabel
the son of Shealtiel, and his brethren, and builded the altar of the God of Israel,
to offer burnt offerings thereon, as *it is* written in the law of Moses the man of God.
3 And they set the altar upon his bases; for fear *was* upon them because of the peo-
ple of those countries: and they offered burnt offerings thereon unto the LORD, *even*
4 burnt offerings morning and evening. They kept also the feast of tabernacles, as
it is written, and *offered* the daily burnt offerings by number, according to the cus-
5 tom, as the duty of every day required; And afterward *offered* the continual burnt
offering, both of the new moons, and of all the set feasts of the LORD that were con-
secrated, and of every one that willingly offered a freewill offering unto the LORD.
6 From the first day of the seventh month began they to offer burnt offerings unto the
7 LORD. But the foundation of the temple of the LORD was not *yet* laid. They gave
money also unto the masons, and to the carpenters; and meat, and drink, and oil,
unto them of Zidon, and to them of Tyre, to bring cedar trees from Lebanon to the
sea of Joppa, according to the grant that they had of Cyrus king of Persia.

II. *Laying of the Corner-stone of the New Temple.* Vers. 8–13.

8 Now in the second year of their coming unto the house of God at Jerusalem, in
the second month, began Zerubbabel the son of Shealtiel, and Jeshua the son of
Jozadak, and the remnant of their brethren the priests and the Levites, and all they
that were come out of the captivity unto Jerusalem; and appointed the Levites,
from twenty years old and upward, to set forward the work of the house of the
9 LORD. Then stood Jeshua *with* his sons and his brethren, Kadmiel and his sons,
the sons of Judah, together, to set forward the workmen in the house of God: the
10 sons of Henadad, *with* their sons and their brethren the Levites. And when the
builders laid the foundation of the temple of the LORD, they set the priests in their
apparel with trumpets, and the Levites the sons of Asaph with cymbals, to praise
11 the LORD, after the ordinance of David king of Israel. And they sang together by
course in praising and giving thanks unto the LORD; because *he is* good, for his
mercy *endureth* for ever toward Israel. And all the people shouted with a great
shout, when they praised the LORD, because the foundation of the house of the

12 LORD was laid. But many of the priests and Levites and chief of the fathers, *who*
were ancient men, that had seen the first house, when the foundation of this house
was laid before their eyes, wept with a loud voice; and many shouted aloud for joy:
13 So that the people could not discern the noise of the shout of joy from the noise of
the weeping of the people: for the people shouted with a loud shout, and the noise
was heard afar off.

EXEGETICAL AND CRITICAL.

The history itself now follows the historical foundations. The most prominent and interesting feature of the narrative is the readiness and zeal of the new congregation, with reference to the temple and its worship, the re-establishment of which was their proper work, and indeed first of all in vers. 1–3 in the building of the altar.

Ver. 1. **And when the seventh month was come.**—The author calls attention to the zeal of all, without exception; especially also of those dwelling outside of Jerusalem. He means, of course, the seventh month of the same year in which the returning exiles arrived in Jerusalem, else he would have been obliged to define it more closely. Besides, it is clear from ver. 8, that the following year was the second after their arrival. The seventh month was properly the festival month, and accordingly the time in which it must be shown how zealous the new congregation was with reference to the service of God. The new year's day, the atonement day and feast of tabernacles fell on this month.—**And the children of Israel were in the cities.**—This clause is meant to indicate that they had already attained a certain degree of rest, but at the same time they had obtained a possession and a labor therein, which might have readily detained them; at any rate that they were again obliged to leave their own affairs and assemble together,—this, however, merely for the purpose of at once uniting in showing that they would not now allow themselves to be detained by anything from the celebration of the feasts of the law. It is clear from verse 6 that they did not wait until the feast of tabernacles, the 15th of the month, as it was prescribed in the law, but already on the day of the new moon came together, yea, in part already some days earlier, so that the building of the altar, which was for the first time undertaken on their coming together, might be ready for the day of the new moon.—**The people gathered themselves together as one man.**—This primarily means "as if inspired by *one* will," thus, "with one spirit" (Keil) ὁμοθυμαδόν, 1 Esdras v. 46, thence also as much as to say "entirely" (Berth.). For the verbal repetition of this verse in Neh. vii. 73, and chap. viii. 1, where an entirely different event was thereby to be introduced, and for the additional clause, which Esdras improperly has appended here, after Neh. viii. 1, see note on Neh. viii. 1.

Ver. 2. **Jeshua,** *etc.*, **stood up and built the altar,** *etc.*—This clause indicates the zeal of the heads of the congregation at Jerusalem, which very well corresponded with that of the people as a whole, but which yet has something striking in it, if as is the most natural interpretation, the future, with ו consec., expresses chronological sequence. We are to suppose that they had not first caused the people to come together, but already before had gone to work in building the altar.

Ver. 3. This verse more closely defines the previous one, and in its first half is designed for an explanation of the hesitation of Jeshua and the rest, in its second half for an explanation of what was meant by offering offerings according to the law.—**And they set the altar upon his base**—that is, on the foundation that was present long before for it. The sense of על מכונתו is without doubt essentially the same as על מכונו in chap. ii. 68. The qeri of the punctators has the more usual plural of the masculine form, which occurs also in Ps. civ. 5; the plural, however, is unsuitable here, because there can be no reference to different foundations, and still less to different pedestals for the altar. Comp. מכונתן, Zech. v. 11. It is manifest that there is here an indication that they made their work as easy as possible, and sought to finish it as soon as they could. For if it was also natural that they should re-erect the temple on its old foundations, partly because the place could not be arbitrarily changed, partly because the difficult substructures might still, without doubt, be very well made use of, yet with the altar it might easily have been entirely different. Under favorable circumstances they might have been obliged to re-establish it on an entirely new foundation, since the old foundation, probably, was no longer intact. Hence the explanatory clause is added: why they had not previously gone to work:—**For** (they did it) **because fear was upon them, because of the people of those countries**; properly fear or terror, which was on them. The בְּ here expresses the condition in which they were (comp. Ewald, § 217 *f*, and § 299 *b*), or more accurately, it states under what circumstances the action proceeded. At any rate it can also be explained with Ewald, § 295 *f*: in anxiety it was incumbent upon them (עֲלֵיהֶם) namely, to build. The conjecture of Ewald (*Gesch.* IV., S. 131), that the suffix of עֲלֵיהֶם refers to the people of the lands and the reference is to their coming together to Israel in a friendly spirit, in accordance with Esdras v. 49, is entirely inadmissible. Accordingly they had not ventured to undertake anything greater or more public, because they feared the hostility of the surrounding nations, so long as the congregation was not assembled in greater numbers, and they had even now to fear hostile interruption in a greater undertaking. The explanation of J. H. Mich. and Keil: They re-established altar and worship in order to secure for themselves the divine protection against the peoples, of whom they were afraid, not only requires us to supply too much, but also is opposed by the fact that we should expect, if this view were correct, that they already previously would have gone to work upon the erection of the altar, and have offered sacrifices, especially those of the daily sacrifice. The peoples are certainly the neighboring peoples, comp. chap. ix. 1; x. 2.—**And offered thereon burnt offerings**, *etc.*—They sought to act in accordance with the law before all in offering the daily sacrifices. The sing. ויעל is to be referred to the one upon whom the offering of the sacrifice was chiefly incumbent, the priest in service at the time,—it is the indefinite subject. Perhaps however the plural of the qeri is more appropriate. The burnt offerings for the morning and evening are those belonging to every morning and evening. Those on the weekly Sabbath and feast days were required to be offered in various numbers. Comp. Ex. xxix. 38 sq.; Numb. xxviii. 3 sq. The prominence given to the burnt offering alone is to be explained from the fact that these chiefly came into consideration, since the daily sacrifices, as well as those of the feasts, were chiefly burnt offerings, as then the burnt offering was regarded in general as the principal sacrifice. But at any rate they were entirely appropriate, in as much as they were the sacrifices of homage, through which the congregation might best express what they now above all had to confess, that they had Jehovah for their Lord, and prayed to Him as such.

In vers. 4, 5 the congregation attests its sacred zeal by the celebration of the feast of tabernacles, and by other ceremonies of worship. The burnt offering of the "day by day," or "every day" is that prescribed for the various days of the feast of tabernacles. במספר = numbered, *pro numero in singulos dies definito* (J. H. Mich.), comp. 1 Chron. ix. 28; xxiii. 31; Ezra viii. 34. כמשפט = according to law; in Num. xxix. 18, 21, 24, 27, 30, 33, to which passages there is a reference here, it is somewhat more definite, in *their* number, according to the law במספרם כמשפט. דבר יום ביומו is in apposition = the matter of the day in its day, *opus dies in die suo* (Vulg. and J. H. Michaelis), comp. Nehem. xi. 23. Bertheau explains this expression as in accordance with יום ביום (vi. 9) as the duty to be done day by day, but this is opposed by the fact that ביומו has the suffix. Compare for these prescribed sacrifices Num. xxviii. and xxix., in accordance with which there must be offered on the first day of the feast of tabernacles thirteen bullocks, on the second day twelve, and so on.

Ver. 5. **And afterward** (they offered) **the daily burnt offering.**—Here we must supply the verb, they offered. Since according to ver. 6 they began to offer burnt offerings on the first day of the seventh month, the meaning cannot be that they did not begin with the daily burnt offerings until after the feast of tabernacles (against Berth.), as if on the first day they had merely offered the offerings of the new moon, and on the feast of tabernacles the offerings of the feast; but had not yet on the ordinary days offered the daily sacrifices. That is inconceivable, or at least highly improbable. Moreover, the words do not imply that until the feast of tabernacles only the chief offerings had been offered, but not the offerings of the new moon, and as little the offerings of the atonement day (against Keil). Rather it is merely said, that after the sacrifices of the feast of tabernacles the usual order of offerings was again continued, which included the daily offerings, and then also those of the new moon and other feasts.—**And of the new moons**, is briefly, what was proper for the new moons, *etc.*—**And of every one that willingly offered a free-will offering unto the Lord.**—These words refer to all the other free-will offerings brought by the people which were offered, especially on the feast-days (comp. Deut. xvi. 2, 10, 16, 17), but also on other occasions. Moreover, among these offerings the sin offering is certainly included, as it belonged to the new moons, *etc.*, and was necessarily attached to the burnt offerings (comp. Num. xxviii. 15 sq). We are to supply to לחדשים first of all עלה, instead of עלת תמיד. Even the נדבה might also be a burnt offering, Lev. xxii. 18, and especially Ez. xlvi. 12; it only depended upon the form of the offering, namely, whether the gift was entirely consecrated to the Lord, or a festival meal was taken from it for the offerer and his family. Perhaps, however, we are to think finally of the offerings in general, instead of the burnt offering, also of the bloody offering, of which the נדבה was usually a subordinate class (Lev. vii. 16).

Vers. 6, 7. Here begins the anxiety for the building of the temple. From the first day of the seventh month on, they did not lack in zeal in offering burnt offerings, although the foundation of the temple had not yet been laid,—this for an introduction. They now, however, did their best (ver. 7) henceforth towards laying the foundation of the temple. They gave money to the חצבים, who hewed stones, or even cut timber, and to the חרשים, who prepared the stones and the timber, accordingly the workmen, without doubt, from the contributions mentioned in ii. 68 sq. To the Sidonians and Tyrians, however, who are always referred to in connection with the products of Canaan, they gave in return for their cedar wood, food and drink, that is, grain, wine, and oil, just as Solomon also had paid them with the produce of the earth, 1 Kings v. 21-25; 2 Chron. ii. 10-15. Accordingly they had already found or cultivated something in the land which they practically had taken possession of in the spring, from which they had been able to secure a harvest.—**To bring cedar trees from Lebanon to the sea of Joppa** = to Joppa on the sea, as 1 Kings v. 23 and 2 Chron. ii. 15. Bertheau understands by it not exactly Joppa itself, but merely the vicinity, but there certainly was nothing in the way of their landing at Joppa itself. The sand drifts which now render it impossible for ships to approach nearer the coast than half an hour's sail, and the earthquake that seems to have occurred, were probably then not in the way, and by no means hindered the landing from rafts. At other points of that coast the difficulties would have been still greater.—**According to the grant**, *etc.* The permission given them by Cyrus, which to a certain extent rendered the work obligatory to them, was the general permission to build the temple; *implicite* it involved also special permission to put themselves in connection with the Phœnicians for the accomplishment of this purpose. רִשְׁיוֹן is an ἅπ. λεγ., whose meaning is derived from the Aramaic and Rabbinical רְשָׁא, רְשֵׁי, *facultatem habere*, and רְשׁוּ, *facultas*.

Vers. 8-13. The sacred zeal of the congregation showed itself above all at the laying of the foundation of the temple. In the next year the preparation previously necessary had been so far completed, that now they could think of the building itself. When Theophilus (*ad. Antol., Lib.* III.), according to Berosus, designates this second year after the return as the second year of Cyrus, it is perhaps only in consequence of a sort of carelessness. Cyrus had, it is true, given the permission to return already in his first year, but before the return itself could have taken place the necessary consultations and preparations required a considerable time, during which Cyrus' second year already approached. After that they had first allowed the passover feast to pass by, and perhaps also already the grain harvest had been quite well advanced; they proceeded in the second month to lay the foundation.—**Zerubbabel, Jeshua, and the remnant of their brethren.** By these we must understand the entire congregation, at least so far as they were settled in Jerusalem; the remnant of their brethren are brethren in the wider sense, who are immediately more closely defined on the one side as priests and Levites, who at once follow after the high-priest Jeshua, and on the other side all who had come out of the captivity to Jerusalem, having joined Zerubbabel. Accordingly the entire congregation, as well in their leaders as in their multitude, took part in the work.—**Began and appointed the Levites, who were twenty years old and upward.** This might mean, they began to appoint, according to Gesen., § 142, 3 *a*. But according to the context the sense is: they began the building of the temple, in that they appointed the Levite. הֶעֱמִיד is used, especially by our author, in the sense of "appointing to an office." Comp. 1 Chron. xv. 17. *etc.* That they also appointed the Levites at the age of twenty years with the rest, was in accordance with the rule of David, 1 Chron. xxiii. 24 sq., and after the example of Moses (Numb. viii. 24). נַצֵּחַ, in the sense of "direct," with עַל, is, with the exception of the titles of the Psalms and Hab. iii. 19, peculiar to our author. Gusset improperly asserts, with reference to 1 Chron. xxiii. 4, that נַצֵּחַ may also mean "unite with one in a work," but it can only mean to preside over an affair, sometimes also accomplish it.

Ver. 9. The Levites at once gladly did their part in the work entrusted to them by the congregation. The sing. וַיַּעֲמֹד is here hardly to be explained from the fact that the verb, when it precedes, is not so strongly bound to the number of the subject. The sense is rather: Jeshua through his sons and brethren stood. בָּנָיו and also אֶחָיו are not merely used without connectives, which would here be unusual, but are in explanatory apposition with Jeshua. The names designating the fathers' houses are the names of ancient, and, for the most part, fathers of the times before the exile, who now existed only in their sons and brethren; that is, as well in their own posterity as also in that of their younger brothers. Comp. notes on ii. 3. Jeshua and also Kadmiel are, according to ii. 40, two such names, comp. also Neh. x. 10, according to which even in the time of Nehemiah, Jeshua and Kadmiel still existed. This view is not opposed by the fact that "and his sons" is connected by conjunction with Kadmiel. We may understand thereby the older men of this family and their sons. Instead of בְּנֵי יְהוּדָה we are to read, according to ii. 40, without doubt, בְּנֵי־הוֹדַוְיָה. Whether this is in apposition with the two families of Jeshua and Kadmiel, or merely refers to the latter, is as doubtful here as in ii. 40. Probably it is the latter (with Keil against Bertheau). That both, however, had a common ancestor, who was not Hodaviah, but Henadad, may be regarded as resulting from the last words of our verse. It is highly improbable that the clause **as one** (so united and entirely one were they) **to set forward the workman in the house of God** should be followed by the last words of the verse: **the sons of Henadad, their sons and their brethren, the Levites,** with the intention of naming still another third additional family; for they would not have been added on here without connection and without any predicate. Probably they are in apposition to both, to Jeshua and Kadmiel, with their sons. The relationship and connection of both would thus be indicated. In favor of this view is the comprehensive conclusion: their sons and brethren, the Levites, which does not suit a third particular class, but only the Levites in question as a whole. This also explains the reason why in chap. ii. 40 Henadad is not mentioned among the returned exiles alongside of Jeshua and Kadmiel. That in Neh. iii. 24 and x. 10 Binnui is at once designated as a son of Henadad, may rest upon the fact that he belonged neither to Jeshua nor to Kadmiel, but to Henadad, constituting a family of his own, which was sufficiently well represented, and hence not especially named. That no force is to be given to Esdras v. 56 (against Bertheau), where the sons of Henadad are adduced as a special class and are placed before the predicate, is sufficiently clear from the fact that there the sons of Judah (Hodaviah) are likewise treated as a special class (υἱοὶ Ἰωδᾶ τοῦ Ἡλιαδοὺδ). Moreover עֹשֵׂה is a rare form, which is peculiar to our author for עֹשֵׂי. Comp. 1 Chron. xxiii. 24, *etc.*

Vers. 10, 11. The laying of the foundation was accomplished with solemnity and festivity. The perf. with the simple copula וְיִסְּדוּ does not in itself carry on the narrative, but serves, as if the subject preceded and the preterite followed, to give the circumstances of the subsequent statement, so that the sense is: **And when the builders laid the foundations of the tem-**

ple, they appointed the priests, *etc.*—The subjects of יַּעֲמִידוּ are Zerubbabel and Jeshua and the congregation with them. The Kal., the priests stood, which is in Esdras, Sept., and Vulg., instead of the Hiphil, would not be better (Bertheau), unless we should regard this verse as well as the ninth, as carrying on the eighth verse; in other words, if it were parallel with the ninth, which is not the case. Rather it is parallel with the eighth verse, and contains a new appointment, that of the priests and musicians, and then ver. 11 parallel with ver. 9 narrates the activity of those who had been appointed.—**In their apparel.**—We must supply בּוּץ (Byssus) with מְלֻבָּשִׁים, comp. 2 Chron. v. 12; at any rate, the sense is: clothed with official robes. The following "**with trumpets**" does depend upon it. The trumpets, which do not properly have music in view, were entrusted to the priests (Num. x. 10). The music proper was from the time of David incumbent upon particular families of the Levites, especially that of Asaph (1 Chron. xiii. 8; xv. 16, 19). עַל־יְדֵי is, according to the appointment, institution, 1 Chron. xxv. 2.

Ver. 11. **And they sang together by course in praising**, *etc.*—We may take וַיַּעֲנוּ in the usual sense: they began with praising, *etc.;* but may likewise, with the older interpreters, as Clericus and J. H. Michaelis, explain: they responded to one another in responsive songs. Whilst the one choir sang: "Praise the Lord, for He is good," the other answered: "For His mercy endureth forever." They were songs of praise, as Ps. cvi. and cvii., cxviii. and cxxxvi., that they struck up, comp. 1 Chron. xvi. 34, 41; 2 Chron. v. 13; vii. 3, *etc.* עַל הוּסַּד, "over the being founded"=on account of the laying of the foundation. Comp. 2 Chron. iii. 3.

Vers. 12, 13. It is true that strong expressions of sorrow mingled with the joy, yet both sorrow and joy showed equally well the sacred zeal of the congregation in the worship of God. If the exile had begun in the fourth year of Jehoiakim, and the temple had not been destroyed till eighteen years later in 588 B. C., there might now very well be old men present,—since only seventy-two years had passed since that beginning of the exile,—who had seen the old temple, and had still a lively remembrance of it. Even Haggai, in the second year of Darius, when some seventy years (more accurately sixty-six) had passed since the destruction of the temple itself presupposes that one and another had still a remembrance of the old temple. Comp. Hag. ii. 3. בְּיָסְדוֹ is attached by the accents to the previous words, as if יסד were a noun, which meant founding, then permanence. But this noun nowhere else occurs; besides, בְּיָסְדוֹ, as an infin., seems to be connected with the words that follow thus: **When the foundation of this house was laid before their eyes.**—With this interpretation, it is true, the suffix is pleonastic, but in other passages of this author the suffix anticipates with emphasis the subject following it in apposition, comp. chap. ix. 1; 2 Chron. xxvi. 14, *etc.;* Ewald, § 209 *c.* [This is a late Hebrew usage, an Aramaism; so also זֶה without the article and before its noun is emphatic=this same, this very.—Tr.]—**Many old people wept with a loud voice.**—Not, as it were, tears of joy, because they could now again see the house of God arise; so also not merely with tears of emotion, because they on this occasion were again vividly reminded of the evils they had passed through. The relative clause: **that had seen the first house** gives the sense very decidedly: they wept tears of sorrow, because they could not conceal from themselves the fact that the new work, in accordance with all the prevailing circumstances, promised but little to attain unto the glory of the old. In favor of this is also Hag. ii. 3 and Zech. iv. 10. These tears were thus a proof that if only it had been in any way possible, they would gladly have made the new house as glorious as the old. The second clause is then antithetical: **but many shouted aloud for joy**—that is, were in such a joyful condition that they could not but be loud in their expression of joy.

Ver. 13. The meaning of the words: **the people could not discern the noise of the shouts of joy from the noise of the weeping of the people,** can only be that both those who rejoiced and those who wept were alike zealous to express their feelings—so much so indeed that the words which were sung could not be understood.—**For the people shouted with a loud shout and the noise was heard afar off.**—תְּרוּעָה and קוֹל in this clause in distinction from תְּרוּעַת הַשִּׂמְחָה in the first clause, can only mean the cry in general. This confused cry would be to the blame of the new congregation, if the confusion itself had not been the result of sacred enthusiasm for the cause of the Lord. עַד־לְמֵרָחוֹק stands for the more simple לְמֵרָחוֹק as in 2 Chron. xxvi. 15.

THOUGHTS UPON THE HISTORY OF REDEMPTION.

Our chapter presents a beautiful picture of the sacred enthusiasm of the new congregation for the glory of God, and especially of their commendable zeal for the restoration of the temple. In former times pious kings had provided in this way for the worthy worship of God; but now here for the first time we see the congregation as a whole of their own accord stepping forward in this manner. Such an inspiration of heart had without doubt from the first been rendered possible and brought about by the severe judgment which God had sent upon them, and by the hard oppression connected therewith. It was like the break of a lovely spring day, full of new life, after a storm. It did not by any means secure them a result that must be secured by them, without trials and hinderances; but yet they were finally to have a noble and great success, yea, they gained a great importance for the entire subsequent development of the congregation and of the kingdom of God.

Vers. 1–3. That the congregation, as soon as they could be assembled together as such, should feel above all impelled to build the Lord an altar and offer burnt-offerings, was in accordance with the command which Moses had once given to the people to set up on Ebal, the navel of the land, stones and inscribe thereon the law of the Lord (Deut. xxvii. 1–8), and even so with the other command to proclaim on this mountain the curse for the transgressor, and on Gerizim the blessing for the obedient, Deut. xi. 29–32; xxvii. 9–26. If the ancient congregation had by that act placed the land under the divine commandment, and marked it as under the Lord's jurisdiction, and put it under the obligation to obey Him, so the new congregation consecrated themselves by this worship unto Him, as entirely belonging to Him; they confessed by the burnt-offering in a symbolical manner, that what they have, they have from the Lord, and what they are, they are through Him, that thus they must be entirely devoted to Him. As offerings of homage, the burnt-offerings were better calculated than others to inaugurate the new beginning, the spring, which now broke forth for the congregation after the long night of winter.

Ver. 4. It was because of the season of the year in which the congregation had arrived in Canaan that the first feast which they could again celebrate in accordance with the law was the feast of tabernacles. At the same time, however, we may see therein a special providence of God, which was at once lovely and significant to the congregation. The booths adorned with foliage and fruits had previously represented as well the gracious help in the times of the wilderness as also the gracious blessings of harvest in the present (not the tent-life in the wilderness as such, comp. my *Abh. in der deutschen Zeitschrift*, 1857, and my *Komm. zu V. Mos.* XVI., and Keil's *Archäol.* I., S. 412 sqq.); corresponding with this, the booths now gained of themselves a reference, on the one side, to the exhibition of grace during the new prolonged wilderness-time of the exile, which had entered with so much gloom into the midst of the history of Israel; so to speak to the booths of protection and defiance which had arisen for the people by the grace of the Lord even in the heathen world, and on the other side to the new regaining of Canaan, which, to a certain extent, was a security and a pledge of all the further blessings in store for them in this land. They expressed the thanks which they owed to the Lord for both of these blessings in an especially lively and internal manner. This feast of tabernacles was a festal and joyous conclusion of all the preservations, consolations and blessings that were behind them, connected with a joyous glance into the future; it was an evidence that a height had been reached upon which finally even the last height might be attained, an indication that some day, after all their struggles and all their labors, a still more glorious feast of tabernacles, the Messianic, the eternal and truly blessed one, would come. Comp. Zech. xiv.

Vers. 6, 7. The celebration of the feast of tabernacles was followed by the preparation for building the temple in an especially appropriate and beautiful manner. If the Lord had provided His congregation with booths of preservation, of consolation, and of joy, not only now in Canaan, but even also in the times of the wilderness of the exile, how ought they now to have felt impelled from the heart to build Him a tabernacle also, in which His honor might dwell, a tabernacle of God with men, at least with and among His people! The communion with the Lord, which they had already enjoyed, would have been no true one, if it had not been connected with the desire that it should become strengthened and made more intimate, and if this desire had not now engaged in building the temple. That is the great end of all providential guidances, that communion between Himself and men, as it was prepared on His part by His condescension, should become established and enlivened more and more also on the part of men; for the most part naturally through the communion of the heart with Him, but also in order that it might be cherished in the heart, by the establishment, enlargement and completion of the external means and institutions which have been provided by God Himself for the purpose. The blessings and gifts with which He has blessed us should always be employed first and chiefly for this purpose. And how greatly are we shamed in this respect by this weak congregation of returned exiles, who were scarcely able to sow and reap, and who yet had so much left for the building of the temple.

Ver. 7. It was significant also that at this building of the temple again it was not Canaan proper, but the Phœnician Lebanon, that provided the building-material and that corresponding with this heathen workmen and artists also took part in erecting the house of God. It indicates that the rest of the earth also, and corresponding thereto, the rest of mankind, are to render their gifts and capacities, which are more and more to take part in the complete and true worship of the Lord, that the Lord by no means regards them as profane. The rest of the earth and mankind became thereby, to a certain extent, consecrated in advance and designated as one who, if now already in the Old Testament economy, yet still more some day in the fulness of time, would take part in the highest destiny of Israel. Comp. the beautiful remarks of Bähr on 1 Kings v.

Vers. 8, 9. It was not a single head, as once with Solomon, from whom now the building of the temple proceeded; with Zerubbabel and Jeshua, at the same time all the returned exiles equally took part, as it is expressly said. That the entire congregation should take part freely in the highest work of humanity is the great object in view in all the divine providential guidances. Connected with this, however, the congregation gave a Levitical family the charge of conducting the work of building, accordingly in their choice of officers fell in with the regulations made and sanctified by God already long before, and thus certainly took the best action, since indeed in the tribe of Levi the interest in the house of God was still cherished in the most lively manner, and the understanding of what was necessary or appropriate was most surely preserved. That is always the most salutary and beautiful when the free recognition or choice on the part of the congregation and the arrangements objectively present on the part of God harmoniously combine.

Vers. 12, 13. With respect to the expressions of joy and sorrow at the laying of the foundation of the temple, every step by which we attempt to draw near to our highest end, the confirmation of our communion with God, should become a joyous feast. For the nearer we approach this end, the more there comes into view not only the true reverence of the Lord, but also the fulness of redemption and life, of righteousness, of peace, and of joy, involved therein. The farther off we remain therefrom, the more do unrighteousness, discord and mischief threaten to prevail. In fact nothing is so well calculated to exalt the hearts of the children of God from within outward, to fill them with sacred joy and attune them to festivity, as the coming of the kingdom of God. Ewald properly conjectures that at the time of the laying of the foundation (we must understand the times of the building of the temple and those that immediately followed as included therein), many a grand song resounded afresh, as the 118th Psalm, a song of festivity and sacrifice expressing the feelings of that period with such wonderful depth; and that they soon, as they again made pilgrimages to the ancient seat of true religion and the Davidic sovereignty, as well as the sanctuary itself (so Psalm lxxxvii.), as also on the joyous pilgrim-march, sang a rich abundance of new songs of great power and enchanting inwardness, such as had hardly arisen since the time of David in such streaming fullness and creative life (so Ps. cxx.–cxxxiv.). Comp. Ewald, *Gesch.* IV., S. 131, 133. In the profound 116th Psalm: "I love the Lord because he hath heard my voice and my supplications," the voice of joy mingled with sorrow, then so general, has found an appropriate and particular expression, which is so beautiful, that the pious king Fred. William IV. of Prussia, in his last severe affliction, chose it for his prayer. In the cxiii. Psalm, however, "Praise, O ye servants of the Lord, praise the name of the Lord —the Lord is high above all nations, and His glory above the heavens," there is combined, in the same characteristic manner, the thought of the lowliness and poverty that they then so severely felt, and the praise for the exaltation which had now taken place. Especially, however, Psalm cvii. belongs here with its remembrance of all the different afflictions and dangers through which they had passed with God's help and with its constantly recurring refrain: "O that men would praise the Lord for His goodness, and for His wonderful works to the children of men;" and probably also Psalm cvi., with its prayer that the Lord would still further gather them from among the heathen and redeem them from trouble. If we still so often, on our part, have a lack of joy and suffer from depression of spirits, and if even in better hours a pressure remains upon the soul, of which we are at times scarcely clearly conscious, then even this sadness may redound to the glory of God, that is, be a divine sorrow, which has its ground in the fact that we cannot serve God as we would wish, and as would be really worthy of Him. Under such circumstances we should not lack beams of hope, or rather of promise, that would be able to transfigure them.

HOMILETICAL AND PRACTICAL.

Vers. 1–6. The feast of the redeemed: 1) They present their offerings to God; *a*) for the redemption for which they are thankful to the Lord, and for which they owe all to Him; *b*) notwithstanding the hostility of the world, which indeed grieves them and hinders them in many ways externally, but cannot hold them back from that which is essential; *c*) they consecrate themselves by a daily dedication of themselves. 2) They celebrate especially a feast of tabernacles; *a*) as preserved in the desert of the world and delivered therefrom; *b*) as richly blessed in the land of the Lord; *c*) as called to the eternal tabernacles of joy. 3) They advance the building of the house and kingdom of God; *a*) they consecrate for this purpose their possessions and gifts; *b*) they seek therefore also to add thereto that which is suitable in the world—all (1, 2 and 3) on the ground of and according to the prescriptions of the word of God.—Brentius: *Nobis quotidie hoc festum celebrandum est, quod tum celebratur, dum docemus et sentimus, nos esse peregrinos in hoc mundo et in tabernaculis corporis nostri brevi durantibus, nostrum politeuma esse in cœlo.* Starke: How lovely and necessary is brotherly love among the children of God! Especially in the building of the spiritual temple under Christ should there be one heart and one soul, and each one should stand as all and all as one man, Acts ii. 44; iv. 32; Ps. cxxxiii. 2. If we would again properly reform and re-establish the worship of God, God's word must be the law, rule, lamp, and guiding star, Ps. xix. 5; xxiii. 4; cxix. 105. Although believers have the commandment and promise of God before them, yet the human heart is often so weak that it is easily frightened; but we should here be at the same time blind and dumb, and not look to the present state of affairs, but rely upon God's word alone, Prov. xviii. 10.

Vers. 6–10. How the house (kingdom) of God is built: 1) by the offerings of men; *a*) by the possessions and gifts of the congregation; *b*) by appropriating and using that which is useful in the world; *c*) under the protection of the civil authorities ("according to the permission of Cyrus"). 2) By the activity not only of the heads but also of the other members. The heads have their work to do as leaders, but the rest have freely to co-operate, they have to assist those who according to the divine arrangement have the charge of affairs, encourage them and strengthen them. 3) By the faithfulness of officers to their duties. God has ordained officers for the sake of order. There is not only the office of priests, but also that of their helpers, the teachers, and especially also fathers and mothers. —Starke: God distributes His gifts in many ways; to one He gives talents for one work, to another for another, 1 Cor. xii. 7 sq. The spiritual temple should also be urged on in all ranks of society with all energy, in order that the people may be built up into an holy temple in the Lord, Ez. ii. 22. Preachers and magistrates, instructors also, and parents, thus build a temple when they properly teach and preach, preserve discipline and honesty, and bring up the youth to piety.

Vers. 11–13. The joy of the congregation of the Lord: 1) *Its ground*—the laying of the foundation of the house of God; God on His part would have a dwelling among men, for this He has accomcomplished the work of redemption, especially the incarnation, the atonement, and the establishment of the Church; the congregation on their part constitute ever some part of the beginning of the house of God. 2) *Its kind*—it is a festive joy, and expresses itself accordingly in music and songs in praise of the Lord, but is still saddened, because the house of God still continues to lack the true glory. 3) *Its significance*,—its incompleteness of itself, points to its fulfilment.—STARKE: Christ is the true foundation and corner-stone of His church (Ps. cxviii. 22; Isa. xxviii. 16; 1 Cor. iii. 11), in whom we highly rejoice, and on whose account we have to praise God. Experience of previous times often gives an impulse to correct judgment; sometimes however unbelief derives an evil example and support therefrom. The inward joy of the Spirit should suppress all temporal sorrows, so that we should not hear the weeping for the joy.

[SCOTT: The greater difficulties and the more formidable enemies we are exposed to, the more we need the friendship and assistance of God.—In this world joys and sorrows will be blended, for it is a mixed state; hereafter there will be a complete separation.—HENRY: Let worldly business be postponed to the business of religion and it will prosper the better.—They that do not work themselves may yet do good service by quickening and encouraging those that do work.—TR.]

B.—THE INTERRUPTION AND AN ORIGINAL DOCUMENT RESPECTING THE MACHINATIONS OF THE ENEMIES.

CHAPTER IV. 1–24.

I. *The Interruption of the Building of the Temple.* Vers. 1–5.

1 Now when the adversaries of Judah and Benjamin heard that the children of
2 the captivity builded the temple unto the LORD God of Israel; Then they came to
Zerubbabel, and to the chief of the fathers, and said unto them, Let us build with
you: for we seek your God, as ye *do;* and we do sacrifice unto him since the days
3 of Esar-haddon king of Assur, which brought us up hither. But Zerubbabel, and
Jeshua, and the rest of the chief of the fathers of Israel, said unto them, Ye have
nothing to do with us to build a house unto our God; but we ourselves together
will build unto the LORD God of Israel, as king Cyrus the king of Persia hath com-
4 manded us. Then the people of the land weakened the hands of the people of Ju-
5 dah, and troubled them in building, And hired counsellors against them, to frus-
trate their purpose, all the days of Cyrus king of Persia, even until the reign of
Darius king of Persia.

II. *An Original Document respecting the Hostile Machinations.* Vers. 6–24.

6 And in the reign of Ahasuerus, in the beginning of his reign, wrote they *unto him*
7 an accusation against the inhabitants of Judah and Jerusalem. And in the days
of Artaxerxes wrote Bishlam, Mithredath, Tabeel, and the rest of their companions,
unto Artaxerxes king of Persia; and the writing of the letter *was* written in the
8 Syrian tongue, and interpreted in the Syrian tongue. Rehum the chancellor and
Shimshai the scribe wrote a letter against Jerusalem to Artaxerxes the king in this
9 sort: Then *wrote* Rehum the chancellor, and Shimshai the scribe, and the rest of
their companions; the Dinaites, the Apharsathchites, the Tarpelites, the Aphar-
sites, the Archevites, the Babylonians, the Susanchites, the Dehavites, *and* the
10 Elamites, And the rest of the nations whom the great and noble Asnapper brought
over, and set in the cities of Samaria, and the rest *that are* on this side the river,
11 and at such a time. This *is* the copy of the letter that they sent unto him, *even*
unto Artaxerxes the king; Thy servants the men on this side the river, and at such
12 a time. Be it known unto the king, that the Jews which came up from thee to us
are come unto Jerusalem, building the rebellious and the bad city, and have set up

13 the walls *thereof*, and joined the foundations. Be it known now unto the king, that
if this city be builded, and the walls set up *again*, then will they not pay toll,
14 tribute, and custom, and *so* thou shalt endamage the revenue of the kings. Now
because we have maintenance from *the king's* palace, and it was not meet for us to
15 see the king's dishonour, therefore have we sent and certified the king; That search
may be made in the book of the records of thy fathers: so shalt thou find in the
book of the records, and know that this city *is* a rebellious city, and hurtful unto
kings and provinces, and that they have moved sedition within the same of old
16 time: for which cause was this city destroyed. We certify the king that, if this
city be builded *again*, and the walls thereof set up, by this means thou shalt have
17 no portion on this side the river. *Then* sent the king an answer unto Rehum the
chancellor, and *to* Shimshai the scribe, and *to* the rest of their companions that
dwell in Samaria, and *unto* the rest beyond the river, Peace, and at such a time.
18, 19 The letter which ye sent unto us hath been plainly read before me. And I
commanded, and search hath been made, and it is found that this city of old time
hath made insurrection against kings, and *that* rebellion and sedition have been
20 made therein. There have been mighty kings also over Jerusalem, which have
ruled over all *countries* beyond the river; and toll, tribute, and custom was paid
21 unto them. Give ye now commandment to cause these men to cease, and that this
22 city be not builded, until *another* commandment shall be given from me. Take
heed now that ye fail not to do this: why should damage grow to the hurt of the
23 kings? Now when the copy of king Artaxerxes' letter *was* read before Rehum,
and Shimshai the scribe, and their companions, they went up in haste to Jerusalem
24 unto the Jews, and made them to cease by force and power. Then ceased the work
of the house of God which *is* at Jerusalem. So it ceased unto the second year of
the reign of Darius king of Persia.

EXEGETICAL AND CRITICAL.

Vers. 1–5. *The interruption.* Vers. 1–3 first give its occasion. When the enemies of Judah and Benjamin heard of the undertaking in Jerusalem, they wished to unite with them in building. They are called **the adversaries**, not of the children of the captivity, but of **Judah and Benjamin**, because their opposition and hostility had arisen already in pre-exile times, and indeed against the southern kingdom, which was then most suitably called that of Judah and Benjamin. בְּנֵי הַגּוֹלָה—children or members of the captivity, is the name given to the returned exiles in chap. vi. 19 sq.; viii. 35; x. 7, 16, *etc.*; so also briefly הַגּוֹלָה—*e. g.*, chap. i. 11. In order to establish their claim they maintain: **We seek your God as ye** (do).—דָּרַשׁ with לְ or אֶל, also with the simple accusative, is the constant expression for our somewhat colorless expression worship God; properly it is to turn to God with petition or questions, or with desires in general, to apply to Him.—**And sacrifice unto him since the days of Esarhaddon,** *etc.*—The *Kethib:* "we do not offer" cannot well mean: we do not offer to other gods, for then it would be necessary to mention expressly these other gods. If it were original to the text it might perhaps simply have the sense we did not offer at all, not even to Jehovah, since we well knew that Jehovah would accept offering only at the one legitimate place of worship at Jerusalem. Then it would involve the meaning that they would gladly sacrifice to Jehovah, and on this very account desired to take part in building the temple at Jerusalem. But this view is opposed by the fact that they then would without doubt have too openly and boldly gone in the face of all truth, since they certainly had very many altars and sacrificed often enough. Moreover the emphatic position of אֲנַחְנוּ does not accord with this view; besides, in such a case we would expect the perf. זָבַחְנוּ instead of the part. זֹבְחִים. It is very probable that לֹא here, as in fifteen other passages (comp. *e. g.* Ex. xxi. 8; 1 Sam. ii. 3; 2 Sam. xvi. 18; 2 Kings viii. 10) is for לוֹ, in consequence of a mistake, or of design, in that they would state that their sacrifices did not properly deserve the name of sacrifices, as then לוֹ likewise is found in Qeri, and is read by Esdras (αὐτῷ), by Sept., Syriac, and also indeed by the Vulg., which at least does not have the negative. Since the speakers designate themselves as those whom Esar-haddon had brought into their present abode (comp. Bähr on 2 Kings xiv. 37), we have to identify them beyond question with those colonists referred to in 2 Kings xvii., with the Samaritans so-called, whom the king of Assyria, 2 Kings xvii. 24, had brought up out of Babylon, Cutha, and other eastern countries, into the cities of Samaria. These colonists, when they first settled in Canaan, it is true, did not fear Jehovah; it was not till a considerable later period that they asked for an Israelite priest out of Assyria, in order to be instructed by him in the worship of Jehovah; but the words: since the days when Esar-haddon brought us up, are either a somewhat inexact statement, or are to be explained from their efforts to date their worship of Jehovah as far back as possible. Knobel (*Zur Geschichte der Samaritaner, Denkschr. der Gesellsch. für Wissensch. und Kunst in Giessen*, I. 1, S. 147 sqq.), on account of these words, improperly holds them for those who had emigrated from Assyria with the Israelite priests. It is clear from our passage that the colonization spoken of in 2 Kings xvii., if it perhaps had already begun under Sargon and Sennacherib, yet chiefly took place under Esar-haddon. With this agree the cuneiform inscriptions, in accordance with which Esar-haddon had despoiled, not expressly, it is true, the land of the ten tribes, but yet Syria and Phœnicia of their ancient inhabitants, and provided them with new ones, comp. Schrader, *l. c.*, upon our passage.* The occasion of this request of the Samaritans, was the correct recognition of the fact that those who should have the temple at Jerusalem, would be regarded as the leading nation, whilst those who should be excluded from this central point of the worship of the land would appear as less authorized, as intrusive; they likewise no doubt expected, if they were admitted to participation in the building of the temple, as well as to consultation with reference to it, to gain thereby influence in shaping the affairs of the congregation in general. If in addition to this they had also a religious interest in the matter, it was only in order to secure for themselves the favor of the God of the land, whom they recognised as Jehovah, and then therewith also the same possessions and blessings in their new home as the Jews designed for themselves. We cannot regard them as actuated by any higher and purer motive,—for their entire subsequent behaviour, which makes them appear as quite indifferent to religious affairs, and also that which we elsewhere learn of their religion, is opposed to that view. That which is said in 2 Kings xvii. on this subject cannot be understood (as Bähr on that chap.) as stating that they only in part retained their heathen gods, that many had already worshipped Jehovah only, that these latter had worshipped Him, if indeed in the form of a bull, yet, as the only God. There is no distinction between the different classes; for ver. 33 is not, as Bähr translates, "there were *also* worshippers of Jehovah,"—but it is said of all; they feared Jehovah, and served their own gods, and of all it is then likewise said in ver. 34: "they feared not Jehovah;" they prayed to Jehovah only as one of many, only as a limited being, only as an idol, not as the only true God. It is true the question then arises whether this syncretistic stand-point that in no respect can be regarded as even an approximative worship of Jehovah, that in truth was only ordinary heathenism, was still maintained by them in the times subsequent to the exile, whether they had not made an advance in religion beyond it. The question is, how the remnant of the ten tribes, who had maintained themselves in their habitations in the midst of the colonists, especially according to Jer. xli. 4 sq.; and 2 Chron. xxxiv. 9, 10 (comp. Bähr on 2 Kings xvii., S. 401, and Nägelsbach on Jer. xli. 4 sq.), acted both with reference to these colonists in general, and to the claim here made by them. But if the long prevailing opinion were correct that the Samaritans for the most part consisted of the Israelites who remained in the land at the exile, so that they might be regarded as an actual continuation of the people of the ten tribes, and the heathen elements among them had become more and more conformed to the Israelites, we cannot conceive why they did not maintain already now this their external and internal connection with Israel as well as on later occasions when it suited them so to do. That would have been the strongest reason that could have influenced the Jews to admit their claim. For great and respected predecessors, as Hezekiah, 2 Chron. xxx.; and Josiah, 2 Chron. xxxiv. 56, had expressly occupied themselves in attracting the remnants of Israel to the worship of Jehovah at Jerusalem. At first the remnant may have kept themselves concealed from the new comers and the masters of the land, by contenting themselves with the more distant regions and lurking-places of the mountains. They certainly constituted merely despised and scattered bands, which neither sought nor offered any communication, whom therefore the colonists could not trust. Otherwise they would not have had a priest sent to them from Assyria, when they wished to worship Jehovah as the god of the land, comp. 2 Kings xvii. 2. Very soon, it is true, many of them approached the colonists, and mixed with them by marriage; but instead of exerting any influence in shaping them, they rather subordinated themselves—of themselves having quite a strong inclination to heathenism—to the colonists as the more powerful and more favored on the part of the government and united with them in their manners and customs, and also in their religion, so that they more and more disappeared among them. This is very clear partly from the way in which the Samaritans here speak of themselves, partly from their subsequent actions, in that they in contrast to the Jews still preferred to be the representatives of the royal prerogatives of Persia, and designate themselves after their Assyrian places of origin (comp. ver. 7 sq.), but give not the slightest hint of a connection with the ancient Israelites, or of having been in any way modified by them.* Therefore it is improbable that they should have been influenced by these latter in making their claim upon the new congregation, as Berth. and after him Keil supposes. If they subsequently more and more decidedly went over to monotheism and the observa-

* [Also Smith, *the Assyrian Canon*, p. 138, and Rawlinson *in loco*, who says: "There appear to have been at least three colonizations of Samaria by the Assyrian kings. Sargon, soon after his conquest, replaced the captives whom he had carried off by colonists from Babylonia and from Hamath (2 Kings xvii. 24). Later in his reign he added to these first settlers an Arabian element (*Ancient Monarchies*, II., p. 415). Some thirty or forty years afterwards, Esar-haddon, his grandson, largely augmented the population of colonists drawn from various parts of the empire, but especially from the southeast, Susiana, Elymais, and Persia. Thus the later Samaritans were an exceedingly mixed race."—Tr.]

* It was not until very late that their historians invented a return of three hundred thousand men from the Assyrian banishment, and a new establishment of ancient Israel in the midst of the land by this great band, and especially on Mt. Gerizim. (Comp. Abulfatah's *Arab. Chronik.* in Paulus' *Memorabilien*, II., S. 54-100, and in the Samaritan book of Joshua, published at Leyden, in 1848. *Vid.* Ewald IV., S. 125.)

tion of the Mosaic law, they were moved thereto, not by the remnants of Israel, which had blended with them, but by the Jews themselves. They would not remain behind the new congregation in Jerusalem, for they could not conceal from themselves on reflection that the stand-point of the religion of Jehovah, as it was represented in Jerusalem, was higher than their own. And it was for this reason that they then accepted the first Manasseh, and under his direction built the temple on Gerizim, by which circumstance the transformation was as a matter of course still further favored. Besides this there was the entire tendency of those times that was decidedly towards a higher and more spiritual worship of God. Moreover, in addition to such fragments of Israel as were lost among the Samaritans, others still were left in the land who sought to preserve their independence. It is probable that these, who were of themselves more devoted to the religion of Jehovah, let themselves be directed by the judgments that passed over their kingdom, and the contrast that was exhibited between themselves and the colonists, still more decidedly to Jerusalem and the worship there conducted. In favor of this view is the fact that some of them already in the time of Josiah contributed to the restoration of the temple in Jerusalem (2 Chron. xxxiv. 9, 10), and that still after the destruction of the temple eighty men of Shechem, Shiloh, and Samaria came in mourning to bring their gifts to the place where up to this time they had worshipped, Jer. xli. 5, 6. In accordance with some other evidence, there were still at the time such better elements in the northern region of the land. Among those who had separated themselves from the impurities of the nations to unite with the returned exiles in seeking Jehovah (ch. vi. 21) belonged probably at least remnants of Israel as well as of Judah. And this sheds light upon the obscure question, how we are to account for the origin of the Jewish population in Galilee. Bertheau properly remarks with reference to such better elements: "They are the ancestors of a great part of the Jews whom we meet in subsequent times in northern Palestine." There in northern Palestine they had not been dislodged by the colonists, who occupied the cities of Samaria. There, as to their old ancestral abodes, and to their kindred, must those return who now and subsequently gradually returned from any of the ten tribes. It is possible, indeed, that this better remnant of the northern kingdom soon still more decidedly than the Samaritans directed their attention to the temple at Jerusalem. But perhaps they had not yet concluded what relation they should assume to the congregation at Jerusalem; we may suppose that it was in consequence of the impulse that went forth from Jerusalem for them certainly much more than for the Samaritans, that they reflected more deeply upon themselves, and finally attached themselves to the worship at Jerusalem.

Ver. 3. The Jews refused the Samaritans. The sing. ויאמר is used not only because the number of the verb is freer when it precedes the subject, but because Zerubbabel was the chief person who gave the answer; *e. g.* Zerubbabel spake in agreement with Jeshua, *etc.* Jeshua and the heads of the fathers of Israel had united in the answer. ישראל is used with לְ, and accordingly is not the *stat. abs.* of the foregoing האבות, for otherwise this would not have the article, according to the usual combination with ראשי.—**Ye have nothing to do with us to build**, that is, it is not for you and us in common; comp. the expression "what is to me and thee," namely, in common, Jos. xx. 24; Judges xi. 12; 2 Kings iii. 13. In that they say: **house**—not unto God, as chap. i. 4, but **unto our God**, they mean that Jehovah belongs to them more than to the Samaritans, yea, to them alone.—**But we ourselves together**=we as a compact unity, excluding others. They might appeal to the decree of Cyrus in this refusal, since if they were obliged to admit the Samaritans, they would not have gained, according to their feelings and knowledge, that which they had the right to expect from it, namely, an undisturbed worship of Jehovah in all its truth, free from all dangers. It is true it could not escape the congregation, that it was a very serious matter to make those their enemies who had probably connections, consideration and influence at the seat of government, and who naturally regarded themselves as the outposts and guardians of the sovereignty of Persia in Canaan. But nevertheless the dangers to which they would have exposed themselves by a union with these Samaritans who appeared so objectionable, especially in a religious point of view, would have been far greater, and they should not be charged with too great anxiety, or one that cannot be entirely approved (against Ewald, *Gesch.* IV., S. 125, 135). Those who gradually imitated them when they kept themselves pure from their mixed religion, and through them were impelled to a monotheistic development, would, if they had gained an influence and rightful position in Jerusalem from the beginning, have involved them in their heathen doubt and obscurity. Their renunciation of the external advantages which were set before them by the proffered alliance was the result, on the one side, of a correct appreciation of that which they must regard as of the most importance, and on the other side of a candid and humble recognition of their weakness. As a matter of course they were obliged to take an entirely different course with reference to the remnants of the northern kingdom, when these in another way began to seek Jehovah again in sincerity, and on this account desired to be admitted into Jerusalem. That they did not fail in this particular we see in the circumstance that the Galilean ever had an undisputed admission.

Vers. 4, 5. The consequence of this refusal was the interruption of the building of the temple. The Samaritans are called the people of the land in ver. 4 because they, at least until this time had been the proper inhabitants of the land, and at all events constituted the chief part of the population. As such they were strong enough to slacken the hands of the people of Judah, that is, the people now inhabiting Judah.

יְהוּדָה, already in pre-exile times the name of the southern kingdom is used here also as the name of the country (comp. ver. 6). הָיָה with the part. (slackening and affrighting) expresses the continuance of the action; the second participle is explanatory of the first, מְבַלְהִים לִבְנוֹת, affrighting with reference to building=from building. The *Kethib* מְבַלְהִים is sufficiently established by the noun בַּלָּהָה (Isa. xvii. 14) and by the Syriac; the *Qeri*, מְבַהֲלִים, prefers the usual form בַּהֵל.—Without doubt they threatened the Jews with violence, and with punishment on the part of the government, as soon as they had frustrated the edict of Cyrus.—**They hired counsellors against them**—for a cancelling of the edict according to ver. 5, in that they were able to influence probably the ministers to whom chap. vii. 28 and viii. 25 refer, or other influential persons, to give advice to Cyrus unfavorable to the Jews. At court they naturally did not understand how it could be that those who were as much the inhabitants of the land as the returned exiles, and therefore seemed entitled to the God of the land, should be excluded. If Cyrus had seen in Jehovah his own supreme God, it must have been all the more annoying to him that those who apparently had the best intentions of worshipping Him, should be rejected. It would seem as if the reason why the Jews opposed the union could only be a national and political one, and the suspicion was quite natural, that they already designed to form not merely a religious community, but also had national and political designs, that they thus gave an entirely false interpretation to the decree of Cyrus. The part. סֹכְרִים is in continuation of the part. of the previous verse; סָכַר is a later form of שָׂכַר. The time during which they succeeded in frustrating the purposes of the Jews, (for which הָפֵר is to a certain extext the *term. techn.*), consisted of about fourteen years—from about the third year of Cyrus in Babylon (comp. Dan. x. 2 sq.) until the second of Darius, comp. Hag. i. 1.

Vers. 6–22 contains the original document respecting the hostile efforts of the Samaritans. The author adds what the Samaritans did and accomplished in the time of Ahasuerus and Artaxerxes, and the question arises first of all, what kings were meant under these names?* Most ancient and modern interpreters, (comp. J. H. Michaelis, *in loco.*) had supposed that the author from ver. 6 onward would explain why the building of the temple was discontinued for so long a time, as stated in ver. 5, that he then entered into the period between Cyrus and Darius. They were led to this opinion by ver. 24, which leads over to Darius, and what happened under him, in such a manner that it seems certainly, at first, as if the kings mentioned here in vers. 6 and 7 had ruled before him. Luther, from this point of view, united this 6th verse by "for" to the previous verse, instead of by the conjunction "and," and some, as Hartmann in the *Chron. bibl.*, have appealed to this "for" as if it stood in the original text. Ahasuerus must, accordingly, have been Cambyses, Artaxerxes, Pseudo-Smerdis (so still Ewald, *Gesch.* IV., S. 137, and Köhler in *Komm. zu. den. nachexil. Proph.**). But the strongest objections at once arise against this view. How is it that these two kings should have names given them that they bear no where else? How can we suppose that whilst all other Assyrian, Chaldean, and Persian kings bear essentially the same names among the Israelites with which they elsewhere appear, these two kings on one occasion should have had entirely different names among the Jews from those among their own people; for among the Persians Cambyses, so far as we know, only bore the name of Cambyses (old Persian *Kambudschja*), Smerdis however, after whom the Ps. Smerdis named himself, had only that of Tanyoxares or Tanyoxarkes (*Cyrop.* VIII. 7, and Ctesias, *Pers. fr.* 8–13), or also Orapastes (Justin. *Hist.* I. 9), which name cannot be identified with אַרְתַּחְשַׁשְׂתָּא. This supposition is still less admissible, in that both these names every where else in the Old Test. designate other kings, and the same as those who had the corresponding names among the Persians. Ahasuerus, in the book of Esther, as is now generally recognized, is Xerxes; in Dan. ix. 1, the Median king Cyaxares. These two Greek terms, Xerxes and Cyaxares, may be readily derived from the Persian fundamental forms of these names, which we find in the cuneiform inscriptions, *Khsay* or *Khsay-arsa*, by modification of vowels. So also the Hebrew term אחשורוש. However ארתחשסתא is in Ezra vii. and viii. and so also in the book of Nehemiah, without question, Artaxerxes (Machrochir). It is true that it is there written ארתחשסתא (with שס), in our passage, however, תרתחששתא (with שש); but a different person cannot be inferred from this difference in writing. This is clear from vi. 14, where the name is written as it is here, and yet must be referred to a Persian king ruling subsequently to Darius—certainly, therefore, to Artaxerxes Machrochir. In connection with these names that are used in our section, some other marks beside which point beyond Darius, gain importance. If the sixth verse really came as is supposed to speak explanatory of the previous interval of time, it would at least have been more natural to connect with the conjunct. "for," as indeed Luther, without reason, has supplied it, rather than by "and." At the outset it is improbable that Pseudo-Smerdis should have had time during his brief reign (only seven months) to reply to his officers in the manner narrated in vers. 7–23; namely, after an accurate investigation with reference to the previous conduct of the Jews. In the letter of the Samaritans, or rather of the Persian officers among them, to the king, it no longer has to do with the building

* Kleinert already in the *Beitragen der Dorp. Professoren Theol.*, 1832, Bd. 1, had to a certain extent pointed to the correct opinion, which has been commonly recognized, as in my article "*Cyrus der Grosse*" *Stud. u. Krit.* 1853, S. 624 sqq.; by Baihinger. *Stud. u. Krit.* 1857, S. 87 sqq.; by Hengst., *Christologie* II., S. 143; by Berth. and Keil in their Commentaries, *et al.*.

* [So also Rawlinson *in loco*, who refers to the "well-known fact of history," that Persian kings had often two names.—Tr.]

of the temple, but only with that of the city and its walls, which is all the more remarkable, as in the letter to Darius in chap. v. 6 sq. the temple throughout is in the foreground. Furthermore Bertheau properly reminds us in notes on ver. 4 that if the transaction with these kings had already previously transpired, the question of the Persian officers in the time of Darius, who had given the Jews commandment to build the house of God, would not have been very appropriate. Moreover the Jews would have spoken of the steps of the Samaritans and the prohibition of ארתחשׁשתא when it must have been obligatory upon them to explain to the Persian officers in chap. v. 16 why the building already begun under Cyrus had not been completed. By all these circumstances we are compelled to understand by אחשׁורושׁ really Xerxes, and by ארתחשׁשתא really Artaxerxes, and to refer our section accordingly to the period subsequent to Darius. If it is objected to this view that the answer of ארתחשׁשתא does not accord with the sending of Ezra under Artaxerxes in chap. vii.; so far as the one was unfavorable to the Jews and the other favorable, the fact is overlooked that in his answer (ver. 21) the king expressly reserves another command, which possibly would ordain the building of the city and its walls. When, however, Ewald (*Gesch.* IV. S. 138) asserts that in the time of Artaxerxes no intelligent person could any longer speak thus of the building of the city and its walls, as is the case in the letter of the Samaritans, the book of Nehemiah shows how very necessary it still was that the city should be built up, and the walls re-established even after Ezra. That which really appears to be against the view here advocated, is the manner in which ver. 24 passes over from this king to Darius. By the use of one and the same verb in ver. 21 (give ye now commandment to *cause* these men to *cease*), in ver. 23 (they went up to Jerusalem and *made them cease*) and in ver. 24 (then *ceased* the work) and apparently also by the use of בֵּאדַיִן at the beginning of ver. 24, the twenty-fourth verse is so closely united to the previous context, that it in fact seems to contain the result of that which immediately precedes. Hence then Herzfeld also (*Gesch. Israels* I., S. 303) and Schrader (*Stud. u. Krit.*, 1867, S. 469) have supposed that our section, if it indeed originally extended to the time of Xerxes and Artaxerxes, must be referred by the author of our book, notwithstanding all, to Cambyses and Pseudo Smerdis, who placed it here under an error. But no real necessity for such a doubtful supposition can be found. The verb בטל might be written by the author again, in ver. 24, after that he had used it in vers. 21–23, notwithstanding he was here treating of a previous time. The temporal particle בֵּאדַיִן, moreover, which in itself has the indefinite meaning of "*illo tempore*" can just as well refer to the beginning as to the middle or the end of the time spoken of before. If the twenty-fourth verse had been placed at the beginning of the fifth chapter instead of at the end of the fourth chapter, it would apparently occasion us no difficulty at all in giving it its proper reference. Should it be objected that such an anticipation of later events as the view here advocated involves in vers. 6–23, is in itself improbable, this objection is removed to a certain extent by chap. vi. 14, from which it results that our author was readily inclined to connect together in the closest way Artaxerxes and his time with Darius and the previous times. In this passage, where the elders of Judah in the time of Darius are spoken of, and where it is said of them, they built and completed in consequence of the prophecies of Haggai and Zechariah, and on the commandment of the God of Israel, and on the commandment of Cyrus and Darius, the additional clause "and Artaxerxes" is still more singular than in our passage. As the author there would embrace all who had afforded the congregation justice, protection, and help up to the time of Ezra, so here he might have very well had the intention of at once putting together summarily all the interruptions that were occasioned by the Samaritans. In as much as here the narrative was of their operations, it was really the best place for this purpose. Besides, another reason probably co-operated. The author probably had at his command no other document respecting the machinations of the Samaritans and their success at the court of Persia than this one of the time of Artaxerxes. Since now, as we have shown in the introduction, it was his method to accompany everything as far as possible with original documents, since moreover besides it was of the highest importance to justify by such a document the behaviour of the Jewish congregation towards the Samaritans, which had such great, severe, and long-lasting consequences, he here inserted it, after that he had made the transition through ver. 6 to the latter period, since the disposition of the Samaritans in the somewhat later period here meeting us, was, to a certain extent, an evidence likewise of their previous hostility; and the disturbing interference which they occasioned according to the letter of Artaxerxes, was only the continuation of previous interruptions.

Ver. 6. **And in the reign of Ahasuerus in the beginning of his reign, wrote they an accusation,** *etc.*—This shows the zeal of the Samaritans; at once and at the very outset they sought to prejudice this king against the Jews. If the time of Darius, which had been favorable to the Jews, during which the Samaritans had impatiently waited for a change of affairs, had passed, this zeal can the more readily be explained. שִׂטְנָה, hostility (comp. Gen. xxvi. 21) has here the special meaning of accusation, just as שָׂטָן readily gains the special meaning of accuser. Since the author does not enter into particulars with reference to this writing of accusation, or even say whether it had any results at all, it seems here to be mentioned only in order briefly to show that the Samaritans, even in the subsequent period, were still active, and in order thus to give a transition to the following narrative as the principal thing.

Ver. 7. **And in the days of Artaxerxes wrote Bishlam,** *etc.*—The Jewish congregation probably increased from the time of the building of the temple onward, and under Artaxerxes thought more seriously of re-establishing the walls of the city, which then likewise through

Nehemiah actually took place. Bislam, Mithredath, Tabeel, *etc.*, accordingly went to work anew against them. These names certainly indicate Samaritans who, without being Persian officials, enjoyed just as Sanballat subsequently, a certain degree of consequence. The pure Persian name Mithredath need not astonish us, since even Zerubbabel had a similar one (Sheshbazzar). We should expect instead of כְּנָוָתֵהּ, for which the qeri has the usual form כְּנָוָתֵיהּ, in accordance with vers. 9, 17, 23; chap. v. 3, *etc.*, כְּנָוָתְהוֹן. To whom the sing. suffix properly refers, whether to the first named Bislam or to the last named Tabeel is doubtful, is yet without any real importance. כְּנָת, from which our plural is to be derived (comp. Ewald, § 187 *d*) is contracted from כְּנָוַת as פֹּרָת, Gen. xlix. 22 from פֹּרִיַּת and אָחוֹת for אָחָת from אֲחָיַת or אֲחָוַת (comp. Olsh. § 198 *c*). It is not found elsewhere in Hebrew, and was here without doubt chosen simply with reference to ver. 9; in Aramaic it is more frequent. Formed from כָּנָה it designates those *qui eodem cognomine, sive titulo utitur, sive eodem munere fungitur*, according to Gesen., *Thes.;* in the Peschito it is more frequently employed for *σύνδουλος*.—**And the rest of their companions.**—This is according to ver. 9 sq.: the others who were their companions.—**And the writing of the letter was written in Aramaic.**—כְּתָב is no more here than in Esther iv. 8, to be taken in the improved meaning of copy, (against Berth.) as if the author would say, that only the copy was in Chaldee, but the letter itself in another language. It means only writing, and the sense is, that the writers translated into Aramaic what they had thought in Samaritan or any other language, and therefore also at the same time wrote down in Aramaic, without doubt, for the reason that in Babylon at court, and among the Persian officials in anterior Asia the Aramaic language was the usual one, so to say, the official language, which otherwise would not have been employed in the letter of authority given to Ezra in chap. vii. 12 sq. נִשְׁתְּוָן is of Arian origin, to be compared with the new Persian *nuwischten*, to write, and means letter. Comp. ver. 18. מְתַרְגַּם is part. pass. of תַּרְגֵּם, interpret, translate into another language.

Ver. 8. **Rehum the chancellor and Shimshai the scribe, wrote a letter in this sort.**—Although other authors of a letter are adduced here, yet it is impossible that another third letter should be introduced (against Berth.); for 1) it is inconceivable that the author should have left the contents of the letter referred to in ver. 7 so entirely undetermined. The contents of the letter mentioned in ver. 6 he has at least characterized as an accusation. It is all the more inconceivable since the author has expressly designated the language of the letter mentioned in ver. 17. Without doubt he regarded this as of especial importance. 2) Already the fact that the remark that the letter in ver. 7 was written in Aramaic, is immediately followed by a section in Aramaic, and so also the fact that in accordance with ver. 7, where Samaritans are designated at the outset as authors of the letter; again after the Persian officials in ver. 9, Samaritan tribes are mentioned as taking part in the letter—all this is in favor of the view that it is only the contents of that letter which now follow (comp. Köhler, *Nachexil. Proph.* S. 21). 3) The word כְּנָוָתֵהּ in ver. 7, which is found nowhere else in Hebrew, looks evidently forward to the same word in ver. 9. 4) If another letter were referred to in ver. 8, a connecting copula could no more be lacking here than at the beginning of ver. 7, (Keil). Without doubt the Samaritans mentioned in ver. 7, who had become known to the author elsewhere, had been the proper instigators of the letter, the Persian officials mentioned in ver. 8 merely their instruments. The verb כְּתַב which is likewise used of the former, does not by any means always mean: to write with one's own hand. That the Persian officers had written the letter in combination with the Samaritans is besides expressly declared in a short introduction which had been given to it probably at Jerusalem, when they there added it to other important documents, in the form of an explanatory superscription. This introduction, which so to say had grown together with the document, the author has for accuracy and perspicuity taken up in vers. 8–11, leaving it to the reader to put together correctly the different statements respecting the authorship in the manner indicated. Other interpreters, as Keil and Köhler (*l. c.*) suppose that he found the verses 8–11 *a*, and so also then the following letter itself in the history of the building of the temple written in Chaldee, which he used in vers. 5 and 6. Whether however he really had before him such a document is doubtful, as we have shown in the Introduction, § 2. Besides the abbreviation וּכְעֶנֶת and the like, which stands at the end of ver. 10, is found only in the superscriptions of letters, where things that are self-understood may be omitted (comp. vers. 11, 17), not in a historical narrative.—בְּעֵל טְעֵם = lord of understanding, counsellor, is not a proper name (Esdras, Alex., Syr., Vulg.), but a designation of the office of Rehum [the title apparently of the Persian governor of the Samaritan province. Rawlinson *in loco.*—Tr.], as סָפְרָא, scribe, chancellor, is the designation of the office of Shimshai. ["According to Herodotus (III. 128) every Persian governor was accompanied to his province by a 'royal scribe' or 'secretary' (*γραμματεύς*), who had a separate and independent authority," Rawlinson *in loco.*—Tr.]. אִגְּרָא = אִגֶּרֶת, in later Hebrew. חֲדָא is used as an indef. article, as in the later Hebrew אֶחָד. כְּנֵמָא has, according to Raschi and Ab. Ezra, arisen from כְּ and נֵמָא = נֵימָא = נֵאמַר, comp. in the Talmud אֵימָא, I say תֵּימָא, thou sayest; thus literally: as we say,—then: in the following manner, or also, according as has been stated.

Vers. 9, 10 add to the summary statement of authorship a closer explanation: **Then Rehum . . . . and the rest of their companions.**—The verb "write" is to be supplied from the previous verse. Then the sense is, when they wrote the letter in question, they were active in common with their companions. As their companions, the communities transplanted to Palestine are then adduced according to their native lands in Eastern Asia. The **Dinaites** were perhaps from the Median city Deinaver, which still had this name in a quite late period (Abulf. *Geogr. ed. Par.*, p. 414). Schrader would find it as Da-ya-a-ni, also Da-ya-i-ni in the inscription of the older Tiglath Pileser, who reckons them among the Nahiri, that is, to the Armenians, *l. c.*, S. 246. The **Apharsathchites**, perhaps identical with the Apharsachites in ch. v. 6, were compared by Hiller (*Onom.* p. 655, 745) with the robber Paraetakites (Herod. I. 101; Strabo xv. 3, 12), on the boundary of Media and Persia; Rawlinson regards the Apharsachites as the Afar-Sittaces, according to the inscriptions, and the Apharsachites as the Afar-Sacæ (comp. Rœd. in Gesen. *Thes., app.* p. 107). [But in his Com., *in loco*, Rawlinson regards these two names as only variations of the third form Apharsites, all referring to the same people, the Persians.—Tr.].—The **Tarpelites** remind us of the τάπουροι (*Ptol.* VI. 2, 6) dwelling on the East of Elymais.* The **Apharsites** are identified with the Persians, whose name is here provided with א prosthetic; Hiller (*Onom.* p. 655) thought of the *Parrhasians* in Eastern Media. The **Archevites** had their name probably from אֶרֶךְ (Gen. x. 10), Arku in the inscriptions, the present Warka on the left bank of the Euphrates, south-east of Babylon (comp. Schrad. *l. c.*, S. 18). The **Babylonians** are the inhabitants of Babylon, the **Susanchites** those of Susa, the **Dehavites** (*Qeri* דֶּהָיֵא), the Δάοι of the Greeks (Herod. I. 125), the **Elamites**, those of Elam or Elymais.

Ver. 10. **And the rest of the nations whom the great and noble Asnapper brought over.**—Since the author adds these words as a summing up, it is clear that he could not or would not enumerate all in detail, that he would represent them as all taking part together, and indeed not only so far as they dwelt in Samaria, but further than this also those **in the other lands on this side of the river.**—Thus did all these colonists here act in common, even those who dwelt as it were in Phœnicia and Syria, because they perhaps under all circumstances as foreigners over against the natives felt themselves united by the bond of a common situation, because they perhaps all feared also for their territory, if the Jews should grow into a power, upon which the Israelites dwelling at a greater distance round about might lean. Since here all the colonists are to be mentioned in entirely general terms, we cannot regard it as singular that at this time on the one side entirely different names are mentioned from those in 2 Kings xvii. 24, where only those transported to Samaria are mentioned, that moreover on the other side the Samaritan nations are not so particularly mentioned as in that passage, where instead of the Babylonians in general, people from Babylon, Cuthah, *etc.*, are named. *Asnapper* here might be regarded as another name of Esar-haddon, in ver. 2, and indeed the more as we here have a Chaldee document; yet the supposition of different names for one and the same person is ever a doubtful one. It is not suitable, however, to understand thereby the commander-in-chief of Esar-Haddon [Rawlinson], for the *epith. orn.* "great and noble" are in favor of a king, although the title of king is not expressly added. It is probable therefore that a mutilation of the name Esar-Haddon has taken place.* After the designation of the place: **in the city of Samaria**, the following וּשְׁאָר, *etc.*, may also be merely a designation of place; accordingly the בְּ, which is before קִרְיָה is to be supplied before it, and שְׁאָר is to be taken as neuter of the land or places. עֲבַר־נַהֲרָה, on that side of the river, of the land to the west of the Euphrates, is explained as a now universally prevailing geographical expression. וּכְעֶנֶת contracted into כְּעֶת (comp. ver. 17) = *etc.*, or "the like." Perhaps the author himself already placed this expression of abbreviation at the introduction of the letter, in order to indicate that still other designations of lands are to be thought of as a matter of course; perhaps, however, it is derived from the author of our book, who would not copy that which was to be understood of itself.

Ver. 11. **These are the contents of the letter which they sent.**—Here we have at once announced in the first half of the verse the contents of the letter. It seems that already the beginning of the letter itself was used for this announcement, since it was certainly the style for the letter-writer to designate more closely in a superscription as well himself—which is now no longer the case here—as also the receiver of the letter. For only from such superscriptions can it be explained how at the beginning of every letter in our book almost the same formula occurs, comp. ver. 17; v. 6; vii. 11.—פַּרְשֶׁגֶן, in the book of Esther thrice פַּתְשֶׁגֶן, which two forms are likewise used interchangeably in the Targums, is translated by many after the Sept., Vulg., which, however, are not uniform in their usage, and the rabbin. interpreters as *copy* [so A. V.]. But very properly Benfey (*Monatsnamen*, p. 193 sq.) rendered this meaning doubtful. In ver. 23 it does not suit, since the Persian officers had not received a copy, but the letter itself; and it is no more appropriate to Esther iii. 14; viii. 13, and in Esther iv. 8 another meaning suits at least as well. Accordingly the word seems to have rather the meaning of contents, as then indeed the Vulg. in Esther iii. 14 has rendered it *summa.* Gildermeister (*D. M. Zeitschr.* IV., S. 210) and Haug (Ewald's *bibl. Jahrb.* V., S. 163 sq.) conjectures in the syllable פַּר the Persian *fra*, the Sanscrit *pra*=πρό, pro, the new Persian *far*, in the corresponding פַּת the Zend *paiti* (Sanscrit *prati*)=προτί and ποτί, πρός; in שֶׁגֶן a word like *çenghana*, old Persian *thanhana*, from *cenghdicere, prædicare.*—In the second half of the verse, the

* [Rawlinson *in loco* regards them as colonists from the nation which the Assyrians called *Tuplai*, the Greeks "Tibareni," and the Hebrews generally "Tabal."—Tr.]

* According to Hitzig's faithful disciple Egli, it would be an appellative, that would show us the relationship of the Assyrian with the German and would be essentially the same as the German "*Schnapper.*"

letter begins: **thy servants, the men on this side of the river,** *etc.*—Here also there has been left off what usually stands at the beginning of a letter; the sense is: thy servants wish thee, O king, peace, comp. ver. 17. Alongside of the form of the *Qeri*, עַבְדָךְ, that of the *Kethib*, עַבְדָיךְ, is also justified.

Vers. 12–16. The information given to the king: **Be it known unto the king.**—לֶהֱוֵא for יְהֱוֵא as לֶהֱוֹן for יְהֱוֹן, and לֶהֱוְיָן for יְהֶוְיָן, vii. 25, 26; Dan. ii. 20, 28, 29, 45, *etc.* ל has in Bib. Chald., occasionally also in the Targums, more frequently in the Talmuds, vindicated itself as preformative like נ in Syriac. Comp. Zöck., Dan. ii. 20.*—**That the Jews——unto us have come.**—אֲתוֹ, they have come, is certainly more closely defined by the following participle "building." But yet it is singular that in the time of Artaxerxes there was still mention made of coming. It seems that the coming of the Jews, even after the time of Cyrus, still went on; with the close connection, which those who remained behind maintained with the returned (comp. Zech. vi. 9 sq.; Neh. i. 2 sq.), this might indeed have been pre-supposed as a matter of course.—**Building the rebellious and the bad city, and have set up the walls thereof, and joined the foundations.** מָרָדְתָּא, with metheg in the second syllable, and so with kametz under ר, is hardly a correct reading. We should read either מָרָדְתָּא (so Norzi) with short *o* sound in the second syll. from the form מָרוֹד, which occurs in the Targums, and is given by the Peschito—an intensive formation like Hebrew קַנּוֹא; or מְרַדְתָּא (J. H. Mich.) as *stat. emphat.* of the *stat. abs.*, מָרָדָא (comp. ver. 15). We must certainly prefer the *Qeri* וְשׁוּרַיָּא שַׁכְלִלוּ to ושורי אשכללו. A similar false separation of words is found in 2 Sam. xxi. 12. שכלל is shaphel of כלל, and means to make ready. That the perf. שַׁכְלִלוּ should follow the part., is in historical narrative not unusual; here, however, it has its special reason perhaps in the fact that the Samaritans would co-ordinate this expression: and they have made the walls ready, to the first and principal statement (אֲתוֹ), in order to bring it into suitable prominence. Besides they may be charged in all probability with a kind of exaggeration, even if the perfect was not meant to be taken strictly. If the Jews had now really brought the walls so near to completion, Nehemiah would not have found them still under this same king in the condition described in Neh. ii. Since they yet let an imperfect follow the perfect, they indicate of themselves, as it were involuntarily, that the work still continued; otherwise the transition to the imperfect would be without any reason. יָחִיטוּ might be the imperf. Aphel of חטט, dig, dig out, which is also found in Syriac, since יָחִיט would be for יָחֵט; to dig out the foundations would then be simply=make excavations for the foundations; it might, however, still easier be taken as imperf. Aphel of חוט, properly sew together, then heal, improve; alongside of יָקִים the sharper form יַקִּים is to be maintained, after the analogy of which under the influence of the guttural we have יָחִיט.

* [More properly it is the characteristic of the subjunctive or optative force of the verb. See Luzatto's *Gram. der bib. Chald.*, § 109, and Rigg's *Manual of Chaldee*, p. 65.—TR.]

Ver. 13. **Be it known now unto the king that they will not pay toll, tribute and custom.**—The three usual kinds of taxes are here meant, comp. ver. 20 and vii. 24. מִנְדָּה, for which vi. 8 has מִדָּה, which expression is also usual in Syriac, is etymologically=measure; here, however, the appointed general tax. בְּלוֹ after בלה is perhaps the consumption tax, and הֲלָךְ the toll for highways.—**And that it finally will prepare damage to the king.** —The meaning of אַפְּתֹם, which is entirely disregarded by the ancient versions, is entirely uncertain. The meaning "income" is simply invented by the Jewish interpreters of the middle ages, and is not recommended by vers. 15 and 22 in so far as the kings themselves are those who are there injured. Haug (*l. c.*) compares אורום in the Pehlewi language, which=the last, hindermost, Sansc. *apa*, superl. *apama*, and thus gains for our word the meaning of "finally, at last," which certainly is entirely appropriate. מַלְכִים is a Hebraism, or perhaps only a copyist's mistake for מַלְכִין. תְּהַנְזִק is *tert. fem.* in Aphel, in which conjugation the Bib. Chald. sometimes chooses the prefix ה, which it preserves even in the imperf. and part., comp. תְּהַשְׁכַּח in ver. 15. The subj. is the city of Jerusalem, or the indef. subject, referring to the design of Jerusalem.

Ver. 14. **Now because we have maintenance from the king's palace.**—The writers would here at any rate state a reason for the following statement, that it was not meet for them to see the injury of the king. The rabbinical explanation followed by Luther: "we all, who have destroyed the temple," is therefore not recommended; besides we would then have to expect at least instead of: salt the salt of the temple, scatter salt on the temple, comp. Judges ix. 45; Jer. xvii. 6; Isa. li. 6. To salt the salt of any one probably means to live through any one's bounty, perhaps pay, and therefore be obligated to him, stand in his service. Syriac and Persian expressions accord with this, comp. Gesen., *Thes.*, p. 790. We may also compare *salarium.* Whether the writer as an official really received pay from the palace of the king, or speaks figuratively, we cannot say.* עַרְוַת מַלְכָּא is according to the analogy of the Heb., עֶרְוַת, the uncovering, not in the sense of deprivation, but of dishonoring; the Sept. has properly ἀσχημοσύνη, whilst the Vulg. employs *læsiones.*

* ["The Persian satraps had no salaries, but taxed the provinces for the support of themselves and their courts." Rawlinson *in loco.*—TR.]

It would be a dishonoring of a great king if the Jews should throw off their allegiance (refuse to fulfil their duties). אֲרִיךְ, also in the Talmud=appropriate, fitting, is connected with עֲרַךְ, arrange.—**Therefore have we sent**, namely, this letter, **and made known to the king**, namely, the following.

Ver. 15. **That search may be made in the book of the records of thy fathers.**—Subj. of יְבַקַּר is he whose duty it is to search, the keeper of the archives, properly indef. subj.—דָּכְרָנָה and דִּכְרוֹנָה (comp. vi. 2) is the memorable occurrence from דכר=זכר. In Esther vi. 1; this book is called more completely: the book of the memorable events of the day. The fathers of Artaxerxes are here his predecessors on the throne, and indeed including also those not Medo-Persian, especially the Chaldean, who in this connection come very particularly into consideration. For the rebellions that follow must mean above all those under Jehoiachim and Zedekiah. The manner of expression is properly explained from an inclination of the inhabitants of Western Asia to assume a connection of families between the dynasties that succeeded one another, but also from figurative language, which was all the more natural if Artaxerxes already had had many real ancestors for predecessors on the throne.—**So shalt thou find.**—These words may be taken as depending upon the verb make known in the previous verse, but yet really contains the consequence of the investigation. אֶשְׁתַּדּוּר is *nom. verb.* of Ithpaal of the verb שְׁדַר, uproar; it is found elsewhere only in ver. 19. עָבְדִין, they make (continually) uproar, indefin. subject, they make; in ver. 19 there is made. מִן יוֹמָת עָלְמָא, from the days of old. The fem. form יוֹמָת is also found in Syriac alongside of the masc.; otherwise in Bib. Chald. the masc. יוֹמֵי is used, as then in Heb. likewise the masc. is throughout the usual form, the fem. only occurring in poetry. With the clause: **For which cause was this city destroyed**, we certainly are to look back to the destruction of the city by Nebuchadnezzar. הָחָרְבַת is Hoph., which is used throughout in Bib. Chaldee for the Ittaphal.

Ver. 16. **We certify the king, that if—by this means thou shalt have no portion on this side the river.**—The verse concludes with this inference and summing up. לְקֳבֵל דְּנָה =on this account, in consequence of this circumstance as in Dan. ii. 12. They supposed that the fortified Jerusalem would not merely free itself from taxes, but also appropriate to itself all the territory on the west of the Euphrates, so that the great king would have nothing left, comp. Eccl. ix. 6; 2 Chron. x. 16; Jos. xx. 25, 27.

Vers. 17–22. The writers of the letter had manifestly desired to obtain by means of their information authoritative measures, authorizing them to restrain the Jews. These they obtained. —**The king sent an edict.**—The abrupt way in which the letter of the king is mentioned may be explained from the fact that the same address as in ver. 11 is here used, even if with slight differences. פִּתְגָמָה from the Zend. *patigama* (modern Persian *paigam*, Armenian *pattkam*) is the command, and in this sense has even passed over into the Hebrew, comp. Eccl. viii. 11; Esther i. 20. At its root is the word *paiti* (πρός) and *gam*=go, accordingly=the approaching message (comp. Keil on Dan. iii. 16). Moreover, comp. notes on ver. 10.

Ver. 18. **The letter which ye sent unto us hath been plainly read before me.**—מְפָרַשׁ, Pael part. passive, means here, since the Aramaic without doubt was chosen only because it was used at court, not translated, but explained, or adverbially, plainly, comp. the Pual part. in this sense in Neh. viii. 8, as then this word has the same meaning also in the Talmud.*

Ver. 19. **And I commanded.**—שִׂים properly, Kal passive part.; in Bib. Chaldee is used instead of a *tertia pers. praet. pass.* accordingly, instead of the Ithpael (comp. v. 17; Dan. iv. 3); moreover the Peil part. in Bib. Chald. usually gives a new preterite passive, and is for this purpose conjugated throughout with the afformatives of the verb. Alongside of שִׂים, the form שׂוּם also occurs, in fem. שׂוּמַת, Dan. vi. 18.—**Search hath been made, and it is found that this city—hath made insurrection.**—הִתְנַשְּׂא is here used as in 1 Kings i. 5 in Hebrew, of rising up in rebellion. Comp. ver. 15.

Ver. 20. **There have been mighty kings also over Jerusalem which have ruled.**—The reference is to Uzziah, Jotham, and perhaps David and Solomon, if in any way a rumor of them had come to Babylon and to the Persians.† Since these kings had subjugated the land to the west of the Euphrates, especially the territory of the Moabites and Ammonites and similar tribes, the suspicion was quite natural that Jerusalem would again strive for such a supremacy. בְּ before כֹּל depends upon the previous שַׁלִּיטִין: ruling over all on that side of the river. With reference to the following clause comp. ver. 13.

Ver. 21. **Give ye now commandment,** namely, to those who are building in Jerusalem. טְעֵם is here as in ver. 19, not in the sense of investigation, observation, as in Dan. iii. 12, in connection with שׂוּם עֲל, but in the sense of decision, command, לְבַטָּלָא = that you cause to cease by your command. From this infinitive, as frequently in Hebrew, the construction passes over into the finite verb: **and that this city be not built**. The additional clause: **until a command shall be given from me,** namely, that defined by the context, for building, hence the *stat. emph.* טַעְמָא. This is not a mere phrase,

* [" It is doubtful if the Persian monarchs could ordinarily read (*Ancient Monarchies*, Vol. IV., p. 185). At any rate it was not their habit to read, but to have documents read to them (comp. Esther vi. 1)." Rawlinson *in loco*. —Tr.]

† [Rawlinson *in loco* doubts the reference to David and Solomon, and thinks the reference more probable to Menahem (2 Kings xv. 16), and Josiah (2 Chron. xxxiv. 6, 7; xxxv. 18).—Tr.],

that would make all things dependent upon himself and his words, but a product of his prudence, since he really had in view the possibility of a change. With this agrees very well the earnestness and severity with which in

Ver. 22 he sharpens the previous command: **and be careful**—so זְהִיר, which is especially frequent in Syriac,—**to make a mistake** = that you may not make a mistake with reference to this matter. לְמָה properly "to what" = that not, comp. vii. 23, so also in Syriac. Accordingly the meaning is, that חֲבָלָה, damage, which easily grows as a pest, may not become great.

Ver. 23. The consequences of the royal edict are now added, probably by the same hand, that had added the introductory address of the original document.—**Now when the contents of the letter . . . were read.** A parenthetical clause begins with מִן־דִּי. It is not until אֲזַלוּ that the principal clause continues.—**They went up to Jerusalem, unto the Jews.**—אֲזַל may be connected with לְ and עַל in the sense of "going to or unto" (comp. v. 8 Dan. ii. 24); here both prepositions follow. The subject is supplied from the parenthetical clause. בְּאֶדְרָע, properly, "with arm," or "the power of the arm," but this could not be the meaning here, were it not for וְחָיִל = troops, which is accordingly added. The Sept. renders freely, but not incorrectly (against Keil): *ἐν ἵπποις καὶ δυνάμει*, comp. the Hebrew זְרוֹעַ, Ezra xvii. 9, and זְרוֹעוֹת, or זְרוֹעִים, Dan. xi. 15, 31, where also Keil explains the meaning as warlike powers. Instead of אדרע, almost always דרע occurs without the prosthetic א.

Ver. 24. **Then ceased the work of the house of God.**—This verse already begins the continuation of vers. 1–5, the further history of the building of the temple; at least it is introductory thereto. Our author himself (comp. notes on ver. 6) here gives the results of the hostile effort, but not those of the last struggle, but those of the first under Cyrus, which already results from the idea of בטל, if it is taken in the strict sense. The author would not have gone back to the cessation, were it not that he would come to something that had already connected itself with the first intimation which had occasioned the cessation.*

THOUGHTS UPON THE HISTORY OF REDEMPTION.

Vers. 1–3. (1) The release of Israel and the re-establishment of Jerusalem and the temple connected therewith was a beginning of the fulfilment of the great prophetic promises. Among these promises were those that said that the heathen would come near, to walk in the light of the Lord (especially Mic. iv. 1 sq.; Isa. ii. 2, 24; lx. 1 sq.); they were to take part in the communion with Him, and accordingly in His worship and kingdom, and rejoice in His blessings. When now the Samaritans drew nigh with the request that they might help in building the temple, was not their claim sustained by these prophets? Should not Israel have been ready gladly to contribute their part for the accomplishment of the prophecy, even if it should for the moment be burdensome to them? Did they not have to fear lest they should by a refusal strive against God's own great thoughts and designs which had been expressed long before? If the one prophecy is compared and explained by the other, then it follows, certainly, that this conversion of the heathen was not to be expected until the appearance of the Messiah. But if the Lord had given the one thing that was to come with the better and Messianic times, namely the return to the land of their fathers, could He not then very soon also afford them the other, the appearance of the Messiah itself? At present, indeed, Israel had no other prince than Zerubbabel, who did not even have the majesty of an ordinary king, not to speak of Messianic majesty and glory. But if now the congregation had gained in strength and numbers by the reception of the Samaritans, would it not thereby have also gradually advanced an important stage, and would not other tribes and families also have gradually followed the Samaritans? The congregation was obliged in those times, when so much was but feeble, and began to have but little prospect of improvement (comp. Zech. iv. 10), to look at so many things with the eye of faith, if they would make no mistakes; and grasp them in faith, if they would not lack courage for them from the outset—should they not then have seen here also in faith a beginning, that would have its continuation and completion; should they not have covered over with the veil of mildness and forbearance the many weaknesses which might still adhere to the Samaritans, and have excused them with the hope of better things? They felt themselves too weak to overcome the heathen elements that were natural to them, and to meet the influences which they would exert in case of a union. But should they not have overcome their feeling of weakness in the power of the enthusiasm of their faith? They were obliged to recognise likewise that something of good was in the Samaritans, and were in duty bound to God to trust in Him that He would make the good to prevail over the evil and secure the victory to the truth. Was it not, if they rejected the Samaritans, looking deeper, a lack of faith, unnecessary anxiety, and was not national narrow-mindedness, and uncharitableness mingled therewith? There are many who take this view of it, and are very much inclined to make use of such thoughts with reference to similar things, which are not entirely lacking at present. But however difficult it may appear to take a safe course in such a state of affairs, one thing is sure: The Samaritans had no right to an entrance into the congregation on their assertion that they had already always and from the beginning worshipped the Lord, for on the contrary this could have been the case only in that they

* ["The stoppage of the building by the Pseudo Smerdis is in complete harmony with his character. He was a Magus, devoted to the Magian elemental worship, and opposed to belief in a personal god. His religion did not approve of temples (*Herod.* I., 130); and as he persecuted the Zoroastrian (*Behist. Inscr.*, col. i., par. 14), so would he naturally be inimical to the Jewish faith (comp. *Ancient Monarchies*, Vol. IV., pp. 347, 398)" Rawlinson *in loco*.—Tr.]

could have shown at some period of their history a decisive break with their previous heathenism and a real conversion to Jehovah. Such a conversion, however, of a true and hearty character, such as the prophets had prophesied as taking place in the Messianic time (comp. Isa. xix. 16 sq.) was not at all possible on their part. They needed first for this a turning unto them, a change *on the part of the Lord.* Israel was what it was in consequence of the divine election. The Samaritans also, and indeed all other nations, can become God's people only when God extends His election clearly and effectually unto them likewise. They cannot choose Him, but He must choose them. It was His prerogative in this as in all other things, to take the initiative, if indeed He was the God of revelation, and was to be honored as such. It was necessary that He should reveal Himself in some manner, that He should draw near them and become apprehensible; He must send a mediator, under whom they likewise might find themselves, and in whom there should be a righteousness, a perfection and glory which would be undoubtedly for them, yea, overpowering them, and above all, likewise rendering satisfaction for them, and of a sufficiently representative character; He must do a redemptive act, by which He should purchase and take them to Himself. It was necessary that there should first be a new manifestation, which should lay a new foundation, and even on this account also another instrument than Zerubbabel and Jeshua, coming from heaven, the appearance of the Sun of righteousness itself, with healing in its beams even for the heathen. That the congregation in Jerusalem rightly judged the Samaritans has been attested by the Lord Himself in John iv. 22, as Hengstenberg has well shown in his *Gesch. des Reiches Gottes* ("ye worship ye know not what") and the history itself has shown that they justly estimated that the hour of God had not yet come. This hour did not strike until Christ the Lord authoritatively removed the fence that had been erected between Israel and the heathen.

(2) The congregation had at first for their own sake as well as for the sake of the Samaritans, to adopt an exclusive policy. Whilst, if they had taken the Samaritans into their membership they would have been ruined by the latter through their worldly conformity, now they remained a salt, that in good time might become useful even to them, yea, they became already in advance a warning and an impulse to them, in consequence of which they gradually turned to better things. The good Samaritan in the gospel makes it probable that the Lord found here and there among them, hearts that were less hard than those of the priests and Levites in Jerusalem. The story of the Samaritan who was healed of leprosy, who alone rendered thanks to the Lord, is an evidence that the noblest virtue might easily thrive among them better than among the Jews. The Samaritan woman at Jacob's well and the people of Sychar, then those in Samaria itself (Acts viii.) show a susceptibility for the Saviour, by which they might become true members of the people of God before many in the ancient congregation. Would that those, who as the Samaritans do not worship the true and holy God who does not allow His people to be put to shame, but only their own idols who are easily satisfied, might have a clearer and stronger conception of the chasm that separates them from the true congregation of the Lord! It would be a help for them that they need first of all.

(3) The congregation had to do without an increase such as would have come through the Samaritan element; they must rather remain small and suffer persecutions than abandon unto corruption the blessings entrusted to them. But after that Jesus Christ has come into the world and redemption has been made for all, so that only the innermost inclination of the heart need be brought into consideration, it is much more difficult to properly recognize the Samaritan influence that would press into the Church, and there is need in this respect of a very great and especial care. Above all we must take this to heart, that no one has to be converted *to us,* to *our* opinions and methods, but that every one is to be converted to *Jesus Christ* alone. The two do not coincide as long as we are still in an imperfect state. But at all events *conversion* is the decisive thing. How necessary this is and how fundamental it must be has now become still clearer in the light of Jesus Christ. He who now without conversion thinks that he can take part in the kingdom of God, who disputes the necessity of conversion, the depth of human sinfulness, the strictness of the divine holiness, in that he sets before him the grand aim of humanizing Christianity, reconciling it with culture, would set aside the opposition of the world against the Church, the Church's rigor, narrowness, lack of culture, whilst in truth he seeks to make the Church conformable unto the world—such an one is in fact to be placed on a par with the Samaritans: he is, indeed, because he is more accountable, worse than a Samaritan.—The state of affairs, however, to-day is an entirely different one, inasmuch as Samaritanism is not without, but within the congregation [that is, in the State Churches especially; to a limited extent in the free evangelical churches —Tr.], yea, at times indeed is to be found in those who govern the congregation, where then at any rate the parable of the wheat and tares comes into consideration with reference to the way of judging it and treating it.

Vers. 4, 5. The Samaritans were able for a time to prevent the building of the house of God. But what God would have, must finally come to pass. Just as at a previous time when David could not at once and himself execute his design of building a temple to the Lord (2 Sam. vii.), so the Lord now showed that He did not require under all circumstances that which the world was still able to take away from Him and His people. Thus then the Church should never be discouraged when their enemies triumph for a season, and when it is as if they accomplished nothing, as if they lacked the most necessary things, and walked in a way that is not good. When the progress of their work is rendered more difficult by a thousand persecutions, by the spread of many calumnies and the like, then is the time, as Starke says, to pray the third petition that God would prevent all and every wicked counsel and purpose. But we should not judge by success whether we have chosen the right or the wrong way, but only by God's word and truth. We should not find it too hard to be miserable and poor so long as it pleases God. It so easily happens, as it is elsewhere said, that the better the work, the greater hindrances are found, and that where God proposes something good, the devil does not rest, but sows tares with it (Starke).

Vers. 7–16. It was calumniation when the Samaritans charged the Jews behind their back at the Persian court with pursuing political ends, although in Artaxerxes' time the question was no longer of the temple, but of the city and its walls. The Jews had nothing to do with political deliverance and independence, but with securing their existence and freedom of worship which could hardly be refused them by the Persians. But such slanders were almost a necessity. The Church must ever be prepared for them. The world knows only worldly motives, worldly aims, and cannot but ascribe them also to the Church; with all things that they allow themselves, they make a crime for the Church. But all the more care must the Church take that such calumniations may not gain ground; all the more carefully accordingly must it hold itself aloof from the world and its aims. Otherwise it not only injures itself for the present, but also for the future; it makes itself suspected. For their accusers already, to gain credence for their word, refer to the fact that the Jews had already in former times snatched to themselves a great worldly power. O that the congregation might not be so much defiled by their own and their forefathers' sins! how much more irreproachably, powerfully and charmingly would they be able to carry out their work of missions in the world.

Vers. 17–23. The Persian king Artaxerxes commanded that the building of the walls of Jerusalem should cease. We might ask how it was possible that the only true God, the Lord of heaven and earth, should make the lot of His people, and accordingly the history of His kingdom dependent upon the command of the king of Persia; that He should allow His people, and indeed His cause in general, to fall into such dependence upon men, and indeed heathen? But this is indeed His method. Even the individual is allowed a free and determining influence upon his action. And in the very fact that He limits Himself, makes Himself dependent, lets Himself be satisfied, so that the world may enjoy an independent, true existence, and men may have a real freedom, He shows His highest and best greatness. Only the false God, the one merely conceived, is the entirely unlimited one who takes away every freedom of the creature, who wills and does everything himself, and thereby becomes of the nature of the creature and sinful. It is shown here so truly how that which is truly great and important may be externally weak and inversely.

Ver. 24. When Cyrus had given the congregation permission to return and build the temple of the Lord, it almost appeared as if already heathenism was capable and ready under the circumstances to establish a free church in a free state. But when afterwards the building was obliged to stop and remain so long unfinished, when so to speak the Church must lie down in chains, the saying of the free church in the free state became a fable, and as such must it ever anew prove itself to be. The interests and also the callings of the State and the Church are involved in too many ways and in too close relations for the former not to claim when it has the power an oversight of the latter and an influence upon it. The most favorable thing for the Church is ever the Christian State, which really wishes the Church well and ministers to it; as the last thing, however, it has to expect the antichristian state, which restrains it, persecutes it, and where it is possible, enchains and destroys it.

[The author's view of the relations between Church and State are the usual ones prevailing on the continent of Europe and among State-church men in Great Britain. It has been sufficiently proved, however, in the United States and the British colonies that a free Church in a free State is no fable, but a historical fact, and a condition in which the Church is purest, strongest and most dominant in the land through the Christianizing influence that it freely exerts on all classes of the community. And whilst Church and State are closely related in many questions of morals and religion, in education, in marriage and divorce, the observance of the Sabbath, questions of property, individual rights, *etc.*, and conflict will more or less arise, yet the relations will become more and more accurately defined without interfering with the prerogatives of either. Comp. the section on Church and State in the Evangelical Alliance proceedings, N. Y., 1873.—Tr.]

HOMILETICAL AND PRACTICAL.

Vers. 1–3. The Church cannot receive every one into her communion or suffer all to remain therein. Her duty to excommunicate is shown: 1) From what would happen if she excluded none—they would be made to conform to the world by the worldly-minded; 2) From what happens when they do exclude them—they manifest the worldly disposition in their hearts, and do much damage by their hostility; but they cannot ruin the congregation: the possibility remains that they themselves may be the subjects of saving influences.—Starke: No one should enter into communion in religious matters with strange and false religious opinions, 2 Cor. vi. 14; Tit. iii. 10. Tale-bearers and false and wicked talkers are cursed; for they perplex those who enjoy good peace (Sir. xxviii. 15), and invent villany, Ps. lxiv. 7; cxl. 4. The Church of God and its members suffer greater injury by false friends than by open enemies, Ps. xli. 10; 2 Cor. xi. 26.

Vers. 1–5. The duty of the congregation to be apparently intolerant: 1) Towards whom—even against many who would enjoy its communion; 2) how—excluding that which is excluded by its entire character and then bearing whatever evil is ascribed to them on account of this; 3) for what purpose—in order to preserve its best things and thereby at the proper time likewise offer salvation to their enemies.—Brentius: *Ejusdem farinæ sunt, qui nunc hujus nunc illius religionis sunt. Injustum est; qui fides est persuasio certa de divinis promissionibus. Hi autem, cum hinc inde fluctuent, non habent fidem.*—The foolish behaviour of the world towards the Lord's people: 1) The world would belong to the Lord's people, and yet not be converted unto God; 2) They seek to set aside the worship of the true God, and yet can prosper only in the light that streams forth from it.

Vers. 7–16. The charges raised by the world against the people of God; their apparent justice and their lack of grounds. 1) The congregation builds itself at present not with peaceful, but rebellious disposition: in fact, it must obey God rather than men; but they know also how falsely this word is applied by those who have forgotten that the kingdom of the Lord is not of this world. 2) They have in past times constantly sought after worldly power, and have been guilty of manifold encroachments; in fact, the Church has at first more and more taken a political form and equipped itself with external worldly power; but the consciousness that according to its own idea something different was more appropriate has never been able to be entirely suppressed. 3) The church will, if it have its own way, in future endanger the existence of the state; in fact, it cannot acquiesce in the state as it is; the church must seek to gain power over the king, but in a spiritual sense; not with power, but kindness; not from without, but from within. It would not oppress, but change, transform, glorify.—BRENTIUS: *Vide, mirabilem piorum sortem in hoc sæculo. Pii sunt, propter quos omnia bona hominibus hujus seculi eveniunt. Attamen accusantur, quod soli hi sint, propter quos omnia mala, bella, fames et seditiones eveniant.*—STARKE: God's church has at all times been subjected to false accusations. Christ and His apostles could give sufficient witness of this. Let us only avoid the doing, the lie is good counsel, Acts xxiv. 5 sq.

Vers. 14–24. The church's independence of the state. God makes His church dependent on the world: 1) on its own account to glorify its faith and to exercise its patience; 2) for His own sake in order to bring it to a proper conception of the fact that it does not need external majesty and power, a magnificent cultus, *etc.;* 3) for the sake of the world—that it may learn to see that the church cannot be suppressed by it, that there is something higher than it can reach with all its power.—STARKE: God often lets it happen that a good intention is interrupted by the craft of enemies, in order to try His believers. Magistrates are God's officers. If, however, they do not properly fulfil their office, a severe judgment will pass over them, Wisd. vi. 5, 6. God is a long-suffering God who allows Himself to be interfered with and presents Himself as a hero who is faint-hearted (Jer. xiv. 9), but He will wake up some time, Sir. xvii. 19.

[SCOTT: Every vigorous and successful attempt to revive true religion will excite the opposition of Satan and of the children of disobedience in whom he worketh.—HENRY: The worst enemies Judah and Benjamin had were those that said they were Jews and were not, Rev. iii. 9.—Take heed who we go partners with, and on whose hand we lean. While we trust God with a pious confidence, we must trust men with a prudent jealousy and caution.—See how watchful the church's enemies are to take the first opportunity of doing it a mischief. Let not its friends be less careful to do it a kindness.—A secret enmity to Christ and His gospel is oft gilded over with a pretended affection to Cæsar and his power.—At some times the church has suffered more by the coldness of its friends than by the heat of its enemies; but both together commonly make church work slow work.—TR.]

THIRD SECTION.

The Resumption of the Work of Building the Temple and its completion.

CHAPTERS V. VI.

A.—THE RESUMPTION OF THE WORK AND THE REPORT OF THE OFFICIALS TO DARIUS.

CHAPTER V. 1–17.

I. *The Resumption of the Work of Building the Temple.* Vers. 1–5.

1 THEN the prophets, Haggai the prophet, and Zechariah the son of Iddo, prophe-
sied unto the Jews that *were* in Judah and Jerusalem in the name of the God of
2 Israel, *even* unto them. Then rose up Zerubbabel the son of Shealtiel, and Jeshua
son of Jozadak, and began to build the house of God which *is* at Jerusalem: and
3 with them *were* the prophets of God helping them. At the same time came to them
Tatnai, governor on this side the river, and Shethar-boznai, and their companions,

and said thus unto them, Who hath commanded you to build this house, and to
4 make up this wall? Then said we unto them after this manner, What are the
5 names of the men that make this building? But the eye of their God was upon
the elders of the Jews, that they could not cause them to cease, till the matter came
to Darius: and then they returned answer by letter concerning this *matter*.

II. *The Report of the officials.* Vers. 6–17.

6 The copy of the letter that Tatnai, governor on this side the river, and Shethar-
boznai, and his companions the Apharsachites, which *were* on this side the river,
7 sent unto Darius the king: They sent a letter unto him, wherein was written thus;
8 Unto Darius the king, all peace. Be it known unto the king, that we went into the
province of Judea, to the house of the great God, which is builded with great stones,
and timber is laid in the walls, and this work goeth fast on, and prospereth in their
9 hands. Then asked we those elders, *and* said unto them thus, Who commanded
10 you to build this house, and to make up these walls? We asked their names also,
to certify thee, that we might write the names of the men that *were* the chief of
11 them. And thus they returned us answer, saying, We are the servants of the God
of heaven and earth, and build the house that was builded these many years ago,
12 which a great king of Israel builded and set up. But after that our fathers had
provoked the God of heaven unto wrath, he gave them into the hand of Nebuchad-
nezzar the king of Babylon, the Chaldean, who destroyed this house, and carried
13 the people away into Babylon. But in the first year of Cyrus the king of Babylon,
14 *the same* king Cyrus made a decree to build this house of God. And the vessels
also of gold and silver of the house of God, which Nebuchadnezzar took out of the
temple that *was* in Jerusalem, and brought them into the temple of Babylon, those
did Cyrus the king take out of the temple of Babylon, and they were delivered unto
15 *one*, whose name *was* Sheshbazzar, whom he had made governor; And said unto
him, Take these vessels, go, carry them into the temple that *is* in Jerusalem, and
16 let the house of God be builded in his place. Then came the same Sheshbazzar,
and laid the foundation of the house of God which *is* in Jerusalem: and since that
17 time even until now hath it been in building, and *yet* it is not finished. Now there-
fore, if *it seem* good to the king, let there be search made in the king's treasure
house, which *is* there at Babylon, whether it be *so*, that a decree was made of Cyrus
the king to build this house of God at Jerusalem, and let the king send his plea-
sure to us concerning this matter.

EXEGETICAL AND CRITICAL.

Vers. 1–5. The author now narrates in the closest connection with the last verse of the previous chapter how it came to pass that the work of building, which had been interrupted, was resumed.

Ver. 1. **Then the prophets, Haggai, the prophet and Zechariah.**—We learn also from Haggai himself that the congregation at that time needed prophetic admonition. At first the most of them had, without doubt, with great reluctance allowed the building to remain unfinished, but gradually had lost the desire thereto, caring only for their own interests, such as the erection of their own houses in as beautiful a manner as possible. Notwithstanding this, however, some of them had still such devotion to the Lord and zeal for His worship, that the prophetic office was possible, and there was relatively a great susceptibility for it. נְבִיאָה in Hebrew הַנָּבִיא, seems to have been almost a surname of Haggai, chap. vi. 14; Hag. i. 1. The plural "the prophets," which in the Hebrew text follows Zechariah son of Iddo, as if Haggai had not yet been called prophet, is in favor of this view. The preposition עַל after "prophesied," does not denote hostility, but simply the direction of the address, "unto" (comp. 2 Chron. xx. 37; 1 Kings xxii. 8, *etc.*), as is sufficiently clear from the contents of the prophecies.—**The Jews that were in Judah and Jerusalem.**—Thus they are designated to distinguish them from those who remained behind in Chaldea. At the same time it indicates those who had undertaken the task of building the temple. עֲלֵיהוֹן is a closer designation of the name of God, so that the relative might be supplied before it: **Who was over them** (comp. chap. iii. 3, *etc.*), which characterizes them as those who belonged to God. (Isa. iv. 1 and Jer. iv. 16), who leads them, urges them on and encourages them.*

Ver. 2. **Then rose up Zerubbabel.**—They now had an express command of God, which already in itself was an advantage; now moreover they could no longer doubt that the building

* [Rawlinson *in loco* more properly renders in accordance with the current Hebrew phrase "which was upon them," that is, having God's name called upon them.—Tr.]

would succeed.—**And began to build**.—Properly it should have been: They re-commenced, but we might disregard the fact that בְּנָה readily =rebuild, for the first beginning was so long before, and had had such little success, that it no longer came into consideration.

Ver. 3. **At the same time.**—Now again they were threatened with interruption. בֵּהּ זִמְנָא, at it, the time, = at the same time. Comp. Dan. iii. 7, 9; iv. 33.* Again Persian officials arrive, but at this time only do their duty.—**Tatnai, governor on this side the river**, of the entire province to the west of the Euphrates, outranked Zerubbabel, whom Cyrus had appointed governor of Judah (comp. ver. 14). He was perhaps unacquainted with the mission of Zerubbabel, because he had come into his office at a subsequent period to him.—**Shethar Boznai** who accompanied him, is not designated indeed as Shimshai (chap. iv. 8 sq.), *e. g.*, as scribe or chancellor, but the entire appearance is in favor of his being likewise a magistrate.—**Their companions**, however, who in ver. 6 are especially called his companions, that is, Shethar-Boznai's companions, and are named the Apharsachites, are according to ver. 6 likewise government officials, probably of a lower grade. At this time also the Samaritans may have been at work in that they had called attention to the building of the temple in Jerusalem, but now they were no longer able to fill the officials with hostile sentiments. They simply inquire **who hath commanded you to build this house?**—לִבְנֵא here and in ver. 13 is a singular form, since the infin. in Chald. is מִבְנֵא (comp. vers. 2, 17; ch. vi. 8), or מִבְנְיָה, comp. chapter v. 9. R. Norzi has here and in ver. 13 a dagesh in the ב, but there cannot be an assimilation of the מ because it has a vowel. It may be that the language was not entirely fixed in its usage of מ in the infin., as it is here absent from the infin. in Peal., to which elsewhere it is peculiar, so it has been at times prefixed to the Pael and Aphel, before which it is usually absent, and always to the infinitive of the passive conjugations in the later Targums. Comp. Winer, *Gram.*, § 12. [Luzzatto *Gram.*, § 88.—Tr.]. [Rawlinson, *in loco.* "There was no doubt a formal illegality in the conduct of Zerubbabel and Jeshua; since all edicts of Persian kings continued in force unless revoked by their successors. But they felt justified in disobeying the decree of the Pseudo-Smerdis, because the opposition between his religious views and those of his successors was a matter of notoriety. (See *Ancient Monarchies*, IV. p. 405)."—Tr.]. אֻשַּׁרְנָא, a word of doubtful etymology, is in Esdras rendered by τὴν στέγην ταύτην καὶ τὰ ἄλλα πάντα (the beams and all the rest), in the Sept. on the other hand by τὴν χορηγίαν ταύτην (this sacred service = this building). These derivations in the versions makes it probable that there was no fixed tradition respecting the meaning; the one rendering being as much guess work as the other. The Vulg., Syriac and the Rabbins have explained it as "walls," which might well be the most suitable and correct, having as its root not אשר (Gesen.), but אשן more properly אֻשַּׁן (firm, strong).

Ver. 4. **Then said we unto them.**—Here the Masoretic text gives at once the answer of the Jews. But this text is in more than one respect singular. The first person might be explained, it is true, very well as having come from the use of an ancient document, whose author had taken part in the building. But אמר should be followed by the direct discourse, whilst the indirect is used, so that we must translate, not, then we said, but then said we to them, what the names of the men were. Besides, if the Jews here spake, that is, answered to the question in ver. 3, instead of referring to the names of the men, we should expect another answer. It is natural therefore with Bertheau to conjecture that the text has been corrupted in some way, that is to say that the first person is incorrect, as it were, has come over from ver. 9, instead of which we must read here the third person, so that the Persian officials still continue: *then said they to them, what are the names of the men, etc.*, as from the start we might expect, according to vers. 9 and 10. It is possible then that likewise אֱדַיִן, which would separate almost too much the second part of the address from the first in ver. 3, is a mistake likewise. The Sept. and Esdras already have regarded the verse as a question of the Persian officials, the former translating: τότε ταῦτα εἴποσαν, the latter, in that it passes over entirely the first four words. It is true that the objection might be raised, that then there is no answer on the part of the Jews. But this might have been omitted with reference to ver. 11. The names of the men were important to the officials, for they had to know whom the king was to hold responsible. Instead of שְׁמָהַת the more accurate editions have שְׁמָהָת.

Ver. 5. **The eye of their God was upon the elders of the Jews.**—This is the prelimiminary result, producing for them mildness on the part of the officials, and securing them from interruption. The eye is used instead of the hand, because the Providence and Wisdom of God above all came into consideration. Comp. Ps. xxxiv. 16; Zech. iv. 10; 1 Peter iii. 2. The שָׂבִין, corresponding with the זְקֵנִים in Hebrew, are at the same time the שָׂרִים chap. x. 8.—**Until the report came to Darius, and they then brought back a letter concerning the matter.**—Bertheau understood it as: Until a command arrived from Darius, *etc.* But טְעֵם need not be the royal decree. Although this word does not assume the wider sense of *causa* (Keil), it yet has the meaning of *ratio*, and indeed also in the sense of account (or likewise of consideration) יָהַב טְעֵמָא, Dan. vi. 3 = give account. Thus it may be used here for a report, by which officers would give their king an account of an important occurrence, and their observation of it. The לְ before Darius cannot be a circumlocution of the genitive—it is thus used only in designations of time. On the other hand

* [Suffix with prep. before its noun has this force in Aramaic, Riggs' *Manual*, § 49, 3. Comp. Cowper, *Syriac. Gram.*, § 203, 5.—Tr.]

its use with הֲלָךְ to give the end, is entirely assured. Comp. chap. vii. 13, *etc.* Finally, if it did not mean "to Darius," the הֲלָךְ alone would be too indefinite. As well Esdras as the Septuagint also has, therefore, although rendering freely, properly understood it as a report to Darius. Naturally, however, these words are only preparatory for the following clause: "Until they bring back a letter, *etc.*", which really for the first expresses the limit of time meant. יְהָךְ imperf. of הלך (comp. chap. vi. 5; vii. 13) is referred by Winer, § 25, to a special root הוך. It is possible, however, that as usually the ה is absorbed at the beginning, so here the ל of הלך and thus we have יְהָךְ for יְהָלֵךְ.* The letter to be brought back, was certainly to come from Darius, there is no occasion to think of one from Tatnai, *etc.*, unless it is already supposed that there is a royal command in טְעֵם. The subject of יְתִיבוּן is indefinite "they."

Vers. 6–17. The report of the officers to Cyrus in vers. 6, 7, at first, precisely like chap. iv. 8–11, has the superscription which this letter probably received already in the collection of documents at Jerusalem.—**These are the contents of the letter that Tatnai.—Shethar-boznai and his companions the Apharsachites.**—We must leave in doubt the question why the Apharsachites (comp. iv. 9) are especially mentioned as the companions of Shethar-boznai, which here means either lower officials or as it were men of the same race, or else people especially attached to him.†

Ver. 7. **They sent a report.**—פִּתְגָמָא according to its etymology (comp. iv. 17) is used in the same sense as טְעֵם in ver. 5, *e. g.*, report, message. כֹּלָּא is loosely connected with שְׁלָמָא = peace, hence peace universally = peace in its fulness.

Ver. 8. **Be it known unto the king.**—The letter in iv. 12 began in the same way. The present letter however is distinguished by the fact that it gives first of all a simple objective report. Judah is called a מְדִינָה (see ii. 1), the god of the Jews, **the great God.**—It is not probable however that they, like the Samaritans (iv. 1) actually paid a certain degree of reverence to him, rather the deep reverence of the Jews made such an impression upon them that they supposed He must be an especially great God (namely, for His worshippers). What they say respecting the building, is manifestly to show that the work was well-done, in a strong, stately manner.—**Of great stones.**—אֶבֶן גְּלָל here the accusative of material is the stone which was too heavy to lift, and which could only be rolled along; thus very heavy and large stones (as chap. vi. 4), which were only taken for great buildings, designed to last a very long time. The Sept. emphasizes by its translation λίθοι ἐκλεκτοί, the excellence of the material; Esdras vi. 9, by its translation λίθοι ξεστοὶ πολυτελεῖς at the same time the labor applied to them, as well as their costliness.—**And timber is laid in the walls.**—Berth. understands by this the placing of beams in the walls, that is, in the partitions, [Rawlinson, *in loco*, "party walls"], or likewise the erection of the scaffolding on the outer walls. But the expressions indicate rather the inlaying of the walls with wood work artistically finished (comp. פִּתּוּחֶיהָ Ps. lxxiv. 6), thus according to the view of the writer represent the building as one erected with great care. It is true the work had not made such progress, in fact that the walls, which themselves were first built of the great stones, could have been already inlaid. But it is probable that the zeal, which is clearly enough attested by Haggai, manifested itself likewise in this way, that those skilled in wainscoting went at once to work, since moreover it was necessary to make as great haste as possible on account of the threatened interruption. The haste is expressly referred to by the officials in the last words—**and this work goeth fast on**—אָסְפַּרְנָא (comp. vi. 8, 12, 13; vii. 17, 21, 26) is explained from the Persian, and means properly, very active. אס is probably the ancient Persian *us* or *os*, Sanscrit *ut*, which expresses intensity; as our "very" and *parna* is an adjective from the ancient Persian *par*, Zend *pere* = do, complete. Comp. Haug. a. a. O. The subject of מַצְלַח, **it prospereth** is not the form עֲבִידְתָּא (comp. vi. 14; Dan. vi. 29), but "it."

Vers. 9, 10 then give an account at first of their question.—**Then asked we those elders.**—אִלֵּךְ, those who, as a matter of course, were in Jerusalem at the head, ver. 10, **at their head.**—בְּרָאשֵׁיהֹם is more naturally explained as at their head (comp. 2 Chron. xx. 2), than: in their capacity as their heads (Berth., Keil). [A. V., "*that were the chief of them*"]. The latter interpretation of בְּ is in itself doubtful, especially moreover, since no verb is given with it. The plural, expressed by the vowels, may be explained by the fact that they worked in different groups, namely, by families (comp. Neh. iii.)

Ver. 11 sq. gives the answer of the heads of the Jews.—**And thus they made us the report**, namely, the one required. לֵאמֹר = לְמֵמַר—**We are the servants of the God of heaven.**—The pleonastic suffix of עַבְדוֹהִי emphasizes very strongly the fact, not that *they* above all others and alone are servants of God (Berth.) but that they above all others are servants of the God of heaven, and not of any lower being. They therefore expressly designate God as the God of heaven and earth, that is, the highest; yea, properly the only true God. They would without doubt show the officers that they had good grounds and were very well entitled to build their temple, and that those would do wrong who should oppose their undertaking. On this account therefore they add that their God had had this house long ago, and in it had long ago possessed a worthy place of worship.—**And we**

* [So Luzatto *Gram.*, § 104. This is the better interpretation of the form.—Tr.]

† [Rawlinson, *in loco*, regards them as Persians or foreign settlers in Samaria generally.—Tr.]

build the house that was built.—not הִתְבְּנָא, it was once built, but הֲוָא בְנֵא, it was built and continued to be a place of worship—**these many years ago.**—מִקַּדְמַת דְּנָה = before this (present) time.—**A great king of Israel built and completed it.**—It would have been an evidence against their God if He had not provided Himself with a worthy place of worship in ancient times, and had not made the king of his people great and mighty. They say intentionally not the great king Solomon, but a great king (the genitive relation being expressed by לְ); they thus emphasize better the idea itself, that the king was a great one.

Ver. 12. It is true the temple has been destroyed, but this does not show any weakness in their God, but rather His holiness.—**On this account, because our fathers provoked.**—לָהֵן does not refer to that which precedes, but to what follows, for it is used in its usual sense of "on this account," and is here really = only on this account. It does not follow from the fact that it sometimes has the sense of "but" after negative expressions, that it may also be an adversative particle, and mean "nevertheless," "however," "yet." מִן־דִּי, however, is here not in the temporal sense, [A. V. *after that*], for then it would express very vaguely the idea: since that the fathers had already provoked God long before He abandoned His temple; but it is here in its usual causal sense "because." מִן may be very properly used in this sense, comp. Hebrew כַּאֲשֶׁר, Isa. xliii. 4. סַתַּר = to conceal, then like the Hebrew הִכְחִיד, to destroy. It is true it is only used here in the Bible in this sense, but in the Targums occurs quite frequently. עַמָּה might, if it had the suffix, that is, if the ה were pointed with mappiq, mean simply, "the people of the land;" ארע is often to be supplied. Yet the Massora remarks, that mappiq is not to be written, and R. Norzai and J. H. Mich. have left it out, so that the ה is to be taken as a representative of the א, as is often the case in this book.

Ver. 13. **But in the first year of Cyrus.**—When the predestined time of chastisement had passed the Lord Himself was able to gain recognition from Cyrus, so that now the restoration of His temple has a good and assured foundation. Comp. chaps. i. 2; vi. 3. לִבְּנֵא, as chap. v. 3.

Ver. 14. **And the vessels also—did Cyrus the king take.**—So great was the recognition that Cyrus gave to the true God, that he not only allowed His veneration, but furthered it with offerings, so that the building of the temple, unless the vessels were to remain without a suitable place, became so much the more necessary. הֵיכְלָא is here used as at the first, so naturally also the second and third time in the sense of temple. Comp. בֵּית אֱלָהָיו, chap. ii. 7. וִיהִיבוּ is probably the conjugated passive participle = and they were given, not the active preterite = they gave, for the indefin. subject with sing. (against Berth.). In the last case we would expect הִמּוֹ after the object, which is not elsewhere in such cases omitted: moreover, the yod in the second syllable has usually only an intrans. or passive signification.—**Whose name is Sheshbazzar**—thus indefinitely, as we would say, to Sheshbazzar, as he is called. For this name see chap. i. 8. As in Hag. i. 1, *etc.*, so here Zerubbabel is designated as Pechah, whilst in chap. i. 8 as prince of Judah, נְשִׂיא.

Ver. 15. **And he said unto him, Take these vessels.**—In connection with giving out the vessels Cyrus expressly ordained the building of the temple. Instead of אֵלֶּה, the *Qeri* is here as in 1 Chron. xx. 8, אֵל. The three unconnected imperatives, "take, go forth, lay down," comprehend the three acts, to a certain extent, in *one*, thus expressing likewise the zeal of Cyrus, and the zeal that Sheshbazzar was expected to exhibit. אֲחֵת, notwithstanding the Chateph Pathah, may be merely the imper. Aphel of נחת, of which we have the part. in chap. vi. 1, and the imperf. in chap. vi. 5.—**And let the house of God be built.**—These words are connected with the words **lay them down in the temple** as a necessary complement, by the copula וְ.

Ver. 16. **Then came this Sheshbazzar,** namely from Babylon to Jerusalem, **and laid the foundations,** *etc.*—The copula is also lacking before יְהַב, because the two acts are connected together in the closest way. אֻשַּׁיָּא, as in chap. iv. 12. Here it can only mean the laying of the foundations in chap. iii. 8-10.—**Since that time even until now hath it been in building, and is not yet finished.**—These words were probably designed to let the present activity appear as a simple continuation of the building, ordained by Cyrus, thus also as something entirely justified. At any rate it was entirely in the interest of the Jews to be silent respecting the fact that Cyrus had allowed an interruption to take place, and there is nothing in our representation of the subject opposed to its reality. But had the express prohibition of the Artaxerxes in chap. iv. 17 sq. already preceded, yet the Jews might well have said that it had been occasioned only by the entirely groundless slanders of the Samaritans. Hence they must regard it as their absolute duty to contradict these slanders. שְׁלִם occurs only here in Bib. Chaldee, yet often enough in the Targums and Syriac, and indeed in the sense of "complete and ready."

Ver. 17. **And now, if it seem good to the king, let there be search made in the treasure-house.**—טָב עַל, comp. vii. 18; Dan. vi. 24, as in later Hebrew, טוֹב עַל, Esther i. 19, good according to any one's judgment. גִּנְזַיָּא, Heb. גְּנָזִים (Esth. iii. 9; iv. 7), are the treasures, probably from גנז = כנס, collect, and *dshanasa*, conceal, but at the same time in accordance with the Arian *gaza*, comp. גִּזְבָּר, Ezr. i. 8; on the other hand, גַּנְזַךְ, 1 Chron. xxviii. 11. It is clear from this passage and chap. vi. 1, that written documents were likewise preserved in the treasure-house. —**Whether a command was given by king Cyrus.**—הֵן = whether, as likewise Jer. ii. 10. For שֵׂים, *vid.* chap. iv. 19. רְעוּת, comp. chap. vii. 18, from רעה = רעת, *voluntas*, cpinion.

THOUGHTS UPON THE HISTORY OF REDEMPTION.

Ver. 1. Notwithstanding the great readiness which distinguished the new congregation at first (comp. notes upon chap. iii.), they yet fell into indolence and worldliness as soon as difficulties were placed in the way of their work, comp. Haggai's prophecy. It was even necessary that again God's word should arouse, encourage, strengthen them, and fill them with joy. And indeed the Lord does not fail on His part: wherever any powers whatever are present; if slumbering, He awakens them. The more we need His all-awakening call, and the more that is the result of undeserved grace and faithfulness that shames us, the more willing should we be to hear and follow Him.

Vers. 1–5. Although the new congregation, when they were called upon by the prophets and strengthened by their prophecies, might have readily supposed that the building of the temple would now be finished without stumbling upon difficulties, they were yet obliged presently to submit to an inquiry on the part of the Persian officials, that might again easily result in an interruption. Such trials the Lord Himself sends at the time,—and then often very properly,—when His own word has given the impulse to an undertaking or action. Even then, and then particularly, faith must be strengthened by trials. The congregation at this time did not allow the interference of the Persian officials to surprise them too much; they were not faint-hearted on this account, and did not allow themselves to be deterred thereby from building; in the careful hesitancy of the officials they saw rather the influence and protection of God. Thus is it ever for the church, so long as it is in covenant with the Lord, to regard the hinderances, even if they seem threatening, and easily might be destructive, as yet trifling; and things favorable, even, if they seem at first insignificant, as great and important. We must be inclined thereto by the contentment with which one feels impelled to thankfulness for the little, and the faith in Him who has all things in His hand. It is the very reverse with the world.

Vers. 6–17. The magistracy often, as is clear from chap. iv., allows itself to use calumniators as its instruments. But without regard to the fact that they are obliged to help in realizing the design of God even in such a case, they are easily preserved by their office and their duties from such errors, even if they are worldly and heathen in their character. In our present chapter they act as true magistrates; they quietly listen to the report of the Jews, and bring it without misrepresentation before the king. Brentius rightly remarks: "*vides differentiam inter calumniatores et bonos ac probos viros. Una eademque causa erat ædificii templi, unus idemque populus Judæorum: attamen hujus populi causa aliter refertur ab impiis calumniatoribus aliter a bonis viris.* How much worse off the Jewish congregation would have been, if the Samaritans had had to do with them without the Persian officials! Hence the church should never forget, even if at times it has had to suffer injustice from worldly authorities, to be thankful from the heart to God that there are magistrates after all, comp. Rom. xiii. 1 sq., *etc.*

Vers. 11, 12. The congregation did not keep back their faith, when it came to the point of rendering account of their designs before the magistrates, rather did they lay down an open confession, even before the heathen, without fearing to be laughed at for their assertion that they served the only true God. In order to ward off the objection that their Lord had been without power, they confessed the sinfulness of their fathers, and praised the holiness of God. God's honor was for them more important than the honor of their fathers or of the nation. Well for the church, when the world itself is obliged to give testimony to it, as it here gives to the Jewish congregation, that it has made such a good confession as this. If with such a confession heart and hand accord, it has the power that overcomes the world.

HOMILETICAL AND PRACTICAL.

Vers. 1–5. How does the Lord prevent our being conformed to the world? 1) By His warning word.—Starke: It is the office of faithful teachers to strengthen the faint hands and feeble knees (Isa. xxxv. 3). 2) By the trials that He sends, especially by making the accomplishment of His own word difficult. 3) By providential care and preservation (ver. 5).—Brentius: *Multa hic notanda. Primum, quod Deus sæpenumero nos a bono proposito impedit, non ut non exequamur, sed ut clarius et illustrius exequamur. Deinde, quod sit ingenium vulgi: mox enim putat, numquam fore, ut promoveat* (sc. *Deus opus suum, si aliquamdiu intermittatur*).—The movements that the development and advance of the kingdom of God call forth: 1) The congregation is agitated by the overwhelming voice of God; it gives new courage, and lays hold of the work of building obligatory upon it with new joy.—Starke: Although it involves not a little danger for awhile to accomplish with obedience that which God commands in His word, yet we should obey notwithstanding, and not allow ourselves to be frightened off by any danger. 2) The world is agitated, for it cannot quietly see the events in the kingdom of God, especially when the congregation is subordinated to its civil authority, but it is obliged to assist in furthering the cause of God in its own way. 3) God Himself is agitated. He directs His eye with especial care and wisdom upon the leaders of the congregation, and stretches forth His hand to give protection and help.

Vers. 11, 12. The true confession. 1) The occasion of it—the magistrates call to account,—2) its contents, God's grace and truth and our own sins,—3) its aim, the establishment of a tabernacle of God among men. The true contents of a believing confession. 1) God's gracious acts—He has by them from the most ancient times obtained worship. Starke: If we purify the doctrines with which Christ and His apostles have erected a spiritual temple to God, from human ordinances, we start no new doctrine, but erect again the marred temple of God. 2) Exhibition of the divine holiness. He has imposed upon His church dependence and deficiencies on account of its sins.—STARKE: Even the sins of our forefathers we should not cloak, but where they have erred, confess it. 3) God's assertions of power.—He has wrung a recognition from even a Cyrus, even the mightiest worldly power, and made them serviceable for the re-establishment of His worship.

[SCOTT: Whilst we continue in this world, we shall always have to confess that our sins have provoked the God of heaven unto wrath, and that all our sufferings spring from this source, and all our comforts from His unmerited mercy.—HENRY: Our eye upon God, observing His eye upon us, will keep us to our duty, and encourage us in it when difficulties are never so discouraging. Let the cause of God, and Truth, be fairly stated, and fairly heard, and it will keep its ground.—TR.]

B.—THE ANSWER OF DARIUS, THE COMPLETION OF THE TEMPLE, AND THE FIRST CELEBRATION OF THE PASSOVER.

CHAPTER VI. 1–22.

I. *Darius' Answer.* Vers. 1–12.

1 THEN Darius the king made a decree, and search was made in the house of the
2 rolls, where the treasures were laid up in Babylon. And there was found at Achmetha, in the palace that *is* in the province of the Medes, a roll, and therein *was* a
3 record thus written: In the first year of Cyrus the king, *the same* Cyrus the king made a decree *concerning* the house of God at Jerusalem, Let the house be builded, the place where they offered sacrifices, and let the foundations thereof be strongly laid; the height thereof three-score cubits, *and* the breadth thereof three-score
4 cubits; *With* three rows of great stones, and a row of new timber: and let the ex-
5 penses be given out of the king's house: And also let the golden and silver vessels of the house of God, which Nebuchadnezzar took forth out of the temple which *is* at Jerusalem, and brought unto Babylon, be restored, and brought again unto the temple which *is* at Jerusalem, *every one* to his place, and place *them* in the house
6 of God. Now *therefore*, Tatnai, governor beyond the river, Shethar-boznai, and your companions the Apharsachites, which *are* beyond the river, be ye far from
7 thence: Let the work of this house of God alone; let the governor of the Jews and
8 the elders of the Jews build this house of God in his place. Moreover I make a decree what ye shall do to the elders of these Jews for the building of this house of God: that of the king's goods, *even* of the tribute beyond the river, forthwith
9 expenses be given unto these men, that they be not hindered. And that which they have need of, both young bullocks, and rams, and lambs, for the burnt-offerings of the God of heaven, wheat, salt, wine and oil, according to the appointment of the priests which *are* at Jerusalem, let it be given them day by day without fail:
10 That they may offer sacrifices of sweet savors unto the God of heaven, and pray
11 for the life of the king, and of his sons. Also I have made a decree that whosoever shall alter this word, let timber be pulled down from his house, and being set up,
12 let him be hanged thereon; and let his house be made a dunghill for this. And the God that hath caused his name to dwell there destroy all kings and people, that shall put to their hand to alter *and* to destroy this house of God which *is* at Jerusalem. I Darius have made a decree; let it be done with speed.

II. *The Completion and Dedication of the Temple.* Vers. 13–18.

13 Then Tatnai, governor on this side the river, Shethar-boznai, and their companions, according to that which Darius the king had sent, so they did speedily.
14 And the elders of the Jews builded, and they prospered through the prophesying

of Haggai the prophet and Zechariah the son of Iddo. And they builded, and
finished *it*, according to the commandment of the God of Israel, and according to
15 the commandment of Cyrus, and Darius, and Artaxerxes king of Persia. And
this house was finished on the third day of the month Adar, which was in the sixth
16 year of the reign of Darius the king. And the children of Israel, the priests, and
the Levites, and the rest of the children of the captivity, kept the dedication of
17 this house of God with joy. And offered at the dedication of this house of God
a hundred bullocks, two hundred rams, four hundred lambs; and for a sin-offering
for all Israel, twelve he-goats, according to the number of the tribes of Israel.
18 And they set the priests in their divisions, and the Levites in their courses, for the
service of God, which *is* at Jerusalem; as it is written in the book of Moses.

III. *Celebration of the First Passover-Feast.* Vers. 19–22.

19 And the children of the captivity kept the passover upon the fourteenth *day* of
20 the first month. For the priests and the Levites were purified together, all of them
were pure, and killed the passover for all the children of the captivity, and for
21 their brethren the priests, and for themselves. And the children of Israel, which
were come again out of captivity, and all such as had separated themselves unto
them from the filthiness of the heathen of the land, to seek the LORD God of Israel,
22 did eat. And kept the feast of unleavened bread seven days with joy: for the
LORD had made them joyful, and turned the heart of the king of Assyria unto
them, to strengthen their hands in the work of the house of God, the God of
Israel.

EXEGETICAL AND CRITICAL.

Vers. 1–12. The answer of Darius. Notwithstanding the great importance of the decision that Darius gave in reply to the letter of his officers and the greatness of its results, in that after so long a waiting it finally introduced a new and significant turn of affairs, its introduction is quite brief.—**Then Darius the king made a decree.**—These words seem to refer only to the command to make an investigation; but in reality they serve as an introduction to the decree which was promulgated to Tatnai, *etc.;* comp. v. 6. It is as if the subsequent narrative: **and search was made,** were taken up merely as an explanation of the decree following in ver. 6 sq. Without doubt it was contained in the decree of Darius to Tatnai, as its basis or introduction.—**The house of writings.**—Comp. v. 17.* Here the treasures likewise were laid up. מְהַחֲתִין is participle Aphel of נחת. Comp. chap. v. 15.

Ver. 2. **And there was found at Achmetha.**—Search was made for the writing in Babylon; but it was found in Achmetha, after that there was probably found in the archives at Babylon a reference to the archives of Achmetha for the documents of the time of Cyrus. The letters אחם engraved on coins seem to designate this city. Comp. Mordtmann, *D. M. Zeitschrift,* VIII., S. 14. In ancient Persian, however, Achmetha probably was Hagamatha.—[Rawlinson *in loco:* "in the Behistun inscription Hagmatana."—TR.]—In Greek it is 'Αγβάτανα (Herod. I. 98) or 'Εκβάτανα (Judith i. 14), the summer-residence of the Persian and Parthian kings, built by Deiokes, the capital of Media the great, in the vicinity of the present Hamadan.—**In the palace.**—The archives were especially in the citadel, בִּירָה=ἡ βάρις, which embraced the palace and likewise the other prominent buildings.—**A roll and therein was a record.***—We should expect directly after בְּגַוַּהּ (there is less authority for a kametz in the last syll.) the contents of the writing; indeed דִּכְרוֹנָה (*st. emph.* of דִּכְרוֹן) may have been a superscription in the writing itself about equivalent to: *memorandum;* nevertheless it is here connected with the previous clause as a *memorandum* was written therein. The contents do not follow until vers. 3–5.

Ver. 3 contains first probably stereotype introductory forms; at first the date: **In the first year of king Cyrus** (as in chap. v. 13); then the short preamble: **Cyrus the king made a decree**; then a statement of the contents; then the following words: **the house of God at Jerusalem,** stand alone by themselves, and constitute to a certain extent a title. Then the command: **Let the house be built as a place where offerings are brought and whose foundations are capable of supporting** (namely, the structure).—אֲתַר is placed before the relative clause in *stat. constr.*

* [Rawlinson *in loco:* "A house of writings was discovered at Koyunjik the ancient Nineveh by Mr. Layard in the year 1850—a set of chambers, *i. e.* in the palace devoted exclusively to the storing of public documents. These were in baked clay, and covered the floors to the depth of more than a foot." Many of these writings were removed to the British Museum, where they have been partially arranged and translated by Rawlinson, Smith, Talbot and others. The library was again visited, and many of its treasures removed by Smith in 1873 and '4 and again in 1876. See Assyrian Discoveries of Geo. Smith, New York, 1875.—TR.]

* [Rawlinson *in loco:* "The ancient Persians used parchment for their records as appears from Ctesias (cap. Diod., Sec. II. 32)."—TR.]

as מְקוֹם, Hos. ii. 1, *etc.*. יְאֻשּׁוֹהִי מְסוֹבְלִין is hardly to be explained as: "its foundation they may set up" (Keil), or "may be erected (Ges. in his *Thesaurus*). In this sense the additional clause would be superfluous. We would expect an optative instead of a participle. It is made co-ordinate with the previous relative clause by the participle, and not with the principal clause "let the house of God be built." סבל, which only in very detached passages is like the Heb. נשׂא, in the Targum of Deut. xxiv. 15 and in the Samaritan translation of Gen. xiii. 10, means, as in Hebrew, without doubt also in Chald, first and chiefly, to drag, bear a burden. Accordingly we regard as the safest explanation: whose foundations are burden-bearing, that is, capable of carrying, durable for the buildings erected upon them. Cyrus might have been present to state briefly in his own way the very reason why the house of God in Jerusalem was to be built. It is a place wherein they from ancient times offer offerings, thus a place long ago sanctified, and besides the foundations are still present and in a condition capable of bearing a building upon them. The two participles, thus viewed, are used without regard to tense. The Vulgate and the Rabbins likewise let this conception betray itself since they render: *ponant fundamenta supportantia.* Although it is more natural to suppose that this second relative clause should be synonymous with the first, yet there is no change in the text that could be at all proposed (*e. g.*, אֶשִּׁין for אֻשִּׁין) that would throw any light. Whilst indeed Esdras had *διὰ πυρὸς ἐνδελεχοῦς*, the Sept. seems, although rendering very freely (*κὰι ἔθηκαν ἔπαρμα*) to have followed our text.

In order that the house might be large and elevated enough, Cyrus at once fixed its height and breadth (comp. Dan. iii. 1 for פְּתָיֵהּ), and indeed both, sixty cubits, double that of the temple of Solomon. Comp. 1 Kings vi. 2. Even if in this passage the cubit of commerce of the exile times were meant, whilst in 1 Kings vi. 2, on the other hand, the ancient Mosaic or holy cubit (2 Chron. iii. 3), which according to Ezek. xl. 5; xliii. 13, was a hand's breadth longer than the former,' namely, eighteen and a half Rhenish inches, the difference would still be significant enough. But it is probable that the reference here is to the Mosaic cubit. The measurements for the new temple appear, since they were just double, to have been chosen with reference to those of the old temple, and on their basis. It is probable that Cyrus thought he could not make the matter of the temple his own affair without at least surpassing Solomon to the extent of double. Perhaps this explains why he fixes nothing at all respecting the length. Probably he knew that a greater length than that of the temple of Solomon was not desirable, since otherwise the temple buildings would have taken relatively too much space, and the extent of the courts, which needed much space, be too limited. Since now he could not well go beyond Solomon in this respect, he rather makes no standard at all. The building of Solomon's temple had a length of sixty cubits, twenty for the most holy place, forty for the holy place, and besides a vestibule of ten cubits. This was besides surrounded on the two long sides and in the rear, by wings of five cubits breadth. The length of the temple of Herod was limited to essentially the same measurements. But if they did not wish to exceed these measurements, the sixty cubits breadth could only be applied to measure the *outer* breadth, embracing likewise the wings, unless they would entirely abandon the relations rendered sacred by the tabernacle, and almost throughout retained by the temple of Solomon. The holiest of all had been a cube in both the tabernacle and the temple of Solomon and the holy place again had had double the length of this cube, and this arrangement of the parts seems to have been regarded as the most essential. The *internal* breadth of the second temple could not well amount to more than that of the first temple, or than that which it subsequently had in the temple of Herod, namely, twenty cubits (with Keil and against Merx in Herz.'s *Real-Enc.* XV. S. 513 and Berth.) Thus there remained to the side buildings a considerable space. If we reckon ten cubits for each side, whilst in the temple of Solomon only five cubits had been applied to that purpose, since the breadth in that case would have amounted to twenty cubits in the clear, in all thirty cubits, there still remain twenty cubits for the four walls, which in the temple of Herod likewise took up the same amount of space. Whether accordingly the internal height was likewise limited, whether it at least in the holiest of all was diminished to the measure of the length and breadth, as it were, by the addition of upper chambers, such as had been in the temple of Solomon likewise, these taking up ten cubits in height, we know not. In the temple of Herod there was assigned to the holiest of all, as well as to the holy place, an internal height of sixty cubits, whilst still forty to sixty cubits in height were applied to the upper chambers. And it is possible that Zerubbabel and Jeshua likewise already acted with more freedom with reference to the height, an internal height of only twenty cubits in connection with an external height of sixty cubits, would have been almost too much out of proportion. That they really carried the external height to sixty cubits, seems to follow from Josephus *Arch.* xv. 11, 1.*

Ver. 4 gives still further directions, but it is difficult to understand them.—**Three rows of great stones.**—נִדְבָּךְ is used in the Targ. for the Hebrew טוּר, which is from טור = *circumire*, and means the surrounding wall or walls (Ezek. xlvi. 23), but also the rows (Ex. xxviii. 17, *etc.*; so also indeed 1 Kings vii. 3, 4). Fritzsche on Esdras vi. 25, Keil and Merx (*l. c.*), regard its meaning as row or course, and accordingly understand it to be = the walls, whether of the temple (Fritzsche) or of the inner porch (Keil and Merx)—of the latter it is very appropriately

* When Josephus here lets Herod say that the second temple fell sixty cubits in height below the temple of Solomon, he accords to the second a height of sixty cubits, and to that of Solomon of one hundred and twenty cubits, the latter without doubt on the basis of 2 Chron. iii. 4, where in consequence of an error or copyist's mistake there is given to the hall of the temple of Solomon a height of one hundred and twenty cubits.

said in 1 Kings vi. 36, that Solomon built them: שְׁלָשָׁה טוּרֵי גְזִית וְטוּר כְּרֻתֹת אֲרָזִים, they should have below three layers of hewn stone and a row of cedar beams. But that the walls of the temple building itself, of which alone we can think according to ver. 3, should be built of four such courses is highly improbable, for such an unfinished massive method of building has no where been found in the Orient. But if the walls of the inner court were meant, these would certainly have been mentioned, or if something had been left out that was originally contained in the edict of Cyrus for explanation (Merx), these words would most suitably have been omitted likewise. Moreover טוּר in the above mentioned passage, 1 Kings vi. 36, very probably has a different meaning. It is very worthy of remark, that טוּר as well here as also immediately afterwards, 1 Kings vii. 2, so also in Ezek. xlvi. 23, occurs with reference to four-sided rooms, which were enclosed round about, just as נִדְבָּכִים is used in our passage. Nothing is more appropriate then than to understand thereby the four side enclosures which enclosed the room; whether walls, as in the inner court, 1 Kings vi. 36; Ezek. xlvi. 23, or side buildings that surrounded a four-cornered room, as 1 Kings vii. 2. The sense of 1 Kings vii. 36 is, then, that Solomon provided the inner court on three sides with walls of quarried stone, on the one other side, without doubt the front side, where the chief entrance was, where then there was probably a larger door, with an enclosure of hewn cedar. Our passage, however, then says that three of the temple walls —for it can only refer to these according to ver. 3—were of hewn stone, the other, namely, the front, which must for the most part be composed of a large entrance, was to be made of wood. In confirmation of this view it is sufficient that in the temple of Herod also, the entrance side of the holy place was still composed of one great folding door, sixteen cubits broad. In the same manner then, moreover, was the inner court enclosed, as we conclude from 1 Kings vi. 36.*—**And a row of new timber.**—Instead of חֲדַת = new after אָע = timber, it is appropriate to read חֲדָה=one, as then the Sept. already renders εἷς, yet this numeral is absent also in 1 Kings vi. 36.—**And let the expenses.**—נִפְקְתָא from נְפַק (in Aphel = to give out) is the expense, and indeed here that which was caused by the building of the temple.—**From the house of the king** is according to ver. 8 sq. = from the royal revenues on this side of the river.

Ver. 5 adds the order for the restoration of the temple vessels, that was so important. The sing. יְהָךְ (respecting the form *vid.* V. 5) is explained after the previous plural from the conception of the different vessels as *one* sum total. תַּחֵת, thus written and pointed, is 2d pers. imperf. Aph. with transitive meaning = cause to be delivered, comp. v. 15. If this meaning is to be retained, we must suppose that the edict of Cyrus was addressed to some individual, perhaps Zerubbabel himself, and that Cyrus now turns immediately to him. Yet the transition to the direct address is here somewhat singular and abrupt, and it seems best to take תַּחֵת as 3d pers. fem. imperf. Kal, which indeed should be pointed תֵּחוֹת or at least תֵּחֹת with the indefinite subject.

Ver. 6. The previous edict of Cyrus is now followed by the order of Darius, so favorable and careful in its provisions for the Jews, that it is as if the latter would not only confirm the former's action out of reverence, but even surpass him. If it should be difficult for the little congregation of Jews to conduct the worship in Jerusalem in accordance with the prescriptions of the law, in that a great expense was especially necessary for the offerings, Darius helped them to bear the burden by his great liberality. He at first in vers. 6, 7 arranged that his governor should not hinder the work.—**Now therefore Tatnai,** *etc.*—For the connection with previous context see notes on ver. 1.—**And your companions, your Apharsachites** = those who are your companions, *etc.* For an explanation of the terms comp. v. 3, 6.—**Be (or keep yourself) far from thence,** *e. g.*, interfere not with the imposition of burdens or hindrances.

Ver. 7. **Let alone.**—שְׁבֻק c.accus. = to give way to or permit something.—**The work of this house of God**, namely, that brought in question by you.—**Let the governor——and the elders build.**—וּלְשָׂבֵי is here after פַּחַת clearly a second subject to יִבְנוֹן. לְ is hence used here to introduce a subject which is quite unusual. Comp. perchance Isa. xxxii. 1, and Dan. iv. 33, and indeed without exactly making שָׂבֵי more prominent than פַּחַת.

Ver. 8. Then Darius directs his officers to defray the cost of the building.—**Moreover I make a decree what ye shall do.**—Comp. iv. 19; לְמָא = in reference to that which ye are to do, comp. אֶל־ with צִוָּה, Isa. xxiii. 11; Ps. xci. 11; 2 Kings xx. 1. עִם is used here with עֲבַד in no other way than with עָשָׂה in Heb., comp. Gen. xxiv. 12 sq. It corresponds to some extent with the German "*an*," but expresses still further "in favor of."—**For the building.**—לְמִבְנֵא = in order that they may build. The second half of the verse: **that of the king's goods, even of the tribute,** contains the principal thing that the royal officers were to do, so that ו=and indeed—**With expenses—that they be not hindered.**—אָסְפַּרְנָא as in ver. 8. דִּי־לָא לְבַטָּלָא cannot well mean that there be no stopping, or that it may not come to a stopping of the work (Keil after the Vulgate: *ne impediatur opus*), since no object such as work is mentioned here as in chap. iv. 21 and 23; but it means: which (prescribed action) is not to be brought to an end, or discontinued (Bertheau). Comp. Dan.

* [Ferguson accepts the Sept. δόμος, and understands three stories of stone, with a fourth story of wood-work on the summit. Rawlinson thinks that Cyrus would limit the thickness of the walls to three rows of stone with an inner wooden wainscotting.—Tr.]

vi. 9. This additional clause is to sharpen the previous one.

In vers. 9 and 10 Darius further adds: that his officers shall provide the material of the offerings in order that prayer may be offered for him, and the welfare of his empire in the Jewish manner, in Jerusalem likewise.—**And whatever is necessary**—חַשְׁחָן is fem. pl. (necessary things) from חֲשַׁח for חַשְׁחָן, comp. חַשְׁחִין Dan. iii. 16, and פַּרְסִין Dan. v. 25, according to Winer's *Gr.*, § 34, III. [Riggs' *Gr.*, § 32—Tr.], the vocalization varies.—**Both young bullocks and.**—The following וְ — וְ is properly = as well—as, or also, whether—or. Darius names here various animals and other materials, which may in any way come into consideration, since he leaves the more particular designation of what would be required to the priests at Jerusalem.—**Let it be given them without fail.**—The singular לֶהֱוֵא מִתְיְהֵב (comp. להוא iv. 12) is explained perhaps from the fact that Darius goes back upon כָּה and embraces every individual in an indefinite "it." דִּי־לָא שָׁלוּ means: that there be no interruption, namely, in providing what is necessary, or indeed in the worship. In the translation of the LXX. ὃ ἐὰν ἀιτήσουσι, which overlooks the לָא and in that of the Vulgate *ne sit in aliquo quærimonia*, שָׁלוּ seems to have been derived from שְׁאֵל.

Ver. 10. **In order that they may be offering** (continually) **sacrifices of sweet savour for the life of the king and his sons.**—נִיחוֹחִין are (comp. Dan. ii. 46) sacrifices which afford God a רֵיחַ נִיחוֹחַ (Lev. i. 9, 13, *etc.*), and thereby gain his good will, comp. Jer. xxix. 7; 1 Mac. vii. 37; xii. 11, *etc.*; Josephus, *Arch.* XII. 2, 5; c. *Ap.* II. 5. Darius thereby indicates the same recognition of the Lord to be worshipped in Jerusalem, as Cyrus, without doubt, from the same stand-point. Comp. i. 2.

Vers. 11, 12. Darius here shows as an additional sign, how earnest he was that his will should be carried out, sealing what has been said with a penalty.—**Whosoever shall alter this word.**—The nom. absol. represents a protasis: if any man whatever יְהַשְׁנֵא as in ver. 12; Dan. vi. 9 and 16, change by transgression or also (comp. ver. 12) by doing away with it.—**Let a timber** (beam) **be torn from his house, let him be fastened thereon and crucified.**—זְקַף in itself = raise on high, can just as well mean "empale" or "pierce through," as also, like the Syriac "crucify." Empalement or the piercing through of delinquents on a pointed wooden stake, was the usual punishment among the Assyrians and Persians, comp. Layard, *Nineveh and Babylon*, p. 355, and *Nineveh and its remains*, p. 379, with the plate fig. 58.* Of Darius it is said ἀνεσκολόπισε (Herod. III. 159). Yet the fastening on a cross likewise occurred among the Persians, yet so that the head of the one to be crucified was first cut off. *Vid.* the passages of Herodotus in Brisonii *de regni Persarum princip.*, II., c. 215.—**And let his house be made a dunghill for this**, that is, let it be torn down and changed into a common sewer, comp. 2 Kings x. 27, and Hävernick, *Com.* on Dan. II. 5. נְוָלוּ as נְוָלִי Dan. ii. 5.*

Ver. 12. **And the God that hath caused his name to dwell there, destroy all kings,** *etc.*—יְמַגַּר corresponds with the Heb. מִגֵּר, Ps. lxxxix. 45. The expression, who has caused His name to dwell there, is so decidedly Hebrew in style (comp. Deut. xii. 11, 14, 23; Jer. vii. 12; Neh. i. 9), that we must suppose the author does not impart the decree verbally, or that Darius made use of Jewish help in this entire affair. Even the entire conception that God confined His especial presence to a temple building was entirely unlike the Persian conception, so that the entire proceedings toward the Jews with reference to the temple on the part of Darius, and already on the part of Cyrus, must be referred back to an accommodation of views.—**Who stretches forth his hand to change, to destroy.**—לְהַשְׁנָיָא for which we would expect לְהַשְׁנָיָא is explained by לְחַבָּלָה, which indicates what kind of change of the decree is here thought of. The threat itself, as we have it here, is genuine Persian; it reminds us of the conclusion of the inscription of Darius at Behistun, where the punishment of Ahuramazada is desired to descend upon him who ventures to violate the image and inscription, his blessing on the one who holds them in honor (Berth.). [Rawlinson *in loco*. See *Beh. Ins.*, col. IV., part 17.—Tr.]

Ver. 13. This happy turn of affairs is followed by the completion of the work, on which, as a matter of course, all depended. It is characteristic of the book that this fact should also be narrated in the Chaldee. It is as if the continued use of this language should express the accompanying fact of their dependence upon Persia, which still continued. Yet this was not so depressing in its influence as encouraging, for, according to divine providence, even the mighty princes of Persia co-operated on their part and in their way in the worship of Jehovah. The author first lets the Persian officers take part in the recognition of Jehovah: **According to that which Darius the king had sent so they did speedily.**—כְּנֵמָא, according to the word (of the king) comp. iv. 18, in consequence of the fact that Darius had sent, namely, answer and command. לָקֳבֵל דִּי properly, over against the fact that = considering that, as usually כָּל־קֳבֵל־דִּי.

Ver. 14. The author here reminds us of all those to whom the congregation were especially indebted for the new temple. They were encouraged by (בְּ) the prophesying of the prophets; but it was the command of God, and then that of Cyrus, Darius, Artaxerxes, that had been the source or origin (מִן) of all that happened.

* [Rawlinson says, that crucifixion was the most common form of punishment among the Persians. *Vid. Com. in loco* and *Ancient Monarchies* IV., p. 208; Herod. III. 159; IV. 53. *Beh. Ins.*, col. II., par. 14, *etc.*—Tr.]

* [Houbigant and Dathe prefer the Vulgate rendering: *domus ejus publicetur*, "let his house be confiscated." But the balance of authority is in favor of the translation given above. Rawlinson, *in loco*.—Tr.]

God is mentioned here, and indeed before Cyrus and Darius, since the author goes forth from the fact, that there would have been no command of Cyrus and Darius without God's command. If we had here a simple account of the final completion of the building, it would seem strange that here the author should go back even to Cyrus, still more that the much later Artaxerxes is taken into consideration, who had nothing to do with the building here under consideration. The author, however, instead of giving a simple narrative, would rather express recognition and thanks, and hence could forget none who were deserving of mention. Artaxerxes came into consideration only on account of the gifts which he caused to be brought to Jerusalem by Ezra, vii. 15, 19.

Ver. 15. For a work of such importance the date is properly given. שֵׁיצִיא, for which the *Qeri* gives שֵׁיצִי, is the Shaphel of יְצָא, [so Luzatto, *Gram.*, § 45.—Tr.]; in the Targum שֵׁיצִי has mostly an active sense, yet at times also an intransitive sense, so that it corresponds with our "end;" now transitive and then intransitive. Thus it is hardly necessary to regard שֵׁיצִיא as a Hebraistic passive formation of the Shaphel (Berth. and Keil). By the third day of the month Adar, that is the last month of the year, was the temple finished, since it is probable that they made haste to have time left in this year for a worthy dedication; whilst the Sept. agrees with our text in respect to the third day, Esdras vii. 5 has instead of it the twenty-third day, but probably, only because the author held that the dedication immediately followed the completion, and that it lasted eight days, after the example of the temple of Solomon, 1 Kings viii. 60, and 2 Chron. xxix. 18, and filled up the last eight days of the year. [The sixth year of Darius, according to Rawlinson, was B. C. 516-515.—Tr.]

Vers. 16, 17. The great significance of that which had been attained, and the consciousness of it in the congregation at the time, the author very beautifully shows by what he says respecting the dedication. All observed it (עֲבַד as עָשָׂה, with חֲנֻכָּה, 2 Chron. vii. 9), with joy, and indeed with the offering of a number of sacrifices which, whilst small in comparison with the multitude in Solomon's time (1 Kings viii. 5, 63), thus in accordance with the limited relations of the time, yet might ever be regarded as a glad beginning, showing by the twelve goats for sin-offerings, that they would act in the name of entire Israel, and regain the divine grace for the whole body of the people. Comp. ii. 2; viii. 35. Whether then already remnants of the northern tribes had returned and settled themselves in Juda, or whether there were from former times representatives of these tribes, scattered about in the land, does not come properly into consideration here. The principal thing is, that the new congregation, without doubt in consequence of former prophecies, had no other thought than that those so long separated from them had retained their privilege of being the people of God, and would realize it in some way or other as in olden times. Besides, the offerings prescribed in Num. vii. 11 sq. were here offered in the manner of the law. Comp. 1 Kings viii. 63; 2 Chron. xxix. 20 sq.

Ver. 18. Thus there was again a legal worship, so likewise a legal body of persons to conduct the worship.—**They set up.**—וְהָקִימוּ as וַיַּעֲמִידוּ, iii. 8, namely, to perform the business of the divine worship.—**The priests in their classes, and the Levites in their divisions** (comp. 2 Chron. xxxv. 5, 12; 1 Chron. xxvii. 4), since every class and division had its week. Comp. 2 Kings xi. 9, and 2 Chron. xxiii. 4. That it is expressly added, **as it is written in the book of Moses** (comp. Num. iii. 6; viii. 14), may be in accordance with the legal disposition, which became very soon characteristic of these times, comp. iii. 2; 2 Chron. xxiii. 18; but at the same time this likewise might well come into consideration, that it was so important, that, whilst still so many other things might be dispensed with, yet at least they should again have a worship in accordance with the law.

Vers. 19-22. It is very significant that the author here at the close of this entire section adds an account of the first celebration of the passover after the completion of the temple. This came into consideration certainly not merely as an evidence that in the new temple the divine worship had its regular course with the cycle of feasts (Keil), but before all as a feast, by which the congregation might again show itself so appropriately as the redeemed and favored people of the covenant of the Lord, also again more and more assure itself of the covenant relation, as a conclusion, which at the same time was a beginning assuring a new and glorious continuance and progress. This is quite clear from the confirmation given in ver. 22, by which nothing less than the proper end of the entire previous period of affliction itself is designated as the foundation of this Passover feast. So then the circumstance that the author now returns to the Hebrew language is likewise appropriate—one might say very significant. If the Chaldee language has been used because Chaldee documents had to be placed in order—that is, because the restoration depended first of all on the world power, and that by it the covenant people had been deprived for a while of their covenant jewels, the temple, and divine worship—so now, when the congregation was again constituted as such, and also provided with their temple and their divine worship, and where the narrative might be occupied with this exclusively, there was at least nothing in the way of a return to the Hebrew tongue.

Ver. 20. **For the priests and Levites had purified themselves as one man** (without exception, comp. iii. 9), **they were all clean.**—This has reference not to the cause of the celebration, but its possibility. Priests and Levites had sufficiently prepared themselves, and were now in the condition to fulfil the duties devolved upon them. Defilements, as Lev. xxii. 4 sq. makes them especially prominent with reference to the priests, occurred again and again, and had been certainly more frequent under previous circumstances, where the priests as such had come but little into consideration, but they must now be put aside ere they could fulfil their priestly functions. At any rate, the author means to point out a noble readiness, yea, a holy zeal, on their part. The subjects of יִשְׁחֲטוּ are, as is clear from the following context, those who were to do the slaughtering, *e.g.* of the Levites. Properly, it is true, every father of a family had himself to slay the Paschal lamb, Ex. xii. 6 sq.; but after the time of Hezekiah, when the Levites had undertaken the slaying for all who had not purified themselves (2 Chron. xxx. 11), it seems to have been more and more the custom for the Levites to do the slaughtering for all (comp. 2 Chr. xxxv. 4, 14)—for the priests, because they were so busy elsewhere; and for the rest of the people, because it was so easy for a defilement to happen to them. As in 2 Chron. xxix. 34; xxxv. 15, the priests are designated as their = the Levites' brethren, probably in connection with the increasing importance of the Levites. וְלָהֶם = "and for themselves," as in 2 Chron. xxxv. 14.

Ver. 21. This fair conclusion of the previous times of trial, and this promising beginning of the new congregation was all the grander that the returned did not eat the Passover alone, but also such persons united with them who would separate themselves from the impurities of the people of the land, and seized with a new and holy zeal, would henceforth hold to the Lord.—**And all such as had separated themselves unto them from the filthiness of the heathen of the land.**—גּוֹיֵ הָאָרֶץ, as עַמֵּי הָאָרֶץ, x. 2, 11, are the heathen nations dwelling in Palestine, whilst the heathen in neighboring lands belong to the עַמֵּי הָאֲרָצוֹת, ix. 1, 2; iii. 3. Those who separated themselves from these heathen are not proselytes from heathenism (Aben Ezra, Raschi, Clericus, *et al.*), but descendants of the Jews and Israelites who had remained in the land when the rest of the nation had been carried captive, as all the parallel passages show, comp. ix. 1, 10; x. 2, 10, 11; Neh. ix. 2; x. 29. They had without doubt intermarried with the heathen, and the more they had entered into communion with them, the less were they in a position to observe the Mosaic laws respecting food and purification. To separate themselves from the impurities of the heathen meant for them to forsake altogether communion with the heathen, and seek communion with the Jewish congregation. For לִדְרשׁ comp. iv. 2.

Ver. 22. If eating the passover (namely, in the narrow sense, not in the broader sense, which means to eat the festival offerings in general, comp. Deut. xvi. 3) as a means of appropriating the covenant grace, closely combines seriousness and joy, so the eating of the unleavened bread ministered exclusively to joy and gave full expression to their joyous and elevated feelings. The concluding clause—**for then had the Lord made them joyful, and turned the heart of the king of Assyria unto them**—means to say: for after all the hard sufferings of the exile, and after all the severe trials which had come upon them since the time of Cyrus, the Lord had now, by the re-establishment of the temple, exactly seventy years after its destruction, caused a real and great change of affairs to take place. There was now a new foundation for the celebration of redemption, a second redemption, which was hardly less than the previous one out of Egypt, a redemption out of the firm bonds of Assyria. Darius, the king of Persia, is here called king of Assyria, not only "as ruler of the territory of the previous Persian empire (Keil), or because Assyria from ancient time had been the usual name for all that region (Clericus),* which cannot be proved from Judith ii. 1; but above all, likewise, because Darius, as head of the great empire of the world, properly took the same relative position over against the people of God as the Assyrian and Chaldean kings had once had, because it was properly only a continuation or renewal of the same, and because the thought was now to be expressed that finally that very enemy who had once so fearfully and destructively oppressed the people of God had been changed by the grace of God into a friend, so that he had even himself strengthened the hands of the congregation in re-establishing the destroyed temple (as I have already shown in my article, *Studien und Kritiken*, 1858, S. 51).† חִזֵּק יַד with בְּ as 1 Sam. xxiii. 16.

THOUGHTS UPON THE HISTORY OF REDEMPTION.

Vers. 1–5. 1) It was not alone Cyrus who had previously determined and established in documents the restoration of the temple and its worship, even to the details of the limits of its measurements, the kind of material that should be employed, but also before all God the Lord Himself, as the great prophecy of Ezekiel respecting the new temple (Ezek. xl.–xlvii.) shows. Cyrus was only an instrument of the Lord, and had only given expression to His sovereign will. Thus the congregation, however many hindrances might be placed in their way, although the circumstances might appear different to them, yet having the eye of faith, they had no sufficient reason for despondency, but only the more confidently to look upon the wonderful providence of God, which makes even opposing forces to serve His purpose. Is there not then also with respect to the building of the Christian Church or of the kingdom of God such a divine predestination, which has provided beforehand even to details all and everything that is adapted to the honor of the Lord and the salvation of men; and which in spite of temporary gloom and struggles and apparent defeat, must yet more and more prevail, and be carried out more and more decidedly by princes and peoples whether they be Christian or not? The prophecy of Ezekiel and even the edict of Cyrus are evidences to us that there is such a predestination, and that likewise there has been prepared, so to say, a document which can never be lost or destroyed; for they prove that the temple of God can suffer only temporal, properly only

* [Rawlinson *in loco* mentions as a corresponding fact that Herodotus, with similar inexactness, calls Cyrus the king of the Medes (I. 206).—Tr.]

† [This was in accordance with the constant usage of prophecy in representing all the enemies of the kingdom of God by the most prominent enemy of the prophets' time. This enemy having been the Assyrian in the times of the prophets, it was natural that in thinking of the fulfilment of prophecy, the author should use the prophetic term.—Tr.]

apparent losses, that it must grow and increase and gain one victory after another.

2) It is not enough for the Lord to restore His kingdom and glory when sin and judgments have come in between to disturb them; He causes His kingdom to grow, increase, advance. Where there is life, there is also development, appropriation, struggle and victory. Here is the highest and most powerful, here is the divine life. Cyrus must even surpass a Solomon, with respect to the size of the temple, in order to show that the cause and kingdom of God advances victoriously from century to century through the history of mankind, and ever achieves a higher stage towards the highest and most glorious end. It is true He more and more deprives His Church of external power and pomp; it is to become more and more internal and spiritual, and thus to work. But even this change is a great advance. If the walls which the worldly power has drawn around the Church fall, then we need comfort ourselves with the words of the Lord through Zechariah (iv. 6) in these very times of Darius "not by might and not by power (namely, on the side of men), but by my Spirit," and as an open country shall Jerusalem lie on account of crowds of men and cattle in her. I myself will be to her a wall of fire round about and for glory I will be in her (ii. 8).

Vers. 1–12. The worldly authorities have often lower motives or interests in the steps that they take; it is often merely to increase their authority and their power. Thus the Persian officials when they made inquiry in Jerusalem and reported to Darius would merely prove their watchfulness. The emperor Augustus, when he gave the command Luke ii., would merely accomplish a census of Israel. But the consequences that followed their steps were yet, by God's will, the advancement of His kingdom. The Persian governor here must give the occasion thereto in that the ancient decree of Cyrus is again brought to light, and the new and still more favorable one of Darius in addition is carried into effect.

Vers. 6–12. Earthly kingdoms must perish to make room and prepare the way for the kingdom of God. Thus had the Lord spoken in the second year of Darius, accordingly four years before the completion of the temple, through Hagg. ii. 20 sq. I will shake the heavens and the earth, and overthrow the throne of kingdoms, and destroy the strength of the kingdoms of the heathen, and overthrow the chariots and those that ride in them, that the horses and their riders shall come down, every one by the sword of his brother—and indeed all this in order to erect the promised kingdom of the Messiah. And the angel of the Lord who stood between the myrtle trees (Zech. i. 11, 12), when his messenger announced to him that the whole earth sitteth still, and is at rest, cried out in intercession: Jehovah Sabaoth, how long wilt Thou not have mercy on Jerusalem and the cities of Judah, against which Thou hast had indignation these seventy years, imploring the shaking and destroying of the heathen kingdoms. But these latter must perish only in so far as they stand entirely in the way of the kingdom of God, and will not let that kingdom come at all. At the bottom the interests of the earthly powers and rulers agree very well with those of the kingdom of God. Darius rightly laid great value upon the execution of his edict with reference to the furtherance and support of the worship in Jerusalem. His wish that they should offer sacrifices of sweet savor to the God of heaven in Jerusalem, and pray for his life and the life of his son, not only might, but indeed must be fulfilled, so sure as the congregation of the true God must be grateful, and indeed sincerely and heartily. Comp. Jer. xxix. 7; 1 Macc. xii. 11; 1 Tim. ii. 2. The congregation could be in his way only if it sought again for earthly power and freedom, if it thus had forgotten its proper nature and its true calling. Let the church then earnestly examine itself when it enters into conflict with the State whether it is not going astray from its proper ways. Woe to it if instead of permeating the State more and more with divine thoughts, it itself gives more and more place for human thoughts and human nature; if it regards flesh for its arm and seeks to appropriate to itself that which belongs to the State. If the salt itself has lost its savor, wherewith shall we season? The responsibility of Rome, which would bow the States not under the kingdom of God, but under its own rule which is still so carnal, is great, the greater that thereby so easily the false view is awakened, as if State and Church could not avoid in any way being in conflict with one another.—Already through Cyrus and Darius there was a fulfillment of those great and noble words of Isai. xlix. 23: "Kings shall be thy foster-fathers, and their queens thy nursing-mothers; they shall bow down to thee with their faces toward the earth, and lick up the dust of thy feet." But already now it is manifest that the true fulfillment involves neither on the part of kings a determining influence on the mode of worship, nor on the side of the congregation an external sovereignty over kings.

Vers. 13–15. Much was required, and very many different things must come together from different sides, in order that the building of the house of God might be undertaken, and could be actually finished. Above all it was necessary that it should be in accordance with the will of God the Lord Himself, and then that the rulers of the world should likewise be willing thereunto. The congregation had brought about this dependence on the world by their own sins, and they were now obliged to be satisfied with it. So also it was necessary that the congregation itself should be aroused to true readiness, and be strengthened when wearied by the hindrances that placed themselves in their way. It was therefore necessary that suitable prophetic organs should be found, who might work upon the congregation through the divine word and in the power of the divine Spirit. But much more than this was still, if not exactly necessary, yet highly important, so, for example, that the nearest authorities in Palestine should be distinguished by righteousness or impartiality. And so it finally came to pass, and at last all things worked well together in correspondence with the divine purpose of redemption. We say "finally" and "at last;" but it was now for the first the exactly right time. The temple was ready just seventy years after its destruction, so that the prophecy of the seventy years was now fulfilled exactly thereby. Would that the congregation, the Church, might have like patience with respect to the accomplishment of greater work, the revival of faith in the unbelieving community, or the Christianizing of the heathen world. Would that they might never be over-hasty or attempt to use violence in accomplishing that which can come to pass only when it has been sufficiently prepared, and so to say, is ripe; when likewise it has a real value. Would that they might never regard the time that elapses too long, but rather think that the building of the house of God is the highest and most glorious, and on this very account the most difficult work on earth, which can only be the final result of all other works, arrangements and developments.

Vers. 16–18. 1) The congregation dedicated the house of God with joy. They might have held a fast day instead of a feast of joy. Even now when the work, after many years of effort, stood before them finished, lofty and broad enough, it is true, but far from reaching the magnificence of the old temple, and besides accomplished only through the permission, and indeed the assistance of a foreign heathen king, they might have had a specially vivid realization of the entire wretchedness of their situation according to external appearance. How easily there comes over us men, at the very time when we reach the aim of long-cherished hopes and strivings, dissatisfaction, ill-humor, dejection, instead of joy, because it does not correspond with our ideas! But it is a matter of humility and faith, under all circumstances, to recognize with internal thankfulness that that which has been gained is much more than we could in any way expect, that it is super-abundant grace and mercy; a child-like heart with reference to what is still denied us waits patiently on the Lord, and says to itself that it is perhaps unable to judge correctly respecting what at present does not at all please it. With humble, believing, childlike hearts shall we be able again and again to ascend from the vale of tears to the bright peaks of joy, shall again and again be able to celebrate feasts of dedication and really enjoy the times of refreshment and grace which the Lord gives as the very thing that should be. It is notable and edifying for us to see that those poets of the Psalter, who probably belong to this period, had sufficient joy of faith to comfort and encourage above all their people, the poets of Ps. cxxxv. and cxxxvi., in that they called upon them to praise the Lord on account of His revelation of Himself in nature, but especially for his revelation in history; the poet of Ps. cxlvi., in that he strikes up,

"Bless the Lord, O my soul,"

which is sweetly re-echoed in our

"*Lobe den Herrn, O meine Seele, ich will ihn loben bis in den Tod.*"

Without doubt the congregation then sung Ps. cxviii. with the inmost accord of the heart, although it was really composed somewhat earlier, and especially did they appropriate with greatly agitated hearts the shout of triumph: "The right hand of the Lord is exalted, the right hand of the Lord doeth valiantly—open to me the gates of righteousness; I will go in, and I will praise the Lord—the stone which the builders refused is become the head of the corner." The poet of Ps. cxxxvii., whose heart swells with patriotism and religion, at the same time with freshness and power, yea, almost with passion, cannot but recall, with the most bitter experience, the abode in exile: "By the rivers of Babylon there we sat down; yea we wept," and wish Babylon a just recompense, thus regarding his present situation as so much better. But already the Lord likewise came to the help of their faith, as is clear from this very Psalm, in that even now, when He turned the heart of the king of Assyria towards Israel, and thus brought the period of exile to an end, He delivered over the ancient enemy Babylon to the destroying judgment. Already the same Darius, to whom the restoration is very properly ascribed, had so severely chastised Babylon, that the poet of Ps. cxxxvii. can designate it in ver. 8 as overthrown or laid waste.

2) It was still the highest thing for the congregation of the old covenant to dedicate a temple, in which the Lord would dwell in their midst, yet separated from them, and indeed in the midst of a priesthood, which must still stand to mediate between them and the Lord. To us, the New Testament congregation, much more is granted. On the peaks that we Christians may ascend in humility and faith, we should dedicate temples to the Lord, since He will dwell among us, moreover also internally within us, namely, in our hearts, we should accordingly rejoice in an entirely immediate communion with Him, and all the peace and blessing that are involved therein, and exercise ourselves in a holy priesthood, that is, offer sacrifices of praise through our Lord Jesus Christ, to show forth, *etc.* 1 Peter ii. 9.

3) Vers. 19–22. The Feast of Passover and unleavened bread constituted the conclusion of the old and the beginning of the new period. Through the offering of the Paschal Lamb and the partaking of the Passover meal connected therewith, the congregation of the old Covenant appropriated to itself the forgiveness of God as the God of the covenant, which forgiveness they ever needed, and the preservation conditioned thereon. But through the feast of unleavened bread they vowed, in that the strict abstinence from all leaven was connected therewith, to walk not in the old leaven of wickedness and wantonness, but in the unleavened bread of sincerity and truth. Well for us that we also, where we are truly conscious of our redemption, can celebrate ever anew the feast of passover and unleavened bread, since we also have a paschal lamb, yea, that we can do this in a different way from the Old Testament congregation, since our paschal offering and the sacred meal connected therewith, imparts in a much more powerful manner forgiveness and preservation, since we thus have far more cogent motives to rise into the new and pure life of sincerity and truth.

HOMILETICAL AND PRACTICAL.

Vers. 1-12. That which threatens to become a hindrance must serve for our advantage. 1) When,—if in our undertakings, looking at the final aim, it is to be done for the cause and glory of God. 2) Why,—because the advancement of the cause of God, long in advance and to the minutest detail has been once for all provided for and ordained. 3) How,—the example of predecessors, who have previously taken part in this work, comes into mind and gives their successors a favorable disposition towards the work.—STARKE: It is easy to conceive, moreover, how it must have grieved the Samaritans that they were not only obliged to let the temple be entirely brought to completion, but that also their tribute should be applied to the promotion of the building, and the observation of the divine service with sacrifices. — How important and thankworthy the favorable conduct of even heathen princes has been toward the people of God. 1) That of Cyrus—*a*, He gave to the congregation again their liberty to worship the Lord, and ordered the restoration of the temple; *b*, he thereby gave an example, which determined the conduct of his successors.—STARKE: Great lords should be diligent in the practice of virtue, in order that their successors after their death may have a good example, and that they thereby may gain an everlasting name. Eccl. vii. 1; Prov. xxii. 1. The richest persons should be the first to open their liberal hands when something is to be given for the building of churches and the support of the ministry.—God has the heart of kings also in His hand and can incline them so that they are obliged to have good-will to His children, Dan. ii. 48. 2) The favorable conduct of Darius: *a*) he lets himself be guided by a noble example, yea seeks to surpass it; *b*) he desires the prayers of the congregation; *c*) he used his power in a good and proper manner to help the pious and threaten the wicked.—STARKE: Respecting the duty of subjects to pray for their rulers, even if they are heathen, see 1 Tim. ii. 2; comp. Jer. xxix. 7; 1 Macc. xii. 11. Magistrates should act in their government so as to comfort themselves with the general prayers of their subjects. Regents should make arrangements that prayers should be made to God for their welfare and successful government; for the devil lays many snares for them, but a devout prayer will help them much. The sword, intrusted by God to magistrates, must afford protection to the pious, Rom. xiii. 4.

Vers. 13-15. The building of the temple or kingdom of God is the final result of all the divine guidance: 1) It needs the willingness of the congregation, and on this account also the activity of prophets and preachers; 2) it needs, moreover, kings and their representatives, and on this account also a direction of history, by which God works on their hearts; 3) it needs above all the good and gracious will of God.—STARKE: The Lord has a kingdom and He rules among the heathen, Ps. xxii. 29. He brings the counsel of the heathen to nought, and turns the thoughts of the nations, He disposes their hearts. Ps. xxxiii. 10, 15.

Vers. 16-18. The true joy of dedication. 1) Upon what it is founded: STARKE: My Christian friend, has the spiritual building of the house of God been established in thy soul, then forget not to praise and give thanks. 2) How it is established,—by our taking to ourselves, with humility and gratitude, what the Lord grants, as truly good and salutary, and putting our trust in Him with respect to all that is still lacking. 3) How it expresses itself by true sacrifices, thus by setting to work in the universal priesthood.—STARKE: Our redemption from the kingdom of the devil and the deliverance of the church is the work of God alone; for His hand helps powerfully, Ps. xx. 7. And then for the first will our mouth be full of laughter, and our tongue full with singing, Ps. cxxvi. 2.

Vers. 19-22. The life of him who has consecrated his heart to be a temple of the Lord is a continual passover feast, for he feels himself compelled, 1) ever to take anew grace for grace, fleeing from the death of the curse; 2) ever anew to let himself be sanctified unto sincerity and truth, so that he rises from the death of sin; 3) to rejoice with the holy passover joy of redemption, which God has accomplished in Jesus Christ, and which He will likewise fulfil in Him at last. —[HENRY: Let not the greatest princes despise the prayers of the meanest saints; 'tis *desirable* to have them *for us*, and *dreadful* to have them *against us*.—Whatever we dedicate to God, let it be done with joy, that He will please to accept of it.—The purity of ministers adds much to the beauty of their ministrations, so doth their unity.—TR.]

PART SECOND.

The Congregation as the People of the Lord. Negative Strengthening of their Life in the Law (Ezra's Activity).

CHAPS. VII.–X.

FIRST SECTION.

Ezra's Emigration to Jerusalem.

CHAPS. VII.–VIII.

A.—EZRA'S JOURNEY AND PURPOSE, AND ARTAXERXES' LETTER OF COMMISSION.

CHAP. VII. 1–27.

I. *Ezra's Journey and Purpose.* Vers. 1–10.

1 Now after these things, in the reign of Artaxerxes king of Persia, Ezra the son
2 of Seraiah, the son of Azariah, the son of Hilkiah, The son of Shallum, the son of
3 Zadok, the son of Ahitub, The son of Amariah, the son of Azariah, the son of Ma-
4, 5 rioth, The son of Zerahiah, the son of Uzzi, the son of Bukki, The son of Abishua,
6 the son of Phinehas, the son of Eleazar, the son of Aaron the chief priest: This
Ezra went up from Babylon; and he *was* a ready scribe in the law of Moses, which
the LORD God of Israel had given: and the king granted him all his request, accord-
7 ing to the hand of the LORD his God upon him. And there went up *some* of the
children of Israel, and of the priests, and the Levites, and the singers, and the por-
ters, and the Nethinim, unto Jerusalem, in the seventh year of Artaxerxes the king.
8 And he came to Jerusalem in the fifth month, which *was* in the seventh year of the
9 king. For upon the first *day* of the first month began he to go up from Babylon,
and on the first *day* of the fifth month came he to Jerusalem, according to the good
10 hand of his God upon him. For Ezra had prepared his heart to seek the law of
the LORD, and to do *it*, and to teach in Israel statutes and judgments.

II. *Artaxerxes' Letter of Commission.*

11 Now this *is* the copy of the letter that the king Artaxerxes gave unto Ezra the
priest, the scribe, *even* a scribe of the words of the commandments of the LORD, and
12 of his statutes to Israel. Artaxerxes, king of kings, unto Ezra the priest, a scribe
13 of the law of the God of heaven, perfect *peace*, and at such a time. I make a de-
cree, that all they of the people of Israel, and *of* his priests and Levites, in my realm,
14 which are minded of their own freewill to go up to Jerusalem, go with thee. For-
asmuch as thou art sent of the king, and of his seven counsellors, to inquire concern-
ing Judah and Jerusalem, according to the law of thy God which *is* in thine hand;
15 And to carry the silver and gold, which the king and his counsellors have freely
16 offered unto the God of Israel, whose habitation *is* in Jerusalem, And all the silver
and gold that thou canst find in all the province of Babylon, with the freewill
offering of the people, and of the priests, offering willingly for the house of their
17 God which *is* in Jerusalem: That thou mayest buy speedily with this money bul-
locks, rams, lambs, with their meat-offerings and their drink-offerings, and offer them
18 upon the altar of the house of your God which *is* in Jerusalem. And whatsoever
shall seem good to thee, and to thy brethren, to do with the rest of the silver and

19 the gold, that do after the will of your God. The vessels also that are given thee
for the service of the house of thy God, *those* deliver thou before the God of Jerusa-
20 lem. And whatsoever more shall be needful for the house of thy God, which thou
shalt have occasion to bestow, bestow *it* out of the king's treasure-house. And I,
even I Artaxerxes the king, do make a decree to all the treasurers which *are*
beyond the river, that whatsoever Ezra the priest, the scribe of the law of the God
22 of heaven, shall require of you, it be done speedily, Unto a hundred talents of silver,
and to a hundred measures of wheat, and to a hundred baths of wine, and to a hun-
23 dred baths of oil, and salt without prescribing *how much.* Whatsoever is com-
manded by the God of heaven, let it be diligently done for the house of the God of
heaven: for why should there be wrath against the realm of the king and his sons?
24 Also we certify you, that, touching any of the priests and Levites, singers, porters,
Nethinim, or ministers of this house of God, it shall not be lawful to impose toil,
25 tribute, or custom, upon them. And thou, Ezra, after the wisdom of thy God, that
is in thine hand, set magistrates and judges, which may judge all the people that
are beyond the river, all such as know the laws of thy God; and teach ye them that
26 know *them* not. And whosoever will not do the law of thy God, and the law of the
king, let judgment be executed speedily upon him, whether *it be* unto death, or to
banishment, or to confiscation of goods, or to imprisonment.

III. *Ezra's Thanksgiving.*

27 Blessed *be* the LORD God of our fathers, which hath put *such a thing* as this in
the king's heart, to beautify the house of the LORD which *is* in Jerusalem: And
hath extended mercy unto me before the king, and his counsellors, and before all
the king's mighty princes. And I was strengthened as the hand of my LORD my
God *was* upon me, and I gathered together out of Israel chief men to go up with me.

EXEGETICAL AND CRITICAL.

Our author has no scruples in simply leaping over a period of fully fifty-seven years, in the use of the loose connecting formula: **And after these things** (comp. Gen. xv. 1; xxii. 1, *etc.*). Such gaps the ancient sacred history has again and again; it is silent respecting the time between Joseph and Moses, respecting the time passed by the generation rejected of God in the wilderness, respecting the time of the exile. There was lacking in these times useful material calculated for the edification of the congregation, so much the more then must this have failed in the time subsequent to the building of the temple, when the congregation of Jehovah had been excused from the task of giving their life a civil organization, and accordingly was referred to a quiet life, in which there could be no longer expected, as in former times, new and important manifestations of God. Nevertheless the new beginning of the congregation after the exile, which the book of Ezra would describe, had not been entirely completed by that which had already transpired. It is true the temple and its worship had been re-established by Zerubbabel and Jeshua, but the law was only thereby secured at the basis, an objective validity. With the new and holy zeal that inspired all, at the beginning, it was their earnest endeavor, as we can hardly doubt, to carry the law out likewise subjectively in the domestic and personal life, with more and more completeness and thoroughness. But the vicinity of the heathen, their dependence upon their superior authorities, the manifold intercourse with many of them, which could hardly be avoided, made the temptation easy to be brought into closer association with them, even to intermarry with them, and thereby there was necessarily involved a neglect of the law, especially in its prescription as to food and purity. Besides, the descendants of Zerubbabel, if we may refer Neh. v. 15 to them, were not calculated to offer the congregation a higher support, they rather, in all probability, soon enough entirely withdrew. Thus notwithstanding the temple and its worship, that which was properly the principal thing, the life of the congregation in accordance with the law, yea the congregation itself as such, was soon again brought into question. The thorough subordination to the divine law, on the part of all, was now all the more necessary that it alone could hold the individuals together. What previously had been accomplished by the kingdom in Israel, must now be done by the law. It was necessary that the law, as never before, should be exalted on the throne. And only when a real strengthening of the life in the law had taken place could there be said to be such a new establishment of the congregation as really promised to be the beginning of a new and permanent existence. This re-establishment was now for the first the work of Ezra, and is rightly ascribed to him by a thankful posterity which honored him as a second Moses. Certainly if we look upon the letter of commission which Artaxerxes gave him to take along with him upon his first appearance in chap. viii. it seems as if for him likewise the worship of the temple and its furtherance stood in the foreground. And surely he took great pains in this direction likewise. But both of these, the elevation of the temple worship, that perhaps again threatened to fall into decay, and the strengthening of the congregation in the life in the law, were too closely connected together, that Ezra should have thought the one possible without the other. And his real design was from the beginning very well given in chap. vii. 10: to teach in Israel statutes and judgments; and the letter of commission of Artaxerxes authorized him, in a manner worthy of attention (vii. 25), to set up magistrates and judges, who should provide for the enforcement of the law. In our book he accomplishes the re-establishment at least in a negative way, by the separation of heathen women, in general by the doing away with intermarriage with the heathen; in Neh. (viii.—x.) likewise in a positive way, that is, by renewing the covenant with God on the basis of those prescriptions of the law that were then most important.

Vers. 1–10. Artachshasta, which is here written אַרְתַּחְשַׁסְתְּא, as in ver. 11, and viii. 1; Neh. ii. 1; v. 14; xiii. 6, is surely the same, who in vi. 14 is called אַרְתַּחְשַׁשְׂתְּא (so also chap. iv. 8, 11, 23), and in iv. 7 אַרְתַּחְשַׁשְׂתָּא, namely, Artaxerxes Longimanus. In Neh. xiii. 6, where the same person is certainly meant, since there is no doubt that Ezra and Nehemiah were cotemporaries according to Neh. xii. 36, the reference is to the thirty-second year of his reign. This does not properly refer to Xerxes, whom Josephus (*Arch.* XI. 5, 1) and recently even Fritzsche (comp. Esdras viii. 1), would understand, because it is most natural to think of him after the Darius of the previous chapter, but only to Artaxerxes Longimanus, to whom indeed the name itself refers with sufficient clearness. Ezra sprang, according to the accompanying genealogy from the family of the high-priest through Seraiah. For all the names from Seraiah up to Aaron are of the line of the high-priest (comp. 1 Chron. v. 30–40); only in ver. 3 six members of the line are passed over between Azariah and Meraioth (according to 1 Chron. vi. 7–10), without doubt only for the sake of brevity, as is frequently the case in the longer genealogies. Seraiah, the son of Azariah, the son of Hilkiah, was the high-priest whom Nebuchadnezzar had commanded to be slain at Riblah (2 Kings xxv. 18–21), was thus the father of the high-priest Jehozadak, who was carried into exile (1 Chronicles vi. 14 sq.). It is very notable, however, that Ezra did not spring from Jehozadak in whose line the high-priesthood was inherited, but from a younger son; for else the intervening member between him and Seraiah would not have been left unmentioned. Ezra was probably the great great-grandson of Seraiah; for the high-priest Jeshua who had gone to Jerusalem seventy-eight years before with Zerubbabel, was a grandson of Seraiah. One hundred and thirty years had already passed since the execution of the latter in the year 588.

Ver. 6. **This Ezra went up from Babylon.**—This renews the subject and gives the predicate of ver. 1.—**A ready scribe.**—Since Ezra is designated already at the beginning as a skillful or learned scholar, that talent is ascribed to him, upon which under the present circumstances, the fostering of the life of the congregation most depended. סוֹפֵר, in the ancient writings, writer or secretary, has already obtained the meaning of *γραμματεύς* in Jer. viii. 8, where it is parallel and synonymous with חֲכָמִים. If it became the official name of the chancellor in the sense of scribe, it has in the sense of scholar, as is clear especially from ver. 11, already almost the character of a title of honor for the man of learning. The additional clause: **the king granted him——all his request**, indicates that his journey was no private undertaking, that he rather was provided with a certain authority, and journeyed as an official personage. Yet we must not think of him as governor of Judah; he is nowhere given this title. He had simply the authority to teach as a teacher his knowledge of the law, and at the same time as a superior judge—according to ver. 25, likewise by the setting up of suitably subordinate judges—to vindicate the law.—בַּקָּשָׁה, the request, the petition, except here, is only found in the book of Esther, chap. v. 3, 6. The question how this favoring of Ezra is related to the writing of Artaxerxes given in chap. iv., is best answered by the fact that Ezra's journey occurred somewhat later, that Artaxerxes, since he had been moved to that writing by his officials, had paid more attention to the Jews, and that he furthered Ezra's journey in order to strengthen the Jewish congregation; perhaps also in order to show thereby that he actually was ready to be as just as possible, notwithstanding the prohibition issued respecting the walls of the city. It is shown then by this approval that he would perhaps recall at a suitable time even that prohibition which indeed had been issued at first only provisionally.—**According to the hand of the Lord his God upon him.**—This language which occurs elsewhere only in vers. 9, 28; viii. 18; Neh. ii. 8, 18, and whose foundation is contained in viii. 22, 31, means so much as this, namely: "according to the goodness, providence and grace which ruled over him," namely Ezra, as then this hand of God sometimes is expressly designated as הַטּוֹבָה (ver. 9 and viii. 18) or לְטוֹבָה (viii. 22).

Vers. 7, 8, mentions in addition that Ezra at the same time led to Jerusalem a new increase of the population.—**And there went up some.**—This, in the view of the historian, so involves "with him" that he continues in ver. 8 without any further ceremony with **he came to Jerusalem.** Comp. vers. 13 and 28 and viii. 1. מִן is used partitively in the sense "some of" as chap. ii. 70, *etc.* The Levites in distinction from the priests on the one side, and from the Levites in the broader sense, from the singers and porters on the other side, are those who performed the proper service of the Levites.

Ver. 9. **For upon the first day of the first month he had fixed the departure from Babyion, and on the first of the fifth month came he to Jerusalem.**—This would state the duration of the journey. Instead of יְסֻד we are probably to read יָסַד, and indeed in the sense of *constituo, præcipio*, in which it occurs, especially in Esther i. 8. Probably the punctators had scruples about admitting this unusual sense, especially as they supposed that they could better give the force of הוּא by understanding it as: on the first of the first month *ipsum erat fundamentum profectionis*, as R. Solomon and J. H. Mich. translate; הוּא would thus serve to emphasize the "*fundamentum*" or the beginning in distinction from the completion. But we should expect יְסוֹד instead of יְסֻד, moreover the following בָּא would not connect itself therewith. Besides, on the first of the first month they began to betake themselves to the common place of assembly, whence then the entire company entered upon the proper journey to Palestine on the 12th of the month. Comp. chap. viii. 31.*

Ver. 10. **For Ezra had prepared his heart to seek the law of the Lord, and to do it, and to teach in Israel statutes and judgments.**—This is not to explain the last subordinate clause of ver. 9: according to the good hand of God upon him; but the entire undertaking of the journey. דָּרַשׁ is here in connection with אֶת־תּוֹרַת יְהוָה in the same sense as usual in connection with אֶת־יְהוָה, "adhere to the law as to a Lord and Benefactor." This "adhere to the law" comes into consideration with respect to the following "doctrines" as a necessary foundation, without which the instruction can never be carried on with success. Ezra's design was to bring again to the consciousness of the Jewish congregation, the law which they had in part neglected and consequently likewise forgotten, to direct their life according to it and strengthen their relations thereto.

Ver. 11. Now follows the documentary basis for the summary representation in the foregoing, and indeed first of all the letter of commission given to Ezra by Artaxerxes.—**And these are the contents of the letter.**—For פַּרְשֶׁגֶן, comp. iv. 11, and for נִשְׁתְּוָן, iv. 7. Ezra is called here and in vers. 12 and 21; Neh. viii. 9; xii. 26, first the **priest**, and then afterwards the **scribe**; in x. 10, 16; and Neh. viii. 2 even, only the priest; hence he is then in Esdras likewise constantly designated merely as ὁ ἱερεύς.—**The scribe of the words of the commandments of the Lord and of His statutes to Israel** means: "the scribe who especially occupied himself with the words of the law, and who thus before all was learned with reference to it."

Ver. 12. **Artaxerxes, king of kings, unto Ezra—perfect** (peace).—This is the introductory formula. גְּמִיר cannot be an adjective of סָפַר דָּתָא; it would then thus placed alone by itself have to be in the *stat. emph.* גְּמִירָא.

Yet it cannot before the following וּכְעֶנֶת mean that all that usually belonged to the introductory formula had been completely expressed in the original document (Berth.); in this way it would seem too peculiar. There is as little in favor of the view of Keil that it is an adverb in the sense of "very" belonging to an adjective to be supplied to ספר, as if the sense were: *doctori doctissimo*; the adjective could hardly have failed in such a case. According to ver. 7 we should expect that the letter, conformable to its contents of good will, would have contained in its introductory formula a greeting or wish of peace; so there is to be supplied in thought after גְּמִיר a verb as "he wishes," and the sense is: Artaxerxes wishes, in a complete manner, or abundantly—namely, peace [so Esdras, χαίρειν, followed by A. V. *perfect* (*peace*).—Tr.]

Vers. 13–19 gives the first part of the royal mandate: Let every one of Israel who will, go up with Ezra. Ezra, however, is to encourage further the worship in Jerusalem with the money that was given him for the purpose.

Ver. 13. **I make a decree,** *etc.* Comp. vi. 8. לִמְהָךְ depends upon כָּל־מִתְנַדַּב = that every one who is freely minded to go. יְהָךְ depends upon דִּי **—may go with thee.**—For the infin. מְהָךְ and the future יְהָךְ, comp. v. 5.

Ver. 14 would say: because the commission of the king and his seven counsellors is designed to encourage and strengthen the worship of Jehovah, and accordingly also the condition of His congregation. For the **seven counsellors** who constituted the supreme tribunal of the Persian kings, *vid.* Esther i. 14.* יָעֲטֹהִי, for which we might expect יָעֲטֹהִי because יָעֲטִין corresponds with the Heb. יוֹעֲצִים, and is used as חֻשְׁחַן in vi. 9. Naturally "thou" cannot be at once supplied to שְׁלִיחַ; rather the expression is a general one: the sending is made.—**To inquire concerning Judah according to the law of thy God, which is in thine hand.**—That the second person is prominent here, cannot be strange because, indeed, the whole matter is a communication to Ezra. בַּקָּרָה עַל "to hold investigation over," thus, "revise something," is then at the same time the same as "to put in order."† בְּדָת, which *st. constr.* in Norzi's edition is pointed דָּת, properly: with the law; means: according to the norm of the law. דִּי בִּידָךְ "which is in thy hand," means, "which thou possesseth," is not however to be under-

* [Rawlinson: "The direct distance of Babylon from Jerusalem is no more than about five hundred and twenty miles; and it may therefore seem surprising that the journey should have occupied four months. But no doubt the route followed was that circuitous one by Carchemish and the Orontes valley, which was ordinarily taken by armies or large bodies of men, and which increased the distance to about nine hundred miles. Still the time occupied is long, and must be accounted for by the dangers alluded to, chap. viii. 22, 31, which may have necessitated delays and *detours* to avoid conflicts."—Tr.]

* ["Herodotus relates that there were seven families pre-eminent in Persia, those of the seven conspirators against the Pseudo-Smerdis (III. 84); and it is reasonable to suppose that the heads of these families formed the special council of the king, the 'Achæmenidæ,' or royal family, being represented by the head of the branch next in succession to that of the reigning monarch." Rawlinson *in loco*. See also. *Ancient Monarchies*, Vol. IV., pp. 403 and 404.—Tr.]

† ["Probably the commission was general to inquire into the state of the province. According to Xenophon (*Cyrop.* VIII. 6, § 16) it was a part of the Persian system for the king to send an officer once a year into each province to inspect it and report upon it." Rawlinson *in loco*.—Tr.]

stood as if Ezra had a particular copy of the law, which Artaxerxes hereby would have explained as the ancient and true law of God; after that he had obtained the consent of the more distinguished of the Jews; but it is, as it were, "which thou knowest, understandest, and hast in hand." [Rawlinson, *in loco*, "righteously and justly according to the principle of thy religion."—Tr.]

Ver. 15. **And to carry the silver and gold,** *etc.* For a fuller statement of this, *vid.* viii. 25.

Ver. 16. **All the silver and gold that thou canst find in all the province of Babylon, with the free-will offering of the people and of the priests,** *etc.* The king here presupposes that in addition to himself and his counsellors there would likewise be found others, not Israelites, in the province of Babylon, who would be willing to contribute silver and gold for the support of the Jewish people; and indicates that he has given Ezra permission to take up a collection among them; for what is collected in the province of Babylon in general, is distinguished with sufficient clearness from the gifts of the people and priests, that is to say, the Jews, as is evident from the subsequent clauses. הִתְנַדָּבוּת an abstract formation from infin. Ithpaal, is that which is voluntarily given. מִתְנַדְּבִין, if it were in simple apposition to people and priests, or represented a relative clause, as Berth. supposes, would necessarily have the article; it is rather loosely connected in the sense of: "if they, so far as they voluntarily contribute."

Vers. 17–19. **Even on this account,** properly in view of these things, namely, because this sending is ordained by me to encourage the Jewish congregation and their worship.—**Thou mayest buy speedily with this money bullocks—with their meat and drink offerings**—that is, the meat and drink offerings belonging to the sacrifices according to Num. xv. 1 sq.—**And offer them on the altar.**—The Pael. תְּקָרֵב is used instead of Aphel in vi. 10, 17.

Ver. 18. **And whatsoever shall seem good to thee.**—The thorough organization of the Jewish congregational life might readily render necessary some additional expense, *e. g.* for the decoration of the temple; and Artaxerxes presupposes that the authorities in Jerusalem will be able also to make such arrangements that they may have something left of the gifts for such purposes—**and thy brethren** = the elders in Jerusalem, who also appear in v. and vi. to decide such questions.—**That do after the will of your God**—namely, as it is declared in the law.

Ver. 19. **And the vessels, for the service of the house of thy God deliver completely.**—These vessels are numbered in viii. 25, 27. The noun פָּלְחָן, which is only found here—but comp. פָּלְחֵי in ver. 24—is identical with פּוּלְחָן = "service" of the Syriac and Targums, and corresponds with the Hebrew עֲבוֹדָה. The meaning of הַשְׁלֵם "render completely" is usual in the Aphel in the Syriac, and is connected with the meaning of the Hebrew Piel שִׁלֵּם "pay."—**Before the God of Jerusalem** is essentially the same as "before the God whose dwelling is in Jerusalem." Comp. i. 3: He is the God, who is in Jerusalem.

Vers. 20–24. The second part of the decree orders that the royal treasury of the land beyond the river is to supply whatever else may prove to be necessary.

Ver. 20. **And whatsoever more shall be needful for the house of thy God, which shall occur to thee, as to be given,** that is to say, whatever need may arise when the other means have been exhausted—**shalt thou give out of the house of the treasury of the king**—that is, out of the royal treasury.*

Ver. 21 now gives at once the supplementary order for the treasurer in question; as a command to which Ezra might appeal. This must also be given here.—**By me, Artaxerxes, myself, is decreed.**—The pronoun אֲנָה serves to emphasize the suffix of מִנִּי (comp. Dan. vii. 15), and so also the following noun. The order: **all that Ezra shall require of you,** turns itself directly to the treasurer, because it is thus so much the more clear and impressive.

Ver. 22. **Unto an hundred talents,** states the *limit* to which the giving may extend. The עַד־ (up to one hundred talents) is connected with the phrase: **it shall be done** of ver. 21, so far as this involves: it shall be rendered or given. The כַּכָּר, the talent, weighed three thousand sacred shekels (comp. Ex. xxxviii. 25, 27), the holy shekel was about two marks, the Persian (comp. Xenoph. *Anab.* I. 5, 6) one and a quarter marks. The כֹּר, which occurs already in 1 Ki. v. 2; Ezek. xlv. 14, instead of the Chomer = ten ephahs or baths, thus almost two bushels.—**Salt, which is not prescribed**—which is not stated, not limited to a definite amount. [For the need of these things in the Jewish system of sacrifice, *vid.* vi. 9. "As the Persian tribute was paid partly in money and partly in kind (see note on iv. 13), the treasuries would be able to supply them as readily as they could furnish money." Rawlinson *in loco.*—Tr.]

Ver. 23 gives a still more comprehensive injunction—**all that is in accordance with the command of the God of heaven**—what is demanded according to the divine law—**let it be completely done.**—The ἅπ. λεγ. אַדְרַזְדָּא is regarded by Hitzig and Berth. as compounded of אֲדַר and אַזְדָּא (Hitz. *Comm. on Daniel* II. 5; Bertheau on II. 3) especially because אֲדַר in אֲדַרְגָּזְרַיָּא Dan. iii. 2 can be clearly recognized as an intensive prefix ("very"). Haug, on the other hand, in Ewald's *Bib. Jahrb.* V., S. 152 sq., derives it from the Persian *dorest*, the Zend. root *doreç* = "grow, prosper, become firm," as formed by א *prosth.* in the meaning of "completely, punctually in every thing."—**For why**—דִּי־לְמָה = for wherefore = "in order that not." Comp. iv. 22.

* ["The Persian system of taxing the provinces through the satraps involved the establishment in each province of at least one local treasury. Such treasuries are mentioned occasionally in Greek history (see *Arrian, Exp. Alex.* I. 17; III. 18, 19, *etc.*)." Rawlinson *in loco.*—Tr.]

Ver. 24 gives an additional clause, which is for the consideration of the treasurer likewise.—**And to you it is made known,** *etc.*, מְהוֹדְעִין has an indef. subject, or the active is for the passive; to you is it made known. Those addressed are still the same, as from ver. 21 on, thus the treasurers.—**That all priests,** *etc.*, that is, concerning all priests.—**Ministers of the house of God.**—The פָּלְחֵי בֵּית אֱלָהָא are alongside of the priests not all worshippers of the true God in general, but official persons, perhaps the lowest class [Rawlinson] as we may infer from their position after the Nethinim, or those who are not included in the foregoing classes. Bertheau compares the servants of Solomon, who occur in II. 55, 58, after the Nethinim. For מִנְדָּה, *etc.*, comp. iv. 13. לָא שַׁלִּיט properly = one not having authority, with the infin., and לְ = one who has not power, or: it is not allowed, as frequently in Syriac. לְמִרְמֵא from רְמָא in the Targums for שִׂים. Such a liberation of priests and Levites from taxes, occurred also under Artaxerxes the great. Comp. Joseph. *Arch.*, XV. 3, 3.*

Vers. 25, 26. The third part of the decree authorizes Ezra to set up judges experienced in the law for the entire Jewish people, and impose punishments for infractions of the law; this contains that very matter in which he is to afford the very help to the congregation upon which all now depended, a matter in which Artaxerxes in his good-will made an important step in advance beyond Cyrus and Darius. Since the civil and social life of Israel was so closely connected with their religion by the law, they could not well prosper under judges who had neither appreciation nor understanding of their religion. It might appear strange to us that nothing more is expressly said of the setting up of Jewish judges. But our book, which limits itself to the negative side of confirmation in the law, to the separation of the heathen women, was not the proper place for this. In the book of Nehemiah, which adds the positive side, since the congregation obligate themselves in chap. x. to keep all the important parts of the law, this is implicitly involved.

Ver. 25. **And thou, Ezra, after the wisdom of thy God,** *etc.*—דִּי בִידָךְ as in verse 24, *etc.*, "which thou possessest." מֶנִּי is imper. Pa. "appoint," "set up," for מַנִּי, the less hard *e* sound is more easily uttered, and occurs as a matter of course when it is followed by a second syllable *ma* or *man*.—**Magistrates and judges, which may judge all the people that are beyond the river.**—The imperf. לֶהֱוֹן, with the part. expresses continued action. The people to be judged are as a matter of course the Jewish people. Among them are not only those who know the law of God, but also others who yet for the first time must be instructed in it. We are not to think of the latter as proselytes, nevertheless it refers not only to the Jews of Palestine, but also to those dwelling widely scattered in the land to the West of the Euphrates. They are all to be subject to the judges set up by Ezra; the judges however are, according to the context, to watch over the observation of the Mosaic law, and maintain its authority. This is the foundation for the Jewish tradition of the institution of the great synagogue by Ezra.

Ver. 26. The object of this institution was that judgment might be diligently held over any one who did not keep the law of God and the king.—**The law of the king** can here be joined on to that of God, because so far as it required obedience to the law of God in the foregoing decree, it was transgressed by disobedience. Perhaps it had already been shown, likewise, that where obedience to the law of God ceased, usually also obedience to the royal command vanished. עֲבַד דִּינָה is in the Targ. not unusual for "hold judgment." מִנֵּהּ "out from him" = "over him." The point of beginning is here at the same time the point aimed at. The following הֵן—הֵן = sive—sive—**whether it be unto death or to banishment, whether to confiscation of goods or to imprisonment.**—שְׁרשׁוּ an entirely Syriac form of שְׁרֹשׁ, properly rooting out, is here in distinction from death, banishment, Vulg.: *exilium*, or at least excommunication (comp. x. 8) [Rawlinson], not παιδεία (Sept.). Respecting the punishment in נְכָסִין, treasure, property, as vi. 8, comp. x. 8.

Vers. 27, 28. A closing doxology. Ezra cannot but add to the foregoing decree—whose communication we are without doubt to ascribe to his hand—his praise for the grace of God, which had been so gloriously exhibited in putting this into the heart of the king to beautify the temple in Jerusalem.* נָתַן בְּלֵב as Neh. 12; vii. 15, yet likewise already in 1 Kings x. 24. כָּזֹאת = the like, namely, as is indicated in the foregoing decree. We are to consider that the exaltation of the worship is likewise a glorification of the house of the Lord.

Ver. 28. **And hath extended mercy unto me before the king.**—This is the continuation of the relative clause in ver. 27. The לְ before כָּל־שָׂרֵי puts this word on one and the same footing as the foregoing. Comp. the לְ before שָׂבֵי in vi. 7; that is to say it represents here essentially the לִפְנֵי, which is before הַמֶּלֶךְ. The clause: **And I was strengthened,** which leads over to the narrative, would say "I was able, would feel myself strong,—**and I gathered together** = so that I gathered together out of Israel chief men. These chief men were heads of households or families who, if they should be taken for the emigration to Judah, would naturally take their families with them.

* ["Here the decree of Artaxerxes was more favorable to the Jews than those of all previous Persian monarchs. We hear of a similar exemption of ecclesiastics from tribute, only to a less extent under the Seleucidæ. (Josephus' *Ant. Jud.* XII. 3, § 3)." Rawlinson *in loco*.—Tr.]

* ["This abrupt transition from the words of Artaxerxes to those of Ezra, may be compared with the almost equally abrupt change in vi. 6. The language alters at the same time from Chaldee to Hebrew, continuing henceforth to be Hebrew till the close of the book." Rawlinson *in loco*.—Tr.]

THOUGHTS UPON THE HISTORY OF REDEMPTION.

Vers. 1–10. (1) It seems that there were found among the Jews remaining behind in Babylon, even after Zerubbabel and Jeshua, at different times, such persons as were seized with a holy longing for the land of their fathers, especially for the temple of the Lord, with its lovely divine worship; who also, accordingly, went up thither not merely for a short time, but to remain forever, in order to become members of the congregation of Jerusalem, although many difficulties stood in the way of most of them, and it might be known to all what great deprivations, yea, evil circumstances, were to be endured in Judah. "Woe is me that I sojourn in Mesech, that I dwell in the tents of Kedar." This was certainly in these times the sigh of many with the poet of the 120th Psalm; and "I will lift up mine eyes unto the hills from whence cometh my help" was their subsequent triumphal song with the author of Psalm cxxi. How much more then should Christians be inspired with a holy longing to become pilgrims on the way to heaven, and become members of the upper Jerusalem, seeing that in the city of God, that is above, among the many thousand angels and saints, every lack and every evil circumstance has vanished. Ezra and the others who went up to Jerusalem in order to be able to lift up their eyes to the heights of the earthly Zion, seem to us to be saints. That Christians should strive for the higher aim, that beckons them from heaven, is, after all, only natural, and so much the more are we obliged to charge ourselves with frivolity, if we lose sight of the aim and jewel of our heavenly calling—yea, are in a condition of entire forgetfulness of it.

(2) To reform the congregation when it has fallen away to the world is impossible without a faithfully preserved and unfalsified word of God, which is their heavenly archetype; or rather ever holds before them anew the eternal norm, according to which they are to be fashioned. Even in Jerusalem, even in the most immediate vicinity of the temple, the congregation, when they neglected and forgot the law of God, might fall into a condition in which a reformation was pressingly necessary. And even in the distance, even in Babylon, Ezra, because he was a true student of the Scripture, might be called to be the reformer.

Vers. 11–26. (1) The congregation in the Diaspora had, properly speaking, for the present the great task of awakening in the heathen world—even in heathen princes, in some way a presentiment that true knowledge of God and piety above all were with them, and thereby to beget in the deeper spirits a receptivity as well for the worship of the true God as for the observation of His law. The decree of Artaxerxes, the good-will of the heathen king towards Jerusalem in general, might be an evidence of the important fact that the Diaspora actually fulfilled this allowed task. Thus there is involved therein the prophecy that they were to render this preparatory and mediatorial service for the first time to its proper extent in the Messianic times. This second edict of Artaxerxes was in distinction from the first (chap. iv.), at any rate, an evidence that he was only prejudiced against the supposed political efforts of the Jews, that he had no objection to their worship of the true God, to their existence as a religious congregation; that on the contrary it caused him joy if the worship of God in Jerusalem was promoted in a suitable manner.

(2) Notwithstanding the commands of Artaxerxes respecting what should be done for the improvement of the worship of Jerusalem were so minute, he did not allow himself in the least degree to prescribe that which concerned the internal affairs, which were regulated by the word of God. He exercised only the so-called *jus circa sacra*, and we find this in him, the heathen prince, from good motives. Manifestly, since there is no longer any theocracy, all princes likewise should be thus discreet. For the internal affairs there are higher laws and authorities, in which an earthly authority can never interfere without punishment.

Vers. 27–28. The Lord's praise expressed by Ezra is a thanksgiving that the Lord, by turning the heart of the king and his counsellors, had enabled him to make the journey to Jerusalem. We may, however, find still something more therein. After all he likewise expressed, if only mediately, his joy that the grace of God had succeeded in making such an impression upon the head of the world-monarchy at that time as the congregation, according to its highest task, was to make,—a joy which was well calculated to mark an era in the history of the congregation living in the Diaspora.

HOMILETICAL AND PRACTICAL.

Vers. 1–10. God's care over His congregation. 1) He awakens teachers (if it be necessary, even reformers) and other persons of importance to the divine worship. He wins also the hearts of the rulers, upon whose good-will the success of the teacher is conditioned.—STARKE: It is not enough to build houses and temples of stone, but we must have living instruments, that is, teachers and preachers. Preachers must first of all exhibit in their own life and consecration that which they preach to others of practical truth, as necessary and possible, 1 Cor. ix. 27; 1 Tim. iv. 12, 16.—No one should be presumptuous in any thing; he will then be sure of his calling, and it will give great comfort in all kinds of opposing circumstances.—Magistrates should also contribute their part to the building of churches and schools, and, above all, act with benevolence, because they can best do so; otherwise the heathen will put them to shame in that day. It is a sign of the great grace of God towards a people when He inclines the heart of their rulers to take suitable care that pious teachers be given to them. It is very easy for God to fill His people with blessings, for the earth is His, and the fulness thereof (Ps. xxiv. 1; 1 Chron. xxx. 12), and He has much more to give away than He has already given. 2) He protects and preserves His instruments in the way that they must go ere they can labor with the congregation. 3) He gives in their hearts the impulse and calling to do, as well as to teach His will.—The holy longing for Jerusalem: 1) it urges us out of Babylon to Jerusalem, and wins for us the hearts of such as will sustain us; 2) it provides us with fellow-pilgrims; 3) it causes the journey to succeed.

Vers. 11–26 are to be treated in essentially the same way as the decree of Darius in chap. vi.

Vers. 27–28. The best grounds for thanksgiving to God: 1) God has made the authorities of earth serviceable for the glorifying of His house and name; 2) He has placed His called ones in the position of being active in the enlargement and strengthening of His congregation.—STARKE: It is a noble gift of God, if we have a magistrate who is devoted to the true religion.—The servants of God, it is true, must submit to receive unthankfulness and disfavor for all of their faithfulness from mankind in general and great lords in particular; but if the contrary should be the case, they should recognize the fact with all the more thankfulness.

[HENRY: Moses in Egypt, Ezra in Babylon, and both in *captivity*, were wonderfully fitted for eminent service to the church.—Would we secure our peace and prosperity, let us take care that the *cause of God* be not *starved*.—If any good appear to be in our own hearts, or in the hearts of others, we must own it was God that *put it there*, and bless Him for it.—WORDSWORTH: Even Artaxerxes, a heathen king, is conscious and proclaims his persuasion, that the neglect of God and His service brings down God's anger on a nation.—TR.]

B.—EZRA'S OWN DOCUMENTARY REPORT.

CHAP. VIII. 1–36.

I. *Respecting his Companions.* Vers. 1–14.

1 THESE *are* now the chief of their fathers, and *this is* the genealogy of them that
2 went up with me from Babylon, in the reign of Artaxerxes the king. Of the sons
of Phinehas; Gershom: of the sons of Ithamar; Daniel: of the sons of David; Hat-
3 tush. Of the sons of Shechaniah, of the sons of Pharosh; Zechariah: and with him
4 were reckoned by genealogy of the males a hundred and fifty. Of the sons of Pa-
5 hath-moab; Elihoenai the son of Zerahiah, and with him two hundred males. Of
the sons of Shechaniah; the son of Jahaziel, and with him three hundred males.
6 Of the sons also of Adin; Ebed the son of Jonathan, and with him fifty males.
7 And of the sons of Elam; Jeshaiah the son of Athaliah, and with him seventy
8 males. And of the sons of Shephatiah: Zebadiah the son of Michael, and with
9 him fourscore males. Of the sons of Joab; Obadiah the son of Jehiel, and with him
10 two hundred and eighteen males. And of the sons of Shelomith; the son of Josi-
11 phiah, and with him a hundred and threescore males. And of the sons of Bebai;
12 Zechariah the son of Bebai, and with him twenty and eight males. And of the
sons of Azgad: Johanan the son of Hakkatan, and with him a hundred and ten
13 males. And of the last sons of Adonikam, whose names *are* these, Eliphelet, Jeiel,
14 and Shemaiah, and with them threescore males. Of the sons also of Bigvai; Uthai,
and Zabbud, and with them seventy males.

II. *Respecting a Rendering of this Band Complete.* Vers. 15–20.

15 And I gathered them together to the river that runneth to Ahava; and there
abode we in tents three days: and I viewed the people, and the priests, and found
16 there none of the sons of Levi. Then sent I for Eliezer, for Ariel, for Shemaiah,
and for Elnathan, and for Jarib, and for Elnathan, and for Nathan, and for Zecha-
riah, and for Meshullam, chief men; also for Joiarib, and for Elnathan, men of
17 understanding. And I sent them with commandment unto Iddo the chief at the
place Casiphia, and I told them what they should say unto Iddo, *and* to his brethren
the Nethinim, at the place Casiphia, that they should bring unto us ministers for
18 the house of our God. And by the good hand of our God upon us they brought us
a man of understanding, of the sons of Mahli, the son of Levi, the son of Israel;
19 and Sherebiah, with his sons and his brethren, eighteen; And Hashabiah, and with

20 him Jeshaiah of the sons of Merari, his brethren and their sons, twenty; Also of
the Nethinim, whom David and the princes had appointed for the service of the
Levites, two hundred and twenty Nethinim: all of them were expressed by name.

III. *Respecting the Preparation for the Journey, the Journey and Arrival in Jerusalem.* Vers. 21–36.

21 Then I proclaimed a fast there, at the river of Ahava, that we might afflict our-
selves before our God, to seek of him a right way for us, and for our little ones,
22 and for all our substance. For I was ashamed to require of the king a band of
soldiers and horsemen to help us against the enemy in the way: because we had
spoken unto the king, saying, The hand of our God *is* upon all them for good that
23 seek him; but his power and his wrath *is* against all them that forsake him. So we
24 fasted and besought our God for this: and he was entreated of us. Then I sepa-
rated twelve of the chief of the priests, Sherebiah, Hashabiah, and ten of their
25 brethren with them, And weighed unto them the silver, and the gold, and the ves-
sels, *even* the offering of the house of our God, which the king, and his counsellors,
26 and his lords, and all Israel *there* present, had offered: I even weighed unto their
hand six hundred and fifty talents of silver, and silver vessels a hundred talents,
27 *and* of gold a hundred talents; Also twenty basins of gold, of a thousand drams;
28 and two vessels of fine copper, precious as gold. And I said unto them, Ye *are*
holy unto the LORD; the vessels *are* holy also; and the silver and the gold *are* a
29 freewill offering unto the LORD God of your fathers. Watch ye, and keep *them*,
until ye weigh *them* before the chief of the priests and the Levites, and chief of the
30 fathers of Israel, at Jerusalem, in the chambers of the house of the LORD. So took
the priests and the Levites the weight of the silver, and the gold, and the vessels,
31 to bring *them* to Jerusalem unto the house of our God. Then we departed from
the river of Ahava on the twelfth *day* of the first month, to go unto Jerusalem: and
the hand of our God was upon us, and he delivered us from the hand of the enemy,
32 and of such as lay in wait by the way. And we came to Jerusalem, and abode
33 there three days. Now on the fourth day was the silver and the gold and the ves-
sels weighed in the house of our God by the hand of Meremoth the son of Uriah
the priest; and with him *was* Eleazar the son of Phinehas; and with them *was* Joza-
34 bad the son of Jeshua, and Noadiah the son of Binnui, Levites; By number *and*
35 by weight of every one: and all the weight was written at that time. *Also* the
children of those that had been carried away, which were come out of the captivity,
offered burnt-offerings unto the God of Israel, twelve bullocks for all Israel, ninety
and six rams, seventy and seven lambs, twelve he goats *for* a sin-offering; all *this*
36 *was* a burnt-offering unto the LORD. And they delivered the king's commissions
unto the king's lieutenants, and to the governors on this side the river: and they
furthered the people, and the house of God.

EXEGETICAL AND CRITICAL.

Vers. 1–14. The register of those heads of families who went up to Jerusalem with Ezra is here inserted as a second important document. It originated from Ezra himself, as the use of the first person in ver. 1 shows; it is the foundation on which his narrative of his journey and activity in Jerusalem rests. It is distinguished from the register in chap. ii. by giving not only the names of the families to which those returning belonged, but also the heads themselves of those households who returned. It is as if they became gradually more and more conscious that the existence of the Jewish congregation no longer depended upon nationality, but the free resolution of individuals, that the individual accordingly, that especially the deciding heads of households had an entirely different significance from ever before, and that this their significance might be exhibited by their express mention by name in the sacred history. That the names of families here almost exclusively, yea, if we accept the very natural emendation in vers. 3, 5, 10, are without exception the same as those that occurred already in chap. ii., is explained simply from the fact that of the families which returned with Zerubbabel, households had still remained behind in Babylon, which now with Ezra followed their relatives; and that this very relationship might have been decisive for the resolution to go up with Ezra. It is worthy of note that in this emigration just twelve families were represented. In connection with the importance then ascribed to the number twelve (comp. chap. ii. 1 sq.; vi. 17; viii. 35) Bertheau finds it probable that Ezra's company was to be a representation of the congregation of Israel in its totality. —In Esdras viii. 28–40 are found some other deviations, which now perhaps are worthy of consideration. As regards the sum total of those who returned with Ezra, it amounted to one thousand four hundred and ninety-six men and fifteen heads according to the Massoretic text; but according to Esdras one thousand six hundred and ninety men and thirteen heads without counting the priests and sons of David, whose number is not given, and in comparison with the number of the rest was perhaps but small, since Zerubbabel had already led back with him a relatively large number of priests and sons of David. In the numerical signs corruption might easily creep in, and we must leave it undecided, which statements are more correct.

Ver. 1. **These are now the heads of their fathers, and this is the genealogy of them that went up.**—רָאשֵׁי אֲבֹתֵיהֶם = רָאשֵׁי בֵית־אֲבֹתֵיהֶם, not only here but usually, house of their fathers=their household. The head of the house of their father=the head of the household. In a household, however, the sons are often again fathers, without their forming on this account households of their own. Thus often many fathers belong to the household, and under a common head of the household. Thus the head of the father's houses can easily be head of fathers. The suffix of אֲבֹתֵיהֶם refers without doubt to the totality, that is, to the children of Israel. הִתְיַחֵשׂ is first "record itself;" then the "register of families" is, however, sometimes used for the family itself. It is here added, because the name of the heads of households is to be followed by the name of the family to which they belonged.

Ver. 2. Here are first mentioned two heads of households of two priestly families; of the family of Phineas, who was a son of Eleazar, thus a grandson of Aaron, **Gerson**; and of the family of Ithamar, who was Aaron's younger son (comp. 1 Chron. xxx. and xxix.), **Daniel**; whether the latter is identical with the one mentioned in Neh. x. 7 is uncertain. Both are to be regarded as accompanied by their households; for in ver. 24 Ezra is able to select from the priests who went up with him, twelve to take care of the presents. Then follows a head of a household of the family of David, without doubt the king David, namely, **Hattush**, possibly to be identified with Hattush, the son of Hashaniah (Neh. iii. 10), but to be distinguished from the priest Hattush, Neh. x. 5; xii. 2. It is questionable, however, whether he is not more closely defined by the first words of ver. 3.

Ver. 3. **Of the sons of Shechaniah, of the sons of Pharosh.**—The twice-repeated מִבְּנֵי following one another and unconnected is striking. The Sept. has supplied an "and" before the second, so that it designates at once two families as such to which the head of household next following belongs. But this is certainly only to improve the text which was at that time just the same as ours. Esdras, on the other hand, has Λαθοὺς τοῦ Σεχενιόυ, since it renders the חַטּוּשׁ of ver. 2 by Λαθούς, attached מִבְּנֵי שְׁכַנְיָה of verse 3 as a much closer definition, and besides read the singular בֵּן for מִבְּנֵי. It is very probable that there has been a corruption of the text in this passage, and the conjecture that Esdras makes recommends itself all the more that חַטּוּשׁ in 1 Chron. iii. 22 is adduced as a son of Shemaiah, and therewith also is a grandson of Shechaniah [so Rawlinson. —Tr.] Accordingly we have left in ver. 3 only the family of Pharosh, as such, to which Zechariah with his household belonged. The next clause we may translate: **And with him belonged genealogically one hundred and fifty men**, since התיחש is taken as preterit., and the singular is explained from the fact that it precedes the verb. התיחש might, however, be a noun, so that the sense would be: and with a family, לִזְכָרִים = of men.

Ver. 5. **Of the sons of Shechaniah the son of Jahaziel.**—It is singular that the son of Jahaziel is not mentioned by name. The Sept. has ἀπὸ τῶν υἱῶν Ζαθόης Σεχενίας υἱὸς 'Αζιήλ, and Esdras viii. 32 essentially the same. Ζαθόης seems to be the same as זַתּוּא, Ezra ii. 8. Thus the Sept. and Esdras seem to have read מבני זתוא, so that it is to be translated: of the children of Zattu, Shechaniah, the son of Jahaziel [so Rawlinson.—Tr.]

Ver. 9. Here **the sons of Joab** are treated as a particular family, whilst in chap. ii. 6 they are counted with the sons of Jeshua as of the family of Pahath-Moab. Probably only a few of them belonged to those who returned under Zerubbabel, so that they were then not counted with that family with which they were nearest related, although the number of the children of Pahath-Moab, in consequence of this, became rather large.

Ver. 10. Here the Masoretic text has: **of the sons of Shelomith the son of Josiphiah.**—It is the same as in ver. 5, according to the Sept. and Esdras, and we are to read: Of the sons of Bani (comp. Ezra ii. 10) Shelomith, the son of Josiphiah [so Rawlinson.—Tr.].

Ver. 13. **And of the last sons of Adonikam, whose names are these, Eliphelet,** *etc.*—It is strange that a common head of a household should be mentioned first. Keil supposes that the sons of Adonikam, here referred to, because they did not constitute a proper father's house, are embraced together with the sons of Adonikam, who returned under Zerubbabel, and distinguished from the latter as אַחֲרֹנִים. But all the new comers here mentioned would have united with their fellow-members of the same families who already dwelt in Judah from the time of Zerubbabel. Besides the reference to those who previously returned is so entirely without support that אחרנים cannot well be explained from it. Perhaps the meaning is: not a first-born of the first line, who as such would have been head of the father's house, but only a later born, none of whom had the dignity of a head of a father's house, but only that of subordinate heads of families. Accordingly only lesser divisions of that father's house went up with Ezra. Thus would אחרנים be explained from the same circumstance from which the name of a common head of a household fails. It is true we must then suppose that אחרנים had gained such a general sense in itself that it had become a technical term for those later born.

Ver. 14. Instead of *one* head of the **sons of Bigvai**, two are mentioned, Uthai and Zabbud, yet not as later born sons, but as it seems as real heads of father's houses. The author of Esdras viii. 40 has οὐϑί ὁ τοῦ Ἰσταλκόυρου, so that it might be asked, whether the two names are not to be reduced to one.

Vers. 15–20. Above all Ezra was anxious to gain for the emigration some persons capable of ministering in the worship. Ver. 15 is probably to be translated: **I gathered them together to the river, that runneth to Ahava**, not that floweth into the Ahava. Ahava is probably the name of a place or region, after which the river there flowing was named; in ver. 21 it occurs briefly as נָהָר אַהֲוָא, and in ver. 31 נְהַר אַהֲוָא, which is either: the river of Ahava; or also after the analogy of the נְהַר פְּרָת, the river Ahava. Where we are to seek the river and region is not known; probably, however, in the vicinity of Babylon; probably it is a tributary or canal of the Euphrates, according to Ewald, *Gesch.* IV., S. 154, perhaps the Pallacopas, in favor of which is certainly the name (פלג אהוא), and indeed the more northern, which lay more in a direction towards Canaan.*—**And I viewed the people.**—Respecting the lengthened form by the addition of the ה, וָאָבִינָה here and וָאֶשְׁלְחָה in ver. 16, comp. Ewald, § 232, *g* [Green, § 99, 3.—Tr.].

Ver. 16. The Sept. translates: **And I sent to or for Elieser**, *etc.* [so A. V.]. This might mean in connection with ver. 17: I sent thither in order to have him come and use him as a messenger to Iddo. We may, however, take the ל in this later usage of the language with the Vulg. and many interpreters without hesitation, as *nota accus.*, according to 2 Chron. xvii. 7, where it is used in this very way with שלח, thus: I sent Elieser, *etc.* The first named messengers were רָאשִׁים, probably heads of little communities; the remaining two מְבִינִים, that is, teachers, Neh. viii. 7, 9; 1 Chron. xv. 22; xxviii. 8, *etc.* Keil takes it in a more general sense, judicious, prudent; but this is opposed by its connection with רָאשִׁים and the circumstance that Ezra would have sent men who could make an impression in accordance with their entire position. According to ver. 15 these men did not belong to the Levites, who usually carried on the office of instruction, comp. 1 Chron. xv. 22; xxviii. 8, *etc.* But scholarship in the Scriptures might have gradually become more widely diffused, especially in Babylon. It is possible, also, that they were priests. In chap. x. 15, 18–31, many of the names here mentioned recur again; but probably different persons were meant there.

Ver. 17. **And I sent them with commandment**; thus the *Qeri.* According to the *Kethib*, whether now the ו in ואוצאה be genuine, or first added by the Masoretes, it is to be understood: I had them go forth, עַל־עִדּוֹ הָרֹאשׁ **unto Iddo.**—עַל, according to later usage is for אֶל־. What kind of a head or chief Iddo was, what society he was of, whether merely religious, or also learned, why Ezra did not above all seek to influence Iddo himself to the return to Palestine: all this we must leave undetermined.—**At the place Casiphia.**—We know not, as a matter of course, how we are to take the clause בְּכָסִפְיָא הַמָּקוֹם. The Sept. and Esdras have not regarded כספיא as a proper name. The former has ἐν ἀργυρίῳ τοῦ τόπου, and the latter makes Iddo the head of the treasury without doubt in Babylon. It is probable, if it be a place, it is one in the vicinity of Babylon and Ahava.—**To his brethren**, *etc.*—אָחִיו הַנְּתוּנִים, which thus gives no sense, should probably be: to his brothers (the Levites) and to the Nethinim, namely, besides to himself, I ordered them to go; not to his brothers, the Nethinim [as A. V.]; for that Iddo himself was one of the Nethinim is improbable from his honorable position; that they, moreover, should be designated as his brethren without any natural relationship would be against all analogy.—**To bring us ministers for the house of our God.**—Those are especially meant who, when they had performed the service in the house of God at the feasts, should be able besides to instruct the people in the law.

Ver. 18. **And they brought us.**—וַיָּבִיאוּ is written with dagesh in א as Gen. xliii. 26, as also תָּבִיאּוּ, Lev. xxiii. 17, as then ה ח and ע sometimes occur with dagesh, "*quorum omnium ratio nota est in Arcanis Cabbalæ*," R. Mose bar Nachman in Comm. upon *Jezir* fol. 61.—Under the gracious help of God (יַד, as vii. 6), and through the influence of Iddo, they gained forty Levites and two hundred and twenty Nethinim. First of all the אִישׁ שֶׂכֶל (that this is a proper name is shown by the ו before the following names), a descendant of Mahli, the grandson of Levi (Ex. vi. 16, 19; 1 Chron. vi. 4), then **Sherebiah**, who again occurs in ver. 24 and Neh. viii. 7; ix. 4; also x. 13; xii. 24; then in ver. 19 **Hashabiah**, who likewise is again mentioned in ver. 24; Neh. x. 12; xii. 24, and finally **Jeshaiah**, who does not again meet us in Ezra or Neh.; in ver. 20 the Nethinim, who had been appointed already by Jeshua (comp. note on ii. 43 sq.), then more definitely as it is here alone mentioned, by David and the princes, that is, the high officials, to perform the heavier work for the Levites. The last words of ver. 20

* [Rawlinson: "In the right direction and at about the right distance are found a river and a town bearing the same name, called by the early Greeks *Is.* (*Herod.* I. 179), and by the later 'Αει (*Isid. Chas.*, p. 5), by the Babylonians themselves *Ibi*, and here apparently Ahava. The modern name of the place is *Hit.* It is famous for its bitumen springs, and is situated on the Euphrates at a distance of about eighty miles from Babylon towards the northwest."—Tr.]

mean* according to 1 Chron. xii. 31; they were all expressed by name (particularly), namely, for the going up with Ezra.

Vers. 21–30. The final preparation for the departure; at first the arrangement of the feast. The fasting had the purpose of imploring from God a way straight or level, free from hindrance, thus a prosperous journey. As an evidence of a penitent self-humiliation, it contributed to gain the favor of Him who, since He is throned on high, can only dwell among the lowly (Is. lvii. 15), so already Judges xx. 26; 1 Sam. vii. 6; Joel i. 14; 1 Chron. xx. 3.

Ver. 22. To implore the help of God, had a special impulse in the circumstance that Ezra and his companions had expressed a trust in God before Artaxerxes which they would not have confirmed if they had not especially relied upon God; if they had been willing to claim earthly means of protection. To show this trust in God was certainly important, because Artaxerxes' respect for the Jewish religion might be best strengthened in this very way. They acknowledged that **the hand of our God is upon all them for good that seek Him; but His power and wrath is against all them that forsake Him.**—We might expect the words: for evil; but His strength and His wrath=His power of opposing, is sufficiently clear; it is as if the previous clause were: His goodness and favor are over, *etc.;* so that the words "for good" might have been left out.

Ver. 23. **We fasted and besought our God.**—This should be followed by זאת, and not עַל־זאת. עַל־זאת seems to refer back to ver. 22 in the sense of therefore. Yet it is at least questionable whether it may not after the verb of asking, likewise introduce the object, comp. עַל־זאת with התפלל (Ps. xxxii. 6), and indeed notwithstanding the מִן before אֱלֹהֵינוּ.—**And He let Himself be entreated for us.**—This is at once manifest in the successful progress of the journey.

Ver. 24 sq. The appointment of guardians of the treasures.—**And I separated twelve of the princes of the priests.**—Instead of לְ before שֵׁרֵבְיָה, we are to read וְ with Esdras viii. 54; for Sherebiah, *etc.*, did not belong to the priests, but to the Levites. In addition, therefore, to the twelve princes of the priests, there were accordingly twelve Levites, as those to whom Ezra weighed the treasure and gave it in charge.

Ver. 25. **And I weighed,** *etc.*—ואשקולה is written with ו after ק because the *Sheva* of ק was meant to be heard, and indeed as Chateph Kametz, and it is probable that this form is to have the same vocalization in the next verse, as then J. H. Mich. found it to be so in many MSS. The other view that it was to be spoken with Chateph Patach was held because the ו was lacking after ק, as likewise in Jer. xxxii. 9. The silver and gold were a heave-offering, תְּרוּמָה, that is, a present to the house of God, that the king and his counsellors had set apart, comp. vii. 15, 16, 19. הֵרִים in connection with תְּרוּמָה means: to take off from the other possessions something, in order to consecrate it to God. The article before הֵרִימוּ represents the relative pronoun as 1 Chron. xxvi. 28; xxix. 17; 2 Chron. xxix. 36, *etc.;* comp. Ew. 381, *b.*—הַנִּמְצָאִים (with *kametz* under צ instead of *sheva* on account of pause, comp. Esther i. 5). These are those who were happened upon or met.

Vers. 26, 27. What Ezra weighed, עַל־יָדָם, in their hands, as i. 8. With respect to the talents comp. vii. 22; the darics, ii. 69; the covered cups, i. 10. Finally there were two copper vessels of excellent polish. מֻצְהָב cannot very well be part. Hophal; in connection with נְחֹשֶׁת, it would just as well as the following טוֹבָה have the fem. form. It seems to be a noun formed like מוּצָק, מֻטָּה, מוּעָף (Is. viii. 8, 23) with the meaning of polish. צָהֹב occurs Lev. xiii. 30, 32 of bleached hair, become somewhat fox-like by leprosy; the root, צהב, is, however, certainly connected with זהב, Arab. *sahaba*, and the other roots in צה and צח, whose meaning extends to: to be bright. הַמּוּדוֹת is properly a noun=lovelinesses, comp. כְּלֵי חֲמוּדוֹת, 2 Chron. xx. 25.

Ver. 28. The sacredness of the guardians as such, especially of the treasures entrusted to them as a heave-offering to the Lord is emphasized by Ezra, in order to make them right watchful with reference to them until they shall have delivered them up.

Ver. 29. הַלְּשָׁכוֹת is acc. of direction, but not *stat. constr.* as the article shows. The לְשָׁכוֹת are, because almost exclusively the temple-chambers, sufficiently definite of themselves. בֵּית יְהוָה is in apposition with the foregoing.

Vers. 31–36. The journey and arrival in Jerusalem.—Ver. 31. They began their journey from the river Ahava on the **twelfth day of the first month**. The interval from the first had been occupied by that which is narrated in vers. 16–30. The statement in ver. 15 that they had encamped only three days on the river of Ahava is probably not to be understood as if they after three days had again broken up (Berth.), but indicates either the point of time when that which is mentioned in ver. 15 sq. occurred (comp. v. 32), namely, when Ezra observed the lack of Levites (Keil); or it means to say that after three days they had gone somewhat further on their way, but without leaving the river Ahava, towards a region where they could unite with those coming from Casiphiah, from thence then entering upon their journey proper.

Ver. 32. When then they had come to Jerusalem, according to chap. vii. 9, on the first day of the fifth month, then after a lapse of three and a half months, they remained there three days, that is, rested, until they understood something further, just as Nehemiah in chap. ii.

* [Rawlinson *in loco:* "The writer seems to mean that he had before him a list of the two hundred and twenty, though he did not think it necessary that he should insert it."—Tr.]

11, whilst without doubt they already made preparation for the delivery of the treasures.

Ver. 33. **Now on the fourth day** they weighed out the treasures in the hand (ver. 26) of the priest Meremoth ben Uriah, whom we find again Neh. iii. 4, 21, and probably also Neh. xii. 3, and Eleazar ben Phinehas, who is not further mentioned, and two Levites, Jozabad ben Jeshua, who may be identical with the one mentioned in chap. x. 23, and Noadiah ben Binnui, whose family is mentioned likewise in Neh. x. 10; xii. 8.

Ver. 34. **By number and weight of every one**, that is, as it was for each and every number and weight. The weight was written then at that time, as Neh. iv. 16, in a public document, so that the correct preservation might be confirmed.

Ver. 35. In order now to secure for themselves a good reception with the Lord, they offered above all burnt-offerings, whereby they rendered homage to Him, dedicated themselves to Him (comp. notes upon iii. 3), and indeed for all Israel, in their name and as their representatives, conscious indeed that they had value before God only as a part of this whole, or rather as in union with entire Israel. They offered twelve bullocks (comp. vi. 17), besides ninety-six rams (ninety-six as intensification of twelve) and seventy-seven lambs (seventy-seven as intensification of seven, the number seven expressing the covenant-relation), as a foundation of the burnt-offering, however, twelve he-goats for a sin-offering, because only the reconciled can do homage to the Lord in a proper manner and worthily dedicate themselves to Him.

Ver. 36. In order now to put themselves in a good relation with the satraps and governor in Abar Nahara, they delivered to them the decree of the king. The satraps, אחשדרפנים, Persian (according to the inscription of Behistun), *khshatrapava*, from *khshatrapavan*, from which the noun in the Hebrew expression of the word is explained, prop. =land-protector* (comp. Esth. iii. 12; viii. 9; Dan. iii. 2), come into consideration as military officers, alongside of the governors, פַּחֲווֹת, as the presidents of the civil government.—**And they furthered**, *etc.*—These closing words are certainly to be referred to those Persian magnates, to whom indeed this supporting was commanded by the royal edict, vii. 20–24. נִשָּׂא as i. 4. The Perfect נִשְּׂאוּ with וְ simply continues the narrative as וְקַבְּלוּ in ver. 30.

THOUGHTS UPON THE HISTORY OF REDEMPTION.

Vers. 1–14. So long as God was obliged to dwell in a particular temple, in the midst of His congregation, yet separated from them, mediatorial persons were still necessary, namely, priests, and a worship of sacrifices; Jerusalem must still remain the proper place of worship, and Judah be the holy land as no other land could be. And the congregation in the dispersion must regard it as their sacred duty, over and over again to put themselves in relation to the temple and Jerusalem, and send thither whole bands, in whom the longing for the land of their fathers awoke, to the enlargement of the principal congregation, or yet at least little embassies (comp. Zech. vi. 9), to enliven the communion with it, so likewise to take part, when opportunity offered, either in person, or at least through representatives, in the offering of sacrifice in the legitimate place of sacrifices. This common relation to the one centre and hearthstone of their religious life, constituted a bond, which held the people together in spite of every scattering and spreading out, yes, cultivated the feeling of a grand unity; and even if this bond was only an external one, it yet was all the more important, the weaker the internal bond was in the times of the law and the letter of the law. Christendom is united by the internal bond of *one* common faith and the most comprehensive love. Would then that this may never prove internally weaker! Would that in spite of all distances and separations, all might remain ever truly and vitally conscious of this, that they may constitute more than the people of the old covenant one only great union the body of the Lord! What can be more exalting and strengthening than this consciousness that we do not stand alone, do not struggle alone, do not suffer alone, do not rejoice alone, but that the Lord has in every land a people, a great and united people?

Vers. 15–20. The relation to the God of Revelation who would be conceived, not according to common notions or ideas, but according to His historical manifestation of Himself, and on the ground of the acts of redemption wrought by Him, would be honored according to the regulations given by Himself,—begets by internal necessity the need of instruction and training. It cannot be maintained in any other way than by the parents' making known to their children, and the learned to the unlearned, the Providences and Histories through which the true God has come near to the understanding, and that trained and suitable persons should cultivate the divine service in a proper manner. The idea, that religious knowledge, so far as it is necessary or desirable, makes its appearance in every man of itself, has no place except in the sphere of natural religion, and is connected, if it has become more general in our day, with a falling away from the religion of revelation to the religion of nature. It thus had its good ground that Ezra would not go up to Jerusalem and enter upon the work of elevation of the congregation at that place, without having gained above all a sufficient number of persons for his emigration, who might stand at his side, as instructors and helpers in the worship of God. And for those who would cherish the true religion, it should ever be a chief care to attract suitable teachers and ministers to the church, whilst now, sad to see, it seems as if it were thought that, at any rate, they could be dispensed with.

* [Rawlinson *in loco:* "The word is derived from *khshatra*, "crown," and *pal*, "to protect," the active part of which would be *pana*. It is evident that the Hebrew term represents the older form of the word, and represents it pretty closely. There is a prosthetic *Aleph*, as in *adarkon* and Ahasuerus, and the *tr* of the Persian becomes in the Hebrew *dr;* but otherwise the letters are correctly rendered." Rawlinson refers the satrap to the chief ruler of the Persian provinces, from which the governors (pachavoth), rulers of smaller districts, are distinguished.—TR.]

Vers. 21–30. Already in Is. lii. 11 the encouragement: depart, depart, go ye out from thence, is connected with the admonition, be ye clean, ye that bear the vessels of the Lord. Ezra might even, without this, have felt himself called upon to prepare himself and those who accompanied him by fasting; that is, by self-humiliation, for the journey to Jerusalem. But since he carried with him vessels and treasure designed for the house of the Lord, and in so far sacred; in other words, since his journey ministered not to ordinary, but sacred purposes, by which properly all who took part received a higher significance, purification and sanctification by true and genuine fasting, were an especially indispensable prerequisite. No one can essentially further the cause and honor of God in a free and conscious manner without previously doing what fasting signifies—namely, chastising, yea, overcoming his soul—that is, his old man. He who has accomplished this will then have a keener feeling also for the particular obligation imposed upon him by his calling or his task, especially for the sacred duty conscientiously to watch that that which has been intrusted to us of blessings or gifts shall be truly serviceable for the higher ends for which they were given to us. He will understand the connection between the two when Ezra says: at first, be ye holy to the Lord, and the vessels are holy,—so watch and take care, *etc.*

Vers. 31–36. Men like Ezra, who know that they are instruments in the hand of the Lord, and indeed for the accomplishment of a high mission, may reckon with the confidence of heroes on especial divine protection and support in the midst of all the dangers threatening them: "And although all the devils would withstand us," *etc.* What, however, is secured to them in this respect by God cannot be for them a motive for giving themselves over to a false security, but only become an impulse for them to make use of all that is entrusted to them, with all the more conscientiousness for the accomplishment of its purposes. At the same time they would be very careful, like Ezra, when he ordered the weight of the gifts brought by him to be written down, of securing their good name against any wicked slanders that so easily are raised against them. That the returned exiles so soon offered sacrifice to the Lord, and indeed burnt-offerings, with the sin-offerings belonging to them, expresses, moreover, the knowledge that the mere offering of external gifts, however great they might be, amounted to nothing; that an internal gift, namely, that of the heart, by internal worship, must be added, yea, that it alone, if it be of the true kind, gives worth to all the rest.

When the returned exiles laid claim to protection and support on the part of the magistracy through the handing over the decree of the king to his officers, they subordinated themselves to them thereby at the same time. As they thus through their sacrifice gave to God what belonged to God, so through the decree of Artaxerxes they gave to the state what the state might expect.

HOMILETICAL AND PRACTICAL.

Vers. 15–20. The importance of teachers and other officials in the congregation. 1) Ezra, although there were priests enough in Jerusalem, felt the absence of Levites and other persons of lower rank, who there might care for the divine service, and also instruct the people. 2) He seeks to procure them before he undertakes anything further. 3) He gains them through the experienced help of God.—Starke: That Ezra seeks to supply the lack of Levites, and sends so far for them, shows his zeal for the house of God, and indicates how much we should make of wise ministers of God, should it ever be necessary to bring them from afar. We need also frequently such persons as may fill the lower offices more pressingly than others who sit in exalted stations; and we must have more village-pastors than doctors of theology and superintendents. He who is of a sincere and unenvious disposition in the ministerial office will not always be alone, but can very well endure, yea, desires and assists, that more laborers and colleagues may be procured alongside of him, Num. xi. 29; Matt. ix. 37.

Vers. 21–30. Respecting the true preparation for the most important journey. 1) By fasting or overcoming one's self; 2) By watchfulness with respect to the blessings and gifts that serve to glorify the divine name; 3) By conscientious execution of the higher duties.—Starke: Although Christians are not bound to any particular time of fasting, yet they should ever lead a temperate and moderate life, in order that they may be the more qualified for prayer, 1 Peter iv. 8.—Observe this, ye travellers: Divine protection sought by humble prayer is your safest escort.—God is the best guide (Ps. xci. 11); though we walk in the dark valley, we need not fear, Ps. xxiii. 4. If after the offering of prayer our enterprise goes successsfully on, we ought not to think that it has been without dangers, but confidently believe that our prayer has been heard.

Vers. 31–36. The pilgrims to Zion. 1) Their journey (is towards Jerusalem under God's especial protection); 2) their blessings and gifts (belong to the house and congregation of the Lord); 3) their aim (to offer to the Lord, and indeed, above all themselves, recognizing the authorities of the world). Brentius: *Sunt autem (Christiani), sanctificari in baptismo per fidem in Christum. Unde portare debent sancta vasa, quæ sunt sancta opera. Credere in Christum, sanctum opus est.*

[Henry: All our concerns about *ourselves,* our *families,* our *estates,* 'tis our Wisdom and Duty by Prayer to commit them to God and leave the care of them with Him. Our prayers must always be seconded with endeavors.—'Tis a great ease to one's mind to be discharged from a trust; and a great honor to one's name to be able to make it appear that it hath been faithfully discharged. —Wordsworth: It appears from the narrative that Ezra's God was good, his treasurers faithful, and his companions devout; and that the royal governors furthered his work. Such were the salutary effects of prayer and fasting.—Tr.]

SECOND SECTION.

The Chief Fault of the Time and its Removal.

CHAPS. IX.—X.

A.—THE CHIEF FAULT OF THE TIME AND EZRA'S PENITENTIAL PRAYER.

CHAP. IX. 1–15.

I. *The Chief Fault of the Time, and Ezra's Sorrow for It.* Vers. 1–4.

1 Now when these things were done, the princes came to me, saying, The people of
Israel, and the priests, and the Levites, have not separated themselves from the
people of the lands, *doing* according to their abominations, *even* of the Canaanites,
the Hittites, the Perizzites, the Jebusites, the Ammonites, the Moabites, the Egyp-
2 tians, and the Amorites. For they have taken of their daughters for themselves,
and for their sons: so that the holy seed have mingled themselves with the people
of *those* lands: yea, the hand of the princes and rulers hath been chief in this tres-
3 pass. And when I heard this thing, I rent my garment and my mantle, and
4 plucked off the hair of my head and of my beard, and sat down astonied. Then
were assembled unto me every one that trembled at the words of the God of Israel,
because of the transgression of those that had been carried away · and I sat astonied
until the evening sacrifice.

II. *Ezra's Penitential Prayer.* Vers. 5–15.

5 And at the evening sacrifice I arose up from my heaviness; and having rent my
garment and my mantle, I fell upon my knees, and spread out my hands unto the
6 LORD my God, And said, O my God, I am ashamed and blush to lift up my face
to thee, my God: for our iniquities are increased over *our* head, and our trespass is
7 grown up unto the heavens. Since the days of our fathers *have* we *been* in a great
trespass unto this day; and for our iniquities have we, our kings, *and* our priests,
been delivered into the hand of the kings of the lands, to the sword, to captivity,
8 and to a spoil, and to confusion of face, as *it is* this day. And now for a little space
grace hath been *shewed* from the LORD our God, to leave us a remnant to escape,
and to give us a nail in his holy place, that our God may lighten our eyes, and give
9 us a little reviving in our bondage. For we *were* bondmen; yet our God hath not
forsaken us in our bondage, but hath extended mercy unto us in the sight of the
kings of Persia, to give us a reviving, to set up the house of our God, and to repair
10 the desolations thereof, and to give us a wall in Judah and in Jerusalem. And
now, O our God, what shall we say after this? for we have forsaken thy command-
11 ments, Which thou hast commanded by thy servants the prophets, saying, The land,
unto which ye go to possess it, is an unclean land with the filthiness of the people
of the lands, with their abominations, which have filled it from one end to another
12 with their uncleanness. Now therefore give not your daughters unto their sons,
neither take their daughters unto your sons, nor seek their peace or their wealth
for ever: that ye may be strong, and eat the good of the land, and leave *it* for an
13 inheritance to your children for ever. And after all that is come to pass upon us
for our evil deeds, and for our great trespass, seeing that thou our God hast pun-
ished us less than our iniquities *deserve*, and hast given us *such* deliverance as this;
14 Should we again break thy commandments, and join in affinity with the people of
these abominations? wouldest not thou be angry with us till thou hadst consumed
15 *us*, so that *there should be* no remnant nor escaping? O LORD God of Israel, thou
art righteous; for we remain yet escaped, as *it is* this day: behold, we *are* before
thee in our trespasses; for we cannot stand before thee because of this.

EXEGETICAL AND CRITICAL.

Vers. 1–4. To a positive strengthening of the life in accordance with the law belonged without doubt a long preparatory activity on the part of Ezra. It could not be accomplished by merely external arrangements or contrivances. Rather it was necessary that Ezra should bring about an internal change, excite a holy zeal for the law, as we see it break forth in fact at a later period (Neh. viii.—x.), and thus above all deepen and render more general the knowledge of the law. But already, at the outset, he had to undertake a negative improvement, the removal of a bad state of affairs that threatened their future. It was again the question as previously in the time of Zerubbabel, respecting their relation to the heathen, which was involved in their present political relations, especially their union with heathen under the same government. If, however, the problem in the time of Zerubbabel had been merely to ward off those who would unite with the congregation on the plea of a common worship of Jehovah, now the question was with reference to the exclusion of those with whom union had been established, notwithstanding difference of religion.

Ver. 1. **And after the completion of these things,** *etc.*—כַּלּוֹת is *infin. nomin.* = completion. אֵלֶּה is neuter, referring to the things mentioned in chap. viii. 33–36. This statement of time is somewhat indefinite—yet we are not to suppose that the length of time of the things here narrated was very long after chap. viii. The delivery of the gifts brought with them occurred on the fourth day after Ezra's arrival; thus, on the fourth or fifth day of the fifth month (comp. chap. viii. 32 and chap. vii. 9); the bringing of the offerings, moreover, chap. viii. 35, without doubt soon followed, and so also the delivery of the royal decree to the officials (viii. 36); the support on the part of the latter may be very well mentioned in chap. viii. 36 proleptically, or is to be understood of their promise. If a longer time had elapsed between Ezra's arrival in Jerusalem and chap. ix., it would not have been necessary for the princes of the congregation to have first made complaint respecting the evil circumstances in question, but Ezra would have observed them himself. Accordingly by the ninth month,—on the twentieth day of which, according to chap. x. 9, the first assembly of the people was held respecting the affair here coming into question,—is meant without doubt the ninth of the first year that Ezra passed in Jerusalem. —**The princes came to me.**—הַשָּׂרִים (with the article) are not the princes as a whole—for according to ver. 2 many of them participated in the guilt, and these would not have given information of themselves,—but the princes in distinction from the people. The princes distinguish as such who have not separated themselves, that is, kept themselves separate from the people of the land, three classes, that occur elsewhere, also along side of one another: **the people of Israel**—that is, the common people (יִשְׂרָאֵל is in apposition to הָעָם, comp. Jos. viii. 33; 1 Kings xvi. 21);—**the priests and Levites**—comp. *e. g.* chap. ii. 70.—**The people of the lands** are the ἔθνη, and indeed, first of all, those in the vicinity, comp. chap. vi. 21. For the most part there were, without doubt, remnants of the ancient tribes of Canaan, whose abominations, according to the subsequent narrative, were peculiar to them; but probably during the exile other heathen races also had emigrated into the depopulated Palestine. Ezra and the princes thus, when they required a separation from all these heathen,—that is, excluded an intermarriage with them,—exceeded the letter of the law, which only prohibited intermarriage with the Canaanites (Ex. xxxiv. 16; Deut. vii. 3),—but not because a certain Pharisaism had already made itself felt among them (O. v. Gerlach in his *Biblework*), but because it was absolutely necessary now if the congregation was to be preserved from sinking down into heathenism. The heathen dwelling in close vicinity to them, and not being separated in political affairs, the mixed marriages now threatened, if not positively forbidden, to become disproportionately numerous, whilst in former times they could never have been more than exceptional. And besides, these heathen were now essentially the same as the ancient Canaanites.—**According to their abominations.**—This briefly = as their abominations required. לַכְּנַעֲנִי does not then begin the enumeration of the races in question—which is against not only the accentuation which separates this clause so strongly from the nations, but also the position of the word, for the clause "according to their abominations" would not then have intervened, but should have followed the enumeration; and besides also the לְ before כְּנַעֲנִי—which would have scarcely an analogy in its favor. Rather לַכְּנַעֲנִי, "belonging to the Canaanites;" briefly = as they were peculiar to the Canaanites, the Hittites, *etc.* The abominations are designated by this clause as the ancient ones, condemned by the prophets, and especially by Moses, long before; and all the various names of nations are mentioned because the abominations had been so many and so different among the different races. It was not the purpose to give a complete statement, else the Hivites (comp. Ex. iii. 8; xiii. 5; xxiii. 23) and also the Girgashites (comp. Deut. vii. 1) would also have been mentioned.

Ver. 2. **For they have taken of their daughters, etc.**—namely, wives, comp. chap. x. 44; 2 Chron. xi. 21, *etc.* The object נָשִׁים is in this connection, to a certain extent, to be understood of itself.—**And have mingled themselves as the holy seed with the people of the land.**—This has properly the same subject as the foregoing. The following זֶרַע הַקֹּדֶשׁ is to be placed in apposition with the subject, as it seems; that is to say, although they are a new and holy seed, or shoot, which, after the old tree had fallen by the severe judgments of God, was to grow up into a new and better tree. Since the expression "holy seed" does not occur again elsewhere, it is not doubtful but that there is here a reference back to Isa. vi. 13. That at least the better part of the people had not yet by any means forgotten the ancient prophets, but preserved them at the present time to strengthen their faith, follows already from Haggai and Zechariah, where the Messianic promise, on the basis of the more ancient prophecy, yet again brought forth the richest flowers.—**Yea, the hand of the princes—rulers hath been chief in this trespass.**—In this unfaithfulness the princes had been leaders with their bad example, assuming thereby the responsibility, comp. Deut. xiii. 10. מַעַל, properly unfaithfulness (comp. Lev. v. 15) is spoken of, in so far as they had abandoned the blessing of the purity of Israel and periled thereby the higher blessings connected therewith. סְגָנִים = commanders, chiefs, is a word passing over from the ancient Persian into the Hebrew, comp. Is. xli. 25.

Ver. 3. Ezra could not but express the deepest pain at this information, as well as the greatest displeasure, and indeed with the warmth of Oriental manners; none the less that there must be applied a remedy, only to be carried out with difficulty, and occasioning much sorrow. He expressed his grief by rending (tearing) his under and over-garment (comp. Lev. x. 6 and Josh. vii. 6), his displeasure and anger by plucking out the hair of the head and beard (a part of it), comp. Neh. xiii. 25; that is to say, he hurt himself and disfigured his appearance (comp. Isa. l. 6); if he had only been sad, he would have shaved his head, Job i. 20. In this condition he then sat down staring, שָׁמֵם in Piel expresses the being stiff and dull (hence also the being waste), comp. Isa. lii. 14.

Ver. 4. Ezra's behaviour produced a profound impression upon those who feared God's word; **because of the unfaithfulness** of הַגּוֹלָה, the people of God living in captivity Ezra continued his behaviour herein even when they assembled themselves unto him. According to chap. x. 3 we are not to explain: all who trembled at the word of God on account of the unfaithfulness, *etc.;* although חָרֵד may be connected with עַל (Is. lxvi. 2, where עַל, indeed=אֶל, in the sense of trembling towards, comp. Is. lxvi. 5), but: all who allowed themselves to be frightened by God's words, which referred to the unfaithfulness. God is here called the **God of Israel** because He had in the words in question called for the purity and dignity of Israel.

Vers. 5–15. At the time of the evening sacrifice, however, he arose from his mortification—תַּעֲנִית, humiliation, mortification, which had consisted in giving way to sorrow, but had certainly likewise been connected with fasting, and indeed accompanied with the rending of his over or under-garment; that is to say, in that he still continued or repeated the rending—in order now to spread out his hands to God as those who pray usually did (1 Kings viii., *etc.*), publicly uttering a penitential prayer.

Ver. 6. This penitential prayer would emphasize throughout what great reasons the congregation had of bewaring of the sins in question. He renders prominent in ver. 6 how great guilt they already had upon them without this, and adds in ver. 7 that sin has been the cause of all the misfortune and misery of Israel. He calls to mind in ver. 9 that God's grace had preserved only just such a remnant, but by no means had constituted a situation in which they could dispense with Him. He confesses in vers. 10–12 that God had expressly forbidden the sins now indulged in, and had made nothing less than the strength of the congregation, yea, the very possession of the land, conditional upon their obedience to his command. He then in vers. 13 and 14 raises the painful and sad question, and draws the inference whether, if after so many chastisements, and after such an exhibition of favor, they should again be guilty of such a transgression of the divine command, whether God would not then really become angry unto their entire destruction. He concludes in ver. 15 with the repenting confession that the Lord is righteous, that the congregation, however, cannot stand before Him. Ezra now prays expressly for forgiveness, as we might expect: he ventures not, he is ashamed, as he himself says, to lift up his face to the Lord. But such a penitential prayer and confession of sin is already in itself a pleading for grace; yea, works more powerfully indeed than a petition expressedly uttered. And, at any rate, it is, just as it is, very well calculated, at the same time, to bring the people to the lively consciousness of the perverseness of their sin.

Ver. 6. **I am ashamed and blush.**—בּוֹשׁ and נִכְלַם are joined together for emphasis, as in Jer. xxxi. 19, *etc.*—**For our iniquities are increased over our head.**—Occasioned by the transgression under consideration; all sins and transgressions whatever come to the remembrance of Ezra. He who already has so many sins upon him should take very particular care lest a new one should be added, especially when one has already been brought into such deep misery by the previous ones. רָבוּ from רָבָה has the same meaning as usually רַבּוּ from רָבַב. לְמַעְלָה = upwards, passes over easily in our author to the adverbial sense of "very abundantly" (comp. 1 Chron. xxix. 3), even with רָבָה (comp. 1 Chron. xxiii. 17), but here in connection with ראשׁ retains its meaning as a preposition = beyond. The iniquities are regarded as a flood in which man soon perishes [comp. Ps. xxxviii. 4, and the general use of water to indicate great troubles] [**our trespasses—unto the heaven**—comp. 2 Chron. xxviii. 9; thus the mercy of God is compared in extent with the heavens, *vid.* Ps. xxxvi. 5; lvii. 10, *etc.*—Tr.].

Ver. 7. **And for our iniquities we have been delivered—into the hands of the kings of the lands to the sword,** *etc.*—To translate, with Bertheau, *through* the sword, is remote from the sense, and is not suited to the following "into captivity." The shame is called that of the **face** because it especially works upon the face, as Dan. ix. 7.—**As this day,** namely, teaches or shows; כְּ in connection with הַיּוֹם הַזֶּה is not = about or on, but has a comparative force, as also in Jer. xliv. 6; xxii. 23; 1 Sam. xxii. 8. The present teaches the here asserted delivering over, in so far as the congregation was still a גֹּולָה, comp. ver. 4.

Vers. 8, 9. It is true, the Lord has again allowed His grace to work after His anger, but not so that He could be dispensed with; only through Him has the congregation protection and continuance.—**And now a little moment** (comp. Isa. xxvi. 20) **hath been grace from the Lord our God**—namely, during the time from Cyrus to the present, which seems short in comparison with the long time of the previous chastisement, especially since the latter had begun already with the Assyrians (comp. chap. vi. 22 and Neh. ix. 32), and had properly been continued even to the time of Cyrus. Ezra would not so much praise the greatness of the divine grace, as if his thought had been that transgression ought to have been avoided out of thankfulness (for then he would have expressed himself in an entirely different manner), but he would say that the congregation, whatever it might be, was only through grace; and back of this lies the thought that with it they would forfeit their one and all.—**To leave us a remnant and to give us a peg in his holy place.**—לָנוּ = us, "the people as a whole," in distinction from which the פְּלֵיטָה is the congregation of the returned exiles. The peg, יָתֵד, is to be regarded as one driven into the wall, on which domestic utensils of any kind were hung, comp. Is. xxii. 23 sq.* Hence we cannot understand thereby, either with Bertheau, the congregation itself (to make us a peg = a congregation of a reliable stock), or, with Keil, the temple, which is opposed by the words, "in the holy place;" rather "to give any one a peg in a house" (here in the temple, in the holy place) means to give him a part and right in the house, accept him as a coinhabitant in the house. It comes into consideration that God is often regarded as a Householder, and His people, in a similar manner, often as His family, who dwell with Him in His house (comp. Psalms xv. 1; xxiii. 6; xxvii. 4, *etc.*). We have an example in Isaiah lvi. 5: I will give them hand and name in my house, where the יָד explained in so many different ways may be simply activity or right to be active, in general to stir one's self.—**That our God might lighten our eyes, and give us a little reviving in our bondage.**—The infins. לְהָאִיר and לְתִתֵּנוּ are subordinated to the foregoing infinitives = that he thereby. The subject אֱלֹהֵינוּ appears in an independent position, as especially Isa. v. 24; comp. Ewald, § 307, *c*, because the object עֵינֵינוּ had preceded and intervened between it and the infin. "The eyes enlighten" means to remove the night of trouble and weakness resting upon them, which was, according to that which follows, already indeed a night of death, and indeed by reviving, that is, by bestowing salvation, strength, encouragement, comp. Ps. xiii. 4; Prov. xxix. 13, especially also 1 Sam. 14, 27, 29.—מִחְיָה = preservation of life, or as here, reviving (comp. 2 Chron. xiv. 12), is used here for the adjective "revived," whilst in ver. 9 it retains its abstract meaning. מְעַט is added, without close connection, as Neh. ii. 12; vii. 4. The idea at the basis is, that national ruin is a death of the congregation, and that the re-establishment is an awakening from the dead. This re-establishment was a very incomplete one so long as the dependence on the powers of the world still endured, and the congregation must still be called הַגּוֹלָה. The reference to the prophecies of the prophets is here unmistakable. As the expression "holy seed," already in ver. 2, so also "leave a remant," and the expression "peg," remind us very decidedly of Isaiah, comp. chaps. i. 9; xxii. 23 sq.; lvi. 5; the expression "revival" looks back upon Ezek. xxxvii. 1–14, where the figure on which it is based is carried out with great vividness and power. We see that the pious Israelites subsequent to the exile, Ezra before all, attentively took to heart the ancient prophecies of chastisements, and that which should follow them, in order to apply them without doubt to their own times.

Ver. 9. **And hath extended mercy unto us before the kings of Persia, to give us revival.**—The subject of the "giving" is not the Persian kings (Berth., Keil), which is opposed by the previous verse, and also by the fact itself; but God alone, whose it is alone to slay and make alive. It is not necessary, on this account, to make God the subject of the clause: to **set up the house of our God, and erect its ruins.** This infin. may be subordinated to the foregoing, so that the Jews become the subject = that we, *etc.* The subject of the last infin. **to give us a wall in Judah and Jerusalem,** is surely again God, and not one of the Persian kings (Berth. and Keil). The expression "give a wall" leads of itself more to God, for it is naturally to be understood figuratively, and indeed not of the temple, but in the more general sense of the protection which was afforded the congregation in Judah and Jerusalem against their oppressors, comp. Zech. ii. 5.

Vers. 10–12. The transgression here spoken of cannot be excused at all, with the plea, that it was not expressly forbidden.—**And now, what shall we say?—for we have forsaken thy commandments,**—not: *that* we have forsaken (Berth. and Keil), which would be weak. Ezra means: I may thus ask, for, *etc.*

Ver. 11 may be translated: thou who, or also, **which thou hast commanded by thy servants, the prophets.**—Ezra does not mention Moses in particular, but the prophets in general, not because the commands of the Pentateuch were not mediated or written down by Moses alone, but also by other organs, as Delitzsch in his introduction to Genesis supposes;—whether Ezra knew this, is at least very doubtful,—but because his thought is that God by His prophets has given or again enforced the commandments in manifold and oft-repeated ways, comp. Judg. iii. 6; 1 Kings xi. 2. When a truth is under

* [Rawlinson *in loco* thinks of the tent pin, which is driven into the earth to make the tent firm and secure, Is. xxii. 23, 25.—TR.]

consideration, which is not represented by one prophet, but more or less by all, then it is usual to cite in general, as the author of the book of Kings also does. Moses is meant at any rate, yea chiefly. And this explains the fact that Ezra states the command, not it is true verbally from a passage in the Pentateuch, but yet formularized in a manner only appropriate to the Mosaic period, when they still had to take possession of Canaan. He has in mind before all Deut. vii. 1–3, as there also the entire manner of expression is undeniably that of Deuteronomy, but he draws into consideration, in a free manner, other passages, and indeed even from Leviticus, comp. especially Lev. xviii. 24 sq. נִדָּה, the abominable, for which in Lev. only טֻמְאָה and תּוֹעֲבוֹת occur, is used in the Pentateuch of the impurity of the issues of blood in women, only subsequently by the prophets of other impurities likewise, especially also of ethical impurities (comp. 1 Sam. i. 17; Ezek. vii. 20; xxxvi. 17). It is preferred to its synonyms as an especially strong expression. מִפֶּה אֶל־פֶּה, does not mean, certainly: from side to side (Keil), or from one end to another (Berth., A. V.); for neither the one nor the other meaning has been proved, or etymologically established for פֶּה. In Isa. xix. 7 it is either the mouth, or the bed of the Nile (later in distinction from the bank, as the שָׂפָה). פֶּה is easily the equivalent of person, from person to person, is, however = on or in all persons, =throughout and everywhere. Comp. פֶּה לָפֶה, 2 Kings x. 21; xxi. 16. It is worthy of attention, of course, that this method of expression only occurs of objects which hold men, of land, house and city, or of men themselves.

Ver. 12. **Nor seek their peace nor their wealth forever.**–These words are from Dt. xxiii. 7, where this is said with reference to the Moabites and Ammonites. It almost seems as if Ezra would have justified from the very letter of the law by this citation, his extension of the prohibition of intermarriage to the Moabites and Ammonites. The clause, **that ye may be strong**, reminds us of Deuteron. xi. 8; the next clause, **and eat the good of the land**, of Isa. i. 19; the last clause, however: **and possess it, or take possession of it for your children for ever**, which does not occur in the Pentateuch in this form, rests on the promise that is often repeated, especially in Deuteronomy, that in case of obedience they would live long in the land that the Lord gave them. הוֹרִישׁ means here not give into possession (Berth., Keil), for then it must govern the double accusative (comp. Judg. xi. 34; 2 Chron. xx. 11), but "take into possession, possess." For the children, posterity, that is, permanently.

Vers. 13, 14. Thus there can be no question but that the new transgression is to be decidedly condemned. This follows, as well from the punishment for previous sins, as from the way of pardon.—**And after all that is come upon us for our evil deeds, and for our great trespass.**—The article before בָּא properly represents the relative, as viii. 25; x. 14, 17; for בָּא cannot well be a participle; as such it would be in the plural. The continuation of this clause does not occur already in the second half of the ver. (Berth.); in this case the following כִּי would have to be taken in the sense of, in truth (after all, in truth hast Thou, our God, spared us), then ver. 14 would be in too little connection; it would not appear that two kinds of things, that as well punishment as forgiveness formed the foundation of ver. 14. Rather the second half of the verse verifies the thought, which is involved in the first, that the guilt was very great, and that it properly would have deserved still severer punishment, and thus entirely prepares the way for ver. 14. Its sense is, at any rate, that the punishment has been less than the transgression. The words might mean: **For thou, our God, hast restrained a part of our sins from below**, so that they (namely, through their consequences, the visitations of punishment) have not gone entirely over our head, have not utterly ruined us; for there is no objection to taking מֵעֲוֹנֵנוּ partitively. Already Esdras has thus: *ὁ κουφίσας τὰς ἁμαρτίας ἡμῶν*. In favor of this view is the fact that in this way לְמַטָּה would come into contrast with לְמַעְלָה in ver. 6, in which it is also found elsewhere, Jer. xxxi. 37. At all events, however, we may likewise explain: Thou hast restrained Thine anger or Thy punishment below the measure of our misdeeds, so that the punishment has not been as great as our misdeeds deserved (so J. H. Mich., Gesen., and Keil). לְמַטָּה, indeed, is nowhere else found with מִן, but perhaps only for the reason that it nowhere else is followed by a noun of closer definition. מִן follows, at least, the corresponding לְמַעְלָה, 1 Chron. xxix. 3; the synonymous מִתַּחַת has usually לְ after it.

Ver. 14. **Then should we again break thy commandments, and unite ourselves in marriage with,** *etc.*—This question appeals to the general sentiment, and serves to emphasize very strongly the blamableness of the new transgression.—**Wouldst thou not be angry with us, even to destruction?**— עַד־כַּלֵּה, as 2 Kings xiii. 17, 19.

Ver. 15. **Lord God of Israel, thou art righteous.**—This concluding and confirming confession would not say: Thou art a severe judge, and must interfere against the congregation on account of its decline (Bertheau and Keil). The usual meaning of צַדִּיק (graciously righteous), is against this, and then also the following clause, "**for we have remained over as an escaped remnant,**" which is not = we have remained over *merely* as escaped, but: we have not been utterly ruined. Rather Ezra would say, that no one can reproach God for not doing all that could be expected.—**Behold, we are before thee in our trespasses,** *etc.*—This, the second half of the verse, constitutes a very suitable and logically conclusive antithesis to the foregoing. The more blameless God is the more deserving of punishment Israel's guilt. The yodh in בְּאַשְׁמָתֵינוּ is found in the edition of R. Norzi and J. H. Mich.; but is missing in some MSS., and the pointing corresponds with the latter. Both methods of writing might in this case easily go on alongside of one another; the singular would be favored by ver. 13, but the plural corresponds with the full-toned style of Ezra.—[**We cannot stand before thee,** *e.g.*, as thy holy people, who are privileged to stand before their king.—Tr.]—**Because of this.** עַל־זֹאת = with this new evil deed.

THOUGHTS UPON THE HISTORY OF REDEMPTION.

Vers. 1–3. 1. If we act upon the supposition that the sacred Scriptures, even the Old Testament already, are to give us warning, exhortation, and instruction with reference to every situation and question of church, civil, or domestic life, yea, that the Old Testament very particularly comes into consideration for the details of life, it is natural that we should find in the opposition that Ezra makes in chapters ix. and x. to intermarriage with the heathen, a warning or exhortation with reference to intermarriage with those of a different faith from our own. And in fact that which may be urged against such an application, *e. g.*, that as Christians we rejoice in a greater liberty than the Jews; that mixed marriages have not been forbidden of themselves and under all circumstances, that the Christian church is never threatened with as great dangers as the Jewish congregation in the time of Ezra, that besides the piety of the Christian has a mightier protection and help than the religion of the Old Testament pious—all this is outweighed by the opposing facts. The wife is now on a greater equality with the husband than in ancient times, has a greater influence upon the man himself, as well as in the training of the children, may thus easily become more dangerous. Besides Christianity is much more internal and deep than Old Testament piety, more influential upon the heart and disposition upon all sides, and hence comes much more into consideration with reference to the married life, that rests upon internal communion. It is true there is very seldom in the mixed marriages of our times a question respecting the difference of religion; usually it is only respecting a difference in the confession of faith, or a different degree of vitality of Christian religiousness—and to place marriages of this kind on the same basis as those intermarriages with the heathen would be premature, yea unfair. Heathendom stood in an essential and indeed very positive contrast to Judaism. The different Christian confessions, on the other hand, have the essential things in common with one another. And between those which are distinguished merely by the degree of the vitality of their Christian religiousness, there is often no positive contrast at all; the less vital Christianity may be awakened and strengthened, especially if treated with love. But we must always recognise and take to heart, with reference to Ezra and his behaviour, the fact, that in the conclusion and conduction of a marriage those considerations which have respect to the interests of religion are more important than all others, and therefore a difference of confession, which threatens not to promote but diminish religious ardor, according to the nature of the case, which besides constantly disturbs or of itself renders impossible the internal living together in the highest and holiest spheres, which then likewise has so much that is unendurable with reference to the training of children, and involves so many difficulties; that likewise in the same manner, a lack of any religious faith, that places itself in open conflict with Christianity, that more earnestly considered, is to be regarded as a positively different religion, or wanders into scornfulness and frivolity,—these ought to be real hinderances to marriage for all Christians. As regards the lack of faith, of the kind here referred to, which manifestly must be placed on the same footing at least with heathenism, the apostle did not allow (1 Cor. vii. 12, 13) that a Christian brother should marry an unbelieving wife, or the reverse, but only that he should retain her if he once had her. That a brother should marry an unbelieving (heathen) wife, he seems not to have regarded as at all possible. With reference to marriage with an unbeliever, we are to take to heart what he says in the subsequent context (ver. 16), What knowest thou, O wife, whether thou shalt save thy husband, or what knowest thou, O man, whether thou shalt save thy wife?

2. The question how the congregation was to act towards others of a different faith, was now to be answered for the second time. It is not easy, with reference to this matter, to do exactly the right thing; for Christians, who more decidedly have the task of winning others for their faith, thus in no way should shut themselves off from them, it is still less easy than for the Israelites. But since all depends upon imparting to the others the best that we have, it follows that we must draw back, when this is impossible, especially if we incur the danger of losing this best thing ourselves. Under all circumstances it is self-evident that we should only cherish such an association as we can ever withdraw from if necessary.

3. No error is so conspicuous in the new congregation as that of intermarriage with the heathen. Not only Ezra but Nehemiah had still to contend with it (Neh. x. 31; xiii. 23 sq.), and as the princes, so indeed had the sons of the high-priests taken part in it (comp. chap. x. 18). Without doubt there was a reason in the circumstances themselves. Usually new tasks are imposed as well upon the congregation as a whole, as also upon the individuals in the new relations. A new end is to be attained, and the difficulty of striving after this in the right manner often involves the temptation of approaching it in a false way. The task of the new congregation was to assume such a relation to the neighboring nations from whom they were no longer separated by political boundaries, as that they might ever be in the position in the fulness of time for fulfilling their missionary calling with reference to them. Accordingly the history itself urged onwards to a sort of approximation. Notwithstanding this, however, the institution of false relations, which could only render the accomplishment of their mission impossible, had no excuse.

4. Having lost their political independence, and reduced to a small number, the congregation, even their leaders or princes might have come upon the thought that it was not only allowable, but indeed was advisable, to enter into closer relations with the heathen, who now were separated from them by so very little. They might have hoped that their people, on the basis of such a connection, might exercise a good influence with reference to religion and morals, and in consequence of this the congregation would gain the desirable increase; yet this error would not have been possible, if they had had the true singleness of heart towards the divine command. By the lack of this singleness, those who ought to have been to the rest of the congregation guides to good, became guides to evil. Ezra on his part, who did not lack this singleness, recognised in these very circumstances, with which the princes might justify the transgression under consideration, grounds for just the contrary, for a still more careful separation from the heathen. In fact, just because the congregation were without the protection of a political independence, because moreover they had become weak and despised on account of their small numbers, there was scarcely a doubt that the heathen, instead of allowing themselves to be influenced by the Israelites, would have become the influential factor for them, and they would have jeopardized the very existence of the congregation itself.

5. In a similar manner, as after other great judgments, as, for example, after the deluge, it became manifest after the exile likewise that the delivered, however excellent they proved to be at first, were unable to constitute a really new beginning, which should be pure and sinless, but ever only a continuation of the ancient sinful existence; that there was now no more sinless development, that rather sin breaks forth in new forms in the new relations which have been established by the judging and preserving providence of God, so that it needs ever anew a holy reaction against it on the part of the Lord. Nevertheless, of course, the judging and preserving acts of the Lord are not in vain. The congregation advances through them forwards, if not to a pure, yet to a better development, and their course, even if it is never that of a conqueror who has entirely overcome his hereditary enemy, is yet that of a victorious warrior, who at least beholds the complete victory and its noble prize at the end of his course. Nevertheless, the circumstance that among the princes many recognised the wrong as such, and sought to remove it with the help of Ezra, is a proof that the Lord at this time had provided a number of a better element, who already not only constituted a starting-point for His reaction, but also themselves began to react out of their own midst.

Vers. 5–15. 1. Before Ezra did anything else he expressed his sorrow for the failure of the congregation from the word of God, and indeed particularly by a penitential prayer, in which he included himself most devoutly within the congregation which had transgressed. The first thing with which to begin a true reformation will ever be the feeling of penitence, and in accordance with this a penitential prayer, which issues from the deepest conviction that we are involved in the sinfulness of the congregation, and which has to share in the fear of the threatening judgments, which, however, none the less manifests the sharpest contrast to the sin in question. Such a penitential prayer, especially if it is connected with an humble recognition of the justice of the judgment that is feared, already has also the significance of a prayer for forgiveness, help, and preservation, just as the praise of the Lord as the God who hears prayer, affords redemption and salvation, at the beginning of those very Psalms, that are prayed out of deep need, and run out into a petition for redemption and salvation, is itself already a mighty petition, which in spite of every necessity joyfully praising God, is able without doubt to most powerfully move His paternal heart.

2. Ezra's prayer very suitably unites various things, which must fill us with holy abhorrence of fresh transgressions after redemption; he reminds us at first of the fact that we are deeply involved in sin from our fathers, we might say, already by nature, and thus can not be too much on our guard against it, and at the same time, that it is our sins that have brought about the misery in which we all more or less live; so then that God has given us grace which certainly appears exceedingly great over against our sins and unworthiness, so that it must fill us with thankfulness and urge us to sanctification, which, however, over against the necessities of earth, is a small beginning of better things, easily lost again; furthermore, that the sin, that we might perchance be guilty of, is against God's express command, and can never be justified; that God's visitation of punishment, if we are not warned by His punishment or by His grace unto holiness, must necessarily become greater and more serious. These truths will have a preserving and improving power for the congregation of all times.

HOMILETICAL AND PRACTICAL.

Vers. 1, 2. We have the duty of keeping afar off from others. 1) When? If we can exercise no improving influence, but have to fear lest we be ruined with them. 2) Why? because we have to preserve great blessings for ourselves and others. 3) How? with renunciation of temporal advantages, especially with self-denial.—The importance of a correct choice in marriage: 1) the injury that is done by a bad choice; it is not only temporal, but eternal; 2) the gain that we have in a good choice.—Starke: Marriage with an unbelieving woman is very dangerous, for she can convert a man easier than the man can convert her, 1 Kings x. 4.—What other injuries unequal marriage may accomplish, *vid.* 2 Chron. xviii. 1.—The importance of true family life for the furtherance of church life: 1) Church life is a matter of the free resolution, which must be correctly guided by proper training; 2) church life is conditioned upon learning its advantages, as this is possible, first of all, only in the bosom of the family.

Vers. 5–15. The fundamental principles of true reformatory activity: 1) True simplicity of heart,—we must not allow ourselves to be led astray by the temptations that are often involved with sufficient strength in the relations given by God Himself; we must rather gladly and without reserve bow to the divine word; 2) true sorrow for the present transgressions, however difficult they may be to remove, they must yet be recognized seriously in their true character; 3) true fear of the divine judgment—it is a bitter, but indispensable medicine for the destructive wanderings from duty.—BRENTIUS: *Exprimitur affectus pietatis, qui in unoquoque debet geri erga proximum suum, videlicet quod unusquisque non debet aliter affici erga peccata proximi sui, quam si ipse ea perpetrasset. Sic affectus erat Abraham, erga Sodomitas, sic Samuel erga Saul, sic Daniel erga populum Judaicum. Et hic affectus multorum bonorum autor est, videlicet ne traducamus proximum nostrum, sed oremus pro eo, et castigemus eum, pro officio nostro.*—STARKE: Pious people laugh not at the sins of others, but are sad at heart on their account, Jer. ix.; Gen. xviii. 23; 2 Sam. xv. 35; 2 Cor. xi. 29.—How inexcusable are the fresh transgressions of those who have been redeemed from the misery of sin. 1) Sin has already wrought misery enough. 2) God has shown His grace in delivering from it, which is exceedingly great, but may easily be lost again. 3) He has let us know His will. 4) His visitation of punishment will be still more severe.—STARKE: The strongest walls and the surest fence about a city and village is God's gracious care, Ps. iii. 4–7; Prov. xviii. 10.—By the wickedness of the inhabitants is a land defiled; accordingly let us beware of sin. In the judgments of God we have to recognize His moderation, and thank God for it.—The true penitential prayer: 1) Recognition of sin in its entire greatness and ruin: 2) recognition of the divine grace; 3) recognition of the cleanness of the divine will; 4) recognition of the justice of the judgment to be feared.—Intercession of pastors for their congregations: 1) Out of love in spite of sin; 2) in faith in God's grace; 3) in hope of a hearing.—STARKE: Since Ezra in his prayer sets before him the entire people, he includes himself among them and accepts his share in the sins of the people, comp. Is. lix.; Dan. ix. 5; Neh. i. 6.—Teachers should particularly stand in the gap and seek to ward off the punishment of God by prayer. We often know not for the sake of what believer's prayer God has spared a people and city.

[SCOTT: Silent grief and astonishment sometimes form the most expressive protestation against enormous crimes; and when men speak on such occasions it may be more effectual to address themselves to God than to the offender.—HENRY: A practical disbelief of God's all-sufficiency is at the bottom of all the sorry shifts we make to help ourselves.—The scandalous sins of professors are what we have reason to be *astonished at.*—An eye to God as *our God* will be of great use to us in the exercise of repentance.—There is not a surer or sadder presage of ruin to any people than revolting to sin, to the same sins again after great judgments and great deliverances.—WORDSWORTH: Observe, this confession and prayer of Ezra, the priest and scribe, the friend of the king of Persia, was in a public place, at a time of public resort to the temple. He was not ashamed of repentance and self-humiliation, and he showed publicly that his trust was in God's help, vouchsafed to fervent prayer at the door of God's house.—TR.]

B.—THE REMOVAL OF THE ERROR, AND THE LIST OF THOSE WHO PURIFIED THEMSELVES FROM IT.

CHAP. X. 1–44.

I. *The effect that Ezra's prayer had upon Shechaniah, then upon the princes of the congregation.*

Vers. 1–8.

1 Now when Ezra had prayed, and when he had confessed, weeping and casting
himself down before the house of God, there assembled unto him out of Israel a very
great congregation of men and women and children: for the people wept very sore.
2 And Shechaniah the son of Jehiel, *one* of the sons of Elam, answered and said unto
Ezra, We have trespassed against our God, and have taken strange wives of the
3 people of the land: yet now there is hope in Israel concerning this thing. Now
therefore let us make a covenant with our God to put away all the wives, and such
as are born of them, according to the counsel of my lord, and of those that tremble
4 at the commandment of our God; and let it be done according to the law. Arise;
for *this* matter *belongeth* unto thee: we also *will be* with thee: be of good courage,
5 and do *it*. Then arose Ezra, and made the chief priests, the Levites, and all Israel,
6 to swear that they should do according to this word. And they sware. Then
Ezra rose up from before the house of God, and went into the chamber of Johanan

the son of Eliashib: and *when* he came thither, he did eat no bread, nor drink water:
for he mourned because of the transgression of them that had been carried away.
7 And they made proclamation throughout Judah and Jerusalem unto all the chil-
dren of the captivity, that they should gather themselves together unto Jerusalem;
8 And that whosoever would not come within three days, according to the counsel of
the princes and the elders, all his substance should be forfeited, and himself sepa-
rated from the congregation of those that had been carried away.

II. *The Success of Ezra in the Assembly of the Congregation.* Vers. 9–17.

9 Then all the men of Judah and Benjamin gathered themselves together unto Jeru-
salem within three days. It *was* the ninth month, on the twentieth *day* of the
month; and all the people sat in the street of the house of God, trembling because
10 of *this* matter, and for the great rain. And Ezra the priest stood up, and said unto
them, Ye have transgressed, and have taken strange wives, to increase the trespass
11 of Israel. Now therefore make confession unto the LORD God of your fathers, and
do his pleasure: and separate yourselves from the people of the land, and from the
12 strange wives. Then all the congregation answered and said with a loud voice, As
13 thou hast said, so must we do. But the people *are* many, and *it is* a time of much
rain, and we are not able to stand without, neither *is this* a work of one day or two:
14 for we are many that have transgressed in this thing. Let now our rulers of all the
congregation stand, and let all them which have taken strange wives in our cities
come at appointed times, and with them the elders of every city, and the judges
15 thereof, until the fierce wrath of our God for this matter be turned from us. Only
Jonathan the son of Asahel and Jahaziah the son of Tikvah were employed about
16 this *matter:* and Meshullam and Shabbethai the Levite helped them. And the chil-
dren of the captivity did so. And Ezra the priest, *with* certain chief of the fathers,
after the house of their fathers, and all of them by *their* names, were separated, and
17 sat down in the first day of the tenth month to examine the matter. And they
made an end with all the men that had taken strange wives by the first day of the
first month.

III. *List of those who Separated Themselves from their Wives.* Vers. 18–44.

18 And among the sons of the priests there were found that had taken strange wives:
namely, of the sons of Jeshua the son of Jozadak, and his brethren: Maaseiah, and
19 Eliezer, and Jarib, and Gedaliah. And they gave their hands that they would put
away their wives; and *being* guilty, *they offered* a ram of the flock for their trespass.
20, 21 And of the sons of Immer; Hanani, and Zebadiah. And of the sons of Ha-
22 rim; Maaseiah, and Elijah, and Shemaiah, and Jehiel, and Uzziah. And of the
sons of Pashur; Elioenai, Maaseiah, Ishmael, Nethaneel, Jozabad, and Elasah.
23 Also of the Levites; Jozabad, and Shimei, and Kelaiah, (the same *is* Kelita,)
24 Pethahiah, Judah, and Eliezer. Of the singers also; Eliashib: and of the porters;
25 Shallum, and Telem, and Uri. Moreover of Israel: of the sons of Parosh; Ramiah,
and Jeziah, and Malchiah, and Miamin, and Eleazar, and Malchijah, and Benaiah.
26 And of the sons of Elam; Mattaniah, Zechariah, and Jehiel, and Abdi, and Jere-
27 moth, and Eliah. And of the sons of Zattu; Elioenai, Eliashib, Mattaniah, and
28 Jeremoth, and Zabad, and Aziza. Of the sons also of Bebai; Jehohanan, Hana-
29 niah, Zabbai, *and* Athlai. And of the sons of Bani; Meshullam, Malluch, and
30 Adaiah, Jashub, and Sheal, and Ramoth. And of the sons of Pahath-moab; Adna,
and Chelal, Benaiah, Maaseiah, Mattaniah, Bezaleel, and Binnui, and Manasseh.
31, 32 And *of* the sons of Harim; Eliezer, Ishijah, Malchiah, Shemaiah, Shimeon, Ben-
33 jamin, Malluch, *and* Shemariah. Of the sons of Hashum; Mattenai, Mattathah,
34 Zabad, Eliphelet, Jeremai, Manasseh, *and* Shimei. Of the sons of Bani; Maadai,
35, 36 Amram, and Uel, Benaiah, Bedeiah, Chelluh, Vaniah, Meremoth, Eliashib,
37, 38, 39 Mattaniah, Mattenai, and Jaasau, And Bani, and Binnui, Shimei, And
40, 41 Shelemiah, and Nathan, and Adaiah, Machnadebai, Shashai, Sharai, Azareel,
42, 43 and Shelemiah, Shemariah, Shallum, Amariah, *and* Joseph. Of the sons of
44 Nebo; Jeiel, Mattithiah, Zabad, Zebina, Jadau, and Joel, Benaiah. All these had
taken strange wives: and *some* of them had wives by whom they had children.

EXEGETICAL AND CRITICAL.

Vers. 1–8. This chapter from beginning to end treats of the great results attending the penitential prayer of Ezra in the congregation.

Ver. 1. **Now when Ezra had prayed,** *etc.* —Ezra's prayer is properly designated as a confessing. הִתְוַדּוֹת, comp. notes on ix. 16. מִתְנַפֵּל means: prostrating one's self, lying on the knees, comp. ix. 1.—**Before the house of God,**—elsewhere also "before the face of God," in the court of the temple. That a great crowd gathered together unto him had its reason in the fact that the people wept very much, that is, for sorrow over the evil circumstances into which so many had plunged themselves, and especially were deeply moved with him also in view of the sins by which they had done it, and accordingly also desired assistance. בֶּכֶה, which form only occurs here, depends upon its verb, although it is separated from it by the adverb הַרְבֵּה in the manner of an infin. abs.

Ver. 2. **And Shechaniah——answered,** *etc.*—That Ezra himself did not step forth with a definite demand, that he waited until one of the congregation should make a proposition, did not have its reason in the fact that his position did not entitle him to make such a demand, but in the circumstance that the reformation could only be of worth and thoroughly carried out when it came forth from the congregation itself. Shechaniah here, the son of Jehiel, is to be distinguished from Shechaniah, the son of Jahaziel, in chap. viii. 5. And Jehiel, his father, is probably not identical with the one mentioned in ver. 26. Were it so, Shechaniah would not have scrupled to make a proposition by which his own father would be compelled to dismiss his wife. The sons of Elam, to whom he belonged, occur in ii. 7; viii. 7, and again in ver. 26. He was, and this is significant, no priest, nor prince, but one of the congregation, so that in and with him the congregation itself promptly arose to vindicate the law. הוֹשִׁיב, cause to dwell, is in our chapter (comp. vers. 10, 14, 17, 18), and so also in Neh. xiii. 23, 27, used for the taking home of wives. Shechaniah confesses: We have acted unfaithfully towards the Lord in taking home foreign women (comp. ver. 10 and Neh. xiii. 27), in order to justify Ezra for his strong condemnation of this intermarriage. At the same time he retains hope, עַל־זֹאת = at this transgression (comp. ix. 15), or rather in spite of it. עַל in itself *sensu medio*, may readily have the meaning of "in spite of," comp. Is. liii. 9; Job xvi. 17. מִקְוֶה is here = תִּקְוָה. Shechaniah is of the opinion that a removal of the evil is still possible, and perhaps he already recognized also the fact that the resolution to carry out this difficult thing might give the impulse to a general reformation.

Ver. 3. **Now therefore let us make a covenant with our God**—that is, we will obligate ourselves by a solemn covenant and a sworn vow to God (comp. 2 Chron. xxix. 10) **to put away.**—הוֹצִיא is here the opposite of הוֹשִׁיב— **all the wives**—namely, as a matter of course, all foreign ones—**and such as are born of them**—also to send away the children. This resolution might almost seem to be unnecessarily severe, yet it is a matter of question whether it would not have been harder still to separate the mothers from their children. The little ones still needed their mothers, and the larger ones might easily be a support for their mothers. Moreover, it was to be feared that the children, if they were retained, would constitute a bond between the men and their banished wives that would soon again reassert its power and render possible the return of the wives. We are by no means to conclude from vers. 11–19 that they contented themselves with reference to this proposition, with the removal of their wives. Comp. against this view ver. 44 and Neh. xiii. 23 sq. Moreover, however, that which Shechaniah here in his zeal so comprehensively proposes might yet not be so recognized and required, without exception. There was no sufficient ground for removing sons who were willing to live in accordance with the law, and who were not necessarily to be cast out on account of the mother. —**According to the counsel of the Lord and of those that tremble at the commandment of our Lord.**—That the Lord and those who tremble at His command should be brought together in this way is almost remarkable. The Sept. and Esdras, and after them also De Wette and Bertheau, read accordingly אֲדֹנִי, my Lord, which would be Ezra [so A. V. and Rawlinson.]* But Ezra had not yet given any counsel at all, and besides, it is hardly conceivable that Shechaniah should here speak to him in such a reverent tone, and then in the verses immediately following so familiarly and cheeringly. Already the Vulgate has *juxta voluntatem domini*, and according to De Rossi, quite a number of MSS. read even יְהוָה. The connection of the two expressions, which is in itself somewhat remarkable, would probably say: according to the counsel of the Lord, as it is understood and vindicated by those who tremble at His commandments. Entirely parallel is Acts xv. 28: "for it seemed good to the Holy Ghost and to us." The עֵצָה of the Lord is often elsewhere His decree (comp. Is. v. 19; xix. 17; Ps. cvi. 13); here, however, according to the context, the counsel, which He gives, as Ps. cvii. 11; Prov. i. 25; 2 Kings xvii. 13. Thus mildly Shechaniah expresses himself, however, because a specific command to dismiss the wives, and likewise also their children, was not found in the law, and moreover also partly because the law, in so far as it yet gave an impulse thereto, had a counselling, that is, a precautionary significance with the good of the congregation in view. The clause כַּתּוֹרָה יֵעָשֶׂה is not to be taken in an optative sense [A. V.]—which would be weak—but as a promise: it shall happen according to the law. The fourth verse, moreover, passes over from the tone of comfort

* [Rawlinson *in loco:* "This expression shows the high position which Ezra occupied as the commissioner of the Persian king. His counsel does not appear to have been expressly given, but might be gathered from the general tone of his prayer."—TR.]

to that of promise.—**Arise, for upon thee is the matter.**—This can only mean: upon thee the matter has to depend; thou must carry it out according to thy judgment and conviction.—**And we with thee.**—This means in accordance with the foregoing. And we will be with thee, will help thee.

Vers. 5–8. Now Ezra made use of the favorable sentiment: **he made the princes,** *etc.*, **to swear to do** כַּדָּבָר הַזֶּה, that is, to carry out the proposition of Shechaniah, then however continued his sorrow, and thereby deepened the zeal that had been excited, until he saw the beginning of the execution of the reform.—**Ezra arose from before the house of God,** that is, he left the place in the court, where he had prayed, and **went into the chamber of Johanan, the son of Eliashib,** in order to fast and mourn there. This cell was certainly in the wing that the new temple had gained, and which served for the preservation of the garments of the priests and other articles, but likewise for the provisional abode of the priests and Levites; according to Neh. xiii. 4–9 the high-priest Eliashib had erected a cell for the use of the Ammonite Tobia, as his relative, which he used in his frequent visits to Jerusalem. The names of Johanan and Eliashib frequently occur (comp. vers. 24, 27, 36), one of the twenty-four classes of priests had its name from a more ancient Eliashib, 1 Chron. xxiv. 12. But that an apartment or cell of the temple should be named after a subordinate man of the name of Johanan, as Ewald supposes (*Gesch.* IV., S. 263), is impossible. It is very likely that we are to think of the later high-priest Johanan, and indeed the more so that he was not, it is true, as the one under consideration, a son, but a grandson of Eliashib. The order of high-priests from the time of Zerubbabel was as follows: Jeshua, Joiakim, Eliashib, Joiada, Johanan, Jaddua, comp. Neh. xii. 10 sq., where it is true Jonathan stands in place of Jaddua; where however, according to Neh. xii. 22, 23, Johanan is meant. In the time of Ezra, Joiakim or Eliashib was high-priest. We must probably suppose that the author used a later designation for the previous times as one more intelligible to his readers. The apartment might have been present already in the time of Ezra, which subsequently, perhaps in consequence of a re-building, was named after the high-priest Johanan. The second וַיֵּלֶךְ is a needless repetition, and cannot be at all compared with the twice-repeated וַיָּקָם in verses 5 and 6, which at any rate each time receives a special definiteness by an additional clause, (against Keil).* שָׁם is besides, at any rate very seldom used in the sense of "thither," as it must be taken to be in connection with וַיֵּלֶךְ. The supposition of Cler. and Berth. that we are to read instead of it וַיָּלֶן, and he passed the night or remained there, commends itself very much to our judgment. Already Esdras ix. 1 has: καὶ αὐλισθεὶς ἐκεῖ, the Syriac: and he sat or remained there; the Sept. however: καὶ ἐπορεύθη ἐκεῖ.—**Eat no bread nor drink water** is to fast. Comp. Ex. xxxiv. 28; Deut. ix. 9.

Ver. 7. Thus they, namely, the princes and elders, who according to ver. 8 took the matter in hand—**made proclamation.**—הֶעֱבִיר קוֹל as i. 1,—and indeed probably whilst Ezra was still fasting and mourning, thus immediately after Ezra's penitential prayer and Shechaniah's proposition—that all the members of the congregation should assemble unto Jerusalem.

Ver. 8. **According to the counsel** or resolution **of the princes and the elders,** *etc.*—כַּעֲצַת belongs to the following clause—the ban should fall upon every one's substance who should not come in after three days* to Jerusalem, his possessions were to be forfeited for the benefit of the temple† (Lev. xxvii. 28 and Neh. xii. 28), and he himself however should be at once cast forth from the congregation.

Vers. 9–17. The assembling took place on the twentieth day of the ninth month, namely, in the same year which Ezra had arrived in Jerusalem. (comp. chap. ix. 1), and indeed **in the square** (רְחוֹב) **of the house of God,** probably on the east or south-east side of the temple court, yet not before the water gate. Comp. notes on Neh. viii. 1. If already the affairs themselves, which naturally had not remained concealed from them, were calculated to excite them to the utmost, and depress them, the stormy weather that had set in made their situation utterly miserable. In December it is not only cold, but the rain is accustomed to fall in torrents. Comp. Robinson's *Phy. Geog.*, p. 287.

Vers. 10, 11. When Ezra now held up before them their error and called upon them to give praise unto the Lord, that is, honor Him indeed by the separation from the people of the land, above all from the foreign wives—נָתַן תּוֹדָה as Josh. vii. 19—then the entire assembly (ver. 12) announced with **a loud voice,** accordingly unreservedly resolved—קוֹל גָּדוֹל (the same as בְּקוֹל גָּדוֹל iii. 12) is a closer designation, which is co-ordinated to the subject or the so-called *acc. instrum.*, Gesen., S. 138, *Anm.* 3, comp. Ps. iii. 5, *etc.*—**according as thy words to us we must do.**—Already the Vulgate in accordance with the accents, connects עָלֵינוּ with the foregoing (*juxta tuum verbum ad nos, sic fiat*); we may however in accordance with ver. 4, Neh. xiii. 13; 2 Sam. xviii. 11, likewise connect עָלֵינוּ with what follows, so that the sense is: thus we are in duty bound to do.

Vers. 13, 14. However, it could not be established in this way, namely, by a general declaration, whether many of the guilty would not be

* [It may be as in the A. V., the protasis of a temporal clause, as "*When he came thither.*"—Tr.]

* [Rawlinson *in loco.* "The brevity of this term indicates the narrowness of the area over which the returned Israelites were spread."—Tr.]

† [Rawlinson *in loco:* "The Persians allowed generally to the conquered nations that they should be governed by their own laws. In the present case Ezra had had special permission to appoint magistrates and judges who should judge the people according to the law of his God (vii. 25) and could enforce his views of the law not only by confiscation of goods, but even by death (vii. 26)."—Tr.]

dissatisfied with the step concluded upon, and seek to withdraw from their obligation. If the separation was to be carried out energetically and surely, it must be established in detail who were united in marriage with strange women, and it was necessary that the elders or princes in question should undertake to take care that the resolution of the congregation should everywhere have its proper consequences. Thus it was necessary that there should be confirmations and explanations that demanded a long time. Those who had spoken accordingly continue:—**But the people are many.**—אֲבָל is an adversative particle of limitation. Their meaning is that on account of the large number of the assembly, it is not certain whether they all were really agreed.—**And the time is violent rain.**—This is briefly for: the time is that of the violent rain, just as "thine eyes are doves" Song of Songs, iv. 1.—**And there is no strength to stand without** = we cannot longer stand in the cold.—**And the business is not for one day and not for two,** *etc.*—There are so many cases that must be established and examined into.

Ver. 14. **Let now our princes stand for the entire congregation,** *etc.* — לְכָל־הַקָּהָל serves not as a closer designation of the princes as such who belonged to the entire congregation in distinction from the elders and judges of the separate cities (Berth.), as it has already been taken by the Sept., *στήτωσαν δὴ ἄρχοντες ἡμῶν*, and Esdras: *στήτωσαν δὲ οἱ προηγούμενοι τοῦ πλήθους*. The ל is rather a designation of the *dat. commodi*, and here is equivalent to "in place of." The sense is, let the princes remain in Jerusalem and advise with Ezra; especially however name to him the members of the congregation in question.—**And let every one in our cities who has taken home strange wives, come at fixed times, and with them** (for, with him) **the elders of every city, and the judges thereof.**—The princes are to fix the times for the guilty ones named by them to Ezra, when they have to appear with their elders and judges; the guilty are then to promise to dismiss the wives; the elders and judges however are intrusted with the duty of watching over the performance of their vows. Since the various local congregations might be called at different times, it was possible in this way to dispose of them in Jerusalem in a much shorter period. The article before הוֹשִׁיב again represents the relative as in ver. 17; viii. 25. עִתִּים מְזֻמָּנִים are appointed terms, only here and Neh. x. 35; xiii. 31. זְמָן is a Chaldaism.—**Until they turn away the fierce wrath of our God from us with reference to this matter.**—עַד in the sense of "until," gives no difficulty. For it might be expected of a God who is ever so gracious, that with the cause of the wrath the wrath itself also would cease. The supposition of Bertheau, that עַד with the following ל in the later language is used for the simple ל, thus stating the purpose, cannot be proved from Jos. xiii. 5; 1 Chron. v. 9; xiii. 5, compared with Num. xiii. 21. Also in the clause עַד לַדָּבָר הַזֶּה after wrath, עַד retains its meaning; the sense is: which reaches even to this matter.* Certainly, however, the simple לַדָּבָר הַזֶּה would have sufficed here (comp. Gen. xix. 21; 1 Sam. xxx. 24; Dan. i. 14), just as עַד לְמֵרָחוֹק, 2 Chron. xxvi. 15; Ezra iii. 13, and לְמֵרָחוֹק, 2 Sam. vii. 19 amount to the same thing. With the first words of the verse, "let our princes stand," this clause cannot be connected in the sense of "so long as this matter lasts, (Keil); against this is not only the fact that it would be somewhat superfluous, but also that a new clause: And let every one—come—has come in between.

Vers. 15–17. **Only Jonathan,** *etc.*—If we follow the clear usage of the language we must regard this as in apposition. אַךְ properly "only" (then often it is true "in truth") easily leads to an adversative limitation, and עָמַד עַל means 1 Chron. xxi. 1; 2 Chron. xx. 23; Dan. viii. 25; xi. 14: stand against any person or thing, as sometimes also קוּם עַל. Accordingly Jonathan and Jahaziah withstood the adopted resolution, whether they merely had some objection to the proposed method of dealing with the matter, or were also opposed to the banishment of strange wives itself. Only the circumstance that verse 16 is joined on, without an adversative particle, although it treats of the obedience of the congregation, seems to favor the view that here also an agreement is meant, as then already the Vulgate has: *steterunt super hoc præfecti sunt huic negotio.* But in truth, according to our conception, ver. 16 is not in contrast with ver. 15. All depends upon the emphasis placed upon "only" at the beginning of ver. 15. Not *notwithstanding that,* but *because* only Jonathan, *etc.*, withstood, the congregation did, as a whole, as had been proposed. The present reading in ver. 16 וַיִּבָּדְלוּ Ezra, the priest, men as heads of fathers' houses were separated, is not only opposed by the fact that we should expect with the Sept. and Vulg. the copula before אֲנָשִׁים, since an asyndeton would here be very remarkable, but likewise by the fact that a separation of Ezra could hardly be spoken of, for he was already sufficiently set apart by his entire position. We may therefore with Ewald, *Gesch.* IV., S. 185 and Berth., in accordance with Esdras and the Peschito read וַיַּבְדֵּל לוֹ.—**And Ezra separated for himself,** or at any rate also וַיִּבָּדְלוּ לְעֶזְרָא—there were separated unto Ezra. [So Rawlinson].—**After the fathers' house** = so that every father's house was represented by its head.—**And they all with names,** as viii. 20.—**And they held a session**—so וַיֵּשְׁבוּ here—**on the first day of the tenth month,** thus ten days after the general assembly of the people,

* [Rawlinson after Dathe and Maurer follows two MSS. which read עַל הַדָּבָר הַזֶּה.—Tr.]

to investigate the matter.—Instead of דַּרְיוֹשׁ which is not a Hebrew formation, we are to read the infin. דְּרוֹשׁ.

Ver. 17. **And they made an end with all,** *etc.*, אֲנָשִׁים (men who had taken home strange wives) can hardly be in apposition with בַּכֹּל as the more ancient interpreters would have it; the expression would be too peculiar; moreover the accentuation is against it. No more can אֲנָשִׁים be the object of וַיְכַלּוּ and בַּכֹּל be a designation of place; they brought to an end the men (the hearing of them) in every place (Berth.); אֲנָשִׁים in this case would certainly require the article. The same objection is to be made to the rendering of Keil, "with reference to the men," which in itself moreover already misses the sense. The suspicion that the clause was a title of the following section in ver. 18, and only by mistake was placed here is quite natural, but it is not confirmed by any ancient version. Thus we must regard the entire clause as a brief, loosely attached, closer designation of כֹּל, and understand: *they were ready* with the entire object incumbent upon them, that however was men who, *etc.*—[Rawlinson *in loco:* "In some cases, it may be presumed, they had to summon persons before them who did not wish to part with their foreign wives; in all they had to assure themselves that the wives were foreign; finally they had in every case where they decreed a divorce to make out the 'writing of divorcement,' to which the woman put away was entitled as evidence of her having been a wife and having become free."—Tr.]—**By the first day of the first month,** namely, of the following year. The session thus lasted in all very nearly three months.

Vers. 18–44. Catalogue of the men, who had strange wives, and were obliged to dismiss them. First of all are the priests in vers. 18–22, and indeed in vers. 18 and 19 four of the house of the high-priest.—**Of the sons of Jeshua,** *etc.* This evidently means the high-priest Jeshua, who had come to Jerusalem with Zerubbabel. The sons of his brother were probably only his distant relatives; according to ii. 36, they were, if Jeshua there is the high-priest Jeshua, sons of Jedaiah, thus brother in a broader sense.

Ver. 19. **They gave their hands,** that is, they vowed in a solemn manner by striking hands (comp. 2 Kings x. 15) to dismiss their wives. וַאֲשֵׁמִים might follow as epexegesis = and indeed as guilty. But it is more simple to supply: and they were guilty, that is, as they stood there guilty. The more general law of Lev. v. 14 sq. comes into consideration. They must bring a guilt-offering, because they had committed a מַעַל against Jehovah, for which a satisfaction was possible, and hence must likewise be given; comp. the different opinions respecting the guilt-offering in Keil's *Archäol.* I. S. 244. אֵיל־צֹאן is subordinated as an accusative of closer definition to the previous word. In connection with the following persons we are to supply in thought the promise to dismiss the wives and probably also the offering of a corresponding guilt-offering.—Of the names following in vers. 20–22 some occur again in Neh. viii. 4; x. 2–9, which perhaps designate the same persons. In all eighteen priests were guilty; none of the divisions that had returned with Zerubbabel had kept themselves free from the transgression (comp. ii. 36–39).

In vers. 23 and 24 ten Levites follow, among whom Kelaiah, usually called Kelita (comp. Neh. viii. 7 and x. 11); furthermore Jozabad, who again occurs in Neh. viii. 7.

Vers. 26–44 give the names from the rest of Israel. In all there are eighty-six, distributed among ten of the families named in chapter ii. It is singular that the sons of Bani are mentioned twice in ver. 29 and ver. 34, and probably there is an error in the second Bani, although it already occurs in the reading of the Sept. and Esdras. Whilst of every other family only four, six, seven or eight persons are enumerated in ver. 34 sq. not less than twenty-seven are mentioned as of this family. Furthermore it is singular that the inhabitants of the cities adduced in ii. 21–28 and vers. 33–35 are not expressly mentioned, whilst yet in ver. 7 sq. and ver. 14 those outside the city come into consideration as well as the Jerusalemites. Probably the twenty-seven men mentioned in vers. 34–41 belonged to the different districts of Judah.

Ver. 44 concludes the entire catalogue with a summary statement.—**All these had taken strange wives.**—נשׂאי must be taken as a participle; probably, however, we should read as the perfect נָשְׂאוּ. for the expression נָשָׂא נָשִׁים, comp. ix. 2. No admissible sense can be derived from the last words of the verse; the translation: And there were among them women, and they had, or which had brought sons into the world, by which the masc. suffix of מֵהֶם, and so also the masc. form וַיָּשִׂימוּ, is referred to the wives, gives a statement, which is too self-evident to be correct. But a change which Bertheau proposes: "And there were among them those who sent away wives and sons," does not commend itself, partly because it is in too little connection with the text as we have it, partly because such a clause would likewise be too self-evident after ver. 3.—[Rawlinson adopts the former interp. and says: "The fact is noted as having increased the difficulty of Ezra's task."—Tr.]

THOUGHTS UPON THE HISTORY OF REDEMPTION.

Vers. 1–4. 1. It is certainly worthy of remark that it is not narrated of Ezra that he, as we should expect, expressly and severely denounced the men married to strange wives, but that we are only told of his prayer and confession of sin, in which he includes himself in the number of the guilty. Earnest sorrow for the sin to be denounced in others, and especially persevering prayer in their behalf, which in the nature of the case readily includes intercession, generally makes a deeper impression as well upon the persons themselves as their adherents, than castigating sermons, as then likewise here a great crowd of men, women, and children assembled about the praying and sorrowing Ezra, deeply affected by his sorrow.

2. If a head of a community sorrows in true sympathy and anxiety for his people, the better class of the people do not lack the earnest wish to remove his sorrow, and especially its cause: the love and respect which they entertain for him very easily pass over into this wish, and then there is easily found in the congregation itself a spokesman, who, as here Shechaniah, openly acknowledges the guilt, and correctly expresses what it is necessary to do in order to be free from it. Such a voice, moreover, arising out of the congregation itself, such willingness, springing up of itself, is the best result and reward of the sorrowing one. The willingness of the congregation, thus testified, is thereby at the same time still further intensified and enlarged, and the improvement which then takes place as a free act, has a truly ethical significance.

3. Such a one, who stands in the midst of a congregation, has need not only of a strict conscientiousness, but also of great courage and alacrity, in order to openly designate a sin of which many have been guilty as a sin, and demand the putting of it away. But he who is first convinced that the sin in question is really sin, and that the putting it away is really God's will, should not be frightened by any objection from expressing his conviction, and improving the others, who perhaps are only weak, but not hardened. A lack of conscientiousness and courage in this respect is truly lamentable; it is ominous and ruinous for those in question. Joy in God, on the other hand, has its great blessings under all circumstances, even when, instead of good resulting, at first only opposition, scorn, and persecution are reaped. Besides, a good transaction never remains entirely, at least never very long, wholly without results.

Vers. 5–8. It is indeed possible, yea, usually the case, that the first better feelings which dawn at a reformation are transitory. Many let themselves be carried away by the awakening voices of the better spirits, so that they to a certain extent outrun themselves, and regard themselves as capable of the severest self-sacrifices; but afterwards, when they come to realize the difficulties to be overcome, in all their magnitude, they shrink back from them as quickly as they had before resolved to overcome them. Even because they are so great, they deem themselves excused from carrying out their resolution. And the longer they hesitate the more grounds they find to justify the sins that were to be put away. He who would truly improve a congregation should therefore never be satisfied with a first good resolution on their part; his earnestness, his sorrow, his prayer must endure, and it must be felt by all, that he has no rest and no joy until the good resolution has become act and fact. But if anything, such a perseverance will have the power to deepen and render permanent the penitence of the congregation, so that, as in our history, it takes the steps with earnestness and zeal, that are necessary to carry out the good resolution.

Vers. 9–12. The wife was not in such a high station among the Israelites as among Christians. Polygamy was still allowed. Yet the true relation to God and the recognition of the truth, that the woman had been created in the divine image, already involved, that the position of the man towards the woman was much better than among the heathen Asiatics. The demand that wives and children should be dismissed was at any rate, for the most of the parties concerned, one of the hardest that could at all be made. But a true reformer should not hesitate to demand even the hardest things of the congregation of the Lord, and express his demand with clearness and definiteness. His rule is God's word and will alone. Every modification, weakening, and rendering it easy on his part, renders his work of reformation all the more difficult. For it deprives him of his authority as an instrument of God; he thereby abandons the only safe foundation, besides passes over to act in his own name. It renders it difficult for the congregation to follow him. For to do God's pure and clear will there is ever to be found fresh readiness, but to execute the will of a man, or what he may think proper, does not satisfy. The divine will often demands much—very much—but its accomplishment has a corresponding blessing, but this fails if God's demand is weakened by human devices.

Vers. 13–17. 1. We cannot blame the authorities for assembling the people without delay even in the cold and rainy season of the year. The removal of transgressions against God's law and will admits of no delay. But again, it would not have been justifiable for Ezra to have prepared additional unnecessary burdens for the people, who already had besides enough to bear in the burden they had taken on themselves if He exposed them to the injuries of the storm, so to speak, punished them. Towards him who is willing to impose upon himself every self-denial, even the hardest, for the sake of the word of God, every possible forbearance has ever its proper place. And under all circumstances he who would carry out a difficult work of reformation has to take care that everything moves on in order.

2. From our point of view, the dismissal of strange wives with their children, seems extravagantly severe,—without doubt there were also many in the congregation of that time who found the demand of Ezra beyond measure hard, many who might be ruined by this proceeding. Notwithstanding, if we properly estimate all the circumstances of that period, and especially the great dangers that threatened the very existence of the congregation, we will be obliged to regard Ezra as in the right. We are not always to avoid that which may be a stumbling-block. The point of view which alone decides at last, is ever that the communion with the Lord must be re-established or furthered; all communion and friendship with men must stand in the background. If, when we let the latter retire to the background we be regarded as destitute of consideration and the like, we may easily put up with it. Even the opinion of men already prepares a martyrdom, to which Peter's word may be applied, "happy are ye; for the Spirit of glory and of God resteth upon you." 1 Pet. iv. 14. What a thorough success his proceeding without regard to consequences had is clear from Neh. viii.—x.; for it certainly already gave an

important impulse to the renewal of the covenant there narrated,—it is clear then moreover from Ps. cxi. and cxii., which praise the Lord still for the redemption given to the people, at the same time, however, already are full of praise of the law and the disposition in accordance with the law, especially also from Ps. cxix., if it originated already in this period where the poet, just as Ezra in chap. ix., refers to deadly peril, from which the Lord only has delivered him, or removed him, and the one thought that only in the keeping of the divine commandments is salvation, is given with variation, comp. especially ver. 37 sq.

HOMILETICAL AND PRACTICAL.

Vers. 1–4. The power of sorrow over sin (if it be a true, divine sorrow): 1) It moves the pious to sympathy and sorrow; 2) the more intelligent to the recognition of sin; 3) the guilty, at least in part, to the resolution to put away sin.—The possibility of hope in God: 1) In spite of what circumstances: even when the pious leaders sorrow, and the more intelligent are obliged to admit great transgression; 2) under what conditions: when we are ready to re-establish the communion with God by putting away sin, and again cheer those sorrowing for it.—STARKE: If we have sinned and deserved punishment, we should not despair, or let go every hope, as if we were out and out ruined; but we should confess the sins committed, lament and grieve for them, and take our refuge with the mercy of God.

Vers. 5–8. How will it be better? 1) If he who has to represent the cause of God obligates superiors (fathers and teachers) to do their duty and suffers sorrow so long as they have not accomplished their work.—SEARKE: Preachers should be an example for the people (1 Tim. iv. 12), that they should see their good works and be likewise incited to good.—In the example of the great is a great power for evil and also for good. 2) When the superiors earnestly and zealously take heed to remove the general transgression. 3) When those who would not follow are excluded from communion with the others.—STARKE: Those who publicly sin should be publicly chastised, in order that others also may fear. Preachers should chastise with especial earnestness where there is loose conduct in matter of marriage.—In true conversion we must for God's sake renounce that which is hard and difficult for us to renounce.

Vers. 9–12. True willingness to set aside that which separates from God: 1) on the side of the people—they follow the call of their superiors punctually, with zeal, in spite of external difficulties; 2) on the side of the teacher—he sincerely shows the people their sins, and requires of them also confidently the most difficult things; 3) on the side of those who have sinned—they vow to free themselves from their guilt.—The duty of loving God more than our nearest relatives. 1) When we are to follow it—always and under all circumstances, even when to fulfil it is especially difficult. 2) What it means—especially this, that we do wrong in letting our highest good be imperilled by relatives, by our wives or by our children,—that we are therefore bound to choose the wife, above all, with reference to the Lord; 3) upon what it is based—on our having to give the Lord praise and honor (comp. ver. 11)—BRENTIUS: *Non est quidem matrimonium sine consensu et sine promissione, at illa non sufficiunt. In contractu matrimonii requiretur legis observatio.*

[SCOTT: Genuine humiliation before God and sorrow for sin always produce works meet for repentance.—Fervent affections should not be allowed to subside till our most beloved sins have been renounced.—HENRY: Our weeping for other people's sins may perhaps set them a weeping for themselves, who otherwise would have continued senseless and remorseless.—Then there is hope of people when they are convinced not only that *'tis good* to part with their sins, but that 'tis indispensably *necessary*.—WORDSWORTH: Prayer may preach; the sighs and sobs of the penitent are sometimes the best sermons; but prayers and tears avail not without practice.—TR.]

THE END.

THE BOOK

OF

NEHEMIAH.

CRITICALLY AND THEOLOGICALLY EXPOUNDED,

INCLUDING THE HOMILETICAL SECTIONS OF DR. SCHULTZ,

BY

REV. HOWARD CROSBY, D.D., LL.D.,

CHANCELLOR OF THE UNIVERSITY OF NEW YORK.

THE BOOK OF NEHEMIAH.

INTRODUCTION.

§ 1. THE BOOK AND ITS CONTENTS.

THE Book of Nehemiah holds a conspicuous place in the sacred canon as the last historic composition of the ante-christian period. With the exception of the prophecy of Malachi, it gives us the last clear look at the Jewish state before it reappears in the bright light of the gospels. We see the returned people—a small remnant of the children of Jacob—continuing the national line in the ancestral land toward the Messiah, with holy vitality enough (as it were) for this one purpose, but with a general mortification existing throughout the nation. The ark of the covenant was gone, the Shechinah no longer illuminated the holy of holies, the Urim and Thummim had long ceased, the bulk of the people were lost in captivity from Armenia to Elam, and Israel, instead of being an independent commonwealth, with a mighty and magnificent capital, had become a petty province of Persia, while Jerusalem was but a half-rebuilt ruin. Yet, with all this, prophets were still vouchsafed to the Abrahamic line. Haggai and Zechariah had by the use of their prophetic power certified the special presence of Jehovah at the building of the second temple, and Malachi, more than a century later, urged the people to renewed spirituality in the name of the Lord. From Neh. vi. 10, 12, 14, we are led to believe that between Haggai and Malachi many prophets appeared before returned Israel, although some of them prostituted their divine gift to low and false ends.

This twilight age of Jewry is lighted up by the writings of Ezra and Nehemiah as the evening is often re-illuminated by the absent sun's reflection upon a cloud high in the zenith. They give us an inlook into the style of life assumed by the nation in its lingering decadence. We enter the holy city—we see and hear the men—we note their tendencies, and mark the old, strange mingling of patriotism and devotion with a *philoxeny* that was destructive of both. The narratives bring us into close contact with the people. Nehemiah's words are simple, betraying not the least effort of the rhetorician, but their very homeliness makes the scenes described most life-like. We see throughout the writing of an honest, earnest man,—and through him the history closes with a sublime dignity.

The book of Nehemiah was included by the old Jews with the book of Ezra, and the latter name was given to the two. In the Vulgate the book of Ezra appears as the first book of Esdras, and the book of Nehemiah as the second book of Esdras. The Geneva Bible introduced our present nomenclature, and thus made the Apocryphal third and fourth books of Esdras to be numbered as the first and second.

The language is a pure Hebrew, with here and there such an Aramaism as חָבַל in the sense of "deal corruptly" (chap. i. 7), מִדָּה in the sense of "tribute" (chap. v. 4), and מָלַךְ in the sense of "consult." This book, Ezra and the Chronicles offer to us the same general linguistic appearance. Such ἅπαξ λεγόμενα as יָגִיפוּ (chap. vii. 3) and תַּהֲלֻכֹת (chap. xii. 31) are the peculiarities of the individual writer, and no marks of a different period.

The main subject of the book is the rebuilding of the walls of Jerusalem, which, in the largest sense, if we include the dedication of the walls and the events occurring during the building, occupies nearly ten chapters of the thirteen which compose the book, namely, chap. iii.—chap. xii. 43. Previous to the wall-building we have the account of Nehemiah's concern for the holy city, his earnest prayer for the divine guidance, his request of the king of Persia, his journey (by royal permission and order) to Jerusalem as its governor, his careful examination of the ruined walls, his encouragement of the people to rebuild them and their consent, and his bold front against the neighboring enemies of the Jews. This preliminary narrative occupies the first two chapters. We may divide the next ten chapters regarding the wall-building and the dedication into—(1) The apportionment of the work, chap. iii.; (2) The opposition from enemies without, chap. iv.; (3) The hindrance from domestic dissensions, chap. v.; (4) The opposition by combination between the outer enemies and their Jewish allies. The wall finished, chap. vi.; (5) The ordering of the city. To this end the genealogies are examined, chap. vii. (6) Religious services follow, to wit: the public reading of the law by Ezra and his assistants. Preparation for and keeping the feast of tabernacles, chap. viii.; (7) Extraordinary fast, with confession, chap. ix.; (8) A covenant sealed touching obedience to the law, separation from foreigners, observation of the Sabbath days and years, and support of the temple service, chap. x.; (9) The settlement of the families in the holy city and the other towns, chap. xi.; (10) A preliminary list of priests and Levites. The dedication of the wall, chap. xii. 1–43.

The remainder of the book, *viz.*, chap. xii. 44—chap. xiii., contains an account of the appointment of officers over the treasures, and the ordering of the singers and porters, the thorough separation of Israel from the strangers, according to the law, and lastly (from chap. xiii. 4), an account of Nehemiah's second visit to Jerusalem, and his stern dealing with Eliashib's family for their alliances with Sanballat and Tobiah, together with his other resolute measures of reform. (See the scheme following.)

§ 2. THE AUTHOR AND HIS TIME.

That Nehemiah is the author of the book, all agree. Much of it is written in the first person, and claims thus to be the writing of Nehemiah himself. But while it is agreed that Nehemiah is the author of the book, yet some learned commentators, such as Archdeacon HERVEY, pronounce a large part of the book to have been inserted by other (though authorized) hands. From chap. vii. 6 to xii. 26 inclusive the matter is supposed to be inserted, as also the passage chap. xii. 44–47. KEIL, on the other hand, stoutly argues for Nehemiah's authorship throughout. The truth is probably between these extremes. The genealogy in chap. vii. 6–73 (virtually the same as that in Ezra ii. 1–70) is undoubtedly an inserted public document, and yet in this we can see Nehemiah's hand making the addition of ver. 65 and ver. 70 *b* regarding his own (the Tirshatha's) action in reference to matters alluded to in the older document.* So the record in chap. xii. 1–26 is evidently an insertion, giving lists of priests and Levites from Zerubbabel's day to the time of Alexander the Great (Jaddua—vers. 11, 22), a century after Nehemiah. KEIL's attempt to explain away this latter is labored and unsatisfactory. The rest of the supposed inserted portion we take to be Nehemiah's own. The fact that Nehemiah does not there speak in the first person only parallels his book with that of Daniel, where the first person and the third person are interchangeably used. Ezra's prominence in this part of the narrative is simply caused by Ezra's priestly duties requiring him to be the prominent figure,† and only exhibits Nehemiah's modesty in the record. The resemblance to Ezra's style and the different construction of the prayer in chap. ix. from that in chap. i. are arguments of a very frail character. The general likeness of chap. xi. 3–36 and 1 Chron. ix. 2–34 makes nothing against Nehemiah's authorship of that portion. There is no good reason for denying a regular chronological sequence in this part

* This document, so amended by Nehemiah, has been incorporated in Ezra.

† The Rev. Mr. Haigh has urged a very bold and ingenious theory, but one that will not bear examination,—that Ezra and Nehemiah went to Jerusalem together. (See *Transact. of the Soc. of Bib. Arch.*, Vol. II.)

of the book in perfect consonance with the rest, and we cannot but consider the attempts to throw doubt here on Nehemiah's authorship as an effort of the destructive criticism that is so headlong and heedless in its efforts. Nehemiah* (Heb. נְחֶמְיָה, *Nehemyah*, "compassion of Jehovah") was of the tribe of Judah, and probably of the royal stock. The expressions in chap. i. 6 and ii. 5, together with his special activity in the matter of re-establishing Jerusalem, and his acceptability by his countrymen, and also his high position at the Persian court, all seem to suggest this fact of Nehemiah's birth. His father was Hachaliah, of whom we know nothing. The name Nehemiah was probably a common one. Many have supposed that Nehemiah was a priest, but there is no more satisfactory ground for such a notion than the occurrence of his name, as Tirshatha, before the names of the priests in chap. x. 1. He was cup-bearer to Artaxerxes (Heb. אַרְתַּחְשַׁסְתָּא, *Artahshasta*), king of Persia. This position was a very high one at court, and brought him into close and intimate relations with the monarch, whence came his ability (when his soul was stirred for Jerusalem) to carry out his measures of aid and reform for his beloved ancestral country. His character appears to us as faultless. Patriotism, piety, prudence, perseverance, probity and courage equally marked his administration of affairs. He renounced the luxuries of the Persian court for the hardships of what might almost be called a primitive and frontier life, in order to save his country from physical and moral ruin; in all his varied trials he looked up to the guidance and protection of his God; he used methods with careful discrimination, he pursued his determined course unflinchingly, he set an example of self-abnegation and liberal dealing, and met the enemies without and within the nation with equal firmness and success. The time in which Nehemiah flourished was clearly that of Artaxerxes I. (*Longimanus*). This king's 32d year is mentioned in chap. xiii. 6. Only three kings of Persia had a 32d year in their reigns—Darius I. (*Hystaspis*), Artaxerxes I. (*Longimanus*), and Artaxerxes II. (Mnemon). Now this Artaxerxes could not be Darius, for in Ezra vi. 14 the two names are contrasted, as of different monarchs. Whoever the Artaxerxes may be there, his name in that connection shows that Darius was not known as Artaxerxes. The date of Artaxerxes II. is far too late for the chronological position of Eliashib, as high priest. We are therefore shut up to Artaxerxes I. as the monarch mentioned by Nehemiah. Josephus calls the king Xerxes, but the chronology of Joseph is so wretchedly corrupt in the matter of Nehemiah, Ezra, Sanballat, *etc.*, that it is waste time to give him attention.†

In Artaxerxes I.'s time Persia was in its zenith of splendor and power, although the elements of decay were already beginning to work in the empire. Artaxerxes had come to the throne through the assassination of his father, Xerxes, by the chief of the guard, Artabanus. At the instigation of Artabanus, he put his brother Darius to death as the murderer of his father, but on discovering the designs of Artabanus against himself, he slew the double traitor. He subdued a revolt headed by his brother Hystaspes, reduced rebellious Egypt, and terminated the long hostilities with Greece by the peace of Callias. The empire then enjoyed a period of quiet, which may be regarded as the culminating point of its glory, during which the events of Nehemiah's history occurred.

The name *Artaxerxes* is the Greek and *Artahshasta* is the Hebrew for the old Persian **Artakhshatra** from *Arta* (very) and *Khshatra* (powerful). Herodotus translates it *μέγα ἀρήϊος*. *Khshatra* is allied to the *Khshatram* (empire) of the Behistun inscription (Col. i. Par. 9, 11, 12, 13, 14) and to *Khshayathiya* (king). The second element of the name is not identical with the name Xerxes, which is in old Persian *Khshayarsha.*

* The name Nehemiah occurs twice in the book as referring to others than the author—to Nehemiah, son of Azbuk, in chap. iii. 16, and to Nehemiah, a companion of Zerubbabel in chap. vii. 7.

† Josephus puts both Ezra and Nehemiah in the reign of Xerxes, son of Darius, and speaks of Xerxes' twenty-eighth year! He also makes Nehemiah to be two years and four months building the walls. He puts the story of Esther in the time of Artaxerxes, and makes Sanballat to be appointed satrap at Samaria by Darius Codomannus.

§ 3. SCHEME OF THE BOOK.

I. Before the wall-building (chaps. i., ii.).

1. Nehemiah's sadness (chap. i.).
2. Nehemiah's request of the king (chap. ii. 1–8).
3. Nehemiah's journey (chap. ii. 9–11).
4. Nehemiah's inspection and counsel (chap. ii. 12–20).

II. The wall-building (chap. iii.—xii. 43).

1. The stations (chap. iii.).
2. The opposition from without (chap. iv.).
3. The opposition from within (chap. v.).
4. The craft used by the enemies (chap. vi.).
5. The ordering of the city (chap. vii. 1–4).
6. The genealogy (chap. vii. 5–73).
7. The law-reading on the first of Tisri (chap. viii. 1–12).
8. The preparations for the feast of tabernacles (chap. viii. 13–16).
9. The feast of tabernacles (chap. viii. 17, 18).
10. The extraordinary fast (chaps. ix., x.).
11. The distribution of inhabitants (chap. xi.).
12. The Levitical Genealogy (chap. xii. 1–26).
13. The dedication of the walls (chap. xii. 27–43).

III. After the wall building.

1. Levitical apportionments (chap. xii. 44–47).
2. The separation of the *Erev* (mixed multitude—chap. xiii. 1–3).

* *

3. Nehemiah's reforms twelve years later (chap. xiii. 4–31).

THE BOOK OF NEHEMIAH.

CHAPTER I. 1–11.

1 THE words [history] of Nehemiah, the son of Hachaliah. And it came to pass
in the month Chisleu, in the twentieth year [of Artaxerxes], as I was in Shushan
2 the palace [the citadel of Susa], that Hanani, one of my brethren, came, he and
certain men of Judah; and I asked them concerning the Jews that had escaped
[the Jews, the delivered ones], which were left [over] of the captivity, and con-
3 cerning Jerusalem. And they said unto me, The remnant [the left-over ones]
that are left [over] of the captivity there in the province *are* in great affliction and
reproach: the wall of Jerusalem also *is* broken down, and the gates thereof are
4 burned with fire. And it came to pass, when I heard these words, that I sat down
and wept, and mourned *certain* days, and fasted,[1] and prayed before the God of hea-
5 ven, and said, I beseech thee, O LORD God of heaven, the great and terrible God that
keepeth covenant and mercy [*i. e.* the merciful covenant] for them that love him
6 and observe his commandments: Let thine ear now be attentive, and thine eyes
open, that thou mayst hear the prayer of thy servant, which I pray before thee
now [to-day], day and night, for the children of Israel thy servants, and confess
the sins of the children of Israel, which we have sinned against thee: both I and
7 my father's house have sinned. We have dealt very corruptly[2] against thee, and
have not kept the commandments, nor the statutes, nor the judgments, which thou
8 commandedst thy servant Moses. Remember, I beseech thee the word that thou
commandedst thy servant Moses, saying, *If* ye transgress, I will scatter you abroad
9 among the nations: but *if* ye turn unto me and keep my commandments, and do
them; though there were of you cast out unto the uttermost part of the heaven, yet
will I gather them from thence, and will bring them unto the place that I have
10 chosen to set my name there. Now these *are* thy servants and thy people, whom
11 thou hast redeemed by thy great power, and by thy strong hand. O Lord, I
beseech thee, let now thine ear be attentive to the prayer of thy servant, and to
the prayer of thy servants, who desire to fear thy name: and prosper, I pray thee,
thy servant this day, and grant him mercy in the sight of this man [*i. e.* Artaxer-
xes]. For I was the king's cup-bearer.

TEXTUAL AND GRAMMATICAL.

[1] Ver. 4. וָאֱהִי צָם. Here and in 2 Sam. xii. 23 the participle. Here the auxiliary verb expressed. After יָמִים supply רַבִּים, as in Dan. x. 14.

[2] Ver. 7. חֲבֹל חָבַלְנוּ לָךְ. Aben Ezra and most of the Jewish commentators count this a Chaldaism as in Dan. vi. 23, 24 (22, 23). In Gen. vi. 12 כִּי־הִשְׁחִית כָּל־בָּשָׂר is translated by Onkelos אֲרֵי חַבִּילוּ כָּל בִּשְׂרָא. The meaning of "act corruptly" is, however, found in Job xxxiv. 31. It may be an early Aramaic signification.

EXEGETICAL AND CRITICAL.

The Tidings from Jerusalem.

Ver. 1. The title of the book is contained in its first four (Hebrew) words, *Divre Nehemyah Ben 'Hachalyah*,* *i. e.*, **The words of Nehemiah, the son of Hachaliah.**—Even the prophets sometimes begin their books in this way (see Jer. i. 1, and Amos i. 1), although with them the *Devar Yehovah* (the Word of the Lord) finds its place soon after. The absence of the *Devar Yehovah* here is nothing against the inspired character of the book. Its presence in the prophets is simply a token of their prophetic character, as they speak to the people directly in God's name with a special message. In the historical books, even in the Pentateuch, the sacred foundation of them all, this phrase very naturally is not found. Here, as in 1 Chron. xxix. 29, and elsewhere, "the words of" are really "the words about," or "the history of." In Jer. i. 1, Amos. i. 1, *etc.*, they have the literal meaning. (Dathe rightly "historia Nehemiah"). (For the name and history of Nehemiah, see the Introduction).

The starting-point of Nehemiah's *words* (or history) is **in the month Chisleu, in the twentieth year, in Shushan the palace.**—Chisleu was the ninth month, Abib or Nisan (in which the passover fell) being the first. Chisleu would thus answer to parts of November and December. Josephus makes it (Χασλεῦ) the same as the Macedonian Apellæus (Ant. xii. 7, 6), which was the second month of the Macedonian year, whose first month Dius began at the autumnal equinox. Apellæus would thus be from the latter part of October to the latter part of November. Josephus was probably satisfied in identifying the two months of Chisleu and Apellæus, to find some portion of time belonging equally to both. They certainly did not coincide throughout.

Chisleu is not likely to be a Persian month-name, as has been conjectured. The Behistun inscription gives us eight Persian month-names, to wit., Bagayadish, Viyakhna, Garmapada, Atriyatiya, Anamaka, Thuravahara, Thaigarchish and Adukanish. It is true that in all but the first of these battles are recorded as occurring, so that they are not probably winter months. Yet the style of the names would scarcely warrant us in supposing that Chisleu would be in such a list. As Chisleu appears on a Palmyrene inscription (Chaslul), it may be of Syrian origin. This month-name occurs in the Hebrew only after the captivity, to wit, in this place and in Zech. vii. 1. Fuerst suggests *Chesil* (Orion-Mars) as the base of the name, the name being brought from Babylonia by the exiles; but the name is found in the Assyrian, as are the other (so-supposed) Persian month-names of the Jews, which is strong presumptive evidence of their Shemitic origin.

The "twentieth year" is, as in chap. ii. 1, the twentieth year of Artaxerxes (Heb. *Arta'hshasta*), who reigned from B. C. 465 to 425. The year designated is therefore parts of B. C. 446 and 445, when the "age of Pericles" was beginning in Athens, and when Rome was yet unknown to the world. (For Artaxerxes, see Introduction). "Shushan the palace" (Heb. *Shushan Habbirah*) was the royal portion of the "city Shushan" (Esther iii. 15). Shushan or Susa (now *Sus*) lay between the Eulæus (Ulai) and Shapur rivers, in a well-watered district, and was the capital of Susiana or Cissia, the Scriptural *Elam* (Isa. xi. 11) the country lying between the southern Zagros mountains and the Tigris. It early furnished a dynasty to Babylonia (Gen. xiv. 1), was conquered by Asshur-bani-pal about B. C. 660, and shortly afterward fell to the lot of the later Babylonian Empire. When the Persians had conquered this Empire, Susa was made a royal residence by Darius Hystaspes, who built the great palace, whose ruins now attract the attention of archæologists. Artaxerxes (the king of Nehemiah's time) repaired the palace, whose principal features resembled those of the chief edifice at Persepolis, the older capital of the Persian Empire. The present ruins of Susa cover a space about a mile square, the portion of which near the river Shapur is probably "Shushan the palace."

Athenæus (xii. 8) says, *Κληθῆναι τὰ Σοῦσά φησιν 'Αριστόβουλος καὶ Χάρης διὰ τὴν ὡραιότητα τοῦ τόπου· σοῦσον γὰρ εἶναι τῇ Ελλήνων* (?'Ελυμαίων) *φωνῇ τὸ κρίνον.* So Steph. Byzant, Σοῦσα, *ἀπὸ τῶν κρίνων, ἃ πολλὰ ἐν τῇ χώρᾳ πεφύκει εκείνῃ.* If this be true we must accord it a Shemitic origin, which is against other evidence. Shushan may be a Turanian or an Aryan word, whose likeness to "Shushan" (Shemit. for *lily*) has deceived the old writers. Susa was the court's principal residence, Ecbatana or Persepolis being visited for the summer only, and Babylon being sometimes occupied in the depth of winter.

Ver. 2. Nehemiah is informed of the sad condition of Jerusalem and the colony of Jews in Judea by Hanani and others. His words are **Hanani, one of my brethren, came, he and certain men of Judah,** *etc.* Hanani was literally brother to Nehemiah, as we see from chap. vii. 1. He afterward was appointed one of the assistant governors of Jerusalem by Nehemiah (ch. vii. 2). He is not to be confounded with Hanani, a priest, mentioned in chap. xii. 36, and (perhaps the same) in Ezra x. 20. *Of Judah* may be read *from Judah* as denoting place rather than tribal distinction. The words would thus refer to the verb "came," and naturally introduce Nehemiah's question. That the colony was called "Judah," see chap. ii. 7.

Nehemiah **asked them concerning the Jews that had escaped, which were left of the captivity, and concerning Jerusalem.** Heb. *happelētah asher nisharu min hashshevi* (lit. "the deliverance which were left over from the captivity"). The abstract is used as a concrete collective noun. Although the greater part of the Jews preferred to live in the land to which their ancestors had been carried captive, yet to the pious heart those who returned to the old country were recognized as the "deliverance," or the "delivered ones," "escaped ones." The journey from Jerusalem to Susa by Tadmor or by Tiphsah is over a thousand miles long, and

* The Hebrew is transliterated for the benefit of the English reader.

at the usual rate of Oriental travelling would take at least 45 days. With the natural causes to retard so long a journey, we may safely call it a two months' travel. Ezra, with his caravan, was four months on his journey from Babylon to Jerusalem (Ezra vii. 9).

Ver. 3. Nehemiah's informers tell him that the **remnant** (*han-nisharim*, "the left-over ones") **in the province are in great affliction** (the general word for adversity) **and reproach** (the word explaining the cause of the adversity). They were the objects of scorn and contemptuous treatment from the neighboring peoples. The **wall of Jerusalem** they also represent as **broken down** and its **gates burned.** Nebuchadnezzar had broken down the walls a hundred and forty-two years before (2 Kings xxv. 10) and the attempt to rebuild them had been stopped by the Pseudo-Smerdis (the Artaxerxes of Ezra iv. 7) seventy-six years before this embassy to Nehemiah. After that, in the reign of Darius Hystaspes, the temple had been finished, but the walls seem not to have been touched. The burnt gates were also, doubtless, the old wreck from Nebuchadnezzar's time. There is no reason for supposing that the walls had been rebuilt, and again destroyed. Hanani and the men of Judah add to their statement of the affliction and reproach of the province that the walls still remain in their old ruined condition.

Ver. 4. *Nehemiah's prayer.* The tidings brought by Hanani and the others deeply moved Nehemiah, and led him to a special season of humiliation and prayer. His grief was doubtless increased at the thought that all this evil existed in spite of Ezra's work, for Ezra had gone to Jerusalem thirteen years before. He **sat down and wept and mourned certain days and fasted and prayed.**—That is, he withdrew from his court duties, and spent a period of retirement (comp. Ps. cxxxvii. 1 for the phrase "sat down and wept") in most sincere sorrow, which compelled his fasting and prayer, as its godly manifestations. The phrase **God of heaven** (*Elohe hash-shamayim*) is supposed by some to be only found with the writers of the Babylonish or post-Babylonish period, Daniel, Ezra, Nehemiah, and the author of the 136th Psalm, but we find it in Gen. xxiv. 3, 7, and in Jonah i. 9. The style is repeated in Rev. xi. 13 and xvi. 11 (*ὁ θεὸς τοῦ οὐρανοῦ*). It was a natural epithet to distinguish Jehovah from the gods of earth formed of earthly substances. The phrase cannot properly be called Persian, as the reference in Jonah proves. Moreover, it does not occur in the long Behistun inscription. If it was used by the later Persians, it is as likely to have been taken from the Jews as *vice versâ.*

Ver. 5. **Terrible** is *awe-inspiring*, נוֹרָא, the Niphal participle of יָרֵא (to tremble). **That keepeth covenant and mercy.**—Lit. *That keepeth the covenant and mercy*, by hendiadys for "the covenant of mercy," or "the merciful covenant" established in the world's Messiah, but centrally and typically in the Israelitish system. **Observe his commandments**—or *keep his commandments;* the same verb as before. God keeps the covenant for them who keep His commandments. This is not a doctrine of meritorious works, but of adhering faith. See its explanation in John vi. 28, 29, where the work of God is a sincere faith. The essence of faith is love, whose definition is given in 2 John 6. "The great and terrible God" is a phrase borrowed from Deut. vii. 21, and "that keepeth—— observe his commandments" is from the 9th verse of the same chapter. The Pentateuch has furnished much of the religious phraseology of the nation in all ages. (Comp. Dan. ix. 4.)

Ver. 6. After this address to Jehovah as the awe-inspiring and yet covenant-keeping God, he asks God to hear him as the representative of his nation. The phrase, **let thine ear be attentive, and thine eyes open, that thou mayest hear,** is peculiar. It is derived from Solomon's prayer (1 Kings viii. 29, 52), and has reference, doubtless, to the greater attention paid by the ear when the eyes are opened towards the source of the sound.

Now, day and night.—Lit. *to-day, day and night.* His prayer was oft repeated in the course of these days of separation and mourning at hours of the night, as well as at the usual hours of daily prayer. **Which we have sinned.**—Nehemiah has a clear sense of his identification with his people in sin as in misery. **Both I and my father's house have sinned.**—From this mention of his father's house we have a strong reason to believe that Nehemiah was of the royal house of Judah. It is hard to understand his special mention of his father's house, unless it had been a conspicuous family in the nation. (See the Introduction.)

Ver. 7. **The commandments, nor the statutes, nor the judgments.**—Heb.: *eth-ham-mitzoth weth-hahukkim weth-hammishpatim.* It is almost impossible to draw the distinction between the meanings of these three words. They were probably used in the fulness of the legal style. *Commandment, statute and judgment* are the nearest English equivalents, but here they are all subjected to the verb corresponding to the first noun ("command"), and we must thus loosely refer them to the various forms of the divine commandments. The 119th Psalm seems to use these words as synonymous. (See on ch. ix. 13, 14.)

Ver. 8. **Remember, I beseech thee, the word.**—After the confession of sin comes the plea of God's promise. See Deut. iv. 25–31, xxx. 1–10. Not the words, but the spirit of the promise, is given.

Ver. 11. **Who desire to fear thy name.**—The name of God is His expression in His word or work. The declaration of a *desire to fear God* is a modest assertion of a true fear of God, but with a consciousness of its imperfection. **This man**=King Artaxerxes.—Nearness to God enables Nehemiah to think of the "great king" as only a man. The "this" does not indicate that he was in the king's presence when he prayed, but that he was brought into close relations with the king. **For I was the king's cup-bearer.**—The position of cup-bearer to the king was an exalted one (comp. Gen. xl. 21). *Rab-shakeh* (the name given to one of Sennacherib's envoys to Hezekiah, 2 Kings xviii. 17) means "chief cup-bearer." The monuments of Egypt, Assyria, and Persia show the high rank of the cup-bearer. Nehemiah's high position as cup-bearer is an additional argument for his relationship to the royal family of Judah, for the Oriental despots loved to have men of royal blood to wait upon them. (See Dan. i. 3.) This phrase, "for I was the king's cup-bearer," is added as explanatory of the allusion to the king.

HISTORICAL AND ETHICAL.

1. The interest of Nehemiah in the forlorn condition of Jerusalem had a deep religious character. Patriotism and piety were closely related in a people whose land had been the scene of a theocracy, and in a man of Nehemiah's character the piety is conspicuous in every impulse of his patriotism. It is sad to reflect that when such opportunity for a return to the Holy Land had been given by Cyrus, that only 50,000 Jews availed themselves of it, out of, probably, an aggregate of millions. The manner in which the affairs of the Jewish province dragged from Cyrus' day to the time of Nehemiah, a period of nearly a hundred years, was not due only or chiefly to the opposition of local enemies, supported by the Persian government, but had its chief cause in the apathy and self-seeking of the Jewish people. Nehemiah's piety is thus no type of the religious condition of the Jews of his day, but is a conspicuous exception to the general state of his people.

2. Fasting, with the exception of that on the day of atonement, was with the Jews (before tradition supplanted God's word) left to the suggestion of the occasion. It grew out of a deep grief or an anxious foreboding. Nehemiah's fast, continuing for several days, must have been not a total abstention from food, but a withdrawal from all pleasurable forms of eating, his sorrow rendering him averse to all indulgence in the pleasures of the palate.

3. The "day and night" prayer of Nehemiah was no "vain repetition," as his wounded spirit and his humble faith gave life to every utterance. He had two facts before him—the greatness of God and the sinfulness of God's chosen people. On these he would graft the return of the people and the mercy of God. Some, like himself, were looking Godward, and had not God promised mercy to such? The favor of the Persian monarch would be the expression of God's grace.

4. The rule of obedience ("if ye turn unto me and keep my commandments, and do them," *etc.*) is not the way of salvation, but of continued prosperity. The love of God is assumed in his children. Their happiness now depends on their obedience. "If ye love me, keep my commandments." The Jews were in covenant with God. Keeping commandments had not brought them there, but keeping commandments would fill them with the blessings of the covenant.

HOMILETICAL AND PRACTICAL.

Vers. 1-4. Genuine patriotism. 1) When and where it is roused: both at a distance and in those who, in their prosperity, could easily forget their country and the people to whom they belong. 2) Concerning what it asks: concerning the prosperity of those whom the Lord has preserved or selected, that they should strive for a better future. 3) What it finds the hardest to bear: that its country and people are in distress, and even in reproach, and that they are wanting in power to protect the goods confided to them.

STARKE: In prosperity we should not forget our poor relations or acquaintances, but should ask after them, Gen. xliii. 27. We should make the necessities of the saints our own, and give account of them to others. Rom. xii. 12.

Our greatest and final wish: 1) Concerning what we ask; there remains to us, even in prosperity and high position, if indeed we are godly, still one question, that is, concerning the kingdom of God, and its approach, and indeed only this certainty can satisfy us, that it comes continually more to us, to our families and our people; without it nothing is of worth to us, for without it there is no stability. 2) Concerning what we mourn for; that thus far, always so much the opposite of that takes place which should take place in relation to the kingdom of God. 3) Before whom we bear it: before the Lord with mourning, fasting and prayer.

STARKE: If the saints of God had great love and yearning for their fatherland, the earthly Jerusalem (Ps. li. 20; cxxxvii. 5), how much greater love and yearning should we have for the heavenly Jerusalem! Heb. xii. 22; xiii. 14. Although a Christian is neither bound to the Jewish nor to the Romish fasts of the present day, still he should practice sobriety. 1 Pet. iv. 8. The judgments of God cannot better be averted than by true humiliation, fervent prayer and honest reformation. Gen. xviii. 23 sq.

Vers. 5-11. The nature of the true petition (for Jerusalem, for the Church): 1) It proceeds from true love; is therefore persistent and fervent: Nehemiah prays (ver. 6) day and night for the children of Israel. 2) It rests upon the humble recognition of one's own worthlessness (although standing before God as priest, the petitioner includes himself nevertheless to the inmost with those for whom he prays). 3) It is full of faith, in spite of sin and punishment, on the ground of the divine promise.

The foundations for our faith in the time of oppression: 1) God's promise, after the chastisements which we have merited, to allow mercy again to rule. 2) God's former evident proofs of grace, particularly the greatest, that He has freed us by His great power (*shining deed*), and has made us His servants. 3) God's divine nature itself, which cannot be false to itself, and cannot leave unfinished that which it has begun.

STARKE: The knowledge of God through the law and through the gospel must be united, otherwise the latter makes confident epicurean and rough people; but the former, hesitating and timid doubters (vers. 4, 5). Neither must we excuse the sins and transgressions of our ancestors. Dan. ix. 16.—Whoever stands in the consciousness of the poverty of his spirit does not exclude himself from sinners, but still always humbles himself before God. Dan. ix. 7; 1 Tim. i. 15; 1 John i. 8. God knows our weakness beforehand, and knows that we will stumble in the future. Matt. xxvi. 34. God's choice is unalterable, and He keeps faith forever. Ps. cxlvi. 6; Jer. iii. 12. We should grasp God's promises and favors by true faith, and base ourselves upon them in prayer. Ps. xxvii. 8; Mark xi. 24. We are God's property and servants, and have been dearly bought and freed. 1 Pet. ii. 9. If we wish to obtain anything from men, especially from those in power, we should first seek it in prayer from God, for their hearts also are in God's hand, and He can incline them as He will. Prov. xxi. 1; Esther iv. 16.

Chapter II. 1–20.

1 And it came to pass in the month Nisan in the twentieth year of Artaxerxes
the King *that* wine *was* before him: and I took up the wine and gave *it* unto the
2 king. Now I had not been *beforetime* sad in his presence. Wherefore [and]
the king said unto me, Why *is* thy countenance sad, seeing thou *art* not sick? this
is nothing *else* but sorrow of heart. Then I was very sore afraid, and said unto
3 the king, Let the king live for ever: why should not my countenance be sad, when
the city, the place of my fathers' sepulchres, *lieth* waste, and the gates thereof are
4 consumed with fire? Then the king said unto me, For what dost thou make re-
5 quest? So I prayed to the God of heaven. And I said unto the king, If it please
the king, and if thy servant have found favor in thy sight, that thou wouldest send
6 me unto Judah, unto the city of my father's sepulchres, that I may build it. And
the king said unto me, (the queen also sitting by him,) For how long shall thy
journey be? And when wilt thou return? So it pleased the king to send me; and
7 I set him a time. Moreover I said unto the king, If it please the king, let letters
be given me to the governors beyond the river [Euphrates], that they may convey
8 me over [*i. e.* from country to country] till I come into Judah; and a letter unto
Asaph the keeper of the king's forest, that he may give me timber to make beams
for the gates of the palace which *appertained* to the house [*i. e.* temple], and for
the wall of the city, and for the house [*i. e.* temple] that I shall enter into [to in-
spect]. And the king granted me, according to the good hand of my God upon me.
9 Then I came to the governors beyond the river [Euphrates], and gave them the
king's letters. Now the king had sent captains of the army and horsemen with
10 me. When Sanballat the Horonite and Tobiah the servant, the Ammonite, heard
of it, it grieved them exceedingly that there was come a man to seek the welfare
11 of the children of Israel. So I came to Jerusalem, and was there three days.
12 And I arose in the night, I and some few men with me; neither told I *any* man
what my God had put in my heart to do at Jerusalem: neither *was there any* beast
13 with me, save the beast that I rode upon. And I went out by night by the gate
of the valley, even before the dragon-well and to the dung-port, and viewed the
walls of Jerusalem, which were broken down, and the gates thereof were consumed
14 with fire. Then I went on to the gate of the fountain, and to the king's pool, but
15 *there was* no place for the beast *that was* under me to pass. Then went I up in the
night by the brook, and viewed the wall, and turned back, and entered by the
16 gate of the valley, and *so* returned. And the rulers knew not whither I went, or
what I did; neither had I as yet told *it* to the Jews, nor to the priests, nor to the
nobles, nor to the rulers, nor to the rest that [afterwards] did the work.
17 Then said I unto them, Ye see the distress that we *are* in, how Jerusalem *lieth*
waste, and the gates thereof are burned with fire: come and let us build up the
18 wall of Jerusalem, that we be no more a reproach. Then I told them of the hand
of my God which was good upon me; as also the king's words that he had spoken
unto me. And they said, Let us rise and build. So they strengthened their hands
19 for this good work [*or rather*, for good]. But when Sanballat the Horonite, and
Tobiah the servant, the Ammonite, and Geshem the Arabian heard *it*, they laughed
us to scorn, and despised us, and said, What *is* this thing that ye do? Will ye

20 rebel against the king? Then answered I them, and said unto them, The God of
heaven, he will prosper us; therefore [and] we his servants will arise and build:
but ye have no portion, nor right, nor memorial [*i. e.*, record of remembrance] in
Jerusalem.

TEXTUAL AND GRAMMATICAL.

[1] Ver. 6. שֵׁגָל. Only here and in Ps. xlv. 10. See Exegetical Note.

[2] Ver. 7. עַל־פַּחֲוֹות. This later use of עַל for אֶל, found in Ezra and Esther, is also found in Job frequently. Compare Exeg. Note on ch. i. 7.

[3] Ver. 8. לְקָרוֹת, infin. construct. of the Piel קָרָה, as in ch. iii. 3, 6. So 2 Chron. xxxiv. 11. See also Ps. civ. 3. בִּירָה. This late Hebrew word is applied to the temple in 1 Chron. xxi. 19, and to the royal portion of Susa in Neh. i. 1. (Comp. Ezra. vi. 2.) See Exeg. Note here, and on ch. vii. 2.

[4] Ver. 12. רֹכֵב בָּהּ for רֹכֵב עָלֶיהָ. Comp. Is. lxvi. 20.

[5] Ver. 13. שֹׁבֵר. In LXX. ἦμην συντρίβων. So also in ver. 15. Doubtless the correct reading is, with some MSS. and commentators, שָׂבַר, which, however, never elsewhere occurs in Kal.—הֵם פְּרוּצִים. The open Mem. suggests הַמְפֹּרָצִים as the proper reading. (Comp. ch. i. 3.)

[6] Ver. 14. לַעֲבֹר תַּחְתָּי. A clumsy form for אֲשֶׁר תַּחְתַּי לַעֲבֹר.

[7] Ver. 16. עַד־כֵּן, not "as yet," but "until so," *i. e.* עַד אֲשֶׁר עָשִׂיתִי כֵּן.

[8] Ver. 17. חֶרְפָּה for לְחֶרְפָּה.

[9] Ver. 18. נָקוּם וּבָנִינוּ for נָקוּם וְנִבְנֶה. So in ver. 20.

EXEGETICAL AND CRITICAL.

The Interview with the King.

Ver. 1. **The month Nisan** (called "Abib" in the Pentateuch, Exod. xiii. 4)—the first month of the Hebrew national year. This name Nisan is found in the Assyrian, but its derivation is obscure. It corresponded to parts of our March and April. **The twentieth year of Artaxerxes the king.**—Artaxerxes' reign-years counted from some other month than Nisan, for the preceding Chisleu was in the 20th year. The unlikely supposition (as by BP. PATRICK) that the "twentieth year" of chapter i. 1 refers to Nehemiah's life, is thus unnecessary. (See on chap. i. 1.) **Wine was before him.**—It is the custom among the modern Persians to drink before dinner, accompanying the wine-drinking with the eating of dried fruits. (See RAWLINSON'S *Herod.* I. 133, Sir H. C. R.'s note.) Compare the "banquet of wine" in Esther v. 6. **Now I had not been beforetime sad in his presence.**—Lit. *And I was not sad in his presence.* That is, it was not his wont to be sad in the king's presence. The exactions of Persian monarchs would not endure any independence of conduct in their presence. Everybody was expected to reflect the sunlight of the king's majesty.

Ver. 2. **Wherefore the king said.**—Lit. *And the king said.* The word translated "sad" in vers. 1, 2, 3, and the noun "sorrow" in ver. 2, are very general words for "bad" and "badness." But the bad countenance was the sad countenance (see Gen. xl. 7 for the same phrase).

Ver. 3. **Let the king live for ever.**—Heb. *hammelek l'olam yihyeh.* Compare 1 Kings i. 31; Dan. ii. 4; v. 10; vi. 6, 21. The mere formula of address to an Oriental king, so that even a Daniel used it without compunction. **The city, the place of my fathers' sepulchres.**—Lit. *the city, house of graves of my fathers.* This emphasis of "the house of graves" not only seems to prove Nehemiah a Jerusalemite in descent, *i. e.*, of the tribe of Judah, but also of the royal house. An obscure person would scarcely have chosen such a way of designating the city before the king. (Comp. on chap. i. 6.)

Ver. 4. **For what dost thou make request?**—Lit. *On what account this thou art asking?* The king takes for granted that the look of sadness is an assumed preliminary to asking a favor. There is a true Oriental touch in this. **So I prayed to the God of heaven.**—A beautiful mark of Nehemiah's piety. He first addresses the King of kings, and then the earthly monarch. He knew in whose hands were kings' hearts. For the phrase "God of heaven," see on chap. i. 5.

Ver. 5. **That I may build it.**—This was Nehemiah's first great aim, to rebuild the city. Without walls and fortifications, it was but a large village, exposed to sudden ruin. Could the walls be rebuilt, its permanence would be secured, and the province of Judah have a strong centre. That Nehemiah saw that this was the true course to conserve the special interests of God's people, there can be no doubt. A man of his piety could not rest in the mere external view of things.

Ver. 6. **The queen also sitting by him.**—We have a good illustration of this scene in a sculpture from Asshur-bani-pal's palace (Koyunjik). The king reclines on one side of the table, and is in the act of drinking. The queen *sits* upright in a chair of state at the side of the table, near the king's feet, but facing him. She is also in the act of drinking. Attendants with large fans stand behind each. (See copy of this interesting scene in RAWLINSON'S *Ancient Monar-*

chies, Vol. I., p. 493). That the word "shegal" refers to the principal wife of the king seems clear from its use in Ps. xlv. 10. The chief wife of Artaxerxes at one time was Damaspia, according to Ctesias.

Ver. 7. **The governors.**—Heb. *pahawoth*, from *pechah*, the modern *pacha*, the Oriental name for a viceroy used by Assyrians, Babylonians, and Persians. **Beyond the river**, *i. e.*, the river Euphrates. The course to Judea would leave the Euphrates probably at Tiphsah, 700 miles from Susa or Shushan, whence there would be 400 miles of travel through the Syrian countries before reaching Jerusalem. They were letters to governors or pachas in this Syrian region that Nehemiah requested.

Ver. 8. **Asaph, the keeper of the king's forest**, may have been a Jew, as the name is Israelitish. It may, however, be a form of Aspatha (Esther ix. 7), from the Persian *Aspa* (horse). The word translated "forest" is *pardes*, which is our familiar *paradise*. It is an Aryan word (Zend, *pairidaeza*), and signifies a *walled round* place, a preserve of trees and animals. There was probably a royal park set off for the king in the neighborhood of Jerusalem, and Asaph was its keeper. The word *pardes* is found in the Scriptures only here and in Sol. S. iv. 13 and Eccl. ii. 5. As it is not an old Persian word, but found in the Sanscrit and Armenian, no argument for the late date of Solomon's Song and Ecclesiastes can be derived from it. In Solomon's day, with that king's extensive connections with distant countries, the word may readily have entered into his vocabulary from any Aryan source. **The palace which appertained to the house.**—It is supposed by some that this is the well-known Birah or Baris (afterward Antonia) at the north side of the temple-area. But that was probably constructed at a later date. Nehemiah sought simply to reconstruct the old buildings. Now the palace next to the house (*i. e.*, to the temple, *the* house, as the house of God) was Solomon's palace, inhabited by all the kings after him, which was situated at the south-east corner of the temple-area. (See 2 Chron. xxiii. 12–15). **The house that I shall enter into.**—Not Nehemiah's own house (he was too high-minded to think of that), but the house of God, spoken of before. He desired timber (1) for the palace gates, (2) for the walls, and (3) for the house of God. "That I shall enter into" means "which I shall visit and inspect."

According to the good hand of my God upon me.—For this beautiful expression of piety, compare Ezra vii. 9 and viii. 18. In ver. 18 of this chapter we see it again, slightly varied in form.

The Journey to Jerusalem.

Ver. 9. **The king had sent captains of the army and horsemen with me.**—Nehemiah's high rank made this a matter of course.

Ver. 10. **Sanballat the Horonite.**—There were two Horons ("Beth-horons" in full) in Palestine, a few miles north of Jerusalem. There was also a Horonaim (lit. "the two Horons") in Moab (Isa. xv. 5). Sanballat was probably from the latter, and was a Moabite, as we find his associate is Tobiah, an Ammonite. He was probably satrap or pacha of Samaria under the Persians, and Tobiah was his vizier or chief adviser. The hatred of the Moabites and Ammonites toward Israel, and the equal hatred of the Israelites to Moab and Ammon appear to have grown stronger in the later ages of the Jewish state. In David's time, his family found refuge in Moab, as Elimelech's family had done long before, and Ruth a Moabitess was ancestress of the line of kings in Israel and Judah. After the attack upon Moab by Jehoshaphat and the terrible scene upon the wall of Mesha's capital (2 Kings iii. 27), there was probably nothing but intense bitterness between the children of Lot and the children of Israel. Sanballat and Tobiah represented the Moabitish and Ammonitish hatred.* The origin of the name Sanballat is uncertain. It seems akin to the Assyrian *Assur-uballat*, and may be, in its correct form, "Sinuballat," Sin being the moon (comp. Sin-akhi-irib or Sennacherib), or it may be San-uballat, San being the sun.

Tobiah, the servant, the Ammonite.—Tobiah is a Jewish name (see Ezra ii. 60 and Zech. vi. 10). We could scarcely expect to find the element Jah in the name of an Ammonite. Tobiah was probably a renegade Jew, who had become a slave among the Ammonites, and, by his talents and cunning, had risen into prominence, and was now chief adviser of Sanballat. Hence the epithet, which probably his enemies had fastened on him: "Tobiah the slave."—**It grieved them.**—Samaria had become the leading state west of the Jordan, and any restoration of Jerusalem would threaten this predominance.

Ver. 11. **And was there three days.**—Days, probably, of prayer and observation before any determinate action. (See Ezra viii. 32, for a precisely similar conduct on Ezra's part thirteen years before.)

The Inspection.

Ver. 12. **In the night—few men—neither told I any man.**—These facts and that of only one animal being used in the night-survey show the prudence of Nehemiah, who would avoid calling the attention of Sanballat to any survey of the walls until all was ready for building. Any formal survey made in the day-time would soon have reached Sanballat's ears, for he and Tobiah were both closely allied by marriage-alliances with the Jerusalem Jews (ch. vi. 18 and xiii. 28).

Ver. 13. **The gate of the valley**, *Sha'ar hag-gai* (2 Chron. xxvi. 9; Neh. iii. 13), was probably a gate overlooking the great valley of Hinnom, which is called in Jer. ii. 23 simply "the valley." It was between the Tower of the Furnaces (*Migdal hat-tannurim*) and the Dung-gate. We may place it about twelve hundred feet south of the present Jaffa Gate. — **The dragon-well** (*Ain hattannin*) is perhaps the present great pool, Birket Sultan, along the

* The Sanballat of Josephus is evidently a very different person, living a century later. He may have been a descendant of this one, inheriting his office and his hostile tactics toward the Jews.

eastern side of which and above it would be Nehemiah's course southward from the Jaffa-gate. The strange name (*Fountain of the Sea-monster*) may have been given to it because some curious large water-snake or crocodile was kept in it in Nehemiah's time.—**The dung-port** (*Sha'ar ha-ashpoth*) is rather *the rubbish-gate*, and was probably the gate in the valley before which the rubbish of the city was cast and burned. It was the "east gate" (lit. *pottery-gate*) of Jer. xix. 2. So the Jewish authorities. We may suppose this gate was at the southern extremity of Zion. The false rendering of "dung-port" has given rise to the idea that it was near the temple; that through it the filth from the animals offered in sacrifice was carried. It is possible that this filth may have been carried over the bridge to Zion, and through this gate to the brink of Hinnom's deepest portion, and there dumped with the other rubbish. But the *rubbish-gate* or dung-port was only one thousand cubits from the valley gate (see ch. iii. 13), and no gate near the temple could have been thus near the valley-gate, if the valley-gate were anywhere on the west of the city. We should consider the Rubbish-gate as directly before that part of Hinnom known as Tophet (Jer. vii. 31, 32, and xix. 6, 11, 12, 13, 14). (But see Excursus.)

Ver. 14. **The gate of the fountain,** *Sha'ar ha-ayin*, is certainly a gate in front of the pool of Siloam (see ch. iii. 15). It would be where the ancient wall turned northward beyond its south-eastern corner.—**The king's pool,** *berechath hammelek*, must be the pool of Siloam. Comp. ch. iii. 15. The "virgin's fountain" of to-day is too far away. It probably received this name from its watering the king's garden (ch. iii. 15). See Joseph. *Ant.* 7, 14, 4. Also Jerom. Com. on Jer. vii. 30.

There was no place for the beast that was under me to pass.—The ruin was so great, and the rubbish so accumulated, along Ophel, that Nehemiah could not pursue his course along the wall any further (ver. 15), but was obliged to go down into the valley of the Kidron (**the brook,** *nachal*), up which he went and surveyed the wall, and then turned back and pursued the same route back again to the valley-gate. It is evident that this survey was confined to the southern and eastern walls, which were perhaps the most ruined and the most neglected, as being on the sides of greater natural defence.*

Ver. 16. **Neither had I as yet told it to the Jews.**—Rather: *Neither did I, until I had done thus, tell it to the Jews.*—**The rulers** (*seganim*, a Persian word) were the executive officers of the colony. Neither to the Jews in general nor to the rulers, priests or nobles specially had Nehemiah communicated the fact of his survey. He, however, now summons an assembly, and urges them to build the walls, showing them as arguments God's mercies to him and the king's favor.—**The rest that did the work,** *i. e.* the others engaged in the public service. Or (more probably) it may be proleptic for "those that afterward engaged in the wall-building."

Ver. 18. **So they strengthened their hands for this good work,** or *for good, i. e.*, for a prosperous time.

Ver. 19. **Geshem** or Gashmu (vi. 6), who was third with Sanballat and Tobiah in hostility to the Jews, was perhaps chief of those Arabs whom Sargon had settled in Samaria (see Rawlinson's *Anc. Mon.*, Vol. II., p. 146).

Ver. 20. **Ye have no portion nor right nor memorial in Jerusalem.**—This was Nehemiah's firm protest against the slightest interference on the part of these heathen chiefs. He will not acknowledge their right even to complain, and refuses to answer their false charge implied in their question. With such enemies there should be a clear understanding from the first. One of the strong points of Nehemiah's character was his uncompromising and prompt method in all things.

HISTORICAL AND ETHICAL.

1. Like Joseph and Daniel, Nehemiah carried into a high office near the throne of an Oriental despot the vigor of a holy life. It did not make him a recluse, nor yet a sad-faced servant of the king. His sad visage at this time was a thing remarkable. He had been an acceptable officer of the court, and the king's treatment of his request shows the high favor in which he stood. True religion does not incapacitate one from office, but furnishes the man with a power to please, while it preserves him from the temptations of rank.

2. No doubt there had been from the foundation of the Persian empire a sincere sympathy on the part of the Persians with the Jews. The monotheism of the Jews gained them favor with the Persian throne, and was, doubtless, the chief reason of Cyrus's edict concerning their return to Jerusalem. By the twentieth year of Artaxerxes this sympathy had probably diminished (as under Magian influences it had been previously hindered), and yet the king's readiness to send an escort with Nehemiah (chap. iv. 23), and to make his way easy, may be attributed in part to this traditional regard for the Jewish hostility to polytheism.

3. Nehemiah's secresy was a part of his executive ability. Although he had the king's endorsement, he knew the value of keeping his own counsel, for there were jealous foes around the Jews ready to throw hindrances in his way. Moreover these had allies among the Jews themselves—men high in rank and position—and the distance was so great from the Persian capital that Nehemiah's firman needed great wisdom on his part to make it efficient.

4. The encouragement which Nehemiah held out to his countrymen to rebuild the walls was not simply the king's willingness, but the guiding hand of God. He saw behind the throne of Persia the power of Israel's Jehovah, and sought to strengthen his brethren by the same view. Piety teaches the heart to see second causes as only indicators of the Divine will and action, and law, whether it be from man's mouth or in the

* It is generally thought that Nehemiah made the full circuit of the walls; but, although the language might allow such an interpretation, the want of any hint of another way back (no mention of the Fish-gate or Old-gate or any other prominent land-mark on the north and west side) seems to force us to take *shuv* in the sense of going back in the way he went out.

forces of external nature, is rightly referred to an overruling Providence that guides and guards the people of God. It was this consideration that formed Nehemiah's answer to Sanballat, Tobiah, and Geshem.

HOMILETICAL AND PRACTICAL.

Vers. 1-9. Love towards suffering Jerusalem: 1) Its sorrow (vers. 1, 2), in spite of personal prosperity, and even in the midst of the enjoyments of the royal banquet. 2) Its confession (vers. 2, 3); it is not ashamed of belonging to the congregation of the Lord; neither is it ashamed of its poor brethren, but declares itself candidly as love, and indeed in spite of the danger of displeasing in a very hazardous way. 3) Its petition (vers. 4, 5): it begs for help, first indeed of God the Lord, and then also of men, but particularly for the permission to give its own aid, and that too with self-denial. 4) Its joy (vers. 6, 9): its prayer is not only granted, but it receives almost more than it could hope for. BRENTIUS: *Hæc enim est vera amicitia, quæ in afflictionibus perdurat. Exemplum imitandum: si quid petendum est ab homine, primum a Deo petamus, qui hominis cor nobis amicum reddere potest.*

STARKE: To speak to princes of weighty matters demands great precaution. 2 Sam. xiv. 2. O Soul, if a heathen lord takes a servant's griefs so tenderly to heart, how should not the Father of mercy allow thy griefs to penetrate His heart! Jer. xxxi. 20, 25. The sighs of the godly are powerful petitions before God. Ps. xii. 6. One should not frighten timid supplicants still more, but speedily encourage their petition by generous bounty. Matt. v. 32; Rom. xii. 8. Princes and lords should willingly listen to the complaints of their subjects, and grant as much as possible. 2 Sam. iii. 16. God gives according to His great goodness more than we can hope or ask for. Eph. iii. 20; 1 Kings iii. 13.

The sorrow for suffering Jerusalem: 1) In spite of our own prosperity; 2) On account of the sad position of the congregation; 3) In presence of those who are able to help, and must be gained over.—The self-denial of a patriot: 1) He grieves in spite of his own prosperity, for the misery of his country; 2) He risks his position by a frank confession; 3) He wishes to relinquish his position, in order to aid his fatherland.

STARKE: It is a token of a godless spirit when one does not reverence his fatherland; but it is villainy when one desires to injure it. 2 Macc. v. 8.

Ver. 10. The conduct of the worldly-minded towards the congregation of the Lord: 1) Their latitudinarianism: Sanballat and Tobiah maintained friendship with the Jerusalemites. Chap. vi. 10, 17; xiii. 4-9, 28. 2) Their narrowness: they cannot endure that any one should seek to advance the welfare of the congregation of the Lord, as such.

VENERABLE BEDE: *Notanda animarum rerumque diversitas, quia supra quidem dicti sunt hi, qui remanserunt de captivitate in Juda, in afflictione magna et opprobrio fuisse; sed et Nehemiam longum cum fletu et precibus duxisse jejunium, eo quod muros Hierusalem dissipatos, et portæ illius essent igne combustæ, et nunc versa vice hostes ejusdem sanctæ civitatis contristati et in afflictione sunt magna constituti, eo quod ædificia illius restauranda. Unde colligendum, etiam in hac vita sententiam domini posse compleri, qui cum dixissit: Amen, amen, dico vobis, quia plorabitis et flebitis vos, mundus autem gaudebit, vos autem contristabimini, continuo subjecit: sed tristitia vestra vertetur in gaudium.*

Vers. 11-18. Bright zeal in the concerns of God: 1) It foresees (vers. 11, 12) and hastens at times because dangers threaten; 2) It looks around (vers. 13-15) to fully estimate the difficulty of the work to be performed; 3) it looks, and points, on high (vers. 17, 18), to God's help, to the hand of God, which is extended in favor above it, and therefore succeeds with those whose help is necessary.

VENERABLE BEDE: *Diversa urbis destructæ loca lustrandro pervagatur. . . . . Sic et doctorum est spiritualium, sæpius nocte surgere ac solerte indagine statum sanctæ ecclesiæ quiescentibus ceteris inspicere, ut vigilanter inquirant, qualiter ea, quæ vitiorum bellis . . . . dejecta sunt, castigando emendent et erigant.*

STARKE: When one has suitable means at hand for avoiding the danger, he must not despise them. Josh. ii. 15; 2 Cor. xi. 33. When something is granted to us by the authorities through favor, we must ascribe it to God. When one will perform anything great, he must keep it secret. 1 Sam. xiv. 1. When the Church sleeps, God awakens pious people, who work and watch for its welfare. There is a time for speaking and a time for silence. Well begun is half gained.

Vers. 19, 20. In our work for the kingdom of God what position must we take towards the objections of the world? 1) We must be prepared for scorn, contempt, and anxiety. The worldly-minded consider the aim which we truly have as foolish, as it is too elevated for them; they therefore attribute to us another aim, which is foreign to us; and in this way they give a most suspicious look to our activity. 2) We must not, however, lay any importance upon this; that which they consider foolish is our highest task, that we should keep ourselves unspotted from the world, and therefore concede to them, in so far as they are the world, no part or right in our intercourse.

Vers. 17-20. The admonition to build up the kingdom of God. 1) It complains: you see the distress, *etc.*, for it always finds again the reason that it may pass beyond to the demand: come, let us build, resting upon the former proofs of the Lord, who also has known how to make the kings of the earth serviceable to His ends. 2) It excites the ridicule and the suspicions of the world, but overcomes them through reference to the God of heaven, who causes His people to succeed, but never allows the evil to prevail.—VENERABLE BEDE: *Doctores sancti, immo omnes, qui zelo Dei fervent, in afflictione sunt maxima, quamdiu Hierusalem, hoc est, visionem pacis, quam nobis Dominus reliquit et commendavit, per bella dissensionum cernunt esse desertam, et portas virtutum, quas juxta Esaiam laudatio occupare debuerat, prævalentibus inferorum portis dejectas atque opprobrio habitas contuentur.*—STARKE: It is a good sign when envious people combat a work; for one can conclude from that that it provokes the devil, and that makes us the more joyful. Gen. xxxvii. 4; 1 Sam. xvii. 28. The devil is never idle: therefore when he can undertake nothing actively against the people of God, he makes use of poisonous tongues; but whoever fears God has a secure fortress. Sir. xiv. 26, 31. One should be firm in his confidence in God, and allow nothing to be abstracted from it.

CHAP. III. 1–32.

1 THEN Eliashib, the high-priest, rose up with his brethren the priests, and they
builded the sheep-gate; they sanctified it, and set up the doors of it; even unto the
2 tower of Meah they sanctified it, unto the tower of Hananeel. And next unto
him [*lit.* at his hand] builded the men of Jericho. And next to them [*rather*, next
3 to him, *i. e.*, next to Eliashib] builded Zaccur the son of Imri. But [and] the
fish-gate did the sons of Hassenaah [sons of Senaah] build, who *also* laid the beams
thereof, and set up the doors thereof, the locks [sockets] thereof, and the bars thereof.
4 And next unto them repaired Meremoth the son of Urijah, the son of Koz [Hak-
koz], and next unto them repaired Meshullam, the son of Berechiah, the son
5 of Meshezabeel. And next unto them repaired Zadok, the son of Baana. And
next unto them the Tekoites repaired; but their nobles put not their necks to the
6 work of their Lord. Moreover [and] the old gate repaired Jehoiada the son of
Paseah and Meshullam the son of Besodeiah; they laid the beams thereof, and set
7 up the doors thereof, and the locks [sockets] thereof, and the bars thereof. And
next unto them repaired Melatiah the Gibeonite, and Jadon the Meronothite,
the men of Gibeon and of Mizpah [the Mizpah which belonged] unto the
8 throne of the governor on this side the river. Next unto him repaired Uzziel the
son of Harhaiah, of the goldsmiths. Next unto him also repaired Hananiah the
son of *one of* the apothecaries [the son of Shelemiah of the apothecaries (?)], and
9 they fortified Jerusalem unto the broad wall. And next unto them repaired Re-
phaiah the son of Hur, the ruler of the half part [half the circuit] of Jerusalem.
10 And next unto them repaired Jedaiah the son of Harumaph, even over against his
11 house. And next unto him repaired Hattush the son of Hashabniah. Malchijah
the son of Harim, and Hashub the son of Pahath-moab, repaired the other piece
12 [a second piece], and the tower of the furnaces. And next unto him repaired Shal-
lum the son of Halohesh, the ruler of the half part [half the circuit] of Jerusalem.
13 The valley-gate repaired Hanun and the inhabitants of Zanoah; they built it, and
set up the doors thereof, the locks [sockets] thereof, and the bars thereof, and a
14 thousand cubits on the wall unto the dung-gate [rubbish gate]. But [and] the
dung-gate [rubbish gate] repaired Malchiah the son of Rechab, the ruler of part
[the circuit] of Beth-haccerem; he built it, and set up the doors thereof, the locks
15 thereof and the bars thereof. But [and] the gate of the fountain repaired Shallum
the son of Col-hozeh, the ruler of part [the circuit] of Mizpah; he built it, and co-
vered it, and set up the doors thereof, the locks [sockets] thereof, and the bars
thereof, and the wall of the pool of Siloah [Shelah] by [that appertained to] the
16 king's garden, and unto the stairs that go down from the city of David. After
him repaired Nehemiah the son of Azbuk the ruler of the half part [half the cir-
cuit] of Beth-zur, unto the place over against the sepulchres of David, and to the
17 part that was made, and unto the house of the mighty. After him repaired the
Levites, [under] Rehum the son of Bani. Next unto him repaired Hashabiah the
18 ruler of the half part [half the circuit] of Keilah in his part. After him repaired
their brethren, [under] Bavai the son of Henadad, the ruler of the half part [half
19 the circuit] of Keilah. And next to him repaired Ezer the son of Jeshua, the ruler
of Mizpah, another piece [a second piece] over against the going up to the armory

20 at the turning *of the wall* [armory of the corner]. After him Baruch the son of
Zabbai earnestly repaired the other piece [a second piece], from the turning *of the*
21 *wall* [from the corner] unto the door of the house of Eliashib the high-priest. After
him repaired Meremoth the son of Urijah the son of Koz [Hakkoz] another piece
[a second piece] from the door of the house of Eliashib even to the end of the house
22, 23 of Eliashib. And after him repaired the priests, the men of the plain. After
him repaired Benjamin and Hashub over against their house. After him repaired
24 Azariah the son of Maaseiah the son of Ananiah by his house. After him repaired
Binnui the son of Henadad another piece [a second piece] from the house of Aza-
riah unto the turning *of the wall* [unto the corner], even unto the corner [and unto
25 the turret]. Palal the son of Uzai [repaired] over against the turning *of the wall*
over against the corner], and the tower which lieth out from the king's high house,
that was by the court of the prison. After him Pedaiah the son of Parosh [re-
26 paired.] Moreover [and] the Nethinim dwelt in Ophel unto *the place* over against
27 the water-gate towards the east, and the tower that lieth out. After them [him]
the Tekoites repaired another piece [a second piece], over against the great tower
28 that lieth out, even unto the wall of Ophel. From above the horse-gate repaired
the priests, over against his house. After them (him, *i. e.*, the last one of these
29 priests] repaired Zadok the son of Immer over against his house. After him re-
30 paired also Shemaiah the son of Shechaniah, the keeper of the east gate. After him
repaired Hananiah the son of Shelemiah, and Hanun the sixth son of Zalaph, ano-
ther piece [a second piece]. After him repaired Meshullam the son of Berechiah
31 over against his chamber. After him repaired Malchiah the goldsmith's son unto
the place [house] of the Nethinim and of the merchants over against the gate
32 Miphkad [gate of the visitation] and to the going up of the corner [turret]. And
between the going up of the corner [turret] unto the sheep-gate repaired the gold-
smiths and the merchants.

TEXTUAL AND GRAMMATICAL.

9. פֶּלֶךְ. In this sense of "circuit" the word is Chaldee. See Targum on Josh. xvii. 11. In Heb. it means "staff," or "distaff." See 2 Sam. iii. 29; Prov. xxxi. 19.

13. הַשְׁפּוֹת. The omission of the א is to be noted as comp. with ver. 14. Gesenius considers the א as prosthetic, and makes the root שָׁפַת, but it is as likely to be אָשַׁף.

30. שֵׁנִי, a *lapsus* for שֵׁנִית.

נִשְׁכָּה, here and in ch. xii. 44 and ch. xiii. 1, seems to be a varied form of לִשְׁכָּה.

EXEGETICAL AND CRITICAL.

The Wall-Building.

Ver. 1. **Eliashib the high-priest.**—This man was afterwards closely allied to Jerusalem's enemies, one of his grandsons having married Sanballat's daughter (ch. xiii. 28). His alliance with Tobiah became so close that he prepared a room for Tobiah in the temple (ch. xiii. 4, 7). Eliashib may have excused this desecration on the ground that Tobiah was a Jew by birth. (See on ch. ii. 10.) Eliashib was grandson of Jeshua, who, with Zerubbabel, led the original return. Notwithstanding the unworthiness of this high-priest and his probable want of sympathy with Nehemiah's piety and patriotism, he could not refuse to take the lead in the wall-building. Public opinion was too strong under the appeals of Nehemiah.

The sheep-gate, *Sha'ar hatz-tzon,* must have been by the temple, or else the priests would not have been selected to build it. It is probably the προβατικῇ of John v. 2, translated in E. V. "sheep-market." It seems to have been at the north-eastern corner of the temple-area, in the neighborhood of the present St. Stephen's gate. It might derive its name from the fact that through this gate the sheep and goats (for the word refers to all small cattle) destined for the sacrifices were driven. (See Excursus.)

They sanctified it and set up the doors of it.—This gate is the only one which is said to be sanctified (*kidshuhu*), and we cannot tell whether it was done at once, so soon as it was built by the priests, or afterwards when the doors were set up (ch. vi. 1). The other gates were purified (another verb, *taher*) after the completion of the wall (ch. xii. 30). This seems to indicate a special connection with the temple. It probably opened into the temple-area. The setting up of the doors was not done until afterwards, but is here anticipated.* (See ch. vi. 1.)

The tower of Meah, *migdol ham-meah,* . . . **the tower of Hananeel,** *migdol hananeel.*—These two towers were between the sheep-gate and the fish-gate. They may have occupied the

* This gate and the water-gate and horse-gate and gate Miphkad (vers. 26, 28, 31) all appear to have been within the temple-precinct or its neighborhood, and all appear to have been destitute of locks and bars; for these are spoken of with regard to all the other gates (vers. 3, 6, 13, 14), but not with regard to these. These gates may have been kept constantly open, but guarded by an armed force.

north-eastern corner of the temple-enclosure, and the corner west of that, where the city-wall from the north joined the wall of the temple-enclosure. Hence they would (like the sheep-gate) be both connected with the temple, and hence they were sanctified. (See Excursus.) (**They sanctified it** in the second occurrence seems to refer to the wall including the two towers.)—The tower of Meah may have been the place where the nobles and rulers collected their *hundredth* (ch. v. 11), Meah being the Heb. for the "hundredth:" but?

Ver. 2. **And next unto him builded the men of Jericho. And next to them builded Zaccur the son of Imri.**—This should read literally: *And at his hand builded the men of Jericho, and at his hand builded Zaccur the son of Imri.*—Zaccur may have been leader of the men of Jericho. The English version misleads.

Ver. 3. **The fish-gate,** *Sha'ar had-dagim,* was east of the present Damascus-gate in the north wall. It is mentioned 2 Chron. xxxiii. 14 and Zeph. i. 10. (See Excursus.)

The sons of Hassenaah.—Rather: *the sons of Senaah.* (See Ezra ii. 35.) Senaah was a city, or more likely a large territory (if we are to judge from the large numbers in Ezra, *l. c.*), near Jericho. In the Onomasticon we find a Senna, seven miles north of Jericho.—**The locks thereof** were probably the sockets into which the bars fitted.

Ver. 4. **Meremoth, the son of Urijah,** is the same who is called in Ezra viii. 33 "Meremoth, the son of Uriah the priest." (See ch. x. 5.) He was of the family of **Hakkoz,** written wrongly in E. V. in this place Koz. See 1 Chron. xxiv. 10.

Meshullam, the son of Berechiah, the son of Meshezabeel.—This Meshullam was allied to Tobiah, for Tobiah's son Johanan had married Meshullam's daughter (ch. vi. 18). Nehemiah made the Jews, allied to the enemies of Judah, to commit themselves to the welfare of the city, as against their chosen intimates of the heathen. The "Meshezabeel" may be the same mentioned in ch. x. 21 and xi. 24.—**Zadok, the son of Baana,** seems to be the same as the Zadok of ch. x. 21. Both Meshullam and Zadok were probably of the tribe of Judah.

Ver. 5. **The Tekoites.**—Tekoa (still bearing its old name) is nine miles due south of Jerusalem, and about two miles south-west of the conspicuous Frank Mountain.—**Their nobles put not their necks to the work of their Lord.**—Nehemiah's task was an immense one, to unite a people, in many of whom there was no sympathy with the cause, for a rapid and successful movement. The fashionable part of Jerusalem was in virtual league with the enemies of God. Some of these were constrained (as Eliashib) by circumstances to take part in the work of rebuilding the Holy City, but others (as these Tekoite nobles) resolutely kept aloof.

Ver. 6. **The old gate** must have been in the north wall, east of the present Damascus-gate. Keil reads: "gate of the old wall" with Arnold and Hupfeld, as referring to the old wall in distinction from the "broad wall," which was newer. If we are to read Jeshanah as a genitive, it is possible that the gate was "the gate of Jeshanah" as leading to that town (2 Chron. xiii. 19). (See Excursus.)

Ver. 7. **Meronothite.**—Here and in 1 Chron. xxvii. 30 only. Meronoth may have been a dependent village of Mizpah.—**Unto the throne of the governor on this side the river.**—They did not repair unto (*i. e.* as far as) the throne, *etc.* Then the preposition would have been *'ad,* but it is *l* (*i. e. el*). It connects the description with Mizpah, and describes this Mizpah as belonging to the throne (or sway) of the governor beyond the river (*i. e.* beyond the river from Susa and the empire's centre), or as our version has it "the governor on this side the river." Perhaps this was to distinguish it from the Gilead Mizpah, which was under another governor (Judg. x. 17, *etc.*). In this case the "river" would be the Jordan. Some place Mizpah at Neby Samwil, some at Scopus.

Ver. 8. **The son of one of the apothecaries.**—Probably the name Shelemiah (ver. 30) has dropped out here. The goldsmiths and apothecaries (makers of spices, ointments and perfumes) worked under these leaders. These apothecaries are supposed by some to have been priests (1 Chron. ix. 30).

Fortified Jerusalem.—Here and at ch. iv. 2, the Heb. word *'azab* is translated in E. V. "fortify." Fürst derives it from an original meaning of "knot" or "bind;" hence "fasten" or "repair." Ewald gives it the meaning of "shelter." But in Ex. xxiii. 5 it seems to mean "help," though Fürst there gives it the meaning of "loosen." A common meaning of the word is "to forsake" as in Deut. xxxi. 16. This last meaning Fürst and Gesenius retain in ch. iv. 2 by translating: "will they (the governors) *forsake the matter* to them?" or "will they *allow* them?" May not this general notion be intended here: "they loosened (*i. e.* freed from exposure and peril) Jerusalem?" Keil retains the common meaning of *azab,* and reads: "they (the builders, or else the Chaldeans) left Jerusalem untouched as far as the broad wall."

The broad wall, *hahomah harehavah* (ch. xii. 38) seems to have been a special fortification at the north-west corner of the city. Keil would identify it with the four hundred cubits destroyed by Joash, and afterward rebuilt by Uzziah. (See Excursus.)

Ver. 9. **Ruler of the half part of Jerusalem.**—Compare vers. 12, 14, 15, 16, 17, 18. *Pelek* means a circuit, and is a governmental term. Rephaiah was ruler of half the circuit of Jerusalem, and Shallum (ver. 12) was ruler of the other half. The circuits of Beth-zur and Keilah had each two rulers also (see vers. 16, 17, 18). These circuits were probably districts deriving their names from their chief towns.

Ver. 11. **The other piece,** *middah shenith,* "a second piece," as in vers. 19, 21, 27, 30. The first piece ("first," perhaps, because first assigned to them) which they repaired is mentioned in ver. 23, where Malchijah is called Benjamin. The Harim and the Pahath-moab, who are mentioned as the fathers of Malchijah and Hashub, who repaired this second piece, were probably remote ancestors, Harim being the third of the twenty-four who in David's time gave name to the priestly divisions or courses (1 Chron. xxiv. 8), and Pahath-moab being one of the chiefs of families who came back with Zerubbabel a century before (see ch. vii. 11). The name Pahath-moab (governor of Moab) is one of the evidences of a close connection with Moab on the part of some of the families of Israel. Elimelech's residence in Moab and David's use of Moab as a place of safety for his family are other evidences. (See also 1 Chron. iv. 22 for another allusion.)

The Tower of the Furnaces, *Migdal hattannurim* would naturally fall into the neighborhood of the Jaffa Gate, and may be represented by the north-eastern tower of the citadel, which Dr. Robinson identifies with Herod's tower of Hippicus. (See Excursus.)

Ver. 12. **Shallum, the son of Halohesh.** Halo'hesh, or Hallo'hesh, is another ancestral name, and not that of an immediate father. (See ch. x. 24.) **He and his daughters** not ruling, but building. The zeal of these women is emphasized.

Ver. 13. **The valley-gate.** See on ch. ii. 13. **Hanun and the inhabitants of Zanoah.**—Hanun is called in ver. 30, "the sixth son of Zalaph." Zanoah was about twelve miles west of Jerusalem.

The dung-gate. See on ch. ii. 13.

Ver. 14. **The ruler of part of Beth-haccerem,** or *the ruler of the circuit of Beth-haccerem.* Beth-haccerem was near Tekoa, and was a height where a beacon could be displayed (Jer. vi. 1). It is identified by modern travellers with Jebel Fureidis, or the Frank Mountain.

Ver. 15. **Gate of the Fountain.**—See ch. ii. 14. **Shallum the son of Col-hozeh,** a Judahite (ch. xi. 5). **The ruler of part of Mizpah,** or *the ruler of the circuit of Mizpah.* The circuit of Mizpah, and Mizpah itself, had different rulers. (See ver. 19.) **Covered it.** Probably equivalent to "laid the beams thereof" of vers. 3, 6. **The pool of Siloah, by the king's garden,** *Berĕchath hash Shelah, legan ham-melek.* It is *Shiloah* in Isaiah, and *Shelah* here. The pool is the present Birket Silwan, and probably includes the Birket el-Hamra. It was outside the city, near the Tyropœon valley, where it enters the valley of the Son of Hinnom. Just at this junction was the king's garden (see 2 Kings xxv. 4, and Joseph., *A. J.* 7, 11), watered by this pool. It receives its water through a subterranean canal under the lower end of Ophel (the ridge running south from the temple-area) from the Fountain of the Virgin, on the west side of the Kidron valley. The old wall probably embraced all Zion, running along its southern brow, and stretched over to Ophel, in the neighborhood of the pool of Siloam, the fountain-gate being near by.

The stairs that go down from the city of David would then be an access to the Tyropœon from Zion, ending in this neighborhood of the pool. (See Excursus.)

Ver. 16. **The ruler of the half part of Beth-zur,** or *the ruler of half the circuit of Beth-zur.* Beth-zur is about four miles north of Hebron. **Unto the place over against the sepulchres of David, and to the pool that was made, and unto the house of the mighty.**—The sepulchres of David were probably the same as the sepulchres of the kings (2 Chron. xxviii. 27, *et al.*), and we may place them somewhere on Zion (1 Kings ii. 10). The part of the wall here designated would be that on Ophel, opposite that portion of Zion where the sepulchres were, the valley of the Tyropœon being between. The "pool that was made" may be the present fountain of the Virgin, which perhaps Hezekiah formed with its remarkable galleries (see Capt. Warren's account in "the Recovery of Jerusalem") for the supply of Ophel (see 2 Kings xx. 20). The "house of the mighty" (*beth-hag-geborim*) we have no clue to.

Ver. 17. **The ruler of the half part of Keilah in his part,** or *the ruler of the half circuit of Keilah for his circuit.* Those of the other half-circuit of Keilah are next mentioned.

Ver. 19. **The ruler of Mizpah another piece.**—The first piece is given in ver. 7. **Over against the going up to the armory at the turning of the wall.**—Rather, *from opposite the ascent of the armory of the corner.* The armory of the corner was perhaps at an angle in the eastern Ophel wall.

Ver. 20. **Baruch the son of Zabbai** is honorably mentioned for his distinguished zeal. He worked at a second piece from the corner mentioned above to the high-priest's house, which seems to have been on Ophel. Perhaps this Baruch's first piece of work has slipped from the text. Zabbai may be the same mentioned in Ezra x. 28. Baruch may be the priest of ch. x. 6.

Ver. 21. **Meremoth, the son of Urijah, the son of Koz.**—See on ver. 4. As a conspicuous priest, it was appropriate that he should be connected with the work on the wall in front of the high-priest's house.

Ver. 22. **The men of the plain.**—The word translated "plain" is *kikkar*, which is generally used for the Jordan valley, but in ch. xii. 28 it is used of the environs of Jerusalem. It literally signifies a *circuit.* As no qualifying word or phrase is found here, this *kikkar* is probably the Jordan valley.

Ver. 23. **Benjamin** (see on ver. 11) one of the descendants of Harim. (See Ezra x. 32.) **Hashub** was son (or descendant) of Pahath-moab. (See on ver. 11.) **Their house** may refer only to Benjamin, who was a priest (one of the Bene-Harim), Hashub, perhaps, being in some way allied to him.

Azariah may be the Levite mentioned in ch. viii. 7.

Vers. 24, 25. **Binnui** is the Levite mentioned in chs. x. 9 and xii. 8. **Unto the turning of the wall, even unto the corner.**—Or, *unto the corner of the wall and unto the turret.* By this seems to be intended the corner, where the "tower which lieth out" (ver. 25) formed a projection. Capt. Warren found about four hundred feet south-west of the south-east corner of the temple area the remains of an outlying tower to the wall, which he conjectures may be the "tower which lieth out." This tower is described in the next verse as **the tower which lieth out from the king's high house.**—Solomon's palace, doubtless, occupied the south-east corner of the present Haram. It probably had a high fortified position extending south to the Ophel wall (see Capt. Warren's map). This part was perhaps built by Jotham (2 Chron. xxvii. 3), or Hezekiah (2 Chron. xxxii. 5), or Manasseh (2 Chron. xxxiii. 14). The *height* of Manasseh's building is especially mentioned.

The court of the prison is spoken of in Jer. xxxii. 2 as appertaining to the king's house.

Ver. 26. **Moreover the Nethinim dwelt in Ophel.** Some with the Syriac, insert the relative and read, "the Nethinim who dwelt in Ophel," and then supply the verb "repaired." This is not needed. We may count this an interjected statement, showing what an important site had been given to the Nethinim. See, moreover, the אַחֲרָיו of ver. 27, referring to Pedaiah. **The water-gate** was, perhaps, a gate opening into the subterranean water galleries, lately discovered by Capt. Warren. If so, then the Nethinim dwelt in all Ophel from a point a little north of the Fountain of the Virgin to this "tower which lieth without," that is, along a distance of about eight hundred feet. This position of the water-gate answers to the narrative in ch. xii. 37. (See Excursus.)

The Nethinim (*i. e.*, dedicated ones) were servants of the temple, who performed the menial duties of the precinct. In Josephus they are *ἱερόδουλοι* (temple-servants). They were appointed by David (Ezra viii. 20), as another guild of service (Solomon's servants, or Andhé Shelomoh) was appointed by Solomon (Ezra ii. 58). The Levites, as compared with the priests, were called Nethunim (Num. viii. 19), a word of the same signification as Nethinim. (Comp. the K'tib of Ezra viii. 17.) Perhaps David's Nethinim were the Gibeonites (hewers of wood and drawers of water) restored to their service in a regular manner, after a dispersion of their number in Saul's time. (See 2 Sam. xxi. 2.)

Ver. 27. **The Tekoites** repaired their first piece near the old gate (ver. 5).

The great tower that lieth out is probably the same as "the tower that lieth out" of ver. 25.

The wall of Ophel would be the southern wall of the temple-area where it joined the district of Ophel.

Ver. 28. **The horse-gate** was where Athaliah was slain. It was between the temple and the palace. This would put it about 200 feet north of the present S. E. corner of the Haram. (See 2 Chron. xxiii. 15, and Jer. xxxi. 40). The part from the "wall of Ophel" to the horse-gate (Sha'ar Has-susim) was probably in good order, as it was the wall of the old royal palace, and had been occupied by the governors of the city. Hence it is not mentioned as rebuilt at this time, but the next builders to the Tekoites begin *from above* (*i. e.*, up the Kidron) *the horse-gate.* (See Excursus).

Ver. 29. **The keeper of the east gate.**—This *Sha'ar ham-mizrah* is the *sha'ar hak-kadmoni* of Ezek. xi. 1, one of the inner temple-gates, not a city gate. If this **Shemaiah, the son of Shechaniah,** is the same as the one mentioned in 1 Chron. iii. 22, then he was a descendant of the kings, and his title may have been one of honor only. He may, however, have been another and a Levite.

Ver. 30. **Hananiah.** See on ver. 8. **Hanun another piece.**—See on ver. 13. **Meshullam the son of Berechiah.** See on ver. 4.

Ver. 31. **The place of the Nethinim and of the Merchants over against the gate Miphkad and to the going up of the corner.** Lit. *The house of the Nethinim and the traders opposite the gate of the visitation even to the ascent of the projecting turret.* The "house" of the Nethinim and traders was not their dwelling-place, but, we suppose, the place where under the direction of the Nethinim the traders (see Matt. xxi. 12) brought their doves, *etc.*, for sale to worshippers. We may place it near the north-east angle of the Haram. For the gate Miphkad, see Excursus. The ascent of the turret would be the stairs at the north-east angle leading up to a corner-tower, not far from the sheep gate.

Ver. 32. **The goldsmiths** may have been also connected with these matters of the Nethinim and traders.

For a plan of the walls of the city, see Excursus.

From this outline it will be seen that only those gates whose bars and locks and doors are mentioned do we consider as belonging to the city wall, to wit:

1. Sheep-gate, ver. 1.
2. Fish-gate, ver. 3.
3. Old-gate, ver. 6.
4. Valley-gate, ver. 13.
5. Dung-gate, ver. 14.
6. Fountain-gate, ver. 15.

The other gates are not spoken of as now constructed, and we take them to be inner gates belonging to the inner temple and palace divisions, to wit:

1. Water-gate, ver. 26.
2. Horse-gate, ver. 28.
3. East-gate, ver. 29.
4. Gate Miphkad, ver. 31.

We also consider the wall along the southern brow of Zion to have continued across the Tyropœon to Ophel near the pool of Siloam.

HISTORICAL AND ETHICAL.

1. Eliashib's connection with Sanballat and Tobiah (chap. xiii. 7, 28) must have taken place at a later date, when Nehemiah had returned to Susa, and was not expected to revisit Jerusalem. If the high-priest had already made those scandalous alliances, Nehemiah certainly would have taken him to task, and the record of such reprimand would have been here given. With a heart disaffected, Eliashib nevertheless takes his place in the rebuilding of the wall. His prominence in the work was doubtless a great help to Nehemiah.

2. It is an interesting feature of this wall-building that those whose local interests were far off, as at Jericho, Tekoah, and Beth-zur, took

such deep interest and such conspicuous part in the work. The old love for Zion and for the temple was still warm in the breasts of the returned Jews. They felt that the true life of the nation flowed from Jerusalem as the central heart. Their union in this work was a powerful means of renewing their patriotic affection and strengthening the interests of the commonwealth. Co-working for defence always brings souls together; and when the co-working is in defence of the citadel of religion and country, the strongest bond of union is formed. The wall-buildings formed a strong basis, on which Nehemiah could introduce his reforms.

3. However, there must have been many who refused the service, and were apathetic, if not hostile to the work. Otherwise we should not see some of them engaged doing a *second* piece of the wall, and perhaps a longer list of leaders in the service would be recorded. It is not to be believed that, if the high-priest himself was inclined to ally himself to Sanballat, there were not many others who had no hearty interest in the restoration of Jerusalem's glory. The nobles of Tekoah (ver. 5) were but samples of a large number.

4. And yet, again, the thirty-four leaders whose names are given us cannot be considered as the only chief men engaged in the wall-building. Other prominent men whose names occur later in the book may have held office under them, and hence are here unmentioned.

HOMILETICAL AND PRACTICAL.

Ver. 1. The importance of Zion's walls. 1) For uniting the congregation, the congregation must be able to shut itself off and secure itself to protect its peculiar goods. 2) For exclusion of the world,—the world must be kept at a distance, so long as it only strives to rob the goods of the congregation.

Vers. 1, 2. The precedence of the high-priest in making the city of God secure. 1) He himself is the first to build. 2) By this he consecrates the work of the others. 3) He is a pledge for the success of the work.—The duty of building the walls of Zion. 1) For those in authority (as Nehemiah), who have to incite and uphold the priests and people in their work. 2) For the priests who are not exalted above the common obligation.—3) For the people whose members must not forget in their household and inferior cares, those which are higher and more universal.—BEDE: *Qui portas et turres ædificant, per quas vel cives ingrediantur vel arceantur inimici, ipsi sunt prophetæ, apostoli, evangelistæ, per quos nobis forma et ordo fidei ac rectæ operationis, per quam unitatem ecclesiæ sanctæ intrare debeamus, ministrata est, quorumque verbis, qualiter adversarios veritatis redarguamus ac repellamus, discimus. Qui vero reliquis verbis extruunt, ipsi sunt pastores et doctores.*—STARKE: The clergy should set to work first in building the city of God, and precede others by a good example. The memory of those who have rendered services to the church and to the commonwealth remains, justly, blessed. Prov. 10:7. The most powerful and richest people do, generally, the least in the temporal and spiritual edifice of the city of God. Happy he who willingly puts on the light and easy yoke of Christ at the building of the spiritual Jerusalem.

Ver. 31. The honor of the mechanics and artists. 1) They may be, and shall be at the same time priests of God. 2) Their products can and shall serve for God's honor. 3) Their doing has in itself worth and reward.

Vers. 33–35. Why the world so easily pretends that our work will have no result. 1) Because in truth of ourselves we are not capable of great efforts: only the sacrifice and the power of Christ can make us willing and endow us with perseverance. 2) Because in truth the work is indeed altogether too lofty and glorious,—only the Spirit of Christ can consecrate us to it. 3) Because the world only sees that which is before its eyes; there is, however, something higher.—STARKE: Fleshly-minded spirits consider the undertaking and the work of God's children as contemptible and small, and measure it according to their standard. Wisd. v. 3; 2 Kings xix. 10. There are different degrees among the godless, in regard to their wickedness. The worst are those who not only do wickedly themselves, but also cannot bear to see others doing good, and express their rage in poisonous jeers. John x. 32; Ps. cix. 4.

Vers. 36–38. Prayer is the most powerful weapon against the enemy. 1) It secures to us the best allies. 2) It makes us sure of the weakness of the enemy. If they are God's enemies at the same time, they have God's holiness opposed to them, before which nothing which is evil can endure. 3) It pledges the final victory to us. They can only escape by change of heart.—STARKE: When we are in the greatest straits, there God is our safety, our rock, our strength and refuge, and we must fly to Him in prayer. 2 Chr. xx. 12; Prov. xviii. 10; Nah. i. 3.

Ver. 38. The blessing of the oppression which the scorn of the world exercises upon us. 1) We work the more steadily under it, we do not indeed know how long the evening will permit us to work. 2) The joy in the work increases as surely as it is elevating to bear the disgrace of Christ. 3) The work advances so much the better. STARKE: In the work of the Lord we must confidently proceed, heedless of all opposition. 2 Tim. iv. 3–5. At pleasure's call all work seems small, therefore be not slothful in what you should do. Rom. xii. 11; Prov. vi. 6. If God has given us successful progress in our work, this should be an admonition to us that we should the more boldly persist in pursuing our calling.

CHAPTER IV. 1–23.

1 BUT [and] it came to pass that when Sanballat heard that we builded the wall,
2 he was wroth, and took great indignation, and mocked the Jews. And he spake
before his brethren and the army of Samaria, and said, What do these feeble Jews?
Will they fortify themselves? Will they sacrifice? Will they make an end in a
day [by day, *i. e.*, openly]? Will they revive the stones out of the heaps of the
3 rubbish which are burned? Now [and] Tobiah the Ammonite *was* by him, and
he said, Even that which they build, if a fox go up, he shall even break down their
4 stone wall. Hear, O our God; for we are despised [a contempt]: and turn their
reproach upon their own head, and give them for a prey in the land of captivity.
5 And cover not their iniquity, and let not their sin be blotted out from before thee;
for they have provoked *thee* to anger before [they have acted vexatiously against]
6 the builders. So built we [and we built] the wall; and all the wall was joined
together unto the half thereof: for [and] the people had a mind [heart] to work.
7 But [and] it came to pass, *that* when Sanballat, and Tobiah, and the Arabians, and
the Ammonites, and the Ashdodites, heard that the walls of Jerusalem were made
up [that a bandage was applied to the walls of Jerusalem], *and* that the breaches
8 began to be stopped, then they were very wroth, and conspired all of them together
to come *and* to fight against Jerusalem, and to hinder it [to do wickedness to it].
9 Nevertheless [and] we made our prayer unto our God, and set a watch against them
10 day and night, because of them. And Judah said, The strength of the bearers of
burdens is decayed, and *there is* much rubbish; so that [and] we are not able to
11 build the wall. And our adversaries said, They shall not know, neither see, till we
12 come in the midst among them, and slay them, and cause the work to cease. And
it came to pass, when the Jews which dwelt by them came, they said unto us ten
times, From all places whence ye shall return unto us *they will be upon you* [they
said unto us ten times, *i. e.*, frequently, from all places, Ye shall return unto us].
13 Therefore [and] I set in the lower places [lowest parts] behind the wall [at the
place behind the wall], *and* in the higher places [in the exposed parts], I even set
14 the people after their families with their swords, their spears, and their bows. And
I looked, and rose up, and said unto the nobles, and to the rulers, and to the rest
of the people, Be not ye afraid of them: remember the Lord, *which is* great and
terrible, and fight for your brethren, your sons, and your daughters, your wives,
15 and your houses. And it came to pass when our enemies heard that it was known
unto us, and God had brought their counsel to nought, that we returned all of us to
16 the wall, every one unto his work. And it came to pass from that time forth [from
that day], *that* the half of my servants wrought in the work, and the *other* half of
them held both the spears, the shields, and the bows, and the habergeons; and the
17 rulers *were* behind all the house of Judah. They which builded on the wall and
they that bare burdens, with those that laded, [while carrying] *every one* with one
18 of his hands wrought in the work, and with the other *hand* held a weapon. For
[and] the builders, every one had his sword girded by his side, and *so* builded.
19 And he that sounded the trumpet was by me. And I said unto the nobles, and to
the rulers, and to the rest of the people, The work *is* great and large, and we are
20 separated upon the wall, one far from another. In what place *therefore* ye hear
21 the sound of the trumpet, resort ye thither unto us: our God shall fight for us. So
[and] we labored in the work: and half of them held the spears from the rising of
22 the morning till the stars appeared. Likewise at the same time said I unto the
people, Let every one with his servant lodge within Jerusalem, that [and] in the

23 night they may be a guard to us, and labor on the day [by day]. So [and] neither
I, nor my brethren, nor my servants nor the men of the guard which followed me,
none of us put off our clothes, *saving that* every one put them off for washing.

TEXTUAL AND GRAMMATICAL.

16. The ו seems to be misplaced. It should be with הַמָּגִנִּים, and not with הָרְמָחִים. Or the words may have changed places.

17. In עֹמְשִׂים the שׂ takes the place of ס.

22. Note the absence of ל with מִשְׁמָר and מְלָאכָה.

EXEGETICAL AND CRITICAL.

The Hindrances (1) *From Sanballat and his allies.*

(N. B.—Vers. 1–6 are in the Heb. vers. 33–38 of ch. 3).

Ver. 1. **Mocked the Jews.**—Sanballat was evidently afraid to use violence directly on account of the favor shown by the Persian monarch to the Jews. His great rage could exhibit itself only in mockery.

Ver. 2. **Before his brethren**, *i. e.*, Tobiah and his brethren in council. **The army of Samaria.**—It is likely that Sanballat had actually brought an armed force in sight of the city to intimidate the Jews. In a speech to his officers he uses the language of mockery here given, **Will they fortify themselves?**—Perhaps. *will they help themselves?* Keil, comparing Ps. x. 14, reads it "will they leave it to themselves?" which is harsh. (See on ch. iii. 8 for the use of this word *azab*). **Will they make an end in a day?** Rather, *will they make an end* (*i. e.*, accomplish it) *by day* (*i. e.*, openly). So *bayyom* in Gen. xxxi. 40; Prov. xii. 16; Judg. xiii. 10.

Ver. 3. **Now Tobiah the Ammonite was by him.**—The style of phrase in this verse suggests what we have already supposed, that when Sanballat addressed his armed men he was in sight of Jerusalem, looking with Tobiah and others at the Jews' work.

Ver. 4. **Hear, O our God.**—Eight times in this book Nehemiah interjects a prayer. They are prayers while writing, not while acting. The grounds of this prayer are, (1) God's people are despised; (2) excited to fear by the enemy. As in the imprecatory psalms, there is a prophetic power in this prayer. The prayer anticipates God's justice.

Ver. 5. **They have provoked thee to anger before the builders.** Rather, *they have vexed* (with alarm) *the builders.* So *kaas* in Ezek. xxxii. 9. The *leneged* is that of hostility as in Dan. x. 13.

Ver. 6. **Unto the half thereof** in height. **The people had a mind to work.**—The disaffected (including probably the high-priest or at least many of his family) were a few, and they had to yield to the zeal of the great mass. Patriotism, piety and security made the wall-building a popular work. (The fourth chapter in the Heb divisions begins here).

Ver. 7. **The Arabians.**—Those in Samaria. See on ch. ii. 19. **The Ammonites.**—Tobiah's influence had probably induced many Ammonites to take active part with Sanballat in opposing the Jews. If Sanballat was a Moabite (as we suppose), that fact would account for an Ammonitish alliance, as the two nations of Moab and Ammon were always closely united, especially against Israel. **The Ashdodites**, with the Philistine traditional hatred, remained hostile to the Jews until Jonathan, brother of Judas Maccabeus, three hundred years after this, destroyed Ashdod at the defeat of Apollonius.

That the walls of Jerusalem were made up.—Lit., *that a bandage was applied to the walls of Jerusalem.* So in 2 Chron. xxiv. 13.

Ver. 8. **To hinder it.**—Lit., *to do wickedness to it.* (So the word *to'ah* in Isa. xxxii. 6). These various nationalities might suppose that by acting in concert, they could show to the Persian king they were only acting in his behalf for the safety of the empire against an insurrectionary movement of the Jews. An attack of Sanballat *alone* might readily be understood at court as a matter of personal jealousy and aggrandizement. Hence the confederacy.

Vers. 10–12. **And Judah said .... and our adversaries said ... the Jews which dwelt by them said.** Here were three sources of discouragement: (1) The severity of the work. (2) The threat of destruction by the confederacy. (3) The recall of the country Jews from the work by their timid fellows.

They said unto us ten times, From all places whence ye shall return unto us they will be upon you.—Rather, *They said unto us ten times* (*i. e.*, frequently), *From all places ye shall return unto us.* The Jews from the outside towns that were near the enemy came to Jerusalem and endeavored to make their townsmen desist, through fear of injury from Sanballat. [The Heb. *Asher* as in Esther iii. 4.]

Ver. 13. **Therefore set I in the lower places behind the wall and on the higher places I even set**, *etc.*—Rather, *Therefore set I in the lowest parts at the place behind the wall, in the exposed parts, I even set, etc.* Nehemiah placed detachments, properly armed, at such points of the wall as had attained the least height and were thus most exposed to attack. These detachments were formed of the families who had been working at the portions of the wall where these gaps were. There was a temporary cessation from the work. "The lowest parts" and "the exposed parts" are in apposition. "The higher places" (E. V.) is a mistaken rendering. The word *tsehihi* means "a dry or bare place (comp. Ezek. xxvi. 4–14), and hence by a metaphorical use, an exposed part of the wall.

Ver. 14. **And I looked.**—Implying perhaps an observation of some fear on the part of the different classes of the community. Or it may refer to a simple review of the defenders in their positions.

Ver. 15. **We returned all of us to the wall every one unto his work.**—This shows that there had been a cessation of the work at the first alarm.

Ver. 16. **My servants** cannot be equal to "my subjects" as some hold, for *naar* could not be so used by Nehemiah, nor would he consider the people of Judah in the light of subjects. Nehemiah had probably a special band of men attached to his person, either by order of the king of Persia, or by the will of the people at Jerusalem. To these we suspect reference is here made. There is a distinction made between these and the others. These divided themselves into two parts, the one working while the other kept guard; but the others held a weapon while they wrought (ver. 17). *Habergeon.* Old English for "coat of mail." From *hals* (neck) and *bergen* (to protect).

Ver. 17. Read *The builders of the wall and the burden-bearers while carrying.* The builders and the burden-bearers each bore a javelin (*shelah*) in one hand, the builders (as distinct from the burden-bearers) also wearing a sword, as we see in ver. 18.

Ver. 18. **For.**—Read "And." The signal trumpet was directly under Nehemiah's order, as commander of the defence.

Ver. 22. **Lodge within Jerusalem.**—That is, during the alarm, those that had their homes in the villages and distant towns should now continue night and day in the city.

Ver. 23. Only Nehemiah and his immediate family and attendants are here referred to as not putting off their clothes. It became them to be patterns of watchfulness and and diligence to the rest.—**Saving that every one put them off from washing.**—A puzzling sentence. It is literally "man his weapon the water." The rendering of the E. V. is in accordance with the old Jewish authorities who regard *shilho* as a verb of equivalent meaning with *pashat* (to put off). Probably some words are lost.

HISTORICAL AND ETHICAL.

1. The wrath and great indignation of Sanballat prove the insincerity of his taunts. If the Jews were so feeble a folk in his estimation, he would not have sought an alliance (ver. 8) to fight against them. He had good reason to fear the sudden restoration of the Jewish power, and was merely exercising that which is praised as political wisdom when he used every energy to thwart Nehemiah's purpose. It is probable that in Galilee there existed a growing remnant of Israel (the men of Babylon, Cuthah, Ava, Hamath and Sepharvaim (2 Kings xvii. 24) having been settled by the King of Assyria in *Central* Palestine), who, of course, sympathized with the movement at Jerusalem. Sanballat, situated between these two fragments of Israel, was the more alert to see danger in Israel's growth. Hence his forwardness to move in the matter, for he was evidently the chief mover, although Arabians, Ammonites and Ashdodites were ready enough to take part.

2. The prayer of Nehemiah that the enemy's reproaches might be turned upon their own head, and that their sin might never be forgiven (comp. Ps. lxix. 27, 28, and Jer. xviii. 23), can only be understood by the soul that is so allied to God as to see His judgments proceeding forth from His holiness. The final judgment by the saints as assessors with God (Ps. cxlix. 6–9 and Rev. iii. 21) has the same character. Where the natural mind can only imagine revenge, the spiritual mind sees faith and holiness.

3. Prayer did not slacken the energy of the Jews. They experienced the redoubled zeal and activity which all true prayer produces. They made their prayer to God, and set a watch against their foes day and night. All the natural means whether of mind or matter form channels through which God conveys His grace in answer to prayer. To stop these channels is to cancel prayer. Prayer was never intended to foster idleness or diminish responsibility.

4. The remembrance of the Lord is the sure safe-guard against our afflictions. David says: "I have set the Lord always before me; because He is at my right hand, I shall not be moved" (Ps. xv. 8).

Remembering the Lord is an act of faith, a new grasp upon His divine help, and, at the same time, a purification of the heart. Forgetfulness of God is the unguardedness of the soul.

HOMILETICAL AND PRACTICAL.

Vers. 1–17. Our abiding tasks. 1) From work to conflict. (Vers. 1–8.) a) On account of defying enemies from without and within. b) In spite of faint-hearted friends. c) With faith in the Lord. 2) From conflict to work. Vers. 9–17.) a) Work remains the principal task. b) It can and must be advanced even during the preparation for conflict; the preparation for conflict does not hinder, but makes us active, zealous, and strong. c) Laziness and ease must be renounced, with self denial. STARKE: We must guard ourselves well on all sides, that the devil may not make a breach, for he goes about us like a roaring lion, 1 Pet. v. 8. In the common struggle against Satan and his hosts we must support and help one another. True builders of the church of Christ must not only industriously build, *i. e.*, teach and preach, but also diligently act on the defensive, and resist all the powerful incursions of the devil, and all godless conduct, Tit. i. 9. In the church militant we must work in full armor, and have the sword of the Spirit at hand, that we may be a match for temptations, Eph. vi. 16, 17. God can easily put to naught the crafty attacks of the enemy, Job v. 12.

Vers. 1–8. The assaults of the people of God. 1) How they originate against it. a) Through enemies who threaten to undo His work. b) Through weak friends, who, in spite of, or, on account of watching and prayer, become depressed and dissuaded from the work. 2) How they are to be overcome. a) By readiness for the conflict. b) By confidence in the great, only-to-be-feared God, who fights for His people.—BEDE: *Plane hæc ira hæreticorum, hæc verba eorum sunt, qui se Samaritanos, hoc est, custodes legis*

Dei, frustra cognominant, cum sint maxime Deo contrarii ac legibus ejus, ut pote jamdudum a domo David, hoc est, ab unitate Christi et ecclesiæ per hæreses aut schismata aut mala opera segregati; qui ne sua forte impugnetur atque excludatur impietas, muros fidei ædificari metuunt. . . . Tales solent imbecilles appellare Judæos, hoc est, confessores fidei, et facile a gentibus superandos, dum in quotidiano animarum certamine plus amant vitia quam virtutis victoriæ palnam obtinere.—STARKE: To pray and keep good watch are the best means in the time of danger, Eph. vi. 18. This is the way of many people; they make, indeed, a good start in the Lord's work, but when it becomes hard they draw back, and wish to take no trouble, Matt. xiii. 20, 21. Honest souls should not allow themselves to be frightened back by them. Nothing makes one more courageous in war than to be entirely assured that God is with us, and fights for us, Rom. viii. 31; Ps. xxvii. 1.—Our task at the time of attack. 1) Towards defying enemies—to pray and watch, *i. e.*, to be prepared for conflict (vers. 1–3). 2) Towards depressed friends, who yet increase the defiance of the enemy—to confirm their confidence in Him who alone is to be feared, and to sharpen their consciousness of the duty of the conflict (ver 8).—What attacks befall the servants of the Lord (as Nehemiah) in their work for the honor of God. 1) Through dangers on the part of defiant enemies, who cannot endure the difference between the kingdom of God and the world. 2) From the dejection, hesitation, and foolishness on the part of weak friends, who easily interrupt the work and put it back. 3) Through the breaches in the walls of Jerusalem, which render the defences of the city difficult. —Our duty to watch and pray. 1) Its cause—the malice of the enemy, their power, their aim, the whole attitude of their hearts towards the kingdom of God. 2) Its result: its fulfilment is difficult to many, certainly faithlessness, increased defiance of the enemy, and dissuasion from the work on the part of weak friends are excited; but in contrast to these are a) watchfulness—b) readiness for the conflict—and c) the increasing the confidence in the Lord.—BEDE: *Hoc est unicum adversus hostes universos ecclesiæ suffugium oratio videlicet ad Deum, et industria doctorum qui die noctuque in lege ejus meditantes corda fidelium contra insidias diaboli ac militum ejus prædicando, consolando, exhortando præmuniant.*

Vers. 9–17. What obligation does the enmity of the world against the building of the kingdom of God lay upon us? 1) To advance the building with all our might, in spite of dangers (vers. 9. 10). 2) To be armed while at work (vers. 11, 12). 3) To heed the signal of the leader, when he calls to conflict (vers. 13, 14). 4) Perseverance in the preparation for war (ver. 15); joyful, sacrificing zeal in the work (ver. 16). In all positions severity towards ourselves, particularly towards our love of ease, and laziness.—STARKE: The church always needs those distinguished people, who can comfort the weak in faith, and timorous, and can give them a certain hope in the help of God, 1 Thes. v. 14. In Nehemiah the rulers of the city, and heads of the church, have an example of godliness in his confidence in God—of foresight and diligent watchfulness in his management of this important work, and his arrangement of such good order and war discipline, also of courage and boldness in his proved heroic spirit in the midst of such great fear, danger, and difficulty as that with which he was surrounded on every side in this difficult work. Also in the spiritual conflict it is obligatory upon teachers and watchmen of the church that they should set the example in watchfulness and perception of the public good, and not allow themselves to be annoyed by any trouble. Rev. xvi. 15; Luke xii. 35.

Vers. 11, 12. The preparation for war of the Christian. 1) Why it is necessary the Christian has to build. His building is an attack upon the world, which is irritated by it to the conflict. 2) In what it consists. The Christian bears, even at work, the right weapons. 3) At what it aims. We must and will secure the continuance of the work, and cultivate the feeling of joy and assurance. God will exercise us at the same time in sobriety, self-denial, and activity. Vers. 18–21. The voice of our general in face of the enemy 1) What it takes for granted—that we are prepared for the conflict, even when at work. 2) Of what it reminds us—of the greatness of the work which imposes upon us the building of the kingdom of God in others, and particularly in ourselves; and on the many dangers connected with it. 3) What it demands—that we should heed the signal for conflict, and join ourselves with all the faithful in the strife. 4) What it promises—that God will fight for us, and finally cause our work to succeed.

CHAPTER V. 1–19.

1 AND there was a great cry of the people and of their wives against their brethren
2 the Jews. For there were that said, We, our sons and our daughters *are* many;
therefore we take up corn [*perhaps*, our sons and our daughters we mortgage, that
3 we might buy corn] *for them*, that we may eat and live. *Some* also there were that
said, We have mortgaged our lands, vineyards, and houses, that we might buy
4 corn, because of the dearth. There were also that said, we have borrowed money
5 for the king's tribute, *and that upon* our lands and vineyards. Yet [and] now our

flesh *is* as the flesh of our brethren, our children [sons] as their children [sons]:
and lo, we bring into bondage our sons and our daughters to be servants, and *some*
of our daughters are brought into bondage *already:* neither *is it* in our power [and
our hand is not to God] *to redeem them;* for [and] other men have our lands and
6, 7 vineyards. And I was very angry when I heard their cry and these words. Then
I consulted with myself, and I rebuked the nobles, and the rulers, and said unto
them, Ye exact usury, every one of his brother. And I set a great assembly against
8 them. And I said unto them, We, after our ability, have redeemed our brethren
the Jews, which were sold unto the heathen; and will ye even sell your brethren?
or shall they be sold unto us? Then held they their peace, and found nothing *to*
9 *answer* [and found no word]. Also [and] I said, It is not good that ye do: ought
ye not to walk in the fear of our God because of the reproach of the heathen our
10 enemies? [And] I likewise, *and* my brethren, and my servants might exact of
11 [have lent] them money and corn: I pray you, let us leave off this usury. Re-
store, I pray you, to them, even this day, their lands, their vineyards, their olive
yards, and their houses, also the hundredth *part* of the money, and of the corn, the
12 wine and the oil, that ye exact of [lent] them. Then [and] said they, We will re-
store *them*, and will require nothing of them; so will we do as thou sayest. Then
[And] I called the priests, and took an oath of them, that they should do according
13 to this promise. Also I shook my lap [bosom], and said, So God shake out every
man from his house, and from his labour, that performest not this promise [word],
even thus be he shaken out and emptied [empty]. And all the congregation said,
Amen, and praised the LORD. And the people did according to this promise
14 [word]. Moreover from the time that I was appointed [he (Artaxerxes) appointed
me] to be their governor in the land of Judah, from the twentieth year even unto
the two and thirtieth year of Artaxerxes the king, *that is*, twelve years, I and my
15 brethren have not eaten the bread of the governor. But [And] the former gover-
nors that *had been* before me were chargeable unto the people, and had taken of
them bread and wine, besides forty shekels of silver; yea, even their servants bare
16 rule over the people: but [and] so did not I, because of the fear of God. Yea,
also I continued in the work of this wall, neither bought we any land: and all my
17 servants were gathered thither unto the work. Moreover [And] *there were* at my
table a hundred and fifty of the Jews and rulers, besides [and] those that came
18 unto us from among the heathen that *are* about us. Now [and] *that* which was
prepared *for me* (*i. e.*, at my expense) daily [for one day] *was* one ox *and* six choice
sheep; also fowls were prepared for me (*i. e.*, at my expense), and once in ten days
store [large quantity] of all sorts of wine: yet [and] for *all* this required not I the
19 bread of the governor, because the bondage was heavy upon this people. Think
upon [remember to] me, my God, for good, *according* to [*om. according* to] all that
I have done for this people.

TEXTUAL AND GRAMMATICAL.

[1] Ver. 5. The E. V. rightly supplies an equivalent to לְפֹּרְתֹם.

[2] Ver. 6. וַיִּמָּלֵךְ. This Niphal evidently carries the Chaldee, Syriac, and Samaritan meaning of the verb. Comp. Dan. iv. 24 (27) where the derivative noun is used. The literal translation here is "and my heart was consulted upon me." Why the lexicographers give it a Kal meaning I know not.

[3] Ver. 15. אַחַר is rightly rendered "besides." *After* the forty shekels salary they received the bread and wine.

EXEGETICAL AND CRITICAL.

Hindrances (2) *from the Tyranny of Jews over one another.*

It might at first sight seem as if this episodical chapter was out of place, and should properly follow chap. viii.; but there is no sound reason why we should not consider the complaint to have been made while all were engaged in the important work of fortifying the city, as a time when it would be the easier to remedy the evil under the pressure of the common danger.

Ver. 2. **We, our sons and our daughters, are many,** *etc.* The error of the Heb. text here in writing *rabbim* for *orebim* (requiring only one letter prefixed in the Hebrew) is very evident (according to Houbigant), so that it should read in English, *we have mortgaged our sons and our daughters that we might buy corn.* Compare the structure of the next verse. The complaint was three-fold: 1. We mortgage our children for food. 2. We mortgage our estates for food. 3. We mortgage our estates for the royal tribute. In all these their brethren were the exactors, not only acting tyrannically towards them, but breaking the written law of God in its spirit (Ex. xxii. 25–27) as well as in its letter (see ver. 7).

Ver. 5. *Neither is it in our power.* Lit. "and our hand is not to God." So Gen. xxxi. 29.

Ver. 7. **Then I consulted with myself.**—The Niphal use of *malak* (*wayyimmalek*) is peculiar, and suggests a peculiar sense in this place. The Syriac use of the word as "consult" (see Dan. iv. 24, 27) is probably the right one here. **Ye exact usury.**—The words refer both to the pledges and the interest (ver. 11). **And I set a great assembly against them.**—In the midst of the necessity of the wall-building Nehemiah summons a great mass-meeting of the Jews (see the word *Kehillah* in Deut. xxxiii. 4) to have this fraternal outrage stopped instantly by the force of public opinion.

Ver. 8. The Jewish colony had probably often redeemed Jews from captivity.

Ver. 9. **Because of the reproach of the heathen.**—That is, so as to avoid giving them an opportunity to reproach us.

Ver. 10. **I likewise, and my brethren and my servants might exact of them.**—Rather: *I likewise, that is, my brethren and my servants exact of them,* or rather "lent them." It is a confession of Nehemiah that he too was implicated from the fact that he had found his own family engaged in the oppression. Hence he says: "let *us* leave off this usury." The law expressly forbade lending money to Jews on interest. See Ex. xxii. 25; Lev. xxv. 36; Deut. xxiii. 19. All the lands those rich men had acquired had been obtained in thisway.

Ver. 11. This **hundredth part** was probably a monthly interest, that is, an interest at the rate of twelve per cent. per annum. *That ye exact of them.* Rather: "that ye lent them."

Ver. 12. The moral force of the great assembly produced an immediate conformity to Nehemiah's demand. His action was a master-piece of management. The oath would have greater solemnity as administered by the priests.

Ver. 13. **My lap.**—This is the bosom of the outer garment (*sinus togæ*), which was used as a pocket. (See for this significant action Acts xviii. 6.)

Ver. 14. This verse and those which follow form an interruption of the narrative. They show that Nehemiah was for twelve years governor of Judah, and did not write this history till the expiration of that time. The parallel between Nehemiah and Washington in refusing salary while saving the nation is striking.

Ver. 15. **Forty shekels of silver.**—This (like the interest in ver. 11) is probably to be reckoned for the month. The former governors had received their table and 480 shekels a year as salary. The 480 shekels would be only $360 in amount of silver; but this would represent in value a large official salary in that day.

Ver. 16. A second point to which Nehemiah refers with satisfaction and as a proof of his disinterested conduct is his allowing no speculation in land on his own part or that of his immediate attendants.

Ver. 17. A third point is his free entertainment of a hundred and fifty Jews, and besides this visitors from surrounding nations.

Ver. 18. **The bondage.**—The service needed to the king of Persia and also that which was needed for the restoration of their national welfare.

Ver. 19. **Think upon me, my God,** *etc.*—Rather: *Remember to me for good all which I have done to this people.* It becomes necessary sometimes for a man of God to declare his integrity against the oppositions and insinuations of enemies. In such cases he can without presumption expect God to vindicate His faithfulness. See Paul's words before the Sanhedrim (Acts xxiii. 1), and compare also 2 Cor. i. 12; iv. 4; 2 Tim. i. 3; Heb. xiii. 18.

HISTORICAL AND ETHICAL.

1. The advantage taken in troublous times for men to prey upon their associates and kindred exhibits the deep depravity of human nature. The violence of open enemies and the presence of surrounding dangers should have encouraged the virtue and piety of the Jews by the odiousness of the opposite and their sense of weakness and need of the Divine help. But as often sailors on a wreck, or as men (*e. g.* the Florentines) in the midst of the plague, have given themselves up to debauchery and revelling, so the Jewish remnant, persecuted and straitened, oppressed one another. It was no little bravery in Nehemiah to face these tigers of his own nation, while guarding Jerusalem from the foreign foe. A weak spirit would have reasoned that it was enough to do the latter, and that domestic evils must be endured until a more propitious time for their cure. That "great assembly" was a grand token of Nehemiah's marvellous energy and fertile resources.

2. Nehemiah's refusal of official salary was like Paul's refusal of support at Corinth and Thessalonica (2 Cor. ii. 9; 1 Thess. ii. 9; 2 Thess. iii. 8), a waiving of an undoubted right for the sake of the higher good. *Summum jus summa injuria* is a sentiment which every tender conscience must often put into exercise. It sees that the only right is to give up right. A sublime spirit discerns when *lex,* no longer *rex,* becomes *nex.*

3. Nehemiah's soul was frank with God. There is freedom of access to a throne of grace for every believer (Heb. iv. 16). "Think upon me, my God, for good, according to all that I have done for this people," is not a presumptuous conceit, but a child-like simplicity. The gross mind of the world would confound the two. Where we know that God has led us in paths of righteousness, we may well use that knowledge and encourage our souls by it. Nehemiah had but few around him who could reach high enough to sympathize fully with him, and it was thus his great comfort to pour out his soul, *according to truth,* before the God, whose good hand had guided him. God wishes no mock modesty from us. His grace in our hearts and lives should be acknowledged (comp. 1 Tim. i. 12).

HOMILETICAL AND PRACTICAL.

Vers. 1–13. The most powerful hinderances to the development of the congregation. 1) That they are discords and separations, but especially the complaints of the poor against the rich. 2)

Whence they arise: from want of love. 3) What do they teach: they challenge to a more powerful proving of love, and lead, when such proof is given, to a new impulse in the life of the congregation, but particularly to new praising of the Lord in common.

The old, and ever new, need 1) In what it consists; want, poverty, and misery are ever in the Lord's congregation. 2) Whence this arises, a) From sin (that of others, but also our own), from laziness, discontent, ingratitude, *etc.* b) From God's wise intention: He knows the sins, and wishes to remove them; He wishes to give opportunity to the rich to exercise their love, and to the poor to struggle against their discontent. 3) How it is removed: not through all sorts of new social regulations and laws—not through home missionary societies, in so far as their work is scarcely experienced by the poor as a mark of love, and is easily looked upon by them as help owed to them, but through an awaking of the heart to the proving of true love and benevolence as the Lord ever anew renders possible.—STARKE: God scourges not alone with a single, but also at times with a double rod, and sends one cross and misfortune upon another. Job x. 17. But the godly have great consolations and promises on the other hand. Ps. xxxiii. 19; Ps. xxxvii. 19, 25. Usury against our poor brethren is forbidden. Lev. xxv. 36; Ps. xv. 5; Ez. xviii. 13; xxii. 12; for whoever builds his house with the property of others, gathers stones for his own grave. Sir. xxi. 9. It is a bad case when we show ourselves to our fellow-Christians in such a way that they must sigh and cry to God against us. Gen. xviii. 21; Sir. iv. 6.

Vers. 7–13. What renders the admonition to exercise love effective? 1) Mildness in example. 2) Readiness of the preacher and his friends to take precedence in the example of love (ver. 10). 3) The assurance that God rejects the unloving from His communion, and robs him of His blessing (ver. 13).

STARKE: Anger in office is not, indeed, forbidden, yet one should be angry so as not to sin, Ps. iv. 5, and moderate himself properly. Sir. xxx. 26. As storming showers beat down the grain to the earth, but gentle drops, on the contrary, revive and ripen it, so is it also with speech. Friendly language has more effect than severe rebuke, particularly with the irascible and people of rank, who cannot submit to hard reproof.

Vers. 7–19. How important, but how difficult it is to go forward as an example in true proving of love. 1) How important (vers. 7–13). *a*) When one condemns hard-heartedness, but is himself hard-hearted, he shows that he was not in earnest in his condemnation. b) When one makes claim to the God of love against the unloving, but is himself unloving, he shows that he does not really possess the fear and faith of God, but hypocritically pretends to have it. c) Those who support their word by their actions always make the greatest impression. 2) How difficult. It is not sufficient to exercise love in that one particular in which one desires proofs of love, much more must love, self-denial, and self-sacrifice be shown in every relation (ver. 14), and indeed beyond common obligations (ver. 15), in spite of particular deeds, on account of which one could be entitled to make claims (ver. 16) in spite of the great sacrifice which the willingness for immolation imposes (vers. 17, 18). SCHLUSS: The example of true deeds of love is (ver. 19) particularly also so important on this account because it gives us the assurance and the joyful sentiment of the love and care of God, but it is always on this account so difficult because with sin is joined such want of love, so that we Christians can only find the prayer of Nehemiah (ver. 19) justified in the mouth of Christ, and only for Christ's sake are allowed to dare to beg for God's care and love.—STARKE: When necessity or other cogent reasons demand it, one should willingly forego that which otherwise he would with good reason demand and take. Matt. x. 10; 1 Cor. ix. 18; 1 Tim. v. 18. He never rules well who does not do everything he can. God will reward good works, not according to the worthiness of the merit, but from grace. Luke xvii. 18.

CHAPTER VI. 1–19.

1 Now [and] it came to pass, when Sanballat, and Tobiah, and Geshem the Ara-
bian, and the rest of our enemies, heard that I had builded the wall, and *that* there
was no breach left therein; (though at that time I had not set up the doors upon
2 the gates); that Sanballat and Geshem sent unto me, saying, Come, let us meet
together in *some one of* the villages in the plain of Ono. But [and] they thought
3 to do me mischief. And I sent messengers unto them, saying, I *am* doing a great
work, so that [and] I cannot come down: why should the work cease, whilst I
4 leave it and come down to you? Yet [and] they sent unto me four times after
this sort [word]; and I answered them after the same manner [after this word].
5 Then [and] sent Sanballat his servant unto me in like manner [after this word] the

6 fifth time with an open letter in his hand; wherein *was* written, It is reported
among the heathen [*i. e.*, nations] and Gashmu [*i. e.*, Geshem] saith *it*, *that* thou
and the Jews think to rebel: for which cause thou buildest the wall, that thou
mayest be their king [and thou art to them for king] according to these words.
7 And thou hast also appointed prophets to preach of thee at Jerusalem, saying,
There is a king in Judah, and now shall it be reported to the king according to
these words. Come now therefore [and now come], and let us take counsel together.
8 Then [and] I sent unto him, saying, There are no such things done as thou sayest
[there is not according to these words which thou sayest], but [for] thou feignest
9 them out of thine own heart. For they all made us afraid, saying, Their hands
shall be weakened from the work, that it be not done [and it shall not be done].
10 Now therefore, [And now], *O God*, strengthen my hands. Afterward [and] I
came unto the house of Shemaiah the son of Delaiah the son of Mehetabeel, who
was shut up; and he said, Let us meet together in the house of God, within the
temple, and let us shut the doors of the temple: for they will come [are coming] to
slay thee; yea [and], in the night will they come [are they coming] to slay thee.
11 And I said, Should such a man as I flee? and who is there that being as I am
12 would go into the temple to save his life [and live]? I will not go in. And lo, I
perceived that [And I perceived and lo] God had not sent him, but that [for] he
pronounced this prophecy against me, for [and] Tobiah and Sanballat had hired
13 him. Therefore was he hired, that I should be afraid, and do so, and sin, and *that*
they might have *matter* for an evil report [name], that they might reproach me.
14 My God, think thou upon [remember] Tobiah and Sanballat according to their
works, and on the prophetess Noadiah, and the rest of the prophets, that would
15 have put me in fear. So [and] the wall was finished in the twenty and fifth *day*
16 of *the month* Elul, in fifty and two days. And it came to pass that when all our
enemies heard *thereof*, and all the heathen that *were* about us saw *these things*, they
were much cast down in their own eyes: for [and] they perceived that this work
was wrought of our God.
17 Moreover in those days the nobles of Judah sent many letters unto Tobiah [multiplied their letters passing to Tobiah] and *the letters* of Tobiah came unto them
18 [and those which of Tobiah came unto them]. For *there were* many in Judah
sworn unto him, because he *was* the son-in-law of Shechaniah the son of Arah; and
his son Johanan had taken [to wife] the daughter of Meshullam the son of Bere-
19 chiah. Also they reported his good deeds before me, and uttered my words to
him. *And* Tobiah sent letters to put me in fear.

TEXTUAL AND GRAMMATICAL.

[1] Ver. 2. בַּכְּפִירִים, as if from כְּפִיר, and not from כָּפָר. This peculiarity helps the hypothesis that כְּפִירָה may be intended.

[2] Ver. 3. עֲלֵיהֶם. The use of עַל for אֶל is noticeable. See ver. 17, *et al.*

[3] Ver. 6. גַּשְׁמוּ, for גֶּשֶׁם, not after the analogy of the prop. names in יָהוּ (where the variation is owing to a form of the divine name), but rather to be compared with יֶתֶר (Ex. iv. 18) and יִתְרוֹ (Ex. iii. 1).

[4] Ver. 8. בּוֹדָאם, Aramaic for בּוֹרְאָם. See 1 Kings xii. 33, for the only other use of the verb.

[5] Ver. 13. לְמַעַן is properly "to the intent that." The first one here anticipates the other two, thus "*To this intent* he was hired, *to the intent that, etc.*"

EXEGETICAL AND CRITICAL.

(3) *Hindrances from the Heathen and their Jewish Confederates.*

Ver. 2. The omission of Tobiah's name is an indication that he was merely an attaché of Sanballat. Notice also (in the Heb.) that the prep. is not repeated before Tobiah, as it is before Geshem.—**Villages.**—Some take this as a proper name, *Chephirim.*—**Ono**, with Lod and Hadid, is mentioned in ch. vii. 37 between Jericho and Senaah, as if it might be in the Jordan depression; but the name of Lod is generally identified with Ludd or Lydda in the Sharon plain, twenty-five miles north-west of Jerusalem. If so, the ordinary siting of Ono in that plain is doubtless correct. Eusebius places it at three miles from Lydda.

Why Sanballat should select so distant a spot is puzzling, unless he happened to be stationed there himself at the time. Otherwise he would know that the invitation would arouse Nehemiah's suspicions. There may be another Ono near Chephirah, which is ten miles north-west of Jerusalem, and Chephirim (villages) may stand for Chephirah.

Ver. 5. **An open letter**, that its contents might alarm all the Jews, and create opposition to Nehemiah.

Ver. 6. **Gashmu**, *i. e.* Geshem.—**According to these words.**—Sanballat throughout makes no accusation, but refers to rumor. Nehemiah's answer is (ver. 8): *There is not according to these words which thou sayest*, *i. e.* there is no such rumor.

Strengthen my hands.—This interjected prayer must be taken from Nehemiah's journal at the time. When he writes the narrative, he quotes his ejaculation, as showing where his dependence was at that trying time.

Ver. 10. **Shemaiah** evidently (see ver. 12) was a prophet. The gift of prophecy did not prevent a man from selling himself to lie for others (see 1 Kings xxii. 22).—**Shut up.**—See Jer. xxxvi. 5. He was shut up perhaps in performance of a vow; Keil suggests as a symbol of his charge to Nehemiah. This use of *'azar* is related to the derivative *'azarrah* (a court).

The temple, *i. e.* the innermost building, the temple proper.

Ver. 11. **Would go into the temple to save his life.**—Lit.: "would go into the temple and live." The last clause may refer to the death of any one violating the sanctity of the temple. See Num. xviii. 7. It may also mean what our translators give.

Ver. 13. **Do so and sin**, *i. e.* shut myself up in fear, and enter the holy place, into which only the priests could enter.

Ver. 14. Sanballat evidently had a strong party in Jerusalem, and among them many of prophetic rank hired with his money.

Ver. 15. **Elul** was the sixth month corresponding to parts of August and September.—**Fifty and two days.**—Hence the work was begun on the fourth of Ab, the fifth month. The work went on during the hottest part of the year (say, from July 19th to Sept. 8th).

Ver. 16. The marvellously short time in which the work had been done, and that, too, by Jews, whom Sanballat knew to be divided into mutually hostile parties, impressed him and his coadjutors with the sense of a divine co-operation with Nehemiah.

Josephus turns the fifty-two days into eight hundred and forty days, probably in his desire to tone down the marvellous for his readers.

Ver. 18. **Meshullam.** See ch. iii. 4.

HISTORICAL AND ETHICAL.

1. Nehemiah, when persistently declining the invitation to meet Sanballat at the plain of Ono, exposed himself to the charge of opposing peace measures. This is one of the hardest trials of virtue, to continue steadfast in a true course at the risk of impugned motives and damaged reputation. Sanballat's fifth message and open letter sought to endanger Nehemiah with the king, while it seemed to show Sanballat's devotion to the king's interests. The refusal now to attend a conference would appear the worse. Yet the sturdy patriot and man of God rests upon his integrity and trusts in God. This *persistence* in the right, come what would, makes Nehemiah a *great* man as well as a *good* man.

2. "Shemaiah" was such a common name among the Jews, that it is impossible to identify this prophet with any other person of his name (as *e. g.* the one in Ezra x. 21). He must, however, have been a man of prominence, and one, too, who had been in Nehemiah's confidence, or else the attempt would never have been made by Tobiah and Sanballat through him. It may have been the high position and reputation of Shemaiah that led the prophetess Noadiah and the rest of the prophets (ver. 14) into the false dealings with Nehemiah.

3. The expression of Nehemiah's soul for their punishment from God is the outcry for vindication, which one's very purity of heart demands. In such outcry the persecuted and innocent soul finds rest. Let none confound this with revenge.

4. It is not strange that Sanballat saw that the wall-building was wrought of Israel's God. The trouble with God's enemies is not that their knowledge is defective, but that their hearts are alienated. Evidences are multiplying constantly before them, but produce no change in their opposition. Sanballat was vexed because he was thwarted by the Lord God of Israel. Those fifty-two days of wall-building were clearly to his mind a token of divine assistance; but this knowledge did not stop his opposition.

HOMILETICAL AND PRACTICAL.

Vers. 1–3. Can the enticements of the dissembling world really make any impression upon us? 1) What are they? They all come to this one thing in the end, that we shall care before all for ourselves, that is, for our temporal well-being, and therefore shall descend from our due height as children of God, and they aim not towards our salvation, but towards our destruction. 2) What have we to place in opposition to them? That we have a great work to do, the building of the walls of Jerusalem, that is, the securing the kingdom of God in others, and particularly in ourselves, the spreading and the improvement thereof, only through the most faithful performance of this great, infinite work, can we reach the high goal of our salvation.—Bede: *Nehemias personam fidelium doctorum tenens, nequaquam ad profanos descendere neque eorum hostiis inquinari sentit, sed in conceptis virtutum operibus devotus persistit; et quo acrius terrere nitebantur inimici, eo magis ipse bene operando terribilis eisdem inimicis fieri contendit.*

Vers. 1–9. The behaviour of those who grudge independence to the congregation. 1) They act as if they wish to aid it. 2) They seek to intimidate, as if the representatives of freedom were rendering themselves worthy of suspicion in a dangerous way. 3) Their only design is to rob the congregation of its capable leaders.

Vers. 10–19. The friends of the enemy. 1) They pretend that they are caring for the well-being and the security of the good. 2) They serve the enemy. 3) They only aim at destroying the good leaders.

Vers. 15–19. The most repulsive enemies. 1) They are not those from without who are grieved when the independence of the congregation is secured, and its work crowned with success. 2) They are much rather the false brethren, who always desire to incite the outside enemy anew to disturbing interference by smooth words.—BEDE: *Semper habent electi foris pugnas, intus timores; nec solum apostolis, sed et prophetæ periculis ex genere, periculis ex gentibus, periculis ex falsis fratribus suspectam vitam agebant.* STARKE: What Paul writes concerning false brethren (2 Cor. xi. 26) that has Nehemiah also experienced for his portion. And it is indeed one of the heaviest griefs of the true servants of God, when they must see that that those connected with them in religion, yes, indeed at times their colleagues, who labor with them in the same work, stand in prejudicial intercourse with the enemies of Christ and His church, and yet wish to be considered as co-members, striving for the honor of God. Those whom God awakens for spiritual building should conduct themselves circumspectly and courageously against the snares of the enemy, and not allow themselves to be frightened off by their slander, but cheerfully proceed. In the end the enemy will be cast down with fear in their consciences, and must acknowledge that the work is of God. Acts v. 39. When we wander in the midst of anxiety God refreshes us, and stretches His hand over the rage of His enemies, and helps us with His right hand. Ps. xcvii. 11.

Vers. 1–19. Concerning the most critical and saddest hinderance which opposes us in defence of the congregation. 1) From whom it proceeds. Not principally from the outside enemy, not even then when they feign friendship, and, under the pretence of helping us, aim at the worst, but much more from false prophets, who make common cause with the outside enemy, and yet pretend that they wish to protect us from their snares. They excite our humanity to allow ourselves, for our security or ease, that which can become ruinous to us. 2) How it serves us. Our zeal, our fidelity and perseverance, and our watchfulness must be so much the greater; we shall have opportunity to keep ourselves in sufferings, not for our injury, but for our salvation. 3) How it is to be overcome. Through precaution and fearlessness, through the fear of God in which are united humility and genuine high courage, also through great watchfulness.—STARKE: Great lords, who seek to further the good of the church of God and of the commonwealth, are a thorn in the devil's eye. The cross is often never lifted from the godly, that they may live in continual communion with God. Ah, my God, I have also a great business to perform, namely, to save my soul, and better that of my neighbor. Grant that I may be faithful therein, then shall it go on well and succeed.

CHAPTER VII. 1–73.

1 Now [AND] it came to pass when the wall was built, and I had set up the doors,
2 and the porters and the singers and the Levites were appointed, that I gave my
brother Hanani and Hananiah the ruler of the palace, charge over Jerusalem, for
3 he was [as] a faithful man, and feared God above [*i. e.* more than] many. And
I said unto them, Let not the gates of Jerusalem be opened until the sun be hot;
and while [until] they stand by, let them shut the doors and bar *them:* and appoint watches of the inhabitants of Jerusalem, every one in his watch, and every
4 one *to be* over against his house. Now [And] the city was large [broad on both
hands] and great; but the people *were* few therein, and the houses *were* not builded.
5 And my God put into my heart to gather [and I gathered] together the nobles,
and the rulers, and the people, that they might be reckoned by genealogy. And
I found a register of the genealogy of them which came up at the first, and found
6 written therein. These *are* the children [sons] of the province, that went up out
of the captivity of those that had been carried away [of the carrying away],
whom Nebuchadnezzar the king of Babylon had carried away, and [who]
7 came again to Jerusalem and to Judah, every one unto his city; who came
with Zerubbabel, Jeshua, Nehemiah, Azariah, Raamiah, Nahamani, Mordecai, Bilshan, Mispereth, Bigvai, Nehum, Baanah. The number, *I say,* of the
8 men of the people of Israel *was this;* The children [sons—*so everywhere in this*
9 *list*] of Parosh, two thousand a hundred seventy and two. The children of She-
10 phatiah, three hundred seventy and two. The children of Arah, six hundred fifty
11 and two. The children of Pahath-moab, of the children of Jeshua and Joab, two
12 thousand and eight hundred *and* eighteen. The children of Elam, a thousand two

13 hundred fifty and four. The children of Zattu, eight hundred forty and five.
14, 15 The children of Zaccai, seven hundred and three-score. The children of Binnui, six hundred forty and eight.
16, 17 The children of Bebai, six hundred twenty and eight. The children of Azgad,
18 two thousand three hundred twenty and two. The children of Adonikam, six
19 hundred three-score and seven. The children of Bigvai, two thousand three-score
20, 21 and seven. The children of Adin, six hundred fifty and five. The children
22 of Ater of Hezekiah, ninety and eight. The children of Hashum, three hundred
23 twenty and eight. The children of Bezai, three hundred twenty and four.
24, 25 The children of Hariph, a hundred and twelve. The children of Gibeon, ninety
26 and five. The men of Bethlehem and Netophah, a hundred four-score and eight.
27, 28 The men of Anathoth, a hundred twenty and eight. The men of Beth-azma-
29 veth, forty and two. The men of Kirjath-jearim, Chephirah, and Beeroth, seven
30 hundred forty and three. The men of Ramah and Gaba, six hundred twenty and
31, 32 one. The men of Michmas, a hundred and twenty and two. The men of
33 Beth-el and Ai, a hundred twenty and three. The men of the other Nebo, fifty
34 and two. The children of the other Elam, a thousand two hundred fifty and four.
35, 36 The children of Harim, three hundred and twenty. The children of Jericho,
37 three hundred forty and five. The children of Lod, Hadid, and Ono, seven hun-
38 dred twenty and one. The children of Senaah, three thousand nine hundred and thirty.

39 The priests: The children of Jedaiah, of the house of Jeshua, nine hundred
40, 41 seventy and three. The children of Immer, a thousand fifty and two. The
42 children of Pashur, a thousand two hundred forty and seven. The children of Harim, a thousand and seventeen.

43 The Levites: The children of Jeshua. of Kadmiel, *and* of the children of Hodevah, seventy and four.

44 The singers: The children of Asaph, a hundred forty and eight.

45 The porters: The children of Shallum, the children of Ater, the children of Talmon, the children of Akkub, the children of Hatita, the children of Shobai, a hundred thirty and eight.

46 The Nethinim: The children of Ziha, the children of Hashupha, the children of
47 Tabbaoth, the children of Keros, the children of Sia, the children of Padon,
48 the children of Lebana, the children of Hagaba, the children of Shalmai,
49, 50 the children of Hanan, the children of Giddel, the children of Gahar, the
51 children of Reaiah, the children of Rezin, the children of Nekoda, the children
52 of Gazzam, the children of Uzza, the children of Phaseah, the children of Besai,
53 the children of Meunim, the children of Nephishesim, the children of Bakbuk,
54 the children of Hakupha, the children of Harhur, the children of Bazlith, the
55 children of Mehida, the children of Harsha, the children of Barkos, the children
56 of Sisera, the children of Tamah, the children of Neziah, the children of Hatipha.

57 The children of Solomon's servants: The children of Sotai, the children of So-
58 phereth, the children of Perida, the children of Jaala, the children of Darkon,
59 the children of Giddel, the children of Shephatiah, the children of Hattil, the
60 children of Pochereth of Zebaim, the children of Amon. All the Nethinim and
61 the children of Solomon's servants, *were* three hundred ninety and two. And these *were* they which went up *also* from Tel-melah, Tel-haresha, Cherub, Addon, and Immer: but they could not show their father's house, nor their seed, whether they
62 *were* of Israel. The children of Delaiah, the children of Tobiah, the children of Nekoda, six hundred forty and two.

63 And of the priests: The children of Habaiah, the children of Koz, the children of Barzillai, which took *one* of the daughters of Barzillai the Gileadite to wife, and
64 was called after their name. These sought their register *among* those that were reckoned by genealogy, but it was not found: therefore were they, as polluted, put
65 from the priesthood. And the Tirshatha said unto them, that they should not eat of the most holy things, till there stood *up* a priest with Urim and Thummim.

66 The whole congregation together *was* forty and two thousand three hundred and
67 three-score. Besides their man-servants and their maid-servants, of whom *there*

were seven thousand three hundred thirty and seven: and they had two hundred
68 forty and five singing men and singing women. Their horses, seven hundred thirty
69 and six: their mules, two hundred forty and five: *their* camels, four hundred
thirty and five: six thousand seven hundred and twenty asses.
70 And some of the chief of the fathers gave unto the work. The Tirshatha gave
to the treasure a thousand drams of gold, fifty basins, five hundred and thirty
71 priests' garments. And *some* of the chief of the fathers gave to the treasure of the
work twenty thousand drams of gold, and two thousand and two hundred pounds
72 of silver. And *that* which the rest of the people gave *was* twenty thousand drams
of gold, and two thousand pounds of silver, and three-score and seven priests' gar-
73 ments. So the priests, and the Levites, and the porters, and the singers, and *some*
of the people, and the Nethinim, and all Israel, dwelt in their cities; and when
the seventh month came, the children of Israel *were* in their cities.

TEXTUAL AND GRAMMATICAL.

1 Ver. 3. יְגִיפוּ for יְסַגְּרוּ, ἅπαξ λεγόμενον. The Targum Jonathan on 2 Kings iv. 4, וְסָגַרְתְּ הַדֶּלֶת is וְתַגִּיפִין דָּשָׁא.

EXEGETICAL AND CRITICAL.

The Ordering of the City.

Ver. 1. The setting up of the doors on the gates is anticipated in the description in chap. iii. (See ch. iii. 1, 3, 6, 13, 14, 15.) It occurred after the wall was completed. (Comp. chap. vi. 1). **The porters and the singers and the Levites** (comp. ch. xii. 45-47). For the temple-porters in David's time, see the accounts in 1 Chron. ix. 17–27, and xxvi. 1–19. The Korhites or descendants of Korah, who were porters, were also singers, to whom are inscribed so many psalms. All of these porters and singers were Levites. Hence the threefold titles might not indicate distinct classes, but we might read it as a *hendiatris* "the Levitical singing porters." Yet from the later portions of this book (ch. x. 28; ch. xi. 15–19) we may gather that the singers and porters formed two distinct guilds, separate from one another and separate from the other Levites. Hence the three terms here represent three bodies of men. It is probable that the opening and shutting of the temple-gates were made with song. Perhaps some of the psalms inscribed to the Bene-Korah were so used.

Nehemiah seems to have set these Levitical porters at all the city gates, perhaps to give a more religious aspect to his work of defending Jerusalem.

Ver. 2. **Hanani.**—See ch. i. 2. **Hananiah's** position as **ruler of the palace** (*sar habbirah*) was probably the old office of the monarchy (*'al-habbayith*) which Eliakim held (2 Kings xviii. 37) and which Jotham held while Uzziah still lived (*'al beth-hammelek*, 2 Chron. xxvi. 21). See note on ch. ii. 8. The old office was probably retained and its incumbent acted as vizier or prime officer to the governor. Nehemiah probably contemplated temporary returns to Persia, and therefore consolidated the government in this way, putting faithful men in the highest positions.

Ver. 3. **While they stand by.**—Rather, *until they stand by*. The command is, not to open the gates till high day, and not even then, unless the guard is ready to stand by and defend them. The **watchers** were stationed throughout the city. These were formed of the inhabitants generally.

Ver. 4. **The houses were not builded.**—A general expression. The city was full of waste places.

Ver. 6. Here begins a copy of the list of Zerubbabel's company of ninety years before. See Ezra ii. It continues through this chapter. Verses 6 and 7 form the title of the list. **Province.**—Judea was now a province of the Persian empire.

That went up out of the captivity of those that had been carried away whom Nebuchadnezzar, *etc.*—Rather, *that went up from exile, the captives whom Nebuchadnezzar, etc.*

Ver. 7. **Nehemiah.**—Not the Nehemiah of this book. **Azariah.**—In Ezra ii., *Seraiah.* **Raamiah.**—In Ezra ii., *Reelaiah.* **Nahamani.**—Not mentioned in Ezra ii. Perhaps a mistaken repetition of Nehemiah. **Mispereth.**—In Ezra ii., *Mizpar.* **Nehum.**—In Ezra ii., *Rehum.*

Ver. 10. The 652 of this verse is 775 in Ezra ii.

Ver. 11. The 2818 of this verse is 2812 in Ezra ii.

Ver. 13. The 845 of this verse is 945 in Ezra ii.

Ver. 15. **Binnui.**—In Ezra ii. *Bani.* The 648 of this verse is 642 in Ezra ii.

Ver. 16. The 628 of this verse is 623 in Ezra ii.

Ver. 17. The 2322 of this verse is 1222 in Ezra ii.

Ver. 18. The 667 of this verse is 666 in Ezra ii.

Ver. 19. The 2067 of this verse is 2056 in Ezra ii.

Ver. 20. The 655 of this verse is 454 in Ezra ii.

Ver. 22. The 328 of this verse is 223 in Ezra ii.

Ver. 23. The 324 of this verse is 323 in Ezra ii.

Ver. 24. **Hariph.**—In Ezra ii. *Jorah.*

Ver. 25. **Gibeon.**—In Ezra ii. *Gibbar.*

Ver. 26. The 188 of this verse is 179 in Ezra ii., and divided into two parts. At this verse, when "children" changes to "men," the names of towns (instead of those of fathers) begin.

Ver. 28. **Beth-azmaveth.** In Ezra ii. *Azmaveth.*

Ver. 32. The 123 of this verse is 223 in Ezra ii.

Ver. 33. **The other Nebo** (*Nebo A'her*). In Ezra ii. *Nebo* simply.

Ver. 34. The word "children" resumed, but the names of fathers are resumed for two verses only.

Ver. 37. The 721 of this verse is 725 in Ezra ii.

Ver. 38. The 3930 of this verse is 3630 in Ezra ii. In Ezra we find "the children of Magbish a hundred fifty and six," which is omitted in this copy of Nehemiah.

Ver. 43. **Hodevah.**—In Ezra ii. *Hodaviah.*

Ver. 44. The 148 of this verse is 128 in Ezra ii.

Ver. 45. The 138 of this verse is 139 in Ezra ii.

Ver. 46. **Hashupha.**—Heb. *Hasupha.*

Ver. 47. **Sia.**—In Ezra ii. Siaha.

Ver. 48. In Ezra we find "the children of Akkub, the children of Hagab," which is here omitted. **Shalmai.**—Heb. *Salmai.*

Ver. 52. In Ezra we find "the children of Asnah," which is here omitted. **Nephishesim.**—In Ezra ii. *Nephusim* (K'ri).

Ver. 54. **Bazlith.**—In Ezra ii. *Bazluth.*

Ver. 57. **Perida.**—In Ezra ii. *Peruda.*

Ver. 59. **Amon.**—In Ezra ii. *Ami.*

Ver. 60. Thirty-five families of Nethinim were represented, and ten of Solomon's servants. Hence there was an average of less than nine to each family.

For **the Nethinim** see on ch. iii. 26.

Solomon's servants were doubtless those whom Solomon enslaved of the Canaanites. (See 1 Kings ix. 20, 21). Their descendants were probably regarded as engrafted into Israel, as were the Gibeonites.

Ver. 61. **Addon.**—In Ezra ii. *Addan.*

Ver. 62. The 642 of this verse is 652 in Ezra ii.

Ver. 65. **The Tirshatha.**—This title is given expressly to Nehemiah in ch. viii. 9, but in this list of those who came with Zerubbabel nearly a century before, it, of course, cannot refer to Nehemiah, unless we suppose that both in Ezra's list and in this of Nehemiah's there had been interpolated in the original record this 65th verse, to show a decision made by Nehemiah in his time. If that be the case, which is perfectly possible, then the latter part of the 70th verse is also an interpolation of Nehemiah to show his gifts to the work of separation in his time. If we do not accept this explanation, we must believe that Zerubbabel was the Tirshatha of Nehem. vii., and Ezra ii. FUERST derives the word from *tarash*, and supposes this root means "to fear," or "to reverence," and refers Teresh (Esth. ii. 21) to the same. But may it not be from the more common root *yarash* (to possess)? The Persian *torsh* (revere) is in favor of the former. It is used as synonymous with *pe'hah* (governor). See ch. xii. 26.

Till there stood up a priest with Urim and Thummim.—This seems to be a circumlocution for "forever." The Urim and Thummim (whatever they were) were connected with the High-priest's breastplate (Ex. xxviii. 30) and with the oracular response of God on application by the High-priest (comp. Num. xxvii. 21 and 1 Sam. xxviii. 6). When these responses ceased or when the Urim and Thummim were lost, we cannot tell. We hear nothing of them after David's reign. The prophets seem to have taken their place. The Urim and Thummim being absent, there was no authority in Israel to determine the priestly status of these unregistered ones.

Ver. 66. **The whole congregation together was forty and two thousand three hundred and threescore.**—The numbers given in this chapter, up to this verse, amount to only 31,089. In Ezra ii. the amount is 29,818. If we add to the former sum the number of servants given in ver. 67, we have only 38,671, or 3,689 less than the gross amount of this verse. We have noted the omission in this list of four families. The differences in the numbers of the two lists also show how liable are numbers to be changed in transcription. The grand total, being the same in both lists, is probably correct.

Ver. 67. **Singing men and singing women,** *meshorerim umeshoreroth.* Comp. Eccl. ii. 8. These were probably a guild of servants, dating from Solomon's day.

Ver. 70. **The work** of restoration. **The Tirshatha.**—See on ver. 65.

Ver. 71. The repetition of **the chief of the fathers** seems to support the view of the Tirshatha sentence being an interpolation by Nehemiah. The 20,000 drams of gold here is 61,000 in Ezra ii., and the 2200 pounds here are 5000 pounds there, but if we add the people's gift of ver. 72 (not found in Ezra) we have here 40,000 and 4200 against 61,000 and 5000 there. So the sixty-seven priests' garments here are one hundred there. See remark on numbers in ver. 66.

The children of Israel were in their cities.—This seems to be the real ending of the quotation from the old register of Zerubbabel's day, and then Nehemiah's narration begins again, using almost the same words as Ezra's concerning the first migration. In Ezra it is *wayyeasphu ha'am keish e'hadh*, and in Nehemiah it is *wayyeasphu khol ha'am keish e'hadh.* This likeness was doubtless designed.

HISTORICAL AND ETHICAL.

1. The walls were not to be substitutes for, but encouragements of, watchfulness. A perfect system of opening, shutting, barring and guarding the gates was to follow the successful upbuilding of the city-bulwark. Faithful men were to be put into the highest positions, and a larger number of Jews were to be induced to dwell in Jerusalem in order to its defence. The order, security and growth of Jerusalem, as the city of the Great King, Jehovah of Israel, formed the undivided aim of the son of Hachaliah.

2. The genealogies occupied an important place in Israel. They contained the certificate of church-membership for each Israelite. They

also contained the claims to official dignity that belonged to priest and Levite. The family-idea thus received a marked emphasis in God's redemptive government—an emphasis which is echoed by Malachi (Mal. iv. 6) and the angel that appeared to Zacharias (Luke i. 17). The appearance of the Nethinim in the genealogies is a forcible illustration of the impartial grace of God. That grace which would bring in all the Gentiles as children was foretokened by the brotherly position of the Nethinim (of Gentile blood) among the people of God, the children of Abraham, Isaac and Jacob.

3. Those priests whose names were not in the lists were counted the same as polluted, that is, not simply as having a *blemish* (see Lev. xxi. 17-21), for such priests could eat of the holy things, but as having an *uncleanness* (see Lev. xxii. 3-6), which prevented all contact with holy objects. This shows the prominence of externals in the Jewish religion—a necessary prominence where the externals had a precise spiritual significance. For, after all, it was the spiritual truth which was the basis of such exactness, and by no means the mere intrinsic value of externals.

4. The entire number of Jews who returned in Cyrus' day to Jerusalem was small—about 50,000, out of millions. Piety, patriotism and desire for change were three motives at work in the 50,000. But what a vast mass were unmoved by any of these motives, and were well satisfied with their exile! Some, however, like Daniel, remained from high and holy motives. The Jewish people is a *remnant.*

HOMILETICAL AND PRACTICAL.

The Lord, on His side, appoints watchmen on the walls of Jerusalem, who must allow themselves no rest day or night, and must not even give the Lord Himself any rest until He fortifies Jerusalem, and makes it for a praise in the earth. Isa. lxii. 6, 7. But now, when Jerusalem is scantily rebuilt, Nehemiah appoints watchmen, who shall guard the city and its gates. The first thing necessary for the congregation is praying hearts, whose petitions shall not slacken until the Lord is persuaded; these the Lord Himself must give. But when the prayers have been granted care must be taken for the preservation and using of that which has been granted. That the congregation itself must see to. And that they themselves can and must watch, that they must remain separated from the world, and that they will be secured in the maintenance of their peculiarity and independence, is their honor and joy. 2. There are always two tasks in the congregation, or church, of the Lord. As there are always enemies remaining (so long as the kingdom is not of God and of His Christ), who cannot endure the spread of the blessing, which might proceed from the church, who would much rather indeed win its possessions and gifts, and would wish to make it like the world, so these enemies, especially then, when the powers of life are most active in it, come out to attack it most energetically, and fall upon its representatives most sharply in word and deed, therefore it must always have some to keep watch, to protect it, and fight the enemy. But again: so long as everything is in embryo, and the conclusion has not been reached, and there are yet those to be found capable of receiving and becoming participants in the goods and gifts of the church and in the salvation of the Lord, that is, those who can and will enter the congregation of the Lord, and increase and extend the Lord's kingdom, therefore, just on this account, such are necessary as will be engaged in the winning and reception of new members to the kingdom, who understand the situation, and can point out the spot where they also can build. 3. As Jerusalem, in Nehemiah's time, extended far on both sides, and was scantily populated, so also the city of God in all times has had space for new additions to its population. For, in truth, the rich possessions which God has prepared in His church for mankind, would only then be sufficiently turned to profit when every one called man should enjoy them, and it were itself full and sufficiently built out, and all had entered in. For that God, who has made all things for Himself, and for that Lord who has redeemed all, the totality alone, from which none is lost, forms a sufficiently great people.—BEDE: *Præcepit autem Nehemias, ne aperiantur portæ Hierusalem usque ad calorem solis, hoc est toto tempore noctis, ne videlicet aut obtectus tenebris hostis erumpat, aut certe aliquis incautus exiens ab hoste captus pereat. Quod etiam in hujus sæculi nocte tota custodes animarum debent solerter agere, ne observantia piæ conversationis neglecta diabolus aut cohortem fidelium perturbaturus subintret aut de ipsorum numero fidelium quempiam perditurus rapiat. Apparente autem sole justitiæ et clarescente luce futuræ beatitudinis jam non opus erit claustris continentiæ; quia nec adversariis ultra dabitur facultas impugnandi sive tentandi fideles, utpote sempiterna cum suo principe ultione damnatis. Unde in Apocalypsi sua Joannes de futura ejusdem sanctæ civitatis gloria dicit; et portæ ejus non claudentur per diem; nox enim non erit illic.*—STARKE: This is the final cause why cities and countries, kingdoms and principalities are founded, and filled with people that God may dwell there, and His church may have a certain shelter. God provides help, protection, and rest for His church, and as human protection is very insignificant, God with His angels is the best watchman.

CHAPTER VIII. 1–18.

1 AND all the people gathered themselves together as one man into the street that
was before the water-gate; and they spake unto Ezra the scribe to bring the book
2 of the law of Moses, which the LORD had commanded to Israel. And Ezra the
priest brought the law before the congregation both of men and women, and all
that could hear with understanding [that understood in hearing] upon the first
3 day of the seventh month. And he read therein before the street that was before
the water-gate from the morning until midday [from the light until half of the
day], before the men and the women, and those that could understand [and the
understanding]; and the ears of all the people *were attentive* unto the book of the
4 law. And Ezra the scribe stood upon a pulpit [tower] of wood, which they had
made for that purpose; and beside him stood Mattithiah, and Shema, and Anaiah,
and Urijah, and Hilkiah, and Maaseiah, on his right hand; and on his left hand
Pedaiah, and Mishael, and Malchiah, and Hashum, and Hashbadana, Zechariah
5 *and* Meshullam. And Ezra opened the book in the sight [to the eyes] of all the
people; (for he was above all the people;) and when he opened it, all the people
6 stood up. And Ezra blessed the LORD, the great God. And all the people an-
swered, Amen, Amen, with lifting up their hands: and they bowed their heads,
7 and worshipped the LORD with *their* faces to the ground. Also [and] Jeshua, and
Bani, and Sherebiah, Jamin, Akkub, Shabbethai, Hodijah, Maaseiah, Kelita,
Azariah, Jozabad, Hanan, Pelaiah, and the Levites, caused the people to under-
8 stand the law: and the people *stood* in their place. So [And] they read in the
book in the law of God distinctly, and gave the sense, and caused *them* to under-
9 stand the reading. And Nehemiah, which *is* the Tirshatha, and Ezra the priest
the scribe, and the Levites that taught the people, said unto all the people, This
day *is* holy unto the LORD your God; mourn not, nor weep. For all the people
10 wept, when they heard the words of the law. Then [And] he said unto them, Go
your way, eat the fat [fat things], and drink the sweet [sweet things], and send
portions unto them [him] for whom nothing is prepared: for *this* day *is* holy unto
11 our Lord: neither be ye sorry; for the joy of the LORD is your strength. So
[And] the Levites stilled all the people, saying, Hold your peace, for the day *is*
12 holy; neither be ye grieved. And all the people went their way to eat, and to
drink, and to send portions and to make great mirth, because they had understood
13 the words that were declared unto them. And on the second day were gathered
together the chief of the fathers of all the people, the priests and the Levites, unto
14 Ezra the scribe, even to understand [consider] the words of the law. And they
found written in the law which the LORD had commanded by [by the hand of]
Moses, that the children of Israel should dwell in booths in the feast of the seventh
15 month; and that they should publish and proclaim [cause the voice to be heard
and to pass] in all their cities, and in Jerusalem, saying, Go forth unto the mount,
and fetch olive branches, and pine [oil-tree] branches, and myrtle branches, and
palm branches, and branches of thick [thick-leaved] trees, to make booths, as *it is*
16 written. So [And] the people went forth, and brought *them*, and made themselves
booths, every one upon the roof of his house [upon his roof], and in their courts,
and in the street [square] of the water-gate, and in the street [square] of the gate
17 of Ephraim. And all the congregation of them that were come again out of the
captivity made booths, and sat under the booths: for since the days of Jeshua, the
son of Nun unto that day had not the children of Israel done so. And there was
18 very great gladness. Also [And] day by day, from the first day unto the last
day, he read in the book of the law of God. And they kept the feast seven days;
and on the eighth day was a solemn assembly according unto the manner [statute].

TEXTUAL AND GRAMMATICAL.

[1] Ver. 6. וַיִּקְּדוּ וַיִּשְׁתַּחֲוּוּ. This frequent combination, the former verb being never without the latter, indicates the two steps of the movement: "they stooped and bowed down." The verbs שָׁחָה, שָׁחַח and שׁוּחַ are stronger than קָדַד.

[2] Ver. 7. The Hiphil of בִּין is used in vers. 7, 8, 9, with the true Hiphil force; but in vers. 2, 3, 12, it has the Kal sense.

[3] Ver. 10. לְאֵין נָכוֹן לוֹ for לַאֲשֶׁר אֵין נָכוֹן לוֹ, by suppression of the relative, which is far harsher than the Eng suppression of the antecedent, *e. g.* "Honor to whom honor is due." Comp. 1 Chron. xv. 12.

[4] **Ver. 17.** Notice the alliterative use of the three roots שָׁבָה, יָשַׁב and שׁוּב.

EXEGETICAL AND CRITICAL.

The Instruction of the People.

Ver. 1. **Street.**—Rather "square" or *plaza.* **The water-gate**, according to our view (see on ch. iii. 26 and xii. 37), was an inner gate connected both with the temple and with the subterranean water galleries of Ophel, by which there seems to have been a large open square for public assemblies. (See Excursus). **Ezra the scribe,** *Ezra hassopher.* In the next verse it is **Ezra the priest,** *Ezra hakkohen.* This is the first mention of Ezra in the book of Nehemiah. He had come to Jerusalem thirteen years previously, with about three thousand returning Jews (1754 males), holding a commission from Artaxerxes to appoint magistrates in Judæa. He had forced the Jews to separate from their heathen wives, and had then probably returned to Persia, as we find the Jews had relapsed into their former condition. As we do not meet with his name in Nehemiah till now, it is probable he followed Nehemiah to Judea to assist him in another movement of reform.

Ver. 2. **All that could hear with understanding.**—Lit., *All that understood in hearing, i. e.*, those old enough to understand. **The first day of the seventh month.**—This was a special "Sabbath, a memorial of blowing of trumpets, a holy convocation." (Lev. xxiii. 24). A specific offering was appointed for that day, beside the burnt-offering of the month. (Numb. xxix. 1–6).

Ver. 3. **From morning.**—Lit., *from the light, i. e.*, from daylight or an hour as early as was available. The reading must have occupied at least six hours. About one-quarter of the Pentateuch might be read in that time.

Ver. 4. **Pulpit.**—Probably the same that is called *stairs* in ch. ix. 4. The word here is strictly *tower* and there *ascent.* It was doubtless a very high platform so as to overlook a large crowd. (Comp. ver. 5). **Anaiah.**—See chap. x. 22. **Urijah.**—See ch. iii. 4. **Hilkiah.**—Not the Hilkiah of xii. 7. He lived in Zerubbabel's day. **Maaseiah.**—See xii. 41. **Malchiah.**—See x. 3. **Zechariah.**—See xii. 41. **Meshullam.**—See x. 7. All these named as standing with Ezra may have been priests. If so, the Anaiah of ch. x. 22 must be a different one from this one here named. As far as we can trace the other names, they appear to be priests.

Ver. 7. **Jeshua.**—See ch. x. 9. **Bani.**—See ch. x. 13. **Sherebiah.**—See ch. x. 12. **Jamin.**—Perhaps the Benjamin of ch. iii. 23. **Akkub.**—See ch. xii. 19. **Shabbethai.**—See ch. xi. 16. **Hodijah.**—See ch. x. 10. **Maaseiah.**—Probably not the Maaseiah of ver. 4, or of ch. x. 25, or of ch. xi. 5, but possibly the Maaseiah of ch. iii. 23. **Kelita.**—See ch. x. 10. **Azariah.**—Perhaps the priest mentioned ch. x. 2. **Jozabad.**—See ch. xi. 16. **Hanan.** See ch. x. 10. **Pelaiah.**—See ch. x. 10. **And the Levites,** *i. e., and other Levites,* for the thirteen mentioned were Levites. These Levites seem to have read after Ezra and to have explained it to different parts of the crowd, while the Amens, the lifting up of the hands, the bowing and the worshipping (in ver. 6) occurred at intervals during the reading. The explanation may have been principally of archaic Hebrew words.

Ver. 8. **So they read.**—That is Ezra read and the Levites re-read and explained where necessary.

Ver. 9. **The Tirshatha.**—See on ch. vii. 65. The holiness of the day is used as an argument against mourning. Note the fact that the high-priest on whose mitre was written "Holiness to the Lord," was forbidden to mourn. (See Lev. xxi. 10. Comp. Lev. x. 6).

Ver. 10. **Send portions.**—See the spirit of this enjoined in Deut. xvi. 11, 12, with regard to the Pentecost season.

The joy of the Lord is your strength, *i. e.*, a mirthfulness which springs from right relations to God is an element and sign of spiritual strength.

Ver. 13. **To understand.**—Rather, "to consider."

Ver. 14. **In the feast of the seventh month,** *i. e.*, the feast of tabernacles. See Lev. xxiii. 34-43.

Ver. 15. This is a pregnant sentence, thus: *And that they should publish and proclaim in all their cities* (Lev. xxiii. 4); *so they proclaimed in Jerusalem, etc.* The order is given on the 2d of Tisri, and the work is done in readiness for the 15th. The narrative runs the two together, confusing the time to the careless reader. **Unto the mount,** *i. e.*, mount of Olives. **Pine branches,** *'alê 'etz shemen*, branches of the oil-tree (Isa. xli. 19). Mr. Houghton (in Smith's Dict.) thinks it may be the Zackum or Balanites Ægyptiaca. **Branches of thick trees,** *'ale 'etz 'avoth;* either specifically "branches of the Avoth tree," or branches of tangled trees."

In Lev. xxiii. 40, the command is to use,

1. The fruit of goodly trees.
2. The leaves of palm trees.
3. The boughs of Avoth trees.
4. Willows of the brook.

Here the olive tree, the oil tree, and the myrtle would come under the first head ("fruit" being used for any produce), while the willow-tree is omitted, perhaps because there happened to be none near Jerusalem at that time.

Ver. 16. **Street of the water-gate.**—See on ver. 1. **Street of the gate of Ephraim.**—From 2 Kings xiv. 13 and Neh. ch. xii. 39, we see that this gate was near the north-west corner of the city, between "the broad wall" and the "old gate," the "old gate" and "cornergate" being perhaps the same. According to Keil, the Gate of Ephraim may have been attached to the broad wall and not have been destroyed. Hence it is not mentioned in chap. iii. There was, we may suppose, a large open place in the N. W. part of the city, corresponding to that by the water-gate in the S. E. part.

Ver. 17. **Done so.**—That is, kept the feast of Tabernacles with such gladness.

Ver. 18. **He read,** *i. e.*, Ezra.

They kept the feast, *i. e.*, of tabernacles. They had been from the second day (ver. 13), to this the 15th day of Tisri (Lev. xxiii. 34) preparing for it. The solemn fast-day of the 10th of Tisri had doubtless been excepted. It is passed over without mention in the narrative. **A solemn assembly,** *atzereth* (comp. Lev. xxiii. 36; Num. xxix. 35; Deut. xvi. 8; Jer. ix. 2; Amos v. 21). It seems to have been something more than the "mikra-kodesh" (holy convocation), and yet what more we cannot say. It is applied to the last day of the feast of tabernacles and to the last day of the passover week. JOSEPHUS (*Ant.* 3, 10, 5) applies it to Pentecost (in the Greek form *Asarthá*), as especially belonging to that day, which is the use of the word by the later Jews.

HISTORICAL AND ETHICAL.

1. The constant study of God's word by the people was always, and is still, a distinguishing characteristic of the Jewish nation. The Levites were originally entrusted with the duty of reading the law before Israel every seventh year (Deut. xxxi. 9–13), and when Jehoshaphat (2 Chron. xvii. 7–9) sent Levites throughout all the cities of Judah to teach the people from the book of the law of the Lord, he was doubtless using the Levites in a way familiar to the nation from the first. God's people were to keep in mind that they were not to follow the light of nature, but to consult the divine oracles for all their guidance (Rom. iii. 2).

Redemption was a *plan*, and the Church was a *scheme*, and the soul of the scheme was the written word of God.

2. The tears of penitence naturally lead to joy. When men mourn for sin, the Lord comforts them, saying: "Go your way, eat the fat and drink the sweet." The sinful woman who bathed our Saviour's feet with tears heard him say: "Go in peace" (Luke vii. 50). There may have been much that was only mere excitement, without a religious basis, both in the weeping and the merriment of this month of Tisri; yet we cannot but believe that there was a nucleus of true devotion in the movement, a mark of the holy succession that reached down to Simeon and Anna.

3. The booths of the tabernacle-feasts were memorials of the booth life of Israel (on leaving Egypt) that began at Succoth. The memory would encourage humility and gladness, bringing the thoughts of the people back to first principles, and making them to feel the Divine presence and protection (see Lev. xxiii. 43). The roofs of the houses were battlemented so as to preclude danger (Deut. xxii. 8) and the houses were low. The building of booths on the roofs was therefore a very natural thing. They would not be in the way of the multitude, and would have in each case somewhat of domestic privacy.

HOMILETICAL AND PRACTICAL.

Vers. 1–12. The holiday of the Lord's congregation. 1) Its cause: the exterior one lies in the time, it is the seventh month, the true one in the proofs God has given, since He has secured the existence of the congregation before the world, fortified their city, *etc.* 2) Its celebration. The congregation shows a longing for God's word, uses it in good order, and listens to it with reverence. 3) Its blessing: sadness turned into joy. The ever permanent elements in the true service of God. 1) On the side of the congregation: hunger for the word of God. 2) On the side of the teachers—the right handling of the word of God—commences with the praise of God, which awakens the assenting acknowledgment of the congregation, communication of the divine word, the explanation and application of the same. On both sides resignation to God's word and being.—BEDE: *Rogaverunt ipsi pontificem suum, ut allato libro mandata sibi legis, quæ agere debeant, replicaret, ut cum civitate ædificata, operis quoque placiti Deo structura consurgeret, ne sicut antea propter negligentiam religionis civitatis etiam ruina sequeretur.*—STARKE: Even the common people must take care that they shall have the word of God pure and clear. Young people should be made to listen to the divine word from their childhood, that they may learn to fear God. If in the Old Testament all without exception have been obliged to listen to the law, how inexcusable it is if the papacy does not allow this to the people. Hearers should not become tired and impatient even if the sermon is rather long. The principal part of the service of God consists in praise, and in this we resemble the God-praising angels. The singing of Collects, prayers and Thanksgivings should be in an intelligible language, that the hearer may understand and be able to respond Amen. The Amen in a public assembly should be sung by each and all. If we should bow the knees of our hearts in particular before the Lord, it is proper that in outward gestures also we should show our humility before God. Preachers must not forget prayer in the arrangement of divine service. If teachers publicly kneel down and pray to God, it is proper that the hearers also should fall upon their knees with them. Teachers should aim at lucidity in explaining the word of God. If God gives us a joyful day we should not forget the poor.

Rejoice in the Lord always! That is 1) possible, for in communion with the Lord we have consolation, promise, help, refreshment, *etc.*, in spite of all the calamities and difficulties of earth. 2) Necessary; for every day is holy to the Lord, and our conduct must always honor the Lord. 3) Wholesome; for joy in the Lord is our strength, and puts us in the position to wait with patience, makes us skilful, and guards us from all straying. Joy in the Lord is our strength, for 1) in ourselves we are weak and hesitating. 2) In the fulness of the Lord is grace for grace. 3) Precisely the joy in the Lord is fitted to cause us to have all that is comprehended in strength. With the prayer, gladden me with Thy help, and let my joy in Thee be my strength, can one gain anew each day consolation and joy, whatever task be before him.

Vers. 13–18. The festival of the people. 1) Its foundation—the divine command—God wishes that the congregation should celebrate the holiday. 2) Its form; it exhibits itself also externally; in the Old Testament by booths, which have their signification; in the New Testament through other ceremonies, which are not less full of meaning. 3) Its effect. Resignation to God's word and will, and from that a glorification of the entire life.—STARKE: Christians have in the world no continuing city, and their life is vain and fleeting. Well for them, then, if they strive to dwell in the eternal tents. Heb. xiii. 14. As the Jews had their holidays and festivals, so have we Christians, but upon the condition of Christian freedom. Coloss. ii. 16. The exercise of true religion gives a tranquil heart and joyful conscience; but false worship gives much annoying trouble, and tortures the conscience.

CHAPTER IX. 1–38.

1 Now [And] in the twenty and fourth day of this month the children of Israel
were assembled with fasting, and with sackclothes, and earth upon them [*i. e.*, upon
2 their heads]. And the seed of Israel separated themselves from all strangers [sons
of strangeness], and stood and confessed their sins, and the iniquities of their fathers.
3 And they stood up in their place and read in the book of the law of the LORD their
God *one* fourth part of the day; and *another* fourth part they confessed, and wor-
4 shipped the LORD their God. Then [And] stood up upon the stairs *of* the Levites,
Jeshua, and Bani, Kadmiel, Shebaniah, Bunni, Sherebiah, Bani, *and* Chenani, and
5 cried with a loud voice unto the LORD their God. Then [And] the Levites Je-
shua, and Kadmiel, Bani, Hashabniah, Sherebiah, Hodijah, Shebaniah *and* Petha-
hiah said, Stand up *and* bless the LORD your God for ever and ever [from eternity
to eternity], and blessed be [they blessed] thy glorious name [the name of thy
6 glory], which [and *it*] is exalted above all blessing and praise. Thou, *even thou,*
art LORD alone; thou hast made heaven, the heaven of heavens, with all their host,
the earth, and all *things* that *are* therein, the seas and all that is therein, and thou
7 preservest them all; and the host of heaven worshippeth thee. Thou *art* the LORD
the God, who didst choose Abram, and broughtest him forth out of Ur of the Chal-
8 dees, and gavest him the name of Abraham; and foundest his heart faithful before
thee and madest a [the] covenant with him to give the land of the Canaanites, the
Hittites, the Amorites, and the Perizzites, and the Jebusites, and the Girgashites, to
9 give *it, I say,* to his seed, and hast performed thy words; for thou art righteous:
and didst see the affliction of our fathers in Egypt, and heardest their cry by the
10 Red Sea [Sea of weeds]. And shewedst signs and wonders upon Pharaoh, and on
all his servants, and on all the people of his land: for thou knewest that they dealt
proudly against them. So didst thou [and thou didst] get thee a name, as *it is* this
11 day. And thou didst divide the sea before them, so that [and] they went through
the midst of the sea on the dry land; and their persecutors thou threwest into the
12 deeps, as a stone into the mighty waters. Moreover [and] thou leddest them in the
day by a cloudy pillar; and in the night by a pillar of fire, to give them light in
13 the way wherein they should go. Thou camest down also [And thou camest down]
upon Mount Sinai, and spakest with them from heaven, and gavest them right
14 judgments and true laws [laws of truth], good statutes and commandments: and
madest known unto them thy holy Sabbath, and commandedst them precepts,

15 [and] statutes, and laws, by the hand of Moses thy servant: and gavest them bread
from heaven for their hunger, and broughtest forth water for them out of the rock
for their thirst, and promisedst them that they should go in to possess the land
16 which thou hadst sworn [lifted up thy hand] to give them. But [And] they and
our fathers dealt proudly, and hardened their necks, and hearkened not to thy
17 commandments, and refused to obey, neither were mindful of thy wonders that
thou didst among them; but [and] hardened their necks and in their rebellion appointed a captain to return to their bondage [*in place of* "*in their rebellion,*" in
Egypt]; but thou *art* a God ready to pardon [a God of pardons] gracious and mer-
18 ciful, slow to anger, and of great kindness, and forsookest them not. Yea, when
they had made [Yea, they even made] them a molten calf, and said, This is thy
God that brought thee up out of Egypt, and had wrought [and wrought] great pro-
19 vocations; yet [and] thou in thy manifold mercies forsookest them not in the wil-
derness: the pillar of the cloud departed not from them by day, to lead them in the
way; neither the pillar of [the] fire by night, to show them light, and the way
20 wherein they should go. Thou gavest also [And thou gavest] thy good Spirit to
instruct them, and withheldest not thy manna from their mouth, and gavest them
21 water for their thirst. Yea forty years [And forty years] didst thou sustain them
in the wilderness, *so that* they lacked nothing; their clothes waxed not old, and
22 their feet swelled not. Moreover [And] thou gavest them kingdoms and na-
tions, and didst divide them into corners [*or* districts]: so they possessed the land
of Sihon, and the land of the king of Heshbon [*perhaps,* the land of Sihon, the king
23 of Heshbon], and the land of Og, king of Bashan. Their children also multipliedst
thou [And their children thou didst multiply] as the stars of heaven, and brought-
est them into the land, concerning which thou hadst promised to their fathers, that
24 they should go in to possess *it.* [So [And] the children went in and possessed the
land, and thou subduedst before them the inhabitants of the land; the Canaanites,
and gavest them into their hands, with their kings, and the people of the land, that
25 they might do with them as they would. And they took strong cities, and a fat
land, and possessed houses full of all goods, wells digged [cisterns hewn], vineyards
and oliveyards, and fruit trees in abundance: so [and] they did eat, and were filled,
26 and became fat, and delighted themselves in thy great goodness. Nevertheless
[And] they were disobedient, and rebelled against thee, and cast thy law behind
their backs, and slew thy prophets which testified against them to turn them to thee,
27 and they wrought great provocations. Therefore [And] thou deliveredst them into
the hand of their enemies who vexed them: and in the time of their trouble when
they cried [their oppressors who oppressed them: and in the time of their oppres-
sion they cried] unto thee, [and] thou heardest *them* from heaven; and according
to thy manifold mercies thou gavest them saviours, who saved them out of the hand
28 of their enemies [oppressors]. But after they had rest, they did evil again [they
returned to do evil] before thee: therefore leftest thou [and thou leftest] them in
the hand of their enemies, so that they had the dominion over them yet when
[and] they returned, and cried unto thee, [and] thou heardest *them* from heaven;
29 and many times didst thou deliver them according to thy mercies; and testifiedst
against [to] them, that thou mightest bring them again unto thy law: yet [and]
they dealt proudly, and hearkened not unto thy commandments, but [and] sinned
against thy judgments, which if a man do, he shall live in them [which a man shall
do and live in them], and withdrew the shoulder [gave a resisting shoulder], and
30 hardened their neck, and would not hear [did not hear]. Yet [And] many years
didst thou forbear them [*i. e.*, act forbearingly towards them], and testifiedst against
[to] them by thy Spirit in thy prophets [by the hand of thy prophets]; yet would
they not give ear [and they did not give ear] therefore gavest thou [and thou
31 gavest] them into the hand of the people of the lands. Nevertheless [And] for
thy great mercies' sake [in thy great mercies] thou didst not utterly consume them,
32 nor forsake them; for thou *art* a gracious and merciful God. Now therefore [and
now], our God, the great, the mighty, and the terrible God, who keepest covenant
and mercy [the covenant and the mercy], let not all the trouble [distress] seem
little before thee, that hath come upon us [found us], on our kings, on our princes,

and on our priests, and on our prophets, and on our fathers, and on all thy people,
33 since the time of the kings of Assyria unto this day. Howbeit [And] thou *art* just
in all that is brought [comes] upon us; for thou hast done right, but [and] we have
34 done wickedly: neither have our kings, our princes, our priests, nor our fathers
kept [done] thy law, nor hearkened unto thy commandments and thy testimonies,
35 wherewith thou didst testify against [to] them. For they have not served thee in
their kingdom and in thy great goodness [blessings of prosperity] that thou gavest
them, and in the large and fat land which thou gavest before them, neither turned
36 they from their wicked works. Behold, we *are* servants this day, and [*as*] *for* the
land that thou gavest unto our fathers to eat the fruit thereof and the good thereof,
37 behold, we *are* servants in it: and it yieldeth much increase unto the kings whom
thou hast set over us because of our sins: also [and] they have dominion over our
38 bodies, and over our cattle, at their pleasure, and we *are* in great distress. And
because of all this we make a sure *covenant*, and write *it;* and our princes, Levites,
and priests seal *unto it* [are on the sealed covenant].

TEXTUAL AND GRAMMATICAL.

[1] Ver. 8. כָּרוֹת inf. abs. for כָּרֹת.

[2] Ver. 22. וַעֲמָמִים. This Aramæan form is found in Judges v. 14, where it is poetical.

[3] Ver. 26. נַאֲצוֹת, In this phrase (see 1 Kings xiv. 9; Ezra xxiii. 35, and here) the Tsere becomes Pattahh, as if from גַּו not גֵּו.

[4] Ver. 28. רַבּוֹת עִתִּים for עִתִּים רַבּוֹת.

[5] Ver. 38. אֲמָנָה. That this is not an adjective with בְּרִית understood is evident from its use in chapter xi. 23.

EXEGETICAL AND CRITICAL.

The Confession.

The confession recorded in this chapter uses largely the language of the older Scriptures. For ver. 6 see Ps. lxxxvi. 10; Ex. xx. 11, and Deut. x. 14. For ver. 9, see Ex. iii. 7. For ver. 10, see Jer. xxxii. 20. For ver. 11, see Ex. xv. 5, 10. For ver. 12, see Ex. xiii. 21. For ver. 13, see Ex. xix. 20. For ver. 15, see Ps. cv. 40, 41. For ver. 16, see 2 Kings xvii. 14. For ver. 17, see Ps. lxxviii. 11; Ex. xxxiv. 6. For ver. 25, see Deut. vi. 10, 11. For ver. 27, see Judg. ii. 14, 18. For ver. 29, see Lev. xviii. 5. For ver. 33, see Ps. cvi. 6. For ver. 35 and ver. 36, see Deut. xxviii. 47, 48.

Ver. 1. **The twenty and fourth day of this month.**—The 'Atzereth was the 22d day of Tisri. Two days after is this special day of fasting and confession. It must not be confounded with the *Yom-hak-kippurim* or Day of Atonement, which was the 10th of Tisri.

Earth upon them, *i. e.*, on their heads (see 1 Sam. iv. 12). Both earth and ashes were used on the head as a sign of sorrow. Comp. 2 Sam. xiii. 19. Our Eng. version has written here **sackclothes**, but everywhere else has used *sackcloth* for the Heb. plural.

This fasting, mourning and confession was not a swing of the pendulum to the other extreme from the joy and gladness of the Tabernacle's feast, but the action of the same religious spirit which recognized God's great favors, but which at the same time recognized the great errors of the people.

Ver. 2. The *Bene-nechar* or **strangers** were foreigners who had become mixed with the Jews by commercial interest or by marriage. Comp. chap. xiii. 3, 27.

Ver. 3. **And read.**—Probably as before, Ezra reading from the high platform to the great multitude, and the Levites explaining in different parts of the crowd. **One-fourth part of the day.**—Probably half way to noon. **Another fourth part.**—Probably the rest of the time till noon. Comp. chap. viii. 3.

Ver. 4. **Stairs.**—See on chap. viii. 4. **Jeshua, Bani, Kadmiel, Shebaniah, Sherebiah** appear again in ver. 5, but **Bunni, Bani** (2) and **Chenani** are replaced there by **Hashabniah, Hodijah,** and **Pethahiah.** So there appears to have been two movements. The Levites mentioned in the fourth verse opened the service with a loud cry, perhaps a doxology, and then the Levites mentioned in the fifth verse began the confession. **Bunni** is perhaps *Binnui* of chap. x. 9. **Bani** (2) is perhaps Benina of chap. x. 13. **Chenani** is probably Hanan of chap. x. 10.

Ver. 5. **Hashabniah.**—In chap. x. 11 *Hashabiah.* **Hodijah.**—See chap. x. 10. **Pethahiah.**—Perhaps *Pelaiah* of chap. x. 10. The only Levites mentioned as sealing in chap. x. who are not mentioned here are, then, Kelita, Micha, Rehob, Zaccur, Shebaniah (2), Hodijah (2).

Stand up and bless the Lord your God for ever and ever.—This the eight Levites cry out to the people (some having perhaps seated themselves), and then they make the confession to God, doubtless from a written document prepared for the occasion, so that all the eight speak together, and so make a strong voice to be heard by all. The Hebrew of this confession is quite pure and largely borrowed from the older books.

And blessed be thy glorious name.—Here the Fut. Piel is, with *wav conversive*, an assertion made by Nehemiah himself in an ejaculatory form to God, thus: "The Levites said,

Stand up and bless the Lord, *etc.*, and they [*i. e.*, the people] blessed thy glorious name, which is exalted above all blessing and praise." The words of the people then begin with ver. 6.

Ver. 6. **Heaven of heavens.**—Intensive, for the unseen as well as seen heaven. **Host of heaven**—*i. e.*, the angels.

Ver. 7. **Ur of the Chaldees** cannot be Mugheir by the Persian gulf, as is the present prevailing theory. The Chaldees or Casdim in Abraham's day (or in Moses' day) were not so far south. Ur was more likely in northern Mesopotamia, though scarcely so near to Haran as Oorfa. The Semitic stock to which Abraham belonged seem to belong to northern Mesopotamia.

Ver. 8. The Hivites are left out of this enumeration, perhaps to please their descendants, the Nethinim. (See Josh. ix. 7.)

Ver. 11. **Mighty**—in the sense of violent. Comp. Ex. xv. 5 for the figure.

Vers. 13, 14. **Judgments, laws, statutes, commandments, precepts.**—In Hebrew the words are (in the singular) *mishpah, torah, hok, mitzwah.* The last word is translated in E. V. by "commandments" and "precepts." The *mishpah* has the idea of discrimination and decision in it. The *torah* is a code. The *hok* is a separate decree. The *mitzwah* is a simple order. The adjectives "right," "true," and "good," are exactly appropriate.

Ver. 17. **Appointed a captain.**—In Num. xiv. 4 it is only stated that they proposed to appoint one. The proposition had been really carried out. **In their rebellion.**—LXX.: ἐν Αἰγύπτῳ, reading מצרים for מרים. The LXX. is probably right. Comp. Num. xiv. 4. The words in Heb. come after "to their bondage."

Ver. 18. **This is thy God.**—Here "this thy Elohim," and in Exod. xxxii. 4 "these thy Elohim." In each case only one God is referred to. The plural style of the sentence in Exodus, both as to the demonstrative and the verb, is simply a conformity to the plural *form* of Elohim. The molten calf may have been a copy of Apis or Mnevis, or it may have been a cherub. Indeed Apis and Mnevis may have been Egyptian forms of the primeval cherubim.

Ver. 19. **To show them light and the way wherein they should go.**—Better: *to shed light on them and the way, etc.*

Ver. 20. **Thou gavest also thy good Spirit.**—Referring to the event described in Numb. xi. Comp. Isa. lxiii. 11.

Ver. 22. **And didst divide them into corners.**—Rather: *And didst distribute them into districts.* The words "and the land of the," *weth eretz*, before "king of Heshbon," seem to be an error of transcription. "The land of Sihon, king of Heshbon, and the land of Og, king of Bashan" is probably the right reading (comp. Deut. ii. 26, 30, and 36), or the old formula may have been corrupted, "the land of Sihon, king of the Amorites, who dwelt at Heshbon," Deut. iii. 2, *etc.*

Ver. 24. **With their kings.**—Rather, *both their kings.*

Ver. 25. **Became fat.**—This is Hiphil as in Isa. vi. 10, and must be strictly rendered "made fat," *i. e.*, themselves.

Ver. 26. **Slew thy prophets.**—See 1 Kings xviii. 4; 2 Chron. xxiv. 21.

Ver. 27. **Their enemies who vexed them, and in the time of their trouble.**—Better: *their oppressors, who oppressed them, and in the time of their oppression.*

Ver. 29. **Testifiedst against.**—Rather, *testifiedst to.*—So in ver. 30 and ver. 34.

Ver. 32. **Since the time of the kings of Assyria,** *i. e.*, the days of Pul and Tiglath-pileser (2 Kings xv. 19, 29). This time was more than three centuries before Nehemiah's day.

Ver. 35. **In thy great goodness that thou gavest them.**—That is, *in the great prosperity (from thee) which thou gavest them.* So in ver. 25. "Thy goodness" is not God's moral attribute, but the prosperity He gave them.

Ver. 38. This verse is the first of the tenth ch. in Heb. Although the word "covenant" is inserted, it is warranted by the use of the verb "carath," the full expression being "carath berith."

HISTORICAL AND ETHICAL.

1. If we marvel at the readiness of Israel to fall away into alliances with the heathen, we must also marvel at their readiness to return to their separation before the testimony of their law. There is no greater wonder displayed to us in the books of Ezra and Nehemiah than the speediness of the work of these reformers in drawing away the people of Israel from alliances, where pecuniary interest and personal affection had formed a double and most potent bond. There must have been a prodigious vitality in the old Mosaic commonwealth. No mere philosophic reformers would have dared to venture on so radical a movement against the deep-seated tendencies of the people, and no people but those who had a truly divine side to their life would have hearkened to such a proposition. With all their errors, how much there is to admire in Israel!

2. Every covenant with God must, on man's side, be founded on penitential confession of sin. For God's grace, which is the content of His part of the covenant, cannot enter a soul that harbors its wickedness. When David acknowledged his sin unto God, God's forgiveness poured in upon his soul. (Ps. xxxii. 5.) After this chapter of confession comes the chapter of the covenant, with its natural issues of reform.

3. This confession is a prayer, although it has no petition in it. It is the laying of the soul before God in the attitude of awaiting. Often the best part of a prayer is its rehearsal of God's goodness and our own short-comings. This increases the receptivity of the soul. It removes worldliness, increases faith, makes the spiritual eyesight clearer, and brings it *en rapport* with heaven.

4. The distress of Israel under its political burdens is recognised as part of the discipline which God had exercised over the nation through its entire history. The covenant is not considered as broken by God in all this. He had been faithful. In this way Israel sees God's grace in the midst of the afflictions. An infidel heart would have regarded God as abandoning

His people, and have seen in their vicissitudes only the ordinary fate of nations. Events are to be judged not by their outward appearance, but by the subjective truth, on which they really depend. A godly soul understands this secret, and draws from it great peace and strength.

HOMILETICAL AND PRACTICAL.

Vers. 1–3. The penitential and fast-days of the Lord's congregation. 1) Their time and cause. They must alternate with facts and festivals; even God's favors must prompt us to observe them. 2) Their aim—to confess sins, our own as well as those of our ancestors, and to praise God's mercy as contrasted with them (ver. 2). 3) The manner of their celebration. Occupation with God's holy law forms the foundation which helps us to a right understanding of sin, and a right appreciation of the grace. The aim is penitence, as also faith, which worships the Lord (ver. 3).—BEDE: *Manifestius ostenditur, quanta gratia devotionis omnes eorum personæ novum post festa skenopægia conventum fecerint, ut videlicet se tota intentione a scelerum contagiis expurgatos divino fœderi conjungerent, ipsamque sancti fœderis conditionem et sermone confirmarent et scripto, acsi ab impiorum consortio separati securiores implerent opus, quod jam dudum cœperant; id est, congruos factæ urbis cives de numero piorum instituerent.*—STARKE: Confession of our sins before God is an effect of true contrition for the same. Such confession is necessary 1). As regards God who demands it (Jer. iii. 12, 13), who also wishes to be recognised by men as holy, just, and true, and will not forgive any sin without confession. (Ps. xxxii. 5.) As regards the Mediator; for as He confessed our sins and the sins of the whole world before God, with words and deed through suffering punishment for His people, so must we, much more, confess our own sins, if indeed we wish to be partakers of the merit of Christ. (1 John i. 7, 8.) 3) As regards the Holy Spirit's office of correction, whose work it is to convince the sinner. 4) As regards ourselves, for if we will not confess we remain under God's wrath. (1 John i. 8). 5) As regards our neighbor: for if we have provoked him, such provocation must be done away, and thereby the honor be given to God. God wishes that public assemblies should be held in the church. Heb. x. 15. When we keep penitential and fast-days, or go to the holy communion, we should fast, lay aside all adornment, and appear in plain dress, with honest, humble hearts.

Vers. 4–15. God's faithfulness to the covenant. 1) Its preparative activity. It lets itself far down, and gives the prospect of great and glorious things (vers. 4–8). Its saving activity (vers. 9–11). It takes pity upon misery, overcomes the oppressor, and removes hinderances and perplexities even in nature. 3) Its preserving and perfecting activities. It shows the way, and provides for God's flock, in body and soul, and incites it to appropriate the promises (ver. 8.) The goal of the Old and New Testament covenant life is, the earthly and heavenly inheritance. 1) The promise of the same. At the calling of Abraham; then in the gospel. 2) The way to it. Through the wilderness of Arabia; then through the wilderness of life. 3) The power which proceeds from it, particularly for Israel after it had obtained the same for us already, while we yet hope for it.—STARKE: Our good, heavenly Father gives earthly goods in possession to His children, in order that they may have good hope of the heavenly inheritance.

Vers. 16–25. God's pardoning grace. 1) He does not refuse it in spite of our disobedience (ver. 16), in spite of faithlessness (ver. 17), in spite of open backsliding (ver. 18). Much more, He shows His gracious presence to lead us to the high prize of the calling (ver. 19), gives His good and Holy Spirit for instruction; gives also the bread and water of life for hunger and thirst (ver. 20). 2) He punishes indeed, but affords, even in the time of punishment experiences, proofs, and advances of grace (vers. 21–23). 3) He brings us richly blessed to the prize of the calling (vers. 24, 25).

Vers. 20, 21. God's gracious care. 1) He provides both for bodily and spiritual necessities. 2) He provides it by great and small, startling and insignificant miracles. 3) He provides it during the march through the wilderness, that He may bring His people into Canaan.

Ver. 21. The wisdom of the divine care. 1) Its manner: God often helps, not in a startling, but in an insignificant way, quietly, yes, secretly blessing. 2) Its reason. The faith of His people is best tried, exercised, and strengthened in this way. 3) Its aim. That the godly may accustom themselves in all things, even in the insignificant, to perceive God's helping father hand, and shall learn the art to let all and everything, even the daily common-place, be a cause of thanks and of joy.—STARKE: God punishes the persecutors of His people energetically. Our pillar of cloud, which shows us the way to our everlasting fatherland, is the ministry of the gospel, in which God is truly present and powerful. Although God does not immediately place all the godly in fruitful and pleasant places, nor give them bread from heaven, nor water from the rock, still He gives them, notwithstanding, necessary nourishment and clothing wherewith they should be satisfied. Matt. vi. 31, 32; 1 Tim. vi. 8. The wickedness of mankind is so great when left to itself, that they are not bettered by the divine benefits, but indeed become worse, and in the highest ingratitude towards our God, return evil for good. Although with us is a multitude of sins, with God is plenteous redemption. Ps. cxxx. 7. Let no one therefore say with Cain, My sins are greater than it is possible to forgive. Gen. iv. 13.

Vers. 26–31. God's educating wisdom. 1) God indeed chastises, but He again has mercy (vers. 26, 27). 2) God has mercy many times, but He also admonishes to follow His precepts, in the observance of which man has his life (vers. 28, 29). 3) He admonishes a long while, and punishes and increases His punishment to the utmost if He is not listened to, but nevertheless He never gives him entirely up whom it is possible to help (vers. 30, 31).

Vers. 26–37. The grounds for the petition for forgiveness and mercy. 1) God's unwearied mercy in the past (vers. 26–31). 2) God's justice and our guilt in the present, particularly as they are to be recognised in connection with our troubles (verses 32–35). 3) The greatness of our need and trouble (vers. 36, 37).

Vers. 32–37. The debasement of the congregation at the present time. 1) Wherein it consists. 2) What is its cause. 3) What its aim.—STARKE: It is very consoling to think of the mercy of God which He has shown to our ancestors, for the same God lives yet. We must hold ourselves in true faith to the promises of God, for they will never fail. When the godly are involved in the greatest danger God cares for them the most, and knows how to rescue them. We are chastised by God that we may not be condemned with the world. When God wishes to deliver His people, He does not look at what they have deserved, but at what His immeasurable mercy demands. Those who have provoked God to anger by their sins have little happiness to expect so long as they go on without penitence. True confession—confession of the name of God and believing prayer, are the right means by which the enemy are again to be driven away. Lord, when trouble is present, they seek thee, *etc.* Isa. xxvi. 16. Although a false religion may have a great appearance of sanctity and piety before people, yet is it in the sight of God a great abomination. What beautiful surnames has God. Oh soul! mark them well, that thou mayest remember them when conscience accuses, and when thou art in trouble, that thou mayest not despond.

CHAPTER X. 1–39.

1 Now those that sealed [and on the sealed documents] were Nehemiah, the Tir-
2 shatha, the son of Hachaliah, and Zidkijah [*i. e.*, Zedekiah] Seraiah, Azariah, Je-
3, 4, 5 remiah, Pashur, Amariah, Malchijah, Hattush, Shebaniah, Malluch, Harim,
6, 7 Meremoth, Obadiah, Daniel, Ginnethon, Baruch, Meshullam, Abijah, Mijamin,
8, 9 Maaziah, Bilgai, Shemaiah: these *were* the priests. And the Levites: both Je-
10 shua the son of Azaniah, Binnui of the sons of Henadad, Kadmiel; and their bre-
11 thren, Shebaniah, Hodijah, Kelita, Pelaiah, Hanan, Micha, Rehob, Hashabiah,
12, 13, 14 Zaccur, Sherebiah, Shebaniah, Hodijah, Bani, Beninu. The chief of the
15, 16 people: Parosh, Pahath-moab, Elam, Zatthu, Bani, Bunni, Azgad, Bebai, Ado-
17, 18 nijah, Bigvai, Adin, Ater, Hizkijah [*i. e.*, Hezekiah], Azzur, Hodijah, Hashum,
19, 20, 21 Bezai, Hariph, Anathoth, Nebai, Magpiash, Meshullam, Hezir, Meshezabeel,
22, 23, 24 Zadok, Jaddua, Pelatiah, Hanan, Anaiah, Hoshea, Hananiah, Hashub, Hal-
25, 26 lohesh, Pileha, Shobek, Rehum, Hashabnah, Maaseiah, and Ahijah, Hanan,
27 Anan, Malluch, Harim, Baanah.

28 And the rest of the people, the priests, the Levites, the porters, the singers, the
Nethinim, and all they that had separated themselves from the people of the lands
unto the law of God, their wives, their sons, and their daughters every one having
29 knowledge *and* having understanding; they clave to their brethren, their nobles,
and entered into a curse and into an oath, to walk in God's law, which was given
by [the hand of] Moses the servant of God, and to observe and do all the com-
30 mandments of the LORD our Lord, and his judgments and his statutes; And that
we would not give our daughters unto the people of the land, nor take their daugh-
31 ters for our sons: And *if* the people of the land bring ware or any victuals on the
Sabbath day to sell, *that* we would not buy it of them on the Sabbath or on the
holy day: and that we would leave [*i. e.*, leave the land to lie untilled] the seventh
32 year and the exaction [loan] of every debt [hand]. Also [And] we made ordi-
nances for us, to charge ourselves yearly with the third part of a shekel for the ser-
33 vice of the house of our God; for the shewbread [the bread of arrangement], and
for the continual meat-offering, and for the continual burnt-offering of the Sabbaths,
of the new moons, for the set feasts, and for the holy *things*, and for the sin-offer-
ings, to make an atonement for Israel, and *for* all the work of the house of our God.
34 And we cast the lots among the priests, the Levites, and the people, for the wood-
offering, to bring it into the house of our God, after the houses of our fathers, at
times appointed year by year, to burn upon the altar of the LORD our God, as *it is*
35 written in the law: And to bring the first-fruits of our ground, and the first-fruits

36 of all fruit of all trees, year by year, unto the house of the LORD: also the first-
born of our sons, and of our cattle, as it is written in the law, and the firstlings of
our herds and of our flocks, to bring to the house of our God, unto the priests that
37 minister in the house of our God: and *that* we should bring the first-fruits [begin-
ning] of our dough [groats], and [*of*] our offerings [oblations], and [*of*] the fruit
of all manner of trees, of [new] wine and of oil, unto the priests, to the chambers of
the house of our God; and the tithes of our ground unto the Levites, that the same
Levites might have the tithes [*perhaps*, and they the Levites pay tithes] in all the
38 cities of our tillage [service]. And the priest the son of Aaron shall be with the
Levites, when the Levites take [*perhaps*, pay] tithes: and the Levites shall bring
up the tithe of the tithes [tithe] unto the house of our God, to the chambers, into
39 [belonging unto] the treasure house. For the children [sons] of Israel and the
children [sons] of Levi shall bring the offering [oblation] of the corn, of the new
wine, and [of] the oil, unto the chambers, where are the vessels of the sanctuary,
and the priests that minister, and the porters, and the singers: and we will not for-
sake the house of our God.

TEXTUAL AND GRAMMATICAL.

[1] Ver. 31. וְנִטֹּשׁ אֶתהַשָּׁנָה הַשְּׁבִיעִית וּמַשָּׁא [or וּמַשָּׁא] כָל־יָד. The ellipsis is to be filled from Ex. xxiii. 11. וְהַשְּׁבִיעִת תִּשְׁמְטֶנָּה וּנְטַשְׁתָּהּ, where the pronoun refers to אֶרֶץ of the preceding verse.

[2] Ver. 37. הַמְעַשְּׂרִים here and בַּעְשֵׂר in ver. 38. (Piel part. and Hiph. inf. of עַשֵּׂר), if we follow the analogy of Deut. xiv. 22, and xxvi. 32, must refer to the paying and not to the receiving tithes.

EXEGETICAL AND CRITICAL.

The Covenant.

Vers. 1–8. Because of these twenty-three names fifteen are supposed to be found in the list (ch. xii. 1–7) of the priests who came with Zerubbabel in the preceding century, it is held by many that this list contains only family names, and that these families were represented by descendants in the signing, Ezra, for example, signing for his ancestor Seraiah. But as we find Nehemiah in the list, and also the very Levites (vers. 9–13), who individually stood upon the stairs on the 24th of Tisri (chap. ix. 4, 5), it is better to suppose that the similarity of the names is accidental, and that family names only occur in the list of the people, vers. 14–27, if even there. The only alternative is harsh in two features: first, that the Levites on the stairs should be called, in a plain historical statement, by their family names; and secondly, that family names and personal names should be so strangely mixed. Moreover, it is to be noted that the family names of chap. vii. and of Ezra ii. are not all repeated here. We have abundant evidence of the very common use of the same names among the Israelites, and a theory, which that fact will explain, seems the easier one here.

Vers. 9–27. See above note.

Ver. 28. **The rest of the people**, *i. e.*, besides the chiefs given in vers. 14–27. The word *rest* (Heb. *shear*) seems to carry its force to the other classes enumerated, to wit, *the rest of the priests, etc.;* that is, besides those enumerated. **Every one having knowledge and having understanding.**—This evidently qualifies the general phrase before it. Not all the rest, but those who had knowledge and understanding, joined their brethren in the reform.

Ver. 29. **Clave to their brethren, their nobles.**—That is, to their brethren, the chiefs above mentioned. **Commandments**, *etc.*—See on chap. ix. 13, 14.

Ver. 31. **We would leave the seventh year and the exaction of every debt.**—The verb *natash* (leave) here seems to have a pregnant meaning. *We would leave fallow the land each seventh year* (comp. Exod. xxiii. 11), *and remit at that time* (lit.) *the debt of every hand.* See Deut. xv. 2.

Ver. 32. **The third part of a shekel.**—This tax, thus first laid, became afterward a half shekel. (See Matt. xvii. 24, where the Greek is *didrachma, i. e.*, a half shekel.) The half shekel tax of Ex. xxx. 13 is another matter, not an annual tax, but ransom money to be taken at a census as a mark of the Lord's ownership.

Ver. 33. **The shew-bread.**—Heb. *lehem hammaareketh* (bread of arrangement). The older phrase is *lehem happanim* (bread of the face). **The continual meat-offering.**—Heb. *minhath hattamidh.*—**The continual burnt-offering.**—Heb. *olath hattamidh.* So the shew-bread is called *lehem hattamidh* (Num. iv. 7). So called as oft-recurring in distinction from the occasional offerings. Here, as we see, the offerings are those of each day, **of the sabbaths**, and **of the new moons.**—The **set feasts** are mentioned separately with *lamedh* (for).

Ver. 34. **For the wood-offering.**—Heb. *kurban haetzim.* The feast of the wood-offering (Josephus, *B. J.*, II. 17, 6) on the 14th of Ab arose from this institution of Nehemiah. It was the day when those assigned to the duty brought in the wood for the altar. (See Lev. vi. 12)

Ver. 35. **The first fruits of all fruits of all trees.**—See Lev. xix. 24 and comp. Deut. xxvi. 2.

Ver. 36. **The first born of our sons.**—That is, by bringing redemption-money, as ordered in Numb. xviii. 15, 16. **Cattle.**—Heb. *behemoth.* Here *unclean beasts*, as contrasted with the herds and flocks below. These were also redeemed. (See Num. *l. c.*)

Ver. 37. **First fruits of our dough** (groats or ground meal).—See Num. xv. 20. **Offerings** —*i. e.*, all special offerings. **Chambers.**—Heb. *lishcoth*. The cells or chambers in the courts of the temple. **Might have the tithes.**—Many read *might pay tithes*, anticipating the statement of the next verse. **Tillage.**—There may be a reasonable doubt whether *anodhah* ever means tillage, unless, as in 1 Chron. xxvii. 26, it is qualified by another noun. It may mean here "service" in the relation of servants to God, as elsewhere. To suppose that the cities of work or service must mean the country towns, is scarcely credible.

Ver. 38. **To the chambers, into the treasure house.**—Rather, *to the chambers of the treasure house*, one of the buildings in the temple area. **The tithe of the tithes** belonged to the priests (Num. xviii. 26–28), the children of Aaron.

HISTORICAL AND ETHICAL.

1. The natural leaders of a people are largely responsible for the people's conduct. The priests, Levites, and chiefs, the nobles of the nation readily find a following. Nehemiah, as Tirshatha, puts his own name first to the solemn reform-document, and then he causes the nobles to set their names to the instrument. A reform begun the other way in the lower circles of society is apt to degenerate into the excesses of revolution. The healing salt should be thrown in at the sources of the streams, if the waters are to be cured.

2. The points specially indicated, wherein the reform was most pressing, are (1) marriage alliances, (2) Sabbath-observance, (3) usury, (4) temple-taxes of the third part of a shekel, of first-fruits and of tithes. On these points we may believe the people had been especially remiss. They were the points where their covetousness would operate to undermine their piety, and thus the integrity of the commonwealth. Was not that, which has become a distinctive trait of the Israelitish race, already in Nehemiah's time beginning to develop itself?

3. When a people grow remiss in the support of religious privileges, the foundations of society are shaken. The moral tone of any people can only be cultivated and sustained by systematized methods, for natural depravity must take advantage of the lack of discipline, and prove too strong for morality. Religion, in any true and high sense, is an exotic, and must be tenderly cared for in this sin-grown earth. The zeal of Nehemiah and other reformers for the thorough establishment of religious rites is a wise example to all who come after them. Where the state cannot enforce such a result, public opinion can be made.

HOMILETICAL AND PRACTICAL.

Ver. 1. To what the consideration of the Lord's faithfulness to the covenant leads us: 1) To penitence and conversion which shows itself through obedience. 2) To faith—particularly in the fact that the Lord always keeps His covenant with us, and that it is only necessary that we on our part should confirm and maintain it. 3) To hope that the Lord will set us free, and evermore aid us to the glorious liberty of the children of God.

Vers. 31, 32. The principal duties of the congregation and its members: 1) To keep themselves unspotted, and particularly separated from the world. 2) To practice communion with the Lord, and especially in the way that is beneficial to us in this mortal state. BEDE: *Porro sabbatismus orationum ac devotionis nostræ, in qua vacamus a temporalibus agendis, ut æternitatis gaudia dulcius gustare mereamur, recte diei septimo adsignatur quia futuræ quietem vitæ ac beatæ laudationis imitatur: sed diem sabbathi alienigenæ quærunt profanare, cum terrenæ cogitationes in tempore nostræ orationis importune nos conturbant, et memoria sive delectatione temporalium rerum ab amore intimo nituntur extrahere.—Imponunt asinis vinum, uvas et ficus et omne onus, et inferunt in Hierusalem, cum oblectamentis carnalibus stultos animi nostri motus onerantes, per hæc et hujus modi tentamenta quietem nostri cordis deo debitam violare conantur.* Comp. chap. xiii. 15.

Vers. 33–40. The tasks to which each member of the congregation must submit himself. 1) The offerings which must be made directly to the Lord for the erection of His buildings, expenses of the service, *etc.* 2) The doing that which assists the servants of the Lord. STARKE: My God! I remember that I too made a covenant with Thee at my baptism. I beseech thee seal the same also in me, and give me in my heart the pledge, the Holy Spirit (2 Cor. i. 21, 22; 2 Cor. v. 5). We must not only ourselves have a Christian zeal for true religion, but also incite others to it, and admonish them (Heb. x. 24; Ps. xlix. 2). Marriages with the godless are displeasing to God, and dangerous (1 Tim. ii. 14). Nothing must be so near to us that it withdraws us from the service of God.

CHAPTER XI. 1–36.

1 AND the rulers of the people dwelt at Jerusalem: the rest of the people also
[and the rest of the people] cast lots, to bring one of ten to dwell in Jerusalem, the
2 holy city, and nine parts *to dwell* in [the] *other* cities. And the people blessed all
the men that willingly offered themselves to dwell at Jerusalem.

3 Now [And] these *are* the chief of the province that dwelt in Jerusalem: but in
the cities of Judah dwelt [and which dwelt in the cities of Judah] every one in his
possession in their cities, *to wit*, Israel [*i. e.*, the people], the priests, and the Le-
4 vites, and the Nethinim, and the children [sons] of Solomon's servants. And at
Jerusalem dwelt *certain* of the children [sons] of Judah, and of the children [sons]
of Benjamin. Of the children [sons] of Judah; Athaiah, the son of Uzziah, the
son of Zechariah, the son of Amariah, the son of Shephatiah, the son of Mahala-
5 leel, of the children [sons] of Perez (*i. e.*, Pharez): and Maaseiah, the son of Ba-
ruch, the son of Col-hozeh, the son of Hozaiah, the son of Adaiah, the son of Joia-
6 rib, the son of Zechariah, the son of Shiloni [Shelah's family]. All the sons of Pe-
rez that dwelt at Jerusalem *were* four hundred three-score and eight valiant men.
7 And these are the sons of Benjamin; Sallu the son of Meshullam, the son of
Joed, the son of Pedaiah, the son of Kolaiah, the son of Maaseiah, the son of Ithiel,
8 the son of Jesaiah [*i. e.*, Isaiah]. And after him Gabbai, Sallai, nine hundred
9 twenty and eight. And Joel the son of Zichri *was* their overseer: And Judah the
10 son of Senuah was second over the city [was over the second city]. Of the priests:
11 Jedaiah the son of Joiarib, Jachin. Seraiah, the son of Hilkiah, the son of Me-
shullam, the son of Zadok, the son of Meraioth, the son of Ahitub, *was* the ruler of
12 the house of God. And their brethren that did the work of the house *were* eight
hundred twenty and two: and Adaiah, the son of Jeroham, the son of Pelaliah, the
13 son of Amzi, the son of Zechariah, the son of Pashur, the son of Malchiah, and his
brethren, chief of the fathers, two hundred forty and two: and Amashai, the son
14 of Azareel, the son of Ahasai, the son of Meshillemoth, the son of Immer, and their
brethren, mighty men of valour, a hundred twenty and eight, and their overseer
was Zabdiel, the son of one of the great men [son of the mighty].

15 Also [And] of the Levites: Shemaiah the son of Hashub, the son of Azrikam,
16 the son of Hashabiah, the son of Bunni; and Shabbethai and Jozabad, of the chief
of the Levites *had* the oversight of [*were* over] the outward business of the house of
17 God. And Mattaniah, the son of Micha, the son of Zabdi, the son of Asaph, *was*
the principal to begin the thanksgiving in prayer [*perhaps*, the chief of the praise-
song who gave thanks at prayer-service]: and Bakbukiah the second among his
brethren, and Abda the son of Shammua, the son of Galal, the son of Jeduthun.
18, 19 All the Levites in the holy city *were* two hundred fourscore and four. More-
over [And] the porters, Akkub, Talmon, and their brethren that kept the gates,
were a hundred seventy and two.

20 And the residue of Israel, of the priests, *and* the Levites, *were* in all the cities of
21 Judah, every one in his inheritance. But [And] the Nethinim dwelt in Ophel:
22 and Ziha and Gispa *were* over the Nethinim. The overseer also [and the overseer]
of the Levites at Jerusalem *was* Uzzi, the son of Bani, the son of Hashabiah, the
son of Mattaniah, the son of Micha. [Some] Of the sons of Asaph, the singers
23 were over the business of the house of God. For it [there] was the king's com-
mandment concerning them, that a certain portion should be for the singers [and
a sure ordinance concerning the singers] due for every day [the thing of a day on
24 its day]. And Pethahiah, the son of Meshezabeel, of the children of Zerah, the son
of Judah, was at the king's hand in all matters concerning the people.

25 And [As] for the villages with their fields, *some* of the children [sons] of Judah
dwelt at Kirjath-arba and *in* the villages [daughters] thereof, and at Dibon, and *in*
26 the villages [daughters] thereof, and at Jekabzeel and in the villages thereof, and
27 at Jeshua, and at Moladah, and at Beth-phelet, and at Hazar-shual, and at Beer-
28 sheba, and *in* the villages [daughters] thereof, and at Ziklag, and at Mekonah, and
29 in the villages [daughters] thereof, and at En-rimmon, and at Zareah, and at Jar-
30 muth, Zanoah, Adullam, and *in* their villages, at Lachish and the fields thereof, at
Azekah, and *in* the villages [daughters] thereof. And they dwelt from Beer-sheba
into the valley of Hinnom.

31 The children also of Benjamin [and the sons of Benjamin] from Geba
dwelt at Michmash [dwelt from Geba to Michmash] and Aija, and Bethel, and *in*
32 their villages [daughters], *and* at Anathoth, Nob, Ananiah, Hazor, Ramah, Git-
33, 34, 35 taim, Hadid, Zeboim, Neballat, Lod, and Ono, the valley of craftsmen.
36 And of the Levites *were* divisions *in* Judah, *and* in Benjamin [divisions of Ju-
dah *were* to Benjamin].

TEXTUAL AND GRAMMATICAL.

[1] Ver. 17. הַתְּחִלָּה instead of being an error for הַתְּהִלָּה, may be for בַּתְּחִלָּה, "chief *at the beginning* of prayer he gave thanks."

EXEGETICAL AND CRITICAL.

*The Places of Abode.**

Ver. 1. **The rest of the people also.**—*And the rest of the people*—that is, other than the rulers.

Ver. 2. **That willingly offered themselves**—*i. e.*, those of the people, beside the tenth part chosen by lot, who also consented to dwell in Jerusalem as the place of greatest danger and need. (See chap. vii. 4.)

Ver. 3. The relative construction should be used with both clauses, thus: *now these are the chiefs of the province who dwelt in Jerusalem, and those who dwelt in the cities of Judah (every one in his possession in their cities)—to wit, Israel, etc.* **Israel**—*i. e.*, the people of Israel as contrasted with priests, Levites, *etc.* **The children of Solomon's servants.**—See on chap. vii. 57.

Ver. 4. **Athaiah** was chief of the Bene-Pharets, or children of Perez (Pharez). See Gen. xxxviii. 29; 1 Chron. iv. 1. In 1 Chron. ix. 4 he is called *Uthai*, and his genealogy traced by a different line.

Ver. 5. **Maaseiah** was chief of the Shilonites or children of Shelah. His grandfather Colhozeh is probably the same as the father of Shallun in chap. iii. 15. He is called *Asaiah* in 1 Chron. ix. 5. **Shiloni.**—Heb.: *hash-shiloni.* Not a man's name, but a family's title, to wit, the children of Shelah, Judah's son. See 1 Chron. ix. 5. These descendants of Shelah are counted with those of Pharez. *Athaiah* and *Maaseiah* were thus the chiefs of Judah. *Jeuel* of the sons of Zerah, mentioned in 1 Chron. ix. 6, is omitted here.

Ver. 6. This verse appears to be out of its place. It should precede ver. 5.

* This chapter is intimately connected with chapter vii. 4, showing Nehemiah's plan of increasing the population of the city. The genealogies and then the confession and covenant came in parenthetically—the former as part of the process in the plan, and the latter as chronologically happening while Nehemiah was maturing the plan.

Ver. 7. The family of **Jesaiah** in Benjamin, of which **Sallu** was chief, is not otherwise known. Sallu's pedigree is differently reckoned in 1 Chron. ix. 7. The text in Chronicles is probably defective.

Ver. 8. **Gabbai** and **Sallai** are other Benjamite chiefs.

Ver. 9. **Joel the son of Zichri** was overseer (Heb.: *pakid*, ἐπισκοπος) over both the Judahites and Benjamites of the city. His office was possibly a police one. **Judah the son of Senuah** *was over the second city* (not **second over the city**).—The second city was a well-known part of Jerusalem. It was there Huldah the prophetess lived in Josiah's time. See 2 Kings xxii. 14, where the Eng. vers. has "college" for the Heb. *mishneh.* In Zeph. i. 10 the Eng. vers. has "second." It was probably the part of the city built up north of the temple. The parallel chapter in 1 Chron. (chap. ix.), which seems to be very corrupt in its reading, appears to have "Joel, the son of Zichri," in "Elah, the son of Uzzi, the son of Michri," and to have "Judah, the son of Senuah," in "Hodaviah, the son of Hasenuah," the former a Benjamite, and the latter an ancestor of Sallu. That list also introduces as Benjamites "Ibneiah, the son of Jeroham," and "Meshullam, the son of Shephatiah, the son of Reuel, the son of Ibnijah."

Joel and Judah were the two inspectors or overseers over the Judahites and Benjamites in the entire city.

Vers. 10, 11. There is great confusion in this part of the record, and we are not helped much by 1 Chron. ix. Both lists have been copied probably from a defective record. **Jedaiah, Joiarib** and **Jachin** were the heads of three of the twenty-four courses of priests in David's time (1 Chron. xxiv. 7, 17). **Seraiah** was high-priest before the captivity (1 Chron. vi. 14). These names appear to be fragments of a record which in its fulness showed the heads of these families in Nehemiah's time. The phrase "ruler of the house of God (*negid beth ha-elohim*) can belong to Ahitub or Seraiah. The Eng. vers. wrongly inserts "was." It is a title of the high-priest. See 2 Chron. xxxi. 13. Also compare 1 Chron. ix. 11. Also see 1 Chron. xii. 27, where Jehoiada (*negid* of the Aaronites) seems to be the same as Ahitub the father of Zadok.

In ver. 10 **Jedaiah, the son of Joiarib,** is doubtless wrong, and the form in 1 Chron. ix. 10 should be followed, to wit, *Jedaiah and Jehoiarib.* In ver. 11 (as in 1 Chron. ix. 11) the words **the son of Meraioth** are out of place and should follow "Ahitub," as Meraioth was grandfather (1 Chron. vi. 7) or great-grandfather (Ezra vii. 3) of Ahitub. For this last discrepancy we may suppose the two sequences in the high-priesthood of "Amariah, Ahitub, Zadok" (one before Solomon, and the other after Solomon) are the occasion. One list has taken the latter, where Ahitub's grandfather is Azariah, and the other has taken the former where Ahitub's grandfather is Meraioth. [We use "father" and "grandfather" in the formal sense, denoting the proximity of the names in the records, not the actual relationship.]

Ver. 12. **And their brethren**—*i. e.*, the brethren or kinsfolk of the chiefs of the priests whose names are lost in the above record (as we have seen in the preceding note). **Adaiah** was chief of the children of Malchiah, the head of the fifth course in David's day (1 Chron. xxiv. 9).

Ver. 13. **Chief of the fathers.**—This clause seems to be out of place, for we can hardly suppose that the Malchiah family were all chiefs. Adaiah had 242 in his kinsfolk, over whom he was chief, just as the representatives of the high-priest's family and the families of Jedaiah, Joiarib and Jachin had 822 in their kinsfolk (ver. 12). This phrase "chief of the fathers" belongs to all these head men of families, and was probably at the head of the list originally. It may have found its place here from the analogy of the phrase "mighty men of valour" in ver. 14. See 2 Chron. xxvi. 12 for a collocation of the two phrases. **Amashai** (*Maasiai* in 1 Chron. ix. 12) was chief of the children of Immer, the head of the sixteenth course in David's time. His pedigree in 1 Chron. ix. is merely a corruption of this one.

Ver. 14. **Their brethren.**—Probably an error for "*his* brethren"—that is, Amashai's. **Their overseer was Zabdiel.**—He was *pakid* (see on ver. 9) of all the priests. He is called *son of the mighty ones*—a phrase that seems to denote a remarkable ancestry. The numbers here and in 1 Chron. ix. 13 differ by 568. Errors in numbers and in names are almost necessities in transcribing.

Vers. 15–17. This list of Levites omits the names of *Heresh, Galal* and *Berechiah,* given in 1 Chron. ix. 15, 16; but contains the names of *Shabbethai* and *Jozabad* not mentioned there. In this list (ver. 14) we have **the son of Bunni** (*i. e.*, Bani, one of the families of Merari), where in 1 Chron. ix. 14 we find "of the sons of Merari." **Bakbukiah** here is *Bakbakkar* there. **Zabdi** here is *Zichri* there. **Abda** here is *Obadiah* there. Of the Levitical chiefs, Shabbethai and Jozabad **had the oversight of the outward business of the house of God.**—That is, attended to the secular department of service as directors therein (comp. 1 Chron. xxvi. 29). **The principal to begin the thanksgiving in prayer.**—Literally "the chief of the beginning gave thanks to prayer." Some would read *tehillah* instead of *tehhillah,* a most natural correction. We should then have "the chief of the praise-song [who] gave thanks (as introductory) to prayer."

Ver. 18. These six (or nine) Levitical chiefs had a constituency of 284.

Ver. 19. **Akkub, Talmon.**—The list in 1 Chron. ix. adds Shallum (as chief of all) and Ahiman, and makes the number 212 instead of 172. The account in 1 Chron. is much more extended on this matter of the porters, thus showing that this record (as is that also) is but a fragment of an older document. Both copies have been marred in the transcribing.

Ver. 20. This verse belongs between ver. 24 and ver. 25, after Jerusalem is disposed of.

Ver. 21. **Nethinim—Ophel.**—See on chap. iii. 26.

Ver. 22. The *pakid* (see on ver. 9) of all the Levites, including the Nethinim, was **Uzzi**. The last clause should read: *The singers of the sons of Asaph* (or some of the sons of Asaph, the singers,—see same construction in ver. 25) *were over the business of the house of God.* This "business" is not the "outward business" of ver. 16. If (with Keil) we disregard the Athnahh, we may consider Uzzi's pedigree as going on in this last clause, thus: "the son of Micha, of the sons of Asaph the singers in the service of the house of God." In this case the parallel with ver. 17 would be striking. There may be an omission in that verse before Mattaniah, and this Uzzi may be the first of the three leading singers—Bakbukiah and Abda being the other two. But see next note.

Ver. 23. Read: *for it was the king's commandment concerning them and a sure ordinance for the singers for each day's duty* (lit. "the thing of a day on its day"). Uzzi was *pakid* of the Levites generally, but the Asaphites took turns in directing the Levitical work. This 23d verse—making the singers (in the plural) the main subject, seems to show that our E. V. is right in stopping Uzzi's genealogy (in ver. 22) at Micha, and then beginning a new passage. The Masorites took this view, as the Athnahh with Micha shows. There is probably some confusion between ver. 22 and vers. 15 and 17, if we may judge from the names. Compare the passage in 1 Chron. ix.

Ver. 24. Pethahiah of the Zerahites (or Zarhites) **was at the hand of the king.**—This does not mean that he was at Susa, but that he was the king's special agent. Comp. 1 Chron. xxiii. 28, where the Levites are said to be at the hand of the sons of Aaron. Pethahiah's office may have taken him often to Susa, and he would thus be the go-between between the king and Nehemiah.

Ver. 25. **Kirjath-Arba**—*i. e.*, Hebron (Josh. xiv. 15). **The villages thereof.**—Lit. *the daughters thereof.* The word is a different one from that at the beginning of the verse (*hatzêr*). It is repeated after Dibon, but the other word returns after Jekabzeel. This use of daughters for dependent towns is common in the earlier books. **Dibon.**—Doubtless the *Dimonah* of

Josh. xv. 22. **Jekabzeel.**—The *Kabzeel* of Josh. xv. 21.

Ver. 26. **Jeshua.**—Probably the *Shema* of Josh. xv. 26, the letters in Hebrew being easily mistaken in transcription. **Moladah** is El Milh. **Beth-phelet.**—The *Beth-palet* of Josh. xxi. 27.

Ver. 27. **Hazar-shual**—like all the above, except Hebron and Moladah, is unknown.

Beersheba is Bir es-Seba, twenty-five miles south-west of Hebron, and ten miles west of Moladah.

Ver. 28. **Ziklag**, conspicuous in David's history (1 Sam. xxx.), is supposed to be Asluj, on the road from El Milh to Abdeh. **Mekonah**—possibly a mistake for *Madmannah* of Josh. xv. 30. It only requires a *mem* dropped and a *daleth* changed to a *kaph.*

Ver. 29. **En-rimmon** is spoken of in Josh. xv. 32 as two places. Keil supposes them two towns closely neighboring which finally grew into one. **Zareah.**—*Zoreah* (Josh. xv. 33) or *Zorah* (Judg. xiii. 2) is Zurah, fourteen miles west of Jerusalem. **Jarmuth** is 16 miles south-west of Jerusalem, on the slope of the mountain country, and about eight miles from the Shephelah or Philistine plain. It is 15 miles from Hebron.

Ver. 30. **Zanoah** is Zanua, or, perhaps, Kh. Sanut. **Adullam**—identified by GANNEAU with Sh. Mudhkur, on the east side of Wady Sur, near Socoh. **Lachish**—36 miles south-west of Jerusalem. **Azekah** is Deir el Aashek. From Beersheba unto the valley of Hinnom (or valley of the sons, or son, of Hinnom) is a distance of nearly 50 miles.

Ver. 31. Read: *and the children of Benjamin dwelt from Geba to Michmash and Aija and Bethel and her villages.* **Geba** is Jeba. **Michmash** is Mukhmas. **Aija** or *Ai* is probably Tell el Hajar, as VAN DE VELDE thinks. **Bethel** is Beitin.

Ver. 32. **Anathoth** is Anata, Jeremiah's birth-place. **Nob** is probably Neby Samwil, according to Lieut. CONDER's suggestion (*Quarterly Statement of Pal. Expl. Fund.* London, Jan. 1875). **Ananiah** is unknown.

Ver. 33. **Hazor** is not identified. **Ramah** is Er-Ram. **Gittaim** is unknown.

Ver. 34. **Hadid** is supposed to be near Lydda. **Zeboim** is not identified. **Neballat** is Beit Nebala, near Lydda.

Ver. 35. **Lod** is Lydda (Ludd). **Ono** is believed to be near Lydda, at Kefr Auna. (See VAN DE VELDE.) **The valley of craftsmen**—*i. e.*, Charashim (see 1 Chron. iv. 14) was probably in the vicinity of Lydda.

Ver. 36. Read: *And of the Levites divisions of Judah went to Benjamin.* These Levites were transferred from former stations in Judahite towns to stations in Benjamite towns.

HISTORICAL AND ETHICAL.

1. Jerusalem was peculiarly the post of labor and danger,—of labor, because the fortifications would require constant guarding, and of danger, because the enemies of the Jews would naturally concentrate their efforts against the holy city. A willing offering of any to dwell in Jerusalem was therefore a mark of self-denial for the sake of country and religion. The popular blessing fell upon such. Even those who did not so volunteer could not but admire this devotion, and join in the general admiration. Happy is the people, where there is such a cause for the public favor.

2. The additional population of Jerusalem included men of Judah, men of Benjamin, Levites, and Nethinim. There were, doubtless, remnants of the ten tribes with preserved pedigrees mingled with the returned Jews, as we find four centuries later Phanuel mentioned as of the tribe of Asher (Luke ii. 36), but none of these seem to have been reckoned in the public genealogies. They had not come back with Zerubbabel, for it is not probable that many (if any) from the remnant of the ten tribes went into captivity under Nebuchadnezzar, unless we consider the coming to Jerusalem of "divers of Asher and Manasseh and Zebulun" in Hezekiah's day (2 Chron. xxx. 11) was a coming for a permanent abode. But we may believe, that, after the return, stragglers from the remnant of the northern kingdom joined the Jews at Jerusalem, for that in the north a remnant preserved the truth against all the immigration of heathen nations is evident from the appearance of Galilee in the New Testament period, which could not be owing simply to the Maccabean influences, such as are described in 1 Maccab. v. 21, seq.

HOMILETICAL AND PRACTICAL.

Vers. 1, 2. It might be very difficult for the poorer families of the congregation to find means of subsistence in Jerusalem, as there was no longer a royal court there, and a troop of higher officers, who could afford work and gain to the lower classes. They might find it much easier to get along in the country, where they could cultivate the ground. Nevertheless Nehemiah and the heads of the congregation had to insist upon it that as many as possible should settle again in Jerusalem. For this there were very urgent reasons. It was not the consideration alone that the congregation would only then be worthily represented to the neighboring people, and would only be in part secure, if it possessed a large, mighty, and flourishing chief city, to which, in times of danger, it could withdraw as to a trustworthy asylum. The main point was, that as many as possible of the congregation must live in direct proximity to the Temple and its service, that their connection with God could the better be furthered and fortified, and be promoted and consecrated, which was so desirable for it. There was the consideration that above all upon Zion and the mountain of the house of the Lord rested the promises of the prophets, and that especially from them the law and the word of the Lord should go forth. (Isa. ii. 2–4; Micah iv. 1.) The congregation should feel itself called upon, as much as lay in its power, to help in the fulfilment of such promises, also to further as much as possible, the honoring of the Lord there in Jerusalem. It had certainly in the prophetic word a warrant that the Lord would here protect and bless it. At least equally urgent calls has Christendom not to scatter itself hither and thither into all sorts of sects and communities, neither to be satisfied with the observance of religion in their houses, but to hold faithfully to the one church, which is founded on God's word and provided with His promises, and instead of despising it on account of its insignificance, poverty, and needs, all the more to raise it by all self-consecration and gratitude, even if one should thereby suffer disadvantages, and even dangers, in worldly things, and should draw upon himself slights and persecution. "And let us hold fast the profession of our faith without wavering, for He is faithful that promised; not forsaking the assembling of ourselves together, as the manner of some is." (Heb. x. 23–25.) That in which a sect has appeared to be preferable in power of love and sanctity has proved itself generally, in great part to be mere empty appearance.

Vers. 3–19. It is very worthy of notice that in the numbering of the inhabitants of Jerusalem, not the priests but the tribes of Judah and Benjamin take the lead, and only then follow the priests and Levites; so much the more worthy of notice, because in the new congregation, following the captivity, according to the entire direction which its development took, and according to everything which was considered as of the greatest moment, the high-priests, and the priesthood in general, had a particularly high significance. It is as if the consciousness were indicated, that the priests and Levites, in spite of their distinction, which the Lord had apportioned to them in the affairs of Israel, had been nevertheless nothing at all, if they had not had a congregation near and around them, and if they had not succeeded in obtaining satisfactory fruit for their activity, namely, a genuine and true piety, which should substantially prove they were not there in vain. Would also that Christian priests, that is, preachers of the gospel, might preserve a lively consciousness that it is not enough for them to have fellowship with their brethren in office, that they are nothing, and can profit and signify nothing, if not some, if only a small congregation stand by them, in whom the seed which they sow, springs up, grows, and bears fruit. STARKE: Ver. 3. In every time there are some pious and God-fearing people who separate themselves from the world, and seek the good of their souls rather than of their bodies.

Vers. 25–36. When one looks at the space which the Jewish congregation inhabited round Jerusalem, how very small was the territory occupied by the people of God, the only race which possessed a clear knowledge of the only true and holy God! A few miles, from three to six, north and south, east and west, comprised the entire district. Compared with our countries, yes, even with our provinces, this district appears to us almost as a vanishing nothing. And nevertheless what powers for the subjugation of entire humanity, for the transformation of all its relations, and for the subduing of all circumstances, has God the Lord been able to put in the people of this oasis, in the, at the same time insignificant, and in many respects miserable race, which cultivated the ground there or raised cattle! If any where surely here arises a testimony for Paul's word, "God hath chosen the weak things of the world to confound the things which are mighty." (1 Cor. i. 27.) A consoling promise also for Christendom in those times in which it appears as though it were being compressed on all sides, and when it is in truth losing position after position. Let it lose in length and breadth, in order afterwards to gain so much the more in height. Even the gates of hell cannot swallow up the church of the Lord.

STARKE: Ver. 25. God collects to Himself a church from among many peoples by the word of the gospel, that the heavenly Jerusalem may be filled.

CHAPTER XII. 1–47.

1 Now [And] these *are* the priests and the Levites that went up with Zerubbabel
2 the son of Shealtiel and Jeshua: Seraiah, Jeremiah, Ezra, Amariah, Malluch, Hat-
3, 4, 5 tush, Shechaniah, Rehum, Meremoth, Iddo, Ginnetho, Abijah, Miamin, Maa-
6, 7 diah, Bilgah, Shemaiah, and Joiarib, Jedaiah, Sallu, Amok, Hilkiah, Jedaiah.
These were the chief of the priests and of their brethren in the days of Jeshua.
8 Moreover [And] the Levites: Jeshua, Binnui, Kadmiel, Sherebiah, Judah, *and*
9 Mattaniah, *which was over* the thanksgiving, he and his brethren. Also [And]
10 Bakbukiah and Unni, their brethren, *were* over against them in the watches. And
Jeshua begat Joiakim, Joiakim also [and Joiakim] begat Eliashib, and Eliashib
11, 12 begat Joiada, and Joiada begat Jonathan, and Jonathan begat Jaddua. And
in the days of Joiakim were priests, the chief of the fathers: of Seraiah, Meraiah;
13, 14 of Jeremiah, Hananiah; of Ezra, Meshullam; of Amariah, Jehohanan; of Me-
15 licu, Jonathan; of Shebaniah, Joseph; of Harim, Adna; of Meraioth, Helkai;
16, 17 of Iddo, Zechariah; of Ginnethon, Meshullam; of Abijah, Zichri; of Minia-
18, 19 min, of Moadiah, Piltai; of Bilgah, Shammua; of Shemaiah, Jehonathan; And

20, 21 of Joiarib, Mattenai; of Jedaiah, Uzzi; of Sallai, Kallai; of Amok, Eber; of
22 Hilkiah, Hashabiah; of Jedaiah, Nethaneel. The Levites in the days of Eliashib,
Joiada, and Johanan, and Jaddua were recorded [according to the] chief of the
23 fathers: also [and] the priests, to the reign of Darius the Persian. The sons of
Levi, the chief of the fathers, were written [recorded] in the book of the Chronicles
[book of the events of the times], even until the days of Johanan, the son of Elia-
24 shib. And the chief of the Levites: Hashabiah, Sherebiah, and Jeshua the son of
Kadmiel with their brethren over against them to praise *and* to give thanks, ac-
cording to the commandment of David the man of God, ward over against ward.
25 Mattaniah, and Bakbukiah, [and] Obadiah, [were singers]. Meshullam, Talmon,
Akkub, *were* porters keeping the ward at the thresholds [treasuries] of the gates.
26 These *were* in the days of Joiakim the son of Jeshua, the son of Jozadak, and in
the days of Nehemiah the governor, and of Ezra the priest, the scribe.
27 And at the dedication of the wall of Jerusalem, they sought the Levites out of
all their places to bring them to Jerusalem, to keep the dedication with gladness
[to keep the dedication and festivity], both with thanksgivings and with singing,
28 *with* cymbals, psalteries and with harps. And the sons of the singers gathered them-
selves together, both out of the plain country [circuit] round about Jerusalem, and
29 from the villages of Netophathi; also [and] from the house of Gilgal [Beth-gilgal],
and out of the fields of Geba and Azmaveth: for the singers had builded their vil-
30 lages round about Jerusalem. And the priests and the Levites purified themselves,
31 and purified the people, and the gates, and the wall. Then [And] I brought up
the princes of Judah upon the wall, and appointed two great *companies of them
that gave* thanks, *whereof one* went on the right hand upon the wall toward the dung
32 gate [rubbish gate]. And after them went Hoshaiah, and half of the princes of
33, 34 Judah, and Azariah, Ezra, Meshullam, Judah, and Benjamin, and Shemaiah,
35 and Jeremiah, and *certain* of the priests' sons with trumpets; *namely* [*the priests'
names have fallen out—here follow the Levites' names*] Zechariah the son of Jonathan,
the son of Shemaiah, the son of Mattaniah, the son of Michaiah, the son of Zaccur,
36 the son of Asaph: And his brethren, Shemaiah, and Azarael, Milalai, Gilalai,
Maai, Nethaneel, and Judah, Hanani, with the musical instruments of David the
37 man of God, and Ezra the scribe before them. And at the fountain gate, which
was over against them, [and over the fountain gate and in front of them], they
went up by the stairs of the city of David, at the going up of the wall, above the
house of David, even unto the water gate eastward.
38 And the other *company of them that gave* thanks went over against *them*, and I
after them, and the half of the people, upon the wall from beyond [past] the tower
39 of the furnaces even unto the broad wall; and from above [past] the gate of Eph-
raim, and above [past] the old gate, and above [past] the fish gate, and the tower
of Hananeel, and the tower of Meah, even unto the sheep gate: and they stood
40 still in the prison gate. So [And] stood the two *companies of them that gave* thanks
41 in the house of God, and I, and the half of the rulers with me: And the priests;
Eliakim, Maaseiah, Miniamin, Michaiah, Elioenai, Zechariah, *and* Hananiah with
42 trumpets; and Maaseiah, and Shemaiah, and Eleazar, and Uzzi, and Jehohanan,
and Malchijah, and Elam, and Ezer. And the singers sang loud [made *their voice*
to be heard], with Jezrahiah *their* overseer.
43 Also [And] that day they offered great sacrifices, and rejoiced: for God had
made them rejoice with great joy: [and] the wives also and the children rejoiced:
so that the joy of Jerusalem was heard even afar off.
44 And at that time were some [men] appointed over the chambers [which were]
for the treasures, for the offerings, for the first fruits, and for the tithes to gather
into them out of [according to] the fields of the cities the portions of the law [*i. e.*,
appointed by the law] for the priests and Levites: for Judah rejoiced [the joy of
Judah *was*] for the priests and the Levites that waited [that stood *at their posts*].
45 And both the singers and the porters kept the ward of their God, and the ward of
the purification [And they kept the ward (or charge) of their God, and the ward
of the purification, and so did also the singers and the porters *keep their ward*], ac-
46 cording to the commandment of David, *and* of Solomon his son. For in the days

of David and Asaph [see note] of old, *there were* chief of the singers, and songs of
47 praise and thanksgiving unto God. And all Israel in the days of Zerubbabel, and
in the days of Nehemiah, gave the portions of the singers and the porters, every day his portion [the thing of a day on its day], and they sanctified [dedicated, *as in* 1 *Chron. xxvi.* 28] *holy things* unto the Levites; and the Levites sanctified *them* unto the children of Aaron.

TEXTUAL AND GRAMMATICAL.

[1] Ver. 38. לְמוֹאל for מוֹאֵל from the root יָאַל, according to Ewald. The usual form is מוּל or מוֹל. May it not be from אוּל, formed like a Hoph. participle?

EXEGETICAL AND CRITICAL.

The Dedication of the Walls.

Before the ceremony of the dedication is rehearsed, a preliminary statement regarding the priests and Levites, as chief actors in the dedication, is made.

Vers. 1–9. This is a list of the principal priests and Levites who came with Zerubbabel from Babylon in the preceding century.

We have already spoken of the *accidental* identity of names, in many of these, with those who sealed the Covenant (ch. x. 1–8). If the question is here asked, "Why, then, are not the names of the sealers put down in vers. 12-21, as the representatives of the old priestly houses of Zerubbabel's day?" the reply is that the sealers were in Eliashib's day, but the representatives of the priestly families in vers. 12-21 were of Joiakim's day, Eliashib's father. The persons were not the same, and hence we do not look for the same names. We have three sets of names. In ch. xii. 1-7 we have those of Jeshua's time (*i. e.*, Zerubbabel's); in ch. xii. 12-21, we have also those of Joiakim's day. In ch. x. 1-8 we have those of Eliashib's day.

But another question is raised by the fact that in Ezra ii. 36-39 and Neh. vii. 39-42 only four orders of priests are said to have come up with Zerubbabel, to wit, those of Jedaiah, Immer, Pashur, Harim, *i. e.*, the 2d, 3d, 5th and 16th orders, Pashur representing Malchijah, (see Neh. xi. 12), while here are twenty-two families. The answer is suggested by Keil that those four represent grand families (and not the four priestly orders) and these represent an inferior division into twenty-two, two of the names, Jedaiah and Harim, being accidentally the same with two of the four. I know not, however, why the four courses or orders may not be intended in ch. vii. 39-42 and the twenty-two families belong to these four. Keil's reasoning seems defective.

Ver. 7. **And of their brethren.**—This does not refer to the Levites, for they are especially mentioned immediately afterward. It is a phrase in apposition, thus "chief of the priests, namely, their brethren."

Jeshua or Joshua, the high-priest at the return from Babylon under Cyrus (B. C. 536), nearly a hundred years before.

Ver. 8. We have already shown that the identity of names here with those in ch. x. is accidental. See notes on ch. x. 1-13, and the first note in this chapter. Hence the identification of Judah, Mattaniah and Bakbukiah with Hodijah (ch. x. 10), Mattaniah of ch. xi. 17, and Bakbukiah of ver. 25 (which identification Keil suggests) is an error, as these last three were men of Nehemiah's time (see ver. 26), while the first three were of Jeshua's day, (see vers. 1, 7).

This Mattaniah and his brethren were **over the thanksgiving** (*'al huyyedoth*) in Jeshua's day. The Mattaniah of ch. xi. 17 was "the principal to begin the thanksgiving in prayer" (*rosh hat-tehillah yehodheh lat-tephillah*) in Nehemiah's day. The phrases are not identical. One refers to several men, the other to one.

Ver. 9. Bakbukiah and Unni were chiefs of the Levitical relays, who, in Jeshua's day, kept the watches over against the Levites commissioned to sing the thanksgivings. *Mishmar* must mean a watch or guard, even in ch. xiii. 14 and in Ezek. xxxviii. 7.

Vers. 10, 11. The pedigree of the high-priests from Zerubbabel's time to the time of Alexander the Great, *i. e.*, from B. C. 536 to B. C. 332. As Nehemiah's government of Jerusalem was B. C. 446–434, we have this genealogy carried a century beyond him by a later hand. **Jonathan** is evidently a mistake in transcription for *Johanan*, as in vers. 22 and 23.

Vers. 12–21. A list of the representatives in Joiakim's day of the priestly houses whose names are obtained from those chiefs of the priests who came with Zerubbabel, as given in vers. 1-7.

Melicu = *Malluch*. *Hattush* is omitted (see ver. 2). **Shebaniah** = *Shechaniah*. **Harim** = *Rehum*. **Meraioth** = *Meremoth*. **Miniamin** = *Miamin*. Miniamin's representative is omitted,—dropped accidentally in transcription. **Sallai** = *Sallu*. These changes in a list evidently intended to be a copy of one immediately preceding form a good instance of the uncertainty of names in these old genealogical registers.

Vers. 22, 23. An interjected statement by the later hand. The Levites were regularly to the time of Alexander the Great recorded by the names of their chiefs, and the priests also, that is, to the reign of Darius (Codomannus). But the book of the Chronicles (1 Chron. ix.) only contained their names to Johanan's high-priesthood. That is, probably in Jaddua's time the record was no longer engrossed. Keil's effort to make these verses refer to Nehemiah's time as the ultimate is ingenious but forced. The days of Johanan and the days of Jaddua cannot mean the days in which they were living as young men or boys, but the days of their active high-priesthood. Hence the Darius is not Nothus, but Codomannus.

Vers. 23–26. The Levites in Joiakim's day and in Nehemiah's time. **Hashabiah** = Hashabniah in ch. ix. 5.

Sherebiah (see ch. ix. 5). **Jeshua, the son of Kadmiel.** See ch. ix. 4, where *Jeshua and Bani and Kadmiel* is probably for "Jeshua ben Kadmiel." These were leaders of the singing Levites.

Mattaniah is put probably by mistake among the porters. He was a singer. (see ch. xi. 17). The same remark may be made of Bakbukiah and Obadiah (Abda). See, as before, ch. xi. 17.

Meshullam is *Shallum* in 1 Chron. ix. 17. **Porters keeping the ward at the treasuries of the gates.**—See 1 Chron. xxvi. 15, 17. These were the store-chambers attached to the various gates, inner and outer, belonging to the temple.

Ver. 26. Joiakim was probably high-priest when Ezra arrived at Jerusalem, Eliashib his son soon succeeding.

Ver. 27. The preliminary statements regarding the priests and Levites being ended, here begins the account of the dedication of the walls. **Out of all their places**, for the Levites were scattered throughout the province (see ch. xi. 3). **To keep the dedication with gladness.**—Instead of supposing a preposition wanting, we may take *sim'hah* as a concrete and read *to keep the dedication and festivity.*

Psalteries and **harps** differed but slightly from one another. The *nebel* or psaltery had more strings than the *kinnor* or harp. They both rather resembled our guitar than our harp.

Ver. 28. **The sons of the singers.**—Heb. *Benê hamshorerim.* That is the guild or company of singers of the three great Levitical families of Asaph, Heman and Jeduthun. **The plain country round about Jerusalem.**—Heb. *hakkikkar sevivoth yerushalayim.* There is no plain country round about Jerusalem. The *kikkar* must here be simply "circuit" (περίχωρος). Compare ver. 29.

If *kikkar* is to have here its specific meaning of "the valley of Jordan" (as Keil insists), then we must insert *umin 'hatzrê* between *hakkikkar* and *sevivoth* (for an omission likely to happen) and read "the valley of Jordan and from the villages round about Jerusalem." The idea that the valley of Jordan at Jericho could be said to be *sevivoth yerushalayim* (round about Jerusalem) is absurd.

Netophathi, the gentile noun without article, seems to be for *Netophah*, a place near Bethlehem (ch. vii. 26). Beit Netif, which is fourteen miles west of Bethlehem, seems too far off.

Ver. 29. **And from the house of Gilgal.**—Rather, *and from Beth-haggilgal* or Beth-Gilgal. Although we should look for a Jiljilia or a Beit-Jiljilia for the modern name of this place, yet as no such name occurs near Jerusalem, we may suppose Beit-Jala close to Bethlehem to be the modern representative.

Geba is now Jeba, six or seven miles north of Jerusalem. **Azmaveth** is not identified.

Ver. 30. The purification of priests, Levites, people, gates and wall was accomplished, doubtless, by a series of prescribed sacrifices.

Ver. 31. Read literally, *appointed two great thanksgivings, i. e.,* two great thanksgiving-companies. Perhaps the *thodhoth* in ver. 27 has this concrete meaning.

Judah is used in this verse for the whole people of Israel.

Whereof one went on the right hand.—Literally, *and processions on the right hand.* The whole passage should read, *and appointed two thanksgiving-companies and processions. On the right hand, etc.* (*i. e.*, the one on the right hand).

Although it is not mentioned, yet it is clear that the two processions started at the valley-gate, the same at which Nehemiah had started to examine the ruined walls of the city on his arrival (chap. ii. 13). The valley-gate was at or south of the present Jaffa Gate (see on chap. ii. 13). **Dung-gate.**—(See l. c.)

Vers. 32–34. There followed the one thanksgiving company of Levites to the right (*i. e.*, to the South) one-half the princes of Judah (*i. e.*, chiefs of the entire Jewish people) with Hoshaiah at their head. The names in vers. 33 and 34 are the names of these princes. The names of Judah and Benjamin are not the tribal names.

Ver. 35. **And certain of the priests' sons with trumpets.**—This should close a section, as the names that follow are not of priests but of Levites. The priests' names have probably dropped out. In the corresponding list of the other procession the priests' names are given (see ver. 41). **Priests' Sons, *i. e.*,** sons of the priests, *i. e.*, priests.

Zechariah, an Asaphite, is leader of those who bear the Davidic instruments of music.

Ver. 36. Zechariah had eight with him, as Jezrahiah had eight with him in the other band (see ver. 42).

Ezra the scribe went before all except the thanksgiving-company of ver. 31, just as Nehemiah took this position in the other band (see vers. 38, 40).

Ver. 37. **The fountain-gate** we believe to have been near the pool of Siloam, and **the water-gate** to have been an interior gate not far from the present south wall of the Haram. (See for these and the stairs of the city of David the notes on ch. iii. 15, 26; also see Excur.). We may read this verse, *and over the fountain gate and in front of them they went up over the stairs of the city of David at the going up of the wall above the house of David even unto the water-gate eastward.* We explain this description thus; that the procession kept along the south wall of Zion until it reached a point on the descent of that wall over against the fountain-gate and the pool of Siloam. There it would be *over the fountain-gate.* At this point it turned north ("in front of them"), leaving the main wall and passing up over the line of the great stairs that led up to the city of David (Zion), where an inner wall ran up and along the eastern crest of Zion. This inner wall had a place called *Beth-David* below it on the side of the Tyropœon valley. (Or if *me'al* be translated "past," then the Beth-David may be placed above). The procession would thus pass along Zion's eastern front and cross over to Ophel and the water gate at a point where the Tyropœon was not so deep and broad.

Ver. 38. **And the other company of them that gave thanks.** (See on ver. 31).

Read *and the second thanksgiving company which*

went in the opposite direction, and which I followed and half the people (went) *upon the wall past the tower of the furnaces even to the broad wall.* By "the people" are meant those who formed the procession, not the people at large. The Heb. *me'al* here when used before "the tower of the furnaces" must mean "past." We cannot conceive the procession's passing over a tower. (See note on ver. 37, where the phrase "above the house of David" occurs). For "the tower of the furnaces" and "the broad wall," see on ch. ii. 8, 11. Also see Excursus.

Ver. 39. **The gate of Ephraim** must have been at the north-eastern extremity of the broad wall. **The prison gate** was on the north side of the temple, not connected with the palace prison of Jer. xxxii. 2. See Excursus. (For the other localities here mentioned, see on chap. ii. and Excursus.)

Vers. 40–42. The latter part of ver. 40 and verses 41 and 42 belong before the former part of ver. 40. There may have been an error of transcription, or it may be a roughness of rhetoric.

Comp. ver. 41 with the first part of ver. 35, and verse 42 with vers. 35 and 36.

Ver. 43. **Great sacrifices,** *i. e.*, thank-offerings which were eaten by the offerers in a happy feast, after "the food of the offering made by fire unto the Lord" (Lev. iii.)

Ver. 44.* **At that time.**—Evidently the time of the dedication. **Some.**—Heb. "men." **The treasures** (or stores) comprised the three sorts enumerated, to wit, the first-fruits, the tithes, and the free-will offerings. **Out of the fields.**—Rather, *according to the fields.* **The portions of the law,** *i. e. the portions appointed by the law* (as in margin). **For Judah rejoiced for the priests and Levites that waited.**—Rather, *for Judah rejoiced in the priests and Levites who stood at their posts.* The people gladly gave the prescribed offerings for the priests and Levites, so that there was no sense of burden upon them, nor any friction between the Levites and the people.

Ver. 45. **The singers and the porters** formed two important bodies of Levites. They **kept the ward,** that is, performed their appointed duties. The verse is improperly divided in the E. V. It should read, *And they* (the priests and Levites of ver. 44) *kept the ward of their God and the ward of the purification, and so did also the singers and the porters keep their ward.* The priests and Levites attended to their duties of public worship and purifying, and the singers and porters observed their appropriate functions.

Vers. 46, 47. The *wav* before "Asaph" is generally supposed an error, and the verse is read "for in the days of David, Asaph of old was chief." This will explain the singular "chief," (the plural K'ri being unsupported). But still it is difficult to see why Asaph's headship should be mentioned just here. It may be suggested that the Masorites are wrong, and that the 46th and 47th verses (Silluk being removed) should run together, "all Israel" being subject in both, anticipated in ver. 46, from ver. 47, thus: *for in the days of David and Asaph, of old, chief of the singers and songs of praise and thanksgiving unto God,—and all Israel in the days of Zerubbabel and in the days of Nehemiah gave, etc.* From David's day to Nehemiah's the care of Israel for the Levitical singers and porters was marked.

Sanctified, *i. e., Brought as consecrated or dedicated.* As in 1 Chron. xxvi. 28.

The Levites brought as dedicated to the priests the *tithe* of that which was dedicated to them. (Num. xviii. 26.)

* The opinion that vers. 44–47 are an insertion by another hand than Nehemiah's is founded on the change from the 1st person to the 3d person, and from the assumption that here is described the same transaction as in ch. xiii. 10-13. The former argument is too weak to trust anywhere. (How would it apply to Ezra ch. vii.?) The latter argument is baseless, for the passage xiii. 10-13 refers to a different event.

HISTORICAL AND ETHICAL.

1. Both the Heb. *hanukkah* and the Greek *enkainia* define a "dedication" as the initiation or beginning of a new thing. There is no notion of consecration in the word. There is no grace conferred or new nature implanted. Even in the dedication of the temple, it was only the Lord's miraculous presence which consecrated the place. The dedication of the walls of Jerusalem by Nehemiah and his brethren was simply a joyful religious celebration of the work achieved under the gracious providence of God. The priests indeed purified the walls, but so they purified the people. Everything Jewish was purified; so that this purification is no distinct part of the dedication. The primal element in the dedication was joy, exhibited in music, vocal and instrumental, and in thanksgiving. There was a formal recognition of God's mercy and loving-kindness by the assembled people.

2. The culminating point in the day's observance was certainly when the two processions, after each passing over half the wall, met at the temple and united their praises with new emphasis, while "great sacrifices" were offered on the brazen altar. The high position of the temple would add much to the imposing character of this service.

3. The ministers of religion were not considered as useless, "non-producing" men by the godly Jews. Even the singers were reckoned worthy of a public support. It is a low, materialistic philosophy that cannot see the moral importance of leaders and teachers of religion in a community, and that without them material accumulation will only expedite national destruction.

HOMILETICAL AND PRACTICAL.

Vers. 1–26. It was without doubt a matter of piety that in the time after the exile, they restored more and more the old classes of priests and Levites which had existed before the exile. It was a necessity for the congregation, which deserved all consideration, to have again an equally manifold-numbered, complete equipment for the establishment of the beautiful service of the Lord, as before the exile. It was also for the priests and Levites themselves most important and wholesome that they should find themselves together again in the old divisions, and should also acknowledge their venerable ancestors as their heads. Who can estimate the blessing there is, when descendants remain conscious that they are preceded by many and ancient ancestors in piety and the service of God, when in families piety too becomes a matter of tradition, when the children know that parents and grandparents have prayed for them, and particularly for their spiritual prosperity, and when they feel themselves called upon by this to pray again in turn for their children and grandchildren. It was an enviable time when in the Christian church likewise there were Aaronic families, when the children received an impulse from the example of parents and ancestors to devote themselves to the service of the word, and when the parents knew no higher joy than to see their children advancing to the same high office which their fathers had occupied. The first condition of a proper, worthy exercise of the office, which shall be rich in blessing, is indeed the pouring out of the Spirit, and the Spirit breathes where He listeth, but even in the Christian church the ordained ways hold an important position by the side of extraordinary ones. In connection with the fact that the number of the priests' classes was about the same as before the exile, Beda's remark is applicable: "*Sic sæpe sancta ecclesia ex detrimentis suis majora recepit incrementa, cum uno per incuriam lapso in peccatum plures exemplo ejus territi ad persistendum in castitate fidei fiunt cautiores. Sæpe idem ipsi, qui peccaverunt, majores post actam pœnitentiam bonorum operum fructus ferre incipiunt, quam ante incursum peccati ferre consuerant. Sæpe ab hæreticis ecclesia vastata, postquam instantia catholicorum doctorum lucem veritatis recepit, plures ad cognoscendam tuendamque rationem recuperantes ejusdem veritatis filios procreavit. Neque enim unquam beati patres Athanasius, Ambrosius, Hilarius, Augustinus, et ceteri tales tot et tam magnificos in sanctam scripturam tractatus conderent, si non contra fidem rectam tam multifarius hæreticorum fuisset error ortus.*"

Vers. 27–43. The feast of dedication. 1. Whose part is it? The congregation's, to which God has anew given protection and power against its enemies, but also the individual believer's, when the Lord has secured to him his position, and has even enclosed it with a wall. 2. How is it to be celebrated? In that we purify ourselves from all that displeases the Lord, that we thankfully consecrate His gifts, that is, put them at His service, that we rejoice in them as a proof of the grace that desires our salvation, and thereby cause our faith to be strengthened, *etc.* 3. What blessing has it? It appropriates thus truly God's gifts to us, and enkindles thus our zeal to honor God with new desire by consecration, devotion, and homage.—BEDA: *Facta autem civitas sancta dedicatur, cum, completo in fine sæculi numero electorum, ecclesia universaliter in cœlis ad visionem sui conditoris introducitur.*—How must the congregation celebrate the feast of dedication? 1. With joyful thanks, that the power and salvation of the Lord has surrounded them as a wall for their protection against the world, and for their separation from the same. 2. With firm trust, that the Lord will still farther protect them. 3. With the sincere vow to hold themselves separate from the world, and to live to the Lord. True joy. 1. Its right, the God who has given us life, wishes also that it shall move joyfully; the God who always anew overwhelms us with favors, wishes that they should fulfil their mission, that is, make us happy, in the end holy. 2. Its occasion is God's grace, which has strengthened, protected, assured, or elevated our lower or higher life. The chief sites in Jerusalem testified to this, and in the Christian church, yes, indeed, in our lives, all the heights testify thereof. 3. Its kind—it raises itself to God, is a joy in Him, that is, becomes a service to God and our neighbor.—BEDE: *Requiruntur et Levitæ spirituales, hoc est, assumpti in sortem regni de omnibus locis suis, quando mittet filius hominis angelos suos et congregabit electos suos a quatuor ventis, a summo terræ usque ad summum cœli. Faciunt illi dedicationem in lætitia, cantico, gratiarum actione, atque in organis musicorum variis, cum in perceptione æternæ vitæ invicem gaudebunt.*—STARKE: Dedications shall take place with praise and thanks, singing and praying, not with sins and wantonness. That should be the delight and joy of our hearts when we see that the city of God, that is, the Christian church, is protected by God within by the defence of faithful authorities. (Ps. lviii. 2.) Christian joy, at the proper time, does not displease God.

Vers. 44–47. What is also needful: 1. That there should be teachers and servants in the church. 2. That they should perform their service without being hindered in it by lower cares. 3. That the congregation should joyfully supply them with what is necessary for their support.—BEDE: *Hujus autem capituli nobis expositio allegorica in promptu est; quia dominus statuit eos, qui evangelium annuntiant, de evangelio vivere. Sed væ illis sacerdotibus ac ministris sanctorum, qui sumptus quidem cum gaudio debitos sumere a populo delectantur, sed nihil pro ejusdem populi student salute laborare, non aliquid sacri ducatus ei recte vivendo præbere, non de suavitate regni cœlestis ei quippiam dulce prædicando canere, sed nec januam ei supernæ civitatis aperire, municipatum in cœlis habendo, verum potius occludere perverse agendo probantur.*—STARKE: It is God's will and command that with the treasure of the godly word and for the maintenance of the same, we should make a provision that churches, schools, and those who serve in them may be supported. (1 Chr. xxvii. 20; 2 Chr. xxiv. 8; xxxi. 4; xxxiv. 9.)

CHAP. XIII. 1–30.

1 On that day [of dedication] they read [it was read] in the book of Moses in the
audience [ears] of the people; and therein was found written, that the Ammonite
2 and the Moabite should not come into the congregation of God for ever; because
they met not the children of Israel with bread and with water, but [and] hired Ba-
laam against them, that he should curse them: howbeit [and] our God turned the
3 curse into a blessing. Now [And] it came to pass, when they had heard the law,
that they separated from Israel all the mixed multitude.

[Events of 12 years' later date].

4 And before this, [in the face of this], Eliashib the priest, having the oversight
of [being set over] the chamber [chambers] of the house of our God *was* allied unto
5 Tobiah: And he had prepared [and he prepared] for him a great chamber, where
aforetime they laid the meat-offerings, the frankincense, and the vessels, and the
tithes of the corn, the new wine, and the oil, which was commanded *to be given* to
6 the Levites, and the singers, and the porters; and the offerings of the priests. But
[and] in all this *time* was not I at Jerusalem; for in the two and thirtieth year of
Artaxerxes, king of Babylon, came I unto the king, and after certain days [at the
7 end of days] obtained I leave of the king: And I came to Jerusalem, and under-
stood of the evil that Eliashib did for Tobiah, in preparing him a chamber in the
8 courts of the house of God. And it grieved me sore: therefore [and] I cast forth
9 all the household stuff of Tobiah out of the chamber. Then [and] I commanded,
and they cleansed the chambers: and thither brought I again the vessels of the
10 house of God, with the meat-offerings and the frankincense. And I perceived that
the portions of the Levites had not been given *them:* for [and] the Levites and the
11 singers, that did the work, were fled every one to his field. Then [and] contended
I with the rulers, and said, Why is the house of God forsaken? And I gathered
12 them [*i. e.*, the Levites and singers] together, and set them in their place. Then
brought all Judah [And all Judah brought] the tithe of the corn and the new wine
13 and the oil unto the treasuries. And I made treasurers over the treasuries, Shele-
miah the priest, and Zadok the scribe, and of the Levites, Pedaiah: and next to
them [at their hand] *was* Hanan the son of Zaccur, the son of Mattaniah: for they
were counted faithful, and their office was [and it was upon them] to distribute unto
14 their brethren. Remember me, O my God, concerning this, and wipe not out my
good deeds [kindnesses] that I have done for the house of my God, and for the
15 offices thereof. In those days saw I in Judah *some* treading wine-presses on the sab-
bath, and bringing in sheaves, and lading asses; as also [and besides] wine, grapes,
and figs, and all *manner of* burdens, which they brought [and bringing them] into
Jerusalem on the sabbath day: and I testified *against them* in the day wherein they
16 sold victuals. There dwelt men of Tyre also therein [And the Tyrians dwelt
therein], which brought fish, and all manner of ware, and sold on the sabbath unto
17 the children of Judah, and in Jerusalem. Then [And] I contended with the nobles
of Judah, and said unto them, What evil thing is this that ye do, and profane the
18 sabbath day? Did not your fathers thus, and did not our God bring all this evil
upon us, and upon this city? yet [and] ye bring more wrath upon Israel by pro-
19 faning the sabbath. And it came to pass that when the gates of Jerusalem began
to be dark [were shaded] before the sabbath, I commanded that the gates should be
shut [and the gates were shut], and charged [commanded] that they should not be
opened till after the sabbath, and *some* of my servants set I at the gates, *that* there
20 should no burden be brought in on the sabbath day. So [and] the merchants and
21 sellers of all kinds of ware lodged without Jerusalem once or [and] twice. Then

[and] I testified against them, and said unto them, Why lodge ye about [before] the
wall? if ye do *so* again, I will lay hands on you. From that time forth came they no
22 *more* on the sabbath. And I commanded the Levites that they should cleanse them-
selves, and *that* they should come *and* keep the gates, to sanctify the sabbath day.
Remember me, O my God, *concerning* this also, and spare [pity] me according to
the greatness [abundance] of thy mercy.
23 In those days saw I also [the] Jews *that* had married [carried to dwell *with them*]
24 wives of Ashdod, of Ammon, *and* of Moab: and their children spake half in the
speech of Ashdod (and could not speak [were not acquainted with speaking] in the
Jews' language), but [and] according to the language [tongue] of each people [of
25 people and people]. And I contended with them, and cursed them, and smote
certain [men] of them, and plucked off [tore out] their hair, and made them swear
by God, *saying*, Ye shall not give your daughters unto their sons, nor take their
26 daughters unto your sons, or for yourselves. Did not Solomon, king of Israel, sin
by these things? yet [and] among many nations was there no king like him, who
[and he] was beloved of his God, and God made him king over all Israel: never-
27 theless even him did outlandish [foreign] women cause to sin. Shall we then [and
shall we] hearken unto you to do [hear that ye do] all this great evil, to transgress
28 against our God in marrying [carrying to dwell *with us*] strange wives? And *one*
of the sons of Joiada, the son of Eliashib the high-priest *was* son-in-law to Sanbal-
29 lat the Horonite; therefore [and] I chased him from me. Remember them, O
God, because they have defiled [on account of the defilings of] the priesthood, and
30 the covenant of the priesthood, and of the Levites. Thus cleansed I [And I
cleansed] them from all strangers, and appointed the wards of the priests and the
Levites, every one in his business; and for the wood-offering, at times appointed,
and for the first-fruits. Remember me, O God, for good.

TEXTUAL AND GRAMMATICAL.

[1] [Ver. 6. נִשְׁאַלְתִּי. The lexicographers interpret this Niphal as Kal. But both here and in 1 Sam. xx. 6, 28 (the only places where the Niph. occurs), the meaning "to receive permission" seems to be necessary. It would be a quasi passive of the Kal meaning.

[2] Ver. 19. אֲשֶׁר omitted before לֹא־יָבוֹא.

[3] Ver. 22. שֹׁמְרִים. Wav omitted. Yet we may read "come *as* keepers of the gates."

[4] Ver. 24. וּבְנֵיהֶם stands absolutely, for מְדַבֵּר being singular takes חֲצִי as its nominative.

EXEGETICAL AND CRITICAL.

Ver. 1. **On that day**, *i. e.* the day of dedication of the walls, as in xii. 43, 44.

The part of the law which forbade mingling with the other nations was specially read on the dedication-day. Deut. xxiii. 3 would naturally be read, as also Deut. vii. 1–6. The reference to the former passage here uses the words *adh olam* (forever), which are not found alone in Deuteronomy. There it reads: "Even to their tenth generation shall they not enter into the congregation of the Lord *forever*," where the "forever" seems to signify the perpetuity of this ordinance, and not the perpetuity of their exclusion. It is quoted here in brief, without any design to change the meaning. No Moabite or Ammonite family could be admitted to the privileges of Jewry until in the tenth generation after quitting heathenism and formally allying itself with Israel.

Ver. 2. The reference to Deut. xxiii. 3–5 continues through this verse, the passage being condensed throughout. In the Heb. we have the singular, *he hired* (*i. e.* Balak) as in Deut. xxiii. 4.

Ver. 3. The result of this reading was a careful exclusion of the mixed multitude (*erev*) from Israel. This was a different act from that of the 24th of Tisri. Then Israel separated itself *from the strangers*. Now they separate the *erev from Israel*. The former was a withdrawal; this an expulsion. For *erev*, see Ex. xii. 38.

Nehemiah's Reform Movement on his Return to Jerusalem.

Ver. 4. **Before this.**—This should be "in the presence of this" (*in conspectu ejus*), with the circumstantial and not the temporal signification of *liphne mizzeh*. For Eliashib's evil conduct occurred while Nehemiah was away on his visit to Susa in Artaxerxes' thirty-second year, and *not before* the dedication-day. The meaning is, that Eliashib, the high-priest, notwithstanding all this reform wrought by Nehemiah in Artaxerxes' twentieth year, *in the face of it all*, dared, twelve years after, when Nehemiah was far away, to introduce Tobiah into the courts of the temple.

Nehemiah closes his record with a brief sketch of a new reform movement which he had to make twelve years later, owing to a long absence from Jerusalem at the Persian Court, in which time evil men had sought to undo his former work.

Between ver. 3 and ver. 4 we have therefore a gap of twelve years in the chronology.

We have no reason to suppose that Eliashib allied himself with Tobiah or (through his grandson) with Sanballat until this season of Nehemiah's absence, when Eliashib may have supposed that he would never return.

Nehemiah in all probability did not write this book of his doings at Jerusalem till late in life, when his second visit to Jerusalem was a thing of the past, as well as his first visit.

Eliashib, the priest (*i. e.* the high-priest), **having the oversight of the chamber of the house of our God.**—The participle is *being set over* (as in the margin). The "chamber" (*lishcah*) is used collectively for the "chambers." As high-priest, he would have control of all the various buildings in the temple-courts where the treasures of corn, oil and wine were preserved.

Was allied to Tobiah.—In what way we know not. *Karov letoviyyah.* A predicate adjective after so long a sentence, not in apposition ("being allied"), but as in E. V. a distinct assertion ("was allied"). A new fact is stated, and we are led to believe that this alliance marked a fearful period of falling away, after Nehemiah had turned his back. If it had existed before, we should have had mention made of it.

Ver. 5. A second fact in the miserable business. The high-priest prepared for Tobiah a great chamber, probably by knocking many into one (see ver. 9), in which Tobiah resided when at Jerusalem (see ver. 8). This desecration Eliashib may have defended on the score of Tobiah being by blood a Jew (see on ch. ii. 10), and the necessity of keeping on good terms with the influential men of the surrounding provinces.

These chambers had held all the unbloody sacrificial offerings and the tithes.

The Levites are distinguished from the singers and porters, although the singers and porters were Levites. So, on the other hand, the Levites are distinguished from the priests, although the priests were Levites. The Levites, as here designated, were those engaged in the more immediate sacrificial services, in attendance on the priests.

Ver. 6. **In the two and thirtieth year of Artaxerxes, king of Babylon,** *i. e.* in B. C. 434–3. Probably the "time set" by Nehemiah and approved by the king (ch. ii. 6) was twelve years. At the expiration of this term he was obliged to leave the superintendence of affairs at Jerusalem and return to the court. Artaxerxes is called "king of Babylon," instead of "king of Persia," probably because at this time of Nehemiah's return the court was removed to Babylon for some special state reason.

After certain days.—Lit. *at the end of days,* a very general expression, and may here mean several years.

Obtained I leave, to wit, to return to Jerusalem.

Ver. 8. This decided action shows that Nehemiah returned with full powers from the Court.

Ver. 9. **The chambers.** See on ver. 5. The tithes are omitted in the enumeration, because, as we see by the next verse, the people had ceased paying tithes, and hence there were none to put in the store-chambers.

Ver. 10. **For the Levites,** *etc.*, **were fled.** Rather: *and the Levites, etc., were fled.* They fled to their own fields to work for their living, because their tithes were withheld. Their own fields were those belonging to the Levitical cities.—**The singers, that did the work,** is a pregnant phrase for "the singers *and porters* who performed service."

Ver. 11. **The rulers** (*seganim*). The Pers. word does not necessarily refer to rulers set over the people by the Persians, although it may include such, but extends to all who might exercise authority by birth, election or otherwise. The Pers. word is used as a familiar term for magistrates.

Set them in their place.—That is, *put the Levites back into their positions.*

Ver. 12. **Unto the treasuries** (or storehouses). Or *for stores.*

Ver. 13. **I made treasurers.**—The Hiphil of *Atzar,* "to store." Lit.: "I caused to store over the store-houses." That is: "I placed men over the store-houses, whom I caused to store the stores in them."

Shelemiah.—See ch. iii. 30.

Zadok.—See ch. iii. 29.

Pedaiah.—See ch. iii. 26 and ch. viii. 4.

Next to them.—Lit. *at their hand,* as their assistant.

Ver. 14. This prayer is not one of self-glorification, but of faith in God's truth. A man who knows he is doing right in the sight of God can say so to God without presumption. It is a testimony of God's grace, and he can rejoice in it.

Ver. 15. **In those days** of my return to Jerusalem. The Sabbath had become desecrated in Nehemiah's absence, so that in some cases the works of the farm were wrought on that day, and produce brought to Jerusalem, and there sold on the Sabbath.

Ver. 16. Tyrian traders in fish and other products were plying their trade in the city on the Sabbath.

Ver. 17. **The nobles** (*horim*), not the "rulers" of ver. 11, but the higher classes generally.

Ver. 18. See Jer. xvii. 20–27.

Ver. 19. **When the gates of Jerusalem began to be dark before the Sabbath.**—This seems to show that the day among the Jews did not begin at sunset. For here *after sunset when it began to be dark,* it was *before the Sabbath.* Only a special Sabbath was counted from the evening before. See Lev. xxiii. 32.

Ver. 20. **The merchants,** or *traffickers.*—On arriving with their wares, according to their wont, they find the gates shut, and are obliged to pass the night outside the walls until the Sabbath is over.

Ver. 21. When this hint was not enough, Nehemiah sends them word that if they make their appearance again before the gates on the Sabbath to lodge there, they will be arrested. This broke up the evil.

Ver. 22. **Cleanse themselves**, as for a holy service, and so guard the Sabbath by guarding the gates. For the prayer, see on ver. 14.

Ver. 23. **In those days** of my return from Jerusalem. As at ver. 15.

Jews that had married.—With the article, *the Jews that had married.* As the children's speech was affected, these Jews must have lived on the outskirts of the Jewish province near the Philistines, Ammonites and Moabites. For children will always know the prevailing language of a district. **Ashdod** seems to stand for all Philistia, at this time probably the most conspicuous Philistine town.

Ver. 24. **And could not speak in the Jews' language.**—A parenthetical phrase.—The succeeding "but" should be "and."—**Of each people,** *i. e.* Ammon and Moab.

Ver. 25. Here is described the action not of a private man in his ungovernable rage, but of a public officer in the faithful use of his power. Notice the word **contended**. In ver. 11 Nehemiah contends with the rulers regarding the neglect of the tithes; in ver. 17, he contends with the nobles regarding the profanation of the Sabbath, and here he contends with the Jews who had married heathen wives for this open disregard of the law.

Ver. 26. **Beloved of his God.**—Comp. 2 Sam. xii. 24. This does not imply saving grace on God's part or holiness on Solomon's part. It only denotes special favor and privilege. Compare Mark x. 21.

Outlandish, *i. e* foreign.

Ver. 27. **Shall we then hearken unto you to do,** *etc.* (*welakhem hanishma laasoth*).—Lit.: *And for you is it heard to do, etc., i. e.* "do we hear that you do all this great evil?"

Although it is not stated expressly, it is implied in ver. 30, that Nehemiah insisted on a separation from the "outlandish" wives, as did Ezra many years before (Ezra x. 3).

Ver. 28. Finding that Eliashib's grandson had married Sanballat's daughter, Nehemiah makes a public example of so glaring a case of defiance to the law, for here the special sanctity of the priesthood was desecrated (Lev. xxi. 6–8).

I chased him from me (*abrihehu me alai*). Lit.: "I made him flee from off me." Nehemiah forced him to leave Jerusalem, and be no longer a burden to his government.

Ver. 29. The covenant of the priesthood and of the Levites was, first, the general covenant with the tribes as Israel's teachers and God's special servants (Deut. xxxiii. 8–11), and, second the special covenant of priesthood (Lev. xxi. 6–8).

Ver. 30. **Thus cleansed I them from all strangers**.—The irregularities regarding tithes, the Sabbath, and the marriages were all attributable to connection with strangers. When this was stopped, the careful ordering of the priestly and Levitical work was made easy, which had all been disarranged and much neglected in Nehemiah's absence.

Ver. 31. The **wood-offering** (see on ch. x. 34) and the **first-fruits** are mentioned for all the offerings, as those most apt to be neglected.

Remember me, O my God, for good.—See on ver. 14.

HISTORICAL AND ETHICAL.

1. The severe exclusion of the Moabite and Ammonite was an enacted token against sin. Even these blood relations of Israel were to be kept away as polluted, because they showed no sympathy with Israel, and made a deliberate and vile attempt to plunge Israel into sin. A permanent horror was to be erected between Israel and these monsters of iniquity. The key to many of the stern Mosaic statutes is to be found in the necessity of holding up the heinousness of sin, which men are ever ready to make light of. (See the exegetical commentary for an explanation of this statute.)

2. The lapse of Israel on Nehemiah's return to Persia throws into clear light the immense work which Nehemiah had wrought, and the remarkable power of the man. His influence had worked the reform and had upheld it, and when his presence was removed the structure at once began to crack and crumble. A generation later Malachi lamented over the spiritual waste that Judah presented. Great as Nehemiah was, he could not make healthy the diseased body of Jewry. He could only, by the force of his character, rouse the people to a decent semblance of righteousness. And yet, while he was powerless to renew the nation, we may believe that his influence ran down private channels in families and humble houses to the very time of the Messiah, making green lines of spiritual growth amid the arid desert of Judaism.

3. Ezra had effected a reform a dozen years before Nehemiah came to Judah. He had separated the Jews from the heathen people, and in this reform had forced the highest in the land to dissolve their wicked matrimonial alliances. The book of Ezra concludes with this statement. When Nehemiah arrived there was a new separation from strangers effected. (Ch. ix. 2.) Whether the mingling with the heathen had again amounted to marriage alliances we may not say. It may have only involved mercantile partnerships. A dozen years later again on Nehemiah's second visit, there is a necessity for a most stern application of Nehemiah's personal and official power to cure the same old evil, which seems to have been bolder than ever.

4. There are times when good men must assume great severity of manner and allow a holy indignation to fire their souls. Gentleness of style before barefaced villany is weakness and inefficiency. Had Nehemiah acted with a soft and effeminate method, the offenders would have laughed at him. God loves to guide with His eye, but sometimes He uses the thunderbolt.

HOMILETICAL AND PRACTICAL.

Vers. 1–3. The duty of the church to purify itself constantly anew. 1. In regard to those with whom they assimilate themselves; in the Old Testament, in regard to the Ammonites, *etc.*, not on account of their nationality, but on account of their ways; in the church, in regard to those who not only go astray, but also who will not allow themselves to be bettered, and who thus exclude themselves. 2. Whereon it grounds itself; not only on the right of self-preservation, but also upon God's word. 3. What it aims at; namely, that the church set forth more and more what it should be as Christ's spotless bride.

STARKE: One cannot read or preach God's Word too often, for one always finds something which one had not noticed or known before.

What God has commanded one must perform, even though it may seem hard to us, and we may draw upon us the enmity of others in its performance.

Vers. 4–9. The sanctity of holy places. 1. That upon which it is grounded; in the Old Testament, upon the fact that God had connected His peculiar presence with the temple; in the Christian dispensation, upon the fact that God's honor dwells in the churches, that is, is cherished there. 2. What it binds us to; to uphold the churches in a condition corresponding to their aim, or where they are lacking to restore them in a worthy manner. 3. What blessing it has for us; it reminds us of the holiness, the majesty and the glory of our God, and fosters our regard therefor; it works frequently by elevating and edifying, whereas an unworthy desecration of churches only promotes the crudity from which it has sprung. BEDE: *Et tu quidquid inter fideles infidelitatis et immunditiæ reperis continuo projice foras, ut immundatis credentium cordibus, quæ sunt gazophylacia Domini, cum virtutum fuerint plena divitiis, vasa Domini inferantur; hoc est, illa ipsa corda quæ paullo ante vasa erroris fuerant per culpam denuo vasa Domini fiant per correctionem; ibiqua sacrificium bonæ operationis et thus puræ orationis, ubi pridem spelunca erat latronum, inveniatur.*

Vers. 30, 31. The retrospect of a servant of God upon his life and his usefulness. 1. It elevates him, because God's grace was with him, and made him worthy to engage in the cause of God and the salvation of mankind. 2. It humbles him, because he was so unworthy of this grace, and moreover because he has fallen so far short of what he might have been able to accomplish through its means. 3. It drives him to prayer, that God would also be merciful to him at the last for Christ's sake, whose righteousness is also his.

EXCURSUS ON THE GATES, ETC.

1. **The Sheep-Gate.**—Heb. שַׁעַר הַצֹּאן. LXX. ἡ πύλη ἡ προβατική. It is mentioned in Neh. iii. 1, 32, and xii. 39. It is probably the same as ἡ προβατική of John v. 2. In Nehemiah it is mentioned as near to the tower of Meah, and that is near the tower of Hananeel. From the fact that it seems to have had no locks and bars (see Neh. iii. 1, and comp. iii. 3, 6, 13, 14, 15), we conjecture that it led directly into the temple-precinct, where a Levitical guard was always present in place of locks and bars. Its name was doubtless given because through it the flocks were driven for the sacrifices, or because they were kept in pens by this gate. The present St. Stephen's gate is usually supposed to mark the site of the sheep-gate, and if so, the Bethesda pool (John v. 2) would be the Birket Israil, which is now satisfactorily proved not to be a moat. Eusebius describes Bethesda as *two pools*, and the Bordeaux pilgrim (about the same time) speaks of it as *twin fish-pools*. The Birket Israil may have been divided into two by a transverse wall in their day, or they may have counted the Birket Hammam Sitti Mariam, just north of the St. Stephen's gate and outside the walls, as one of the two pools; or, again, they may have intended by Bethesda the twin-pools under the convent of the Sisters of Sion near the north-west corner of the Haram, the position defended by Mr. Geo. Williams. The account in Nehemiah makes it necessary to place the sheep-gate *somewhere* in the region of the St. Stephen's gate; but if our argument concerning the absence of locks and bars is worth anything, we must put the gate to the south of Birket Israil. To add to this necessity, we may doubt if the city wall extended further north than the temple-precinct corner, until long after Nehemiah's day, when Agrippa built the third wall. If the Fountain of the Virgin is Bethesda, as Dr. Robinson thinks, then the προβατική of John v. 2 is another gate than that of Nehemiah, situated on Ophel.

On the whole, we are inclined to place the Sheep-Gate in the *north* wall of the temple-precinct, and in close neighborhood to the Birket Israil. In that case the two towers of Meah and Hananeel would be parts of the old Baris or fortification north of the temple, which afterward became altered and enlarged into Antonia.

2. **The Fish-Gate.**—Heb. שַׁעַר הַדָּגִים.—LXX. ἡ πύλη ἡ ἰχθυηρὰ (ἰχθυρὰ, xii. 39: ἰχθυικὰ, 2 Chron. xxxiii. 14; in Zeph. i. 10, it is πύλη ἀποκεντούντων, *gate of the stabbers*, probably הרגים being read for הדגים). It is mentioned in *ll. cc.* It was between the sheep-gate and the old gate, as we see from the Nehemiah passages. The Zephaniah passage does not help us. The passage in 2 Chronicles seems to describe the building of the second wall (comp. Joseph. v. 4, 2) by Manasseh ("on the west to Gihon in the valley, and *on the east* to the entering in at the fish-gate"). If so, it would put the fish-gate

near the Baris, where that wall ended (Jos. *l. c.*).

3. **The Old Gate.**—Heb. שַׁעַר הַיְשָׁנָה. LXX. ἡ πύλη Ἰασαναί. Keil insists that הַיְשָׁנָה is genitive, and follows Arnold in supplying חוֹמָה, thus calling it "the gate of the old wall." Schultz says: "the gate of the old town." If we take it as a genitive, it may be "the gate of Jeshanah," a name given because the road through it led to Jeshanah in Ephraim (2 Chron. xiii. 19), mentioned by Joseph. Antiq. 8, 11, 3, and 14, 15, 12. The LXX. seem to have taken this view. But it need not be a genitive, as we have in Is. xiv. 31 הֵילִילִי שַׁעַר (the שַׁעַר being treated as feminine) and שַׁעַר הַפְּנִימִית (Ezek. viii. 3).

We are inclined to identify this gate with the "corner gate" of Zech. xiv. 10 and Jer. xxxi. 38 (שַׁעַר הַפִּנָּה or שַׁעַר הַפִּנִּים), and so to let it mark the north-east corner of the city-wall. The cited passages in Zechariah and Jeremiah seem to put the gate in relation with the tower of Hananeel. If the Fish-gate were close to that tower, then it would be very natural to mention the Old Gate or Corner Gate next to the tower, in describing a section of the wall. In 2 Kings xiv. 13 the "corner gate" is only four hundred cubits from the gate of Ephraim, but in which direction we cannot tell. If eastward, then it was very likely the same as the Old Gate; but if westward, then the gate of Ephraim, and the corner-gate may be unmentioned in Nehemiah's account of the rebuilding, because belonging to the undestroyed portion of the wall on the western end of the north wall, which part many suppose is the "broad wall" of Nehemiah. Of course in this case, the corner gate and the old gate are different gates. We can, at any rate, quite confidently claim that the corner-gate was at either the north-east or the north-west corner of the city.

4. **The Valley-Gate.**—Heb. שַׁעַר הַגַּיְא.—LXX. ἡ πύλη τῆς φάραγγος. In ch. ii. 13 ἡ πύλη τοῦ Γωληλὰ (by joining גַיְא and לַיְלָה as one word). This gate (mentioned in ch. ii. 13, 15; iii. 13; 2 Chron. xxvi. 9) was evidently north of the dragon-well (עֵין הַתַּנִּין), wherever that was. If the Birket Sultan is the Dragon well (which is very doubtful), we may put the valley gate about a thousand feet south of the present Jaffa Gate. The "tower of the furnaces" would correspond to the north-east tower of the present citadel, perhaps is identical with this very ancient piece of masonry. It does not seem possible by any scheme to identify the valley-gate with the Gate Gennath of Josephus, for that must have been east of the western starting-point of the first wall, where the name of valley-gate would have been a misnomer. If the valley-gate were just north of the northern end of the Birket Sultan, the Dung-gate would come exactly at the southern extremity of Zion, over the deep ravine of Hinnom. The name of valley-gate was doubtless derived from the broad and deep Wady er Rababi (Hinnom), out to which it led.

The most natural point for a gate on this side the city is where the present Jaffa Gate is. If we put the Valley-gate there, then the Dung-gate will come opposite the Birket Sultan.

5. **The Dung-Gate.**—Heb. שַׁעַר הָאַשְׁפֹּת. In Neh. iii. 13, שַׁעַר הַשְׁפֹּת. LXX. ἡ πύλη τῆς κοπρίας. The Heb. is not so strong a word as the Greek, and may be rendered *Rubbish-gate.** This gate was a thousand cubits from the Valley-gate (ch. iii. 13). The extreme southern point of Zion would be a very natural place, from which to empty rubbish down into the deep valley below. Here we might place the Dung-gate, making it the same as the (later) Gate of the Essenes. With Robinson, we would consider the *Bethso* of Josephus the Heb. בֵּית צוֹאָה or Dung-place. The Dung-gate, however, must be opposite the Birket Sultan, if the Valley-gate is placed at the present Jaffa Gate. See the preceding note.

6. **The Fountain-gate.**—Heb. שַׁעַר הָעַיִן. LXX. ἡ πύλη τῆς πηγῆς. In Neh. ii. 14 ἡ πύλη τοῦ Αἰν (untranslated). In Neh. xii. 37 τοῦ αἰνεῖν by a gross error. That this was close to the pool of Siloam (the "King's pool" of ch. ii. 14, the "pool of Siloah by the king's garden," comp. ch. iii. 15), there can be no doubt. In 2 Kings xxv. 4 it is called "the gate between two walls, which is by the king's garden." It was a gate down in the Tyropœon Valley, and at a corner, as the expression in 2 Kings xxv. 4 indicates.

7. **The Water-gate.** — Heb. שַׁעַר הַמַּיִם. LXX. ἡ πύλη τοῦ ὕδατος. At this gate one procession halted at the dedication-service, while the other halted at the Prison-gate (ch. xii. 37, 39). This would place the Water-gate at the south of the temple, and the Prison-gate at the north of the temple. They could scarcely have been in the city-wall, but were probably gates leading from the inner temple-enclosure to the outer. The water-gate may have derived its name from its leading to the remarkable cisterns lately discovered by Capt. Warren south of the Haram. It will be noticed that nothing is said of rebuilding either of these gates. We would put the Water-gate at the southern limit of the "mountain of the house," near the present entrance to El-Aksa. This accords with the Talmud, Mid. 2, 6.

8. **The Prison-Gate.**—Heb. שַׁעַר הַמַּטָּרָה. This is referred to in the last section. It was probably the same as the שַׁעַר הַמִּפְקָד of ch. iii. 31 (*i. e.* gate of visitation of punishment).

If we follow the course of the second dedicative company (ch. xii. 38, 39), we are constrained to put this gate between the sheep-gate and the temple, probably at the north limit of the "mountain of the house." But in ch. iii. 25 we find the "court of the prison" mentioned, as in Jer. xxxii. 2; xxxiii. 1, and xxxvii. 21. This

* [The "east gate" of Jer. xix. 2 is in Heb. שַׁעַר הַחַרְסוּת, which is indicative of either שַׁעַר הַחַרְסוּת or שַׁעַר הַחַרְסִית. If the former be the right reading, then this gate ("the pottery-gate") may very likely be the same as the dung or rubbish-gate.—Tr.]

was attached to the king's palace, and was therefore at the south of the Haram. This prison, into which Jeremiah was cast, was probably the State-prison, while another prison, near the "prison-gate" (whence it derived its name), was a temple-prison, for offenders against the worship.

9. **The Gate of Ephraim.**—Heb. שַׁעַר אֶפְרַיִם. LXX. ἡ πύλη 'Εφραίμ. Neh. viii. 16; xii. 39; 2 Kings xiv. 13. This gate was four hundred cubits from the corner-gate (wherever that was), and had an open square near it like that at the water-gate. It was also between the broad wall and the old gate. So much the cited passages show. It doubless derived its name from the fact that the main northern road to the Ephraimite country led through it. For a like reason it may have been called the "gate of Benjamin" (Jer. xxxvii. 13; Zech. xiv. 10), the Benjamite country lying north of the city, and the road through this gate leading to its chief cities. This gate was not rebuilt by Nehemiah, because, probably, it was in the "broad wall" (*i. e.*, as Keil and others hold, in that 400 cubits of wall which Joash broke down, and which Uzziah rebuilt in a stronger manner. 2 Chron. xxvi. 9). It probably coincided with the modern Damascus Gate, at which ancient substructions are found.

10. *The first Gate.* Heb. שַׁעַר הָרִאשׁוֹן LXX. ἡ πύλη ἡ πρώτη. (Zech. xiv. 10). From this only mention of this gate, we would naturally place it between Benjamin's gate and the corner gate. If the Old Gate and Corner Gate are the same, then we should have to suppose an important gate on the north of the city not elsewhere mentioned. But may not the peculiar phraseology of the Zechariah passage lead us to identify the first gate and the corner gate? The words are "unto *the place of* the first gate unto the corner gate." That may mean "unto the place where the first city gate is, beginning at the north, to wit, unto the corner gate." The adjective "first" seems more appropriate to distinguish one of a series, than to represent the peculiar name of a gate.

11. *The High Gate.* Heb. שַׁעַר הָעֶלְיוֹן LXX. ἡ πύλη ἡ ὑψηλή (in Jer. xx. 2, πύλη τοῦ ὑπερῴου: in 2 Chron. xxiii. 20, ἡ πύλη ἡ ἐσωτέρα). The passage in Jeremiah calls this the "high gate of Benjamin by the house of the Lord." "The passage in 2 Chron. xxvii. 3 calls it the 'high gate' of the house of the Lord." In 2 Chron. xxiii. 20, we see that it was between the temple and the palace. Of course, then, it was not a gate of the city wall. It is called "gate of the guard" in 2 Kings xi. 6, 19.

12. *The Inner Gate.* Heb. שַׁעַר הַפְּנִימִית. (Ezek. viii. 3).

13. *The New Gate.* Heb. שַׁעַר הֶחָדָשׁ. (Jer. xxxvi. 10).

14. *The Middle Gate.* Heb. שַׁעַר הַתָּוֶךְ. (Jer. xxxix. 3).

15. *The Gate of Sur or of the foundation.* Heb. שַׁעַר סוּר or שַׁעַר הַיְסוֹד. (2 Kings xi. 6; 2 Chr. xxiii. 5).

16. *The East Gate.* Heb. שַׁעַר הַמִּזְרָח. (Neh. iii. 29).

17. *The Horse Gate.* Heb. שַׁעַר הַסּוּסִים. (2 Chron. xxiii. 5; Jer. xxxi. 40. Comp. 2 Kings xi. 16).

These six, together with the gates mentioned by Ezekiel in his vision of the temple, are very evidently, like No. 11, gates of inner walls, and do not belong to the circuit of the city fortifications.

18. *The Corner Gate.* See above, under Nos. 3 and 10.

19. *The Gate of Benjamin.* See above under No. 9.

20. *The Gate Miphkad.* See above under No. 8.

21. *The Tower of Meah.*

22. *The Tower of Hananeel.*

These were evidently near one another, and stood between the Sheep Gate and the Fish Gate. We have supposed that they were towers of the special fortification north of the temple, known afterwards as *Baris*, and in Roman times as *Antonia* (Neh. iii. 1; xii. 39; Jer. xxxi. 38; Zech. xiv. 10).

23. *The Tower of the Furnaces.* Heb. מִגְדַּל הַתַּנּוּרִים. LXX. πύργος τῶν θανουρίμ. The natural point in the circuit for this would be anywhere between the second wall's beginning and the valley gate. What is more likely than the very old N. E. tower of the present citadel (the supposed Hippicus) should be it?

24. *The Broad Wall.* Heb. הַחוֹמָה הָרְחָבָה. LXX. τὸ τεῖχος τὸ πλατύ.

Keil supposes with much probability that this was that four hundred cubits of wall broken down by Joash from the gate of Ephraim to the Corner Gate (2 Kings xiv. 13) and afterwards rebuilt of greater breadth by Uzziah.

25. *The stairs that go down from the city of David.* Heb. הַמַּעֲלוֹת הַיּוֹרְדוֹת מֵעִיר דָּוִיד. These, mentioned in Neh. iii. 15, are again referred to in ch. xii. 37. From the latter passage we should gather that the company marched around the wall as far as the neighborhood of the fountain of Siloam, and then left the wall and passed up the stairs to Zion and along Zion's eastern edge till they crossed over to the water-gate at the temple. We suppose, therefore, that these stairs ascended from the king's gardens to his palace, (the Davidian palace) on Zion (ch. xii. 37, "the house of David").

26. *The Sepulchres of David.* Heb. קִבְרֵי דָוִיד. The places of sepulture of David's family were probably near his own palace on Zion. We should place them at the S. E. corner of the present Zion wall. The wall along Ophel is marked by reference to sites on the opposite side of the Tyropœon.

27. *The Pool that was made.* Heb. הַבְּרֵכָה הָעֲשׂוּיָה. This may be the Fountain of the Virgin, about which there has been so much careful work of human hands in the galleries and cisterns connected with it.

28. *The House of the Mighty.*

29. *The Armory.*

To these we have no clue. They may have been both on Ophel.

The destruction of the city was so complete by Titus, and then by Hadrian, that the gates of the later city can be no guide to the position of those of the ancient city. We must depend on the Scriptures and Josephus, with perhaps a little help from Rabbinical tradition. It seems very clear that the main city wall in Nehemiah's day ran directly from the southern brow of Zion over to Siloam, and then northward along Ophel to the S. E. corner of the Haram. On Ophel there may have been an intricacy of wall, by reason of which the topography in the latter part of ch. iii. is very difficult to explain. As Ophel was a fortress, there may have been several angles in the wall there for strategic purposes.

We have given a crude sketch of the walls, gates, *etc.*, as we suppose them to have existed in the days of Nehemiah, as a help to the understanding of the 3d and 12th chapters.

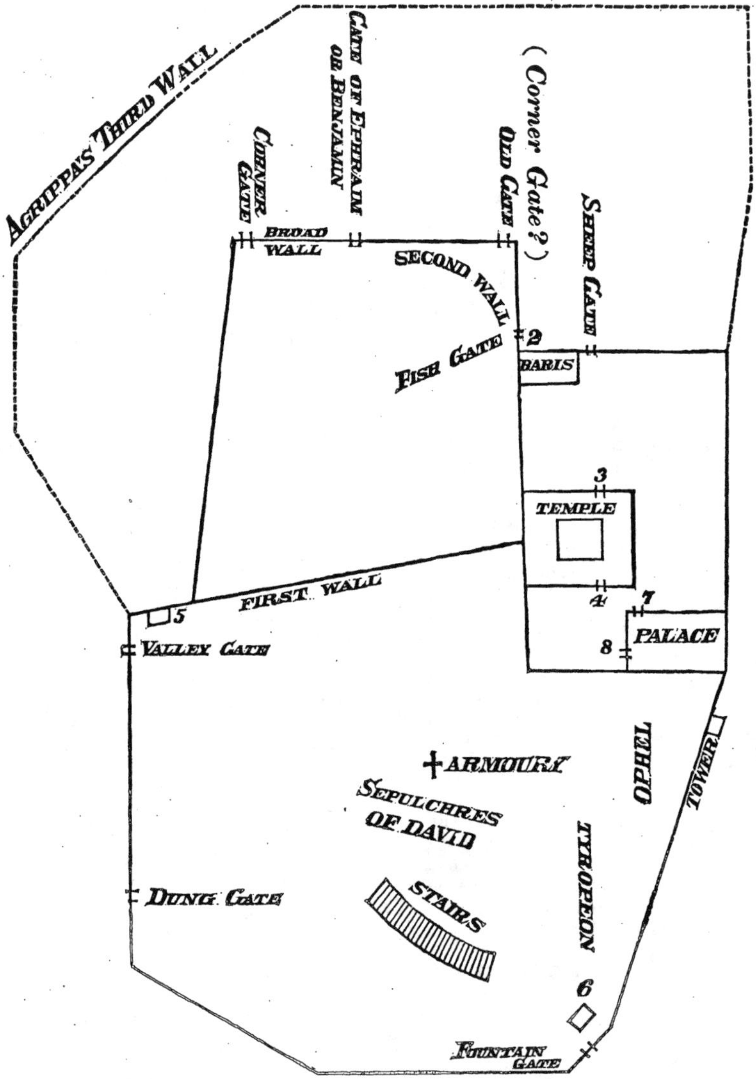

1. Tower of Meah.
2. Tower of Hananeel.
3. Prison Gate (Miphkad).
4. Water Gate.
5. Tower of the Furnaces.
6. Pool of Siloam.
7. Horse Gate.
8. High Gate.

THE END.